Lecture Notes
in Business Information Processing 352

More information about this series at http://www.springer.com/series/7911

Iris Reinhartz-Berger · Jelena Zdravkovic ·
Jens Gulden · Rainer Schmidt (Eds.)

Enterprise, Business-Process and Information Systems Modeling

20th International Conference, BPMDS 2019
24th International Conference, EMMSAD 2019
Held at CAiSE 2019, Rome, Italy, June 3–4, 2019
Proceedings

Springer

Editors
Iris Reinhartz-Berger (iD)
University of Haifa
Haifa, Israel

Jens Gulden (iD)
University of Duisburg-Essen
Essen, Germany

Jelena Zdravkovic (iD)
Stockholm University
Kista, Sweden

Rainer Schmidt
Munich University of Applied Sciences
Munich, Germany

ISSN 1865-1348   ISSN 1865-1356   (electronic)
Lecture Notes in Business Information Processing
ISBN 978-3-030-20617-8   ISBN 978-3-030-20618-5   (eBook)
https://doi.org/10.1007/978-3-030-20618-5

This Springer imprint is published by the registered company Springer Nature Switzerland AG
The registered company address is: Gewerbestrasse 11, 6330 Cham, Switzerland

Preface

This book contains the proceedings of two long-running events held along with the Conference on Advanced Information Systems Engineering (CAiSE) relating to the areas of enterprise, business process, and information systems modeling: the 20th International Conference on Business Process Modeling, Development and Support (BPMDS 2019), and the 24th International Conference on Evaluation and Modeling Methods for Systems Analysis and Development (EMMSAD 2019). The two working conferences had a joint keynote entitled "Modeling and AI: Friends or Foes?," given by Jordi Cabot, Research Professor at the Open University of Catalonia. The abstract of the keynote is included in these proceedings. More information on the individual events and their selection processes can be found below.

BPMDS 2019

The topics addressed by the Business Process Modeling, Development and Support (BPMDS) series are focused on business processes, their conceptualization with the help of modeling languages, and their realization with support of information technology. These topics are among the keystones of information systems theory beyond short-lived fashions. The continued interest in these topics on behalf of the information systems community is reflected by the success of the past BPMDS events, and their promotion from a workshop to a working conference.

The BPMDS series has produced 19 events from 1998 to 2018. From 2011, BPMDS became a two-day working conference attached to CAiSE. The basic principles of the BPMDS series are:

1. BPMDS serves as a meeting place for researchers and practitioners in the areas of business development and business applications (software) development.
2. The aim of the event is mainly discussions, rather than presentations.
3. Each event has a theme that is mandatory for idea papers.
4. Each event's results are, usually, published in a special issue of an international journal.

The goals, format, and history of BPMDS can be found on the website: http://www.bpmds.org/.

BPMDS solicits papers related to business process modeling, development and support (BPMDS) using quality, relevance, originality and applicability as main selection criteria. As a working conference, BPMDS aims to attract *completed research papers* describing mature research, *experience reports* related to using BPMDS in practice, and visionary *idea papers*. To encourage new and emerging challenges and research directions in the area of business process modeling, development and support,

BPMDS has a unique focus theme every year. Papers submitted as idea papers are required to be of relevance to the focus theme, thus providing a mass of new ideas around a relatively narrow but emerging research area. The focus theme for BPMDS 2019 idea papers was "Transformative Business Process Modeling, Development and Support." In line with this, two idea papers published in these proceedings address influential approaches and technologies in the areas of augmented reality, Internet of Things, and blockchain-based smart contracts.

For the 20th edition of the BPMDS conference, we invited interested authors to engage during the two days of BPMDS 2019 in Rome, and to take part in a deep discussion with all participants about the challenges of business transformation in the digitally connected world and the ways *business process modeling, development and support* may provide capabilities to deal with those challenges. The challenges result, among others, from the impacts of the ubiquity of the actors, social networks, new business models, the co-existence of flexibility, exception handling, context awareness and personalization requirements together with other compliance and quality requirements.

Practitioners are producing business process models, researchers are studying and producing business process models, and also are producing new modeling languages when they consider that existing ones are not sufficient. What is beyond? Which kind of analyses can we make using those process models? How can we complete and enhance those process models with annotations, with data coming from everywhere out of the immediate process environment? How can the understanding we gain by working on those models in a sandbox help or facilitate the undergoing business transformation?

BPMDS 2019 received 20 submissions from ten countries (Australia, Chile, Denmark, Estonia, France, Germany, Israel, Italy, Sweden, and Switzerland). Each paper received at least three reviews from the members of the international Program Committee. Eventually, seven full papers and two short papers were accepted, among them six completed research papers, two idea papers addressing the focus theme "Transformative BPMDS," and one experience report. The accepted papers cover a wide spectrum of issues related to business process development, modeling, and support. They are organized under the following section headings:

- Large and Complex Business Process Modeling and Development
- Novel Approaches in Enterprise Modeling
- Execution and Understandability of Declarative Process Models
- Transformative Business Process Modeling, Development, and Support

We wish to thank all the people who submitted papers to BPMDS 2019 for having shared their work with us, as well as the members of the BPMDS 2019 Program Committee, who made a remarkable effort in reviewing the submissions. We also thank the organizers of CAiSE 2019 for their help with the organization of the event, and IFIP WG8.1 for the support.

April 2019   Jens Gulden
                                                         Rainer Schmidt

EMMSAD 2019

The field of information systems and software development has resulted in a rich heritage of modeling paradigms, including software modeling, business process modeling, enterprise modeling, capability modeling, ontology modeling, and domain-specific modeling. These important paradigms, and the specific methods following them, continue to be enriched with extensions, refinements, and even new languages, to deal with new challenges. Even with some attempts toward standardization (e.g., UML for object-oriented software design, ArchiMate for enterprise architecture modeling, and BPMN for business process modeling), new modeling methods are constantly being introduced, especially in order to deal with emerging trends such as compliance and regulations, cloud computing, big data, business analytics, Internet of Things, cyber-physical systems, etc. These topics introduce challenges to modeling as well: scalability, privacy, security, and performance – to list a few, and they may require extending existing modeling methods or developing new ones. Ongoing changes significantly impact the way systems are being analyzed and designed in practice. Moreover, they challenge the evaluation of the modeling methods, which aims to contribute to the knowledge and understanding of their strengths and weaknesses. This knowledge may guide researchers toward the development of the next generation of modeling methods and help practitioners select the modeling methods most appropriate to their needs. A variety of empirical and non-empirical evaluation approaches can be found in the literature: feature comparison, meta-modeling, metrics, paradigmatic analysis, contingency identification, ontological evaluation, surveys, laboratory and field experiments, case studies, action research, and more. Yet, there is a paucity of such research in the literature.

The objective of the EMMSAD conference series is to provide a forum for researchers and practitioners interested in modeling methods for Systems Analysis and Development (SA&D) to meet and exchange research ideas and results. This year, we introduced five tracks that emphasized the variety of EMMSAD topics. Each track involved two chairs whose aim was to encourage submissions in the relevant topics and help during the decision-making phase of the review process. The authors could select multiple tracks for categorizing their papers. The tracks were:

1. Foundations of modeling and method engineering – chaired by Oscar Pastor and Jolita Ralyté
2. Enterprise, business process and capability modeling – chaired by Paul Grefen and Dimitris Karagiannis
3. Information systems and requirements modeling – chaired by Monique Snoeck and Arnon Sturm
4. Domain-specific and ontology modeling – chaired by Tony Clark and Heinrich C. Mayr
5. Evaluation of modeling approaches – chaired by Renata Guizzardi and Jennifer Horkoff

More details can be found at http://www.emmsad.org/.

EMMSAD 2019 received 38 submissions from 21 countries (Argentina, Austria, Bosnia and Herzegovina, Canada, China, France, Germany, India, Israel, Italy, Japan, Latvia, The Netherlands, Norway, South Africa, Spain, Sweden, Switzerland, Turkey, UK, and USA). The division of submissions among tracks was as follows: 11 submission related to foundations of modeling and method engineering, eight to enterprise, business process and capability modeling, 12 to information systems and requirements modeling, 11 to domain-specific and ontology modeling, and eight to evaluation of modeling approaches. Each submitted paper received between three and four reviews. After completing the review process, which involved the track chairs, the following 15 high-quality papers were selected:

1. Foundations of modeling and method engineering:

   - Simon Hacks, Andreas Steffens, Peter Hansen, and Nikhitha Rajashekar. A Continuous Delivery Pipeline for EA Model Evolution
   - Marlies Van Steenbergen, Jeroen van Grondelle, and Lars Rieser. A Situational Approach to Data-Driven Service Innovation
   - Salvador Martinez, Sébastien Gerard, and Jordi Cabot. On the Need for Intellectual Property Protection in Model-Driven Co-Engineering Processes

2. Enterprise, business process, and capability modeling:

   - Georgios Koutsopoulos, Martin Henkel, and Janis Stirna. Dynamic Adaptation of Capabilities: Exploring Meta-model Diversity
   - Mart van Zwienen, Marcela Ruiz, Marlies van Steenbergen, and Veronica Burriel. A Process for Tailoring Domain-Specific Enterprise Architecture Maturity Models
   - Benedikt Reitemeyer and Hans-Georg Fill. Ontology-Driven Enterprise Modeling: A Plugin for the Protégé Platform

3. Information systems and requirements modeling:

   - Xin Dong, Tong Li and Zhiming Ding. Review-Based User Profiling: A Systematic Mapping Study
   - Sunet Eybers, Aurona Gerber, Dominik Bork, and Dimitris Karagiannis. Matching Technology with Enterprise Architecture and Enterprise Architecture Management Tasks Using Task Technology Fit
   - Noa Roy-Hubara, Peretz Shoval, and Arnon Sturm. A Method for Database Selection.

4. Domain-specific and ontology modeling:

   - Andreas L. Opdahl and Bjørnar Tessem. Toward Ontological Support for Journalistic Angles
   - Asha Rajbhoj, Shailesh Deshpande, Jayavardhana Gubbi, Vinay Kulkarni, and Balamuralidhar P. A System for Semi-automatic Construction of Image Processing Pipeline for Complex Problems
   - Ulrich Frank. Specification and Management of Methods — A Case for Multi-Level Modeling

5. Evaluation of modeling approaches:

- Azzam Maraee and Arnon Sturm. The Usage of Constraint Specification Languages: A Controlled Experiment
- Drazen Brdjanin and Stefan Ilic. Dealing with Structural Differences in Serialized BPMN Models
- Ilia Bider and Arian Chalak. Evaluating Usefulness of a Fractal Enterprise Model. Experience Report

The EMMSAD 2019 program further included a session of presentations and a panel on EMMSAD-related topics.

We wish to thank the EMMSAD 2019 authors for having shared their work with us, as well as the members of EMMSAD 2019 Program Committee for their valuable reviews. Special thanks go to the track chairs for their help in EMMSAD advertising and decision-making. Finally, we thank the organizers of CAiSE 2019 for their help with the organization of the event and IFIP WG8.1 for its support.

April 2019

Iris Reinhartz-Berger
Jelena Zdravkovic

BPMDS 2019 Organization

Organizers

Jens Gulden — University of Duisburg-Essen, Germany
Rainer Schmidt — Munich University of Applied Sciences, Germany

Steering Committee

Ilia Bider — Stockholm University and IbisSoft, Sweden
Selmin Nurcan — Université Paris 1 Panthéon - Sorbonne, France
Rainer Schmidt — Munich University of Applied Sciences, Germany
Pnina Soffer — University of Haifa, Israel

Industrial Advisory Board

Ilia Bider — Stockholm University and IbisSoft, Sweden
Pascal Negros — Arch4IE, France
Gil Regev — EPFL and Itecor, Switzerland

Program Committee

João Paulo A. Almeida — Federal University of Espirito Santo, Brazil
Judith Barrios Albornoz — University of Los Andes, Colombia
Kahina Bessai — Loria University of Lorraine, France
Ilia Bider — Stockholm University/IbisSoft, Sweden
Karsten Boehm — FH KufsteinTirol - University of Applied Science, Austria
Dominik Bork — University of Vienna, Austria
Lars Brehm — Munich University of Applied Science, Germany
Cristina Cabanillas — Vienna University of Economics and Business, Austria
Dirk Fahland — Eindhoven University of Technology, The Netherlands
Claude Godart — Loria University of Lorraine, France
Renata Guizzardi — Universidade Federal do Espirito Santo, Brazil
Jens Gulden — University of Duisburg-Essen, Germany
Amin Jalali — Stockholm University, Sweden
Paul Johannesson — Royal Institute of Technology, Sweden
Monika Kaczmarek-Heß — University of Duisburg-Essen, Germany
Marite Kirikova — Riga Technical University, Latvia
Agnes Koschmider — Karlsruhe Institute of Technology, Germany
Marcello La Rosa — The University of Melbourne, Australia
Michael Möhring — Aalen University, Germany
Jens Nimis — University of Applied Sciences Karlsruhe, Germany

Selmin Nurcan	Université Paris 1 Panthéon - Sorbonne, France
Oscar Pastor Lopez	Universitat Politècnica de València, Spain
Elias Pimenidis	University of the West of England, UK
Gregor Polančič	Univerza v Mariboru, Slovenia
Gil Regev	Ecole Polytechnique Fédérale de Lausanne, Switzerland
Manfred Reichert	University of Ulm, Germany
Iris Reinhartz-Berger	University of Haifa, Israel
Stefanie Rinderle-Ma	University of Vienna, Austria
Colette Rolland	Université Paris 1 Panthéon - Sorbonne, France
Michael Rosemann	Queensland University of Technology, Australia
Shazia Sadiq	The University of Queensland, Australia
Rainer Schmidt	Munich University of Applied Sciences, Germany
Stefan Schönig	University of Bayreuth, Germany
Samira Si-Said Cherfi	CEDRIC - Conservatoire National des Arts et Métiers, France
Pnina Soffer	University of Haifa, Israel
Han van der Aa	Humboldt-Universität zu Berlin, Germany
Barbara Weber	University of St. Gallen, Switzerland
Matthias Weidlich	Humboldt-Universität zu Berlin, Germany
Jelena Zdravkovic	Stockholm University, Sweden
Alfred Zimmermann	Reutlingen University, Germany

Additional Reviewers

Augusto, Adriano
Indiono, Conrad
Steinau, Sebastian
Stertz, Florian
Taymouri, Farbod

EMMSAD 2019 Organization

Program Chairs

Iris Reinhartz-Berger   University of Haifa, Israel
Jelena Zdravkovic   Stockholm University, Sweden

Track Chairs

Oscar Pastor Lopez   Universitat Politècnica de València, Spain
Jolita Ralyté   University of Geneva, Switzerland
Paul Grefen   Eindhoven University of Technology, The Netherlands
Dimitris Karagiannis   University of Vienna, Austria
Monique Snoeck   Katholieke Universiteit Leuven, Belgium
Arnon Sturm   Ben-Gurion University, Israel
Tony Clark   Aston University, UK
Heinrich C. Mayr   Alpen-Adria-Universität Klagenfurt, Austria
Renata Guizzardi   Universidade Federal do Espirito Santo, Brazil
Jennifer Horkoff   Chalmers and the University of Gothenburg, Sweden

Advisory Committee

John Krogstie   Norwegian University of Science and Technology, Norway
Henderik A. Proper   Luxembourg Institute of Science and Technology, Luxembourg

Program Committee

Claudia P. Ayala   Universitat Politècnica de Catalunya, Spain
Mira Balaban   Ben-Gurion University of the Negev, Israel
Monalessa Barcellos   UFES
Ladjel Bellatreche   LIAS/ENSMA
Dominik Bork   University of Vienna, Austria
Drazen Brdjanin   University of Banja Luka, Bosnia
Robert Andrei Buchmann   Babe-Bolyai University of Cluj Napoca, Romania
Luis M. Camarinha-Matos   Nova University of Lisbon, Portugal
Nelly Condori-Fernández   Universidade da Coruña, Spain
Dolors Costal   Universitat Politècnica de Catalunya, Spain
Maya Daneva   University of Twente, The Netherlands
Sybren De Kinderen   University of Luxembourg, Austria
Claudio Di Ciccio   Vienna University of Economics and Business, Austria
Elisabetta Di Nitto   Politecnico di Milano, Italy

Stanislaw Wrycza	University of Gdansk, Poland
Marielba Zacarias	Universidade do Algarve, Portugal
Anna Zamansky	University of Haifa, Israel

Additional Reviewers

Faber, Anne
Gall, Manuel
Kleehaus, Martin
Winter, Karolin

Modeling and AI: Friends or Foes?
(Keynote)

Jordi Cabot (ID)

ICREA Barcelona Spain
Universitat Oberta de Catalunya, Barcelona, Spain
jordi.cabot@icrea.cat

Extended Abstract

AI is infiltrating all industries and the software industry is no exception. In fact, as of today, there are already several initiatives claiming the (prospective) applications of AI in the different phases of the software development lifecycle [1, 4, 5], from the requirement analysis and design to the development, testing, deployment and maintenance. But, is this a fad or really the future of software development? And, if so, what role could modeling play in this future?

In this talk, we will review promising applications of AI techniques in conceptual modeling, business process modeling, systems modeling and, in general, any branch of model-driven engineering; and discuss the many challenges that remain to be solved before we see the first real and usable AI-enhanced modeling technique or IDE.

Among other examples, we will discuss how neural networks can kill model transformation languages, how virtual modelers could become our ideal "pair designer" or the use of graph kernels to cluster modeling artefacts [2]. The recently created Modelia[1] initiative aims to support research activities around these topics.

But make no mistake, AI may need us more than we need AI. The future of AI is model-based. During the talk, we will also cover how modeling can help to bring AI to the masses and simplify the fragmented landscape of AI libraries, platforms and tools. As an example, we will see how DSLs (Domain-Specific Languages) can facilitate the definition and generation of AI pipelines and components, such as chatbots [3], by enabling their specification at a higher abstraction level.

References

1. Cabot, J., Clarisó, R., Brambilla, M., Gérard, S.: Cognifying model-driven software engineering. In: Seidl, M., Zschaler, S. (eds.) STAF 2017. LNCS, vol. 10748, pp. 154–160. Springer, Cham (2018)

---

[1] https://modelia.eu/.

2. Clarisó, R., Cabot, J.: Applying graph kernels to model-driven engineering problems. In: Proceedings of the 1st International Workshop on Machine Learning and Software Engineering in Symbiosis, MASES@ASE 2018, pp. 1–5 (2018)
3. Daniel, G., Cabot, J., Deruelle, L., Derras, M.: Multi-platform chatbot modeling and deployment with the jarvis framework. In: 31st International Conference on Advanced Information Systems Engineering, CAiSE 2019 (2019, to appear)
4. Lo Giudice, D.: How AI will change software development and applications. https://www.nhaustralia.com.au/documents/AI_report.pdf
5. Xie, T.: Intelligent software engineering: synergy between AI and software engineering. In: Feng, X., Müller-Olm M., Yang, Z. (eds.) SETTA 2018. LNCS, vol. 10998, pp. 3–7. Springer, Cham (2018)

Contents

Domain-Specific and Ontology Modeling (EMMSAD 2019)

Evaluation of Modeling Approaches (EMMSAD 2019)

Large and Complex Business Process Modeling and Development (BPMDS 2019)

Towards a Knowledge Base of Business Process Redesign: Forming the Structure

Neta Kettler[(⊠)], Pnina Soffer[(⊠)], and Irit Hadar[(⊠)]

University of Haifa, 199 Aba Khoushy Ave., Mount Carmel, Haifa, Israel
Neta.kettler@gmail.com,
{spnina,hadari}@is.haifa.ac.il

Abstract. Many reasons drive organizations to improve their existing business processes. Designing an improvement is complex; it requires familiarity with the process under consideration and vast knowledge and expertise in the field of business processes. Therefore, there is no substitute for an expert judgment while designing a process improvement. Yet, experts' knowledge is limited by their experience. In this paper, we present our vision of supporting more informed expert decisions. This vision is based on designing a knowledge-based solution in order to facilitate sharing experience from past cases gained by various organizations. More specifically, this paper focuses on the first step that is required for constructing a knowledge base: designing its structure. To formulate a representative structure, we studied cases reported in literature and formulated a baseline structure grounded in the reviewed literature. We examined its coverage for additional cases originating in literature and added additional features where needed, until we reached saturation. The proposed structure distinguishes between the features that characterize a situation that leads to a redesign act and the set of improvement actions performed as a result.

Keywords: Business processes · Business processes redesign · Knowledge base

1 Introduction

In today's ever-changing business environment, businesses are often subject to competition, market fluctuations, globalization efforts, and changing regulation by the legislature [5, 22]. These concerns lead organizations to regularly monitor and improve the way they do business, which is directly reflected by their business processes (BP). BP represent a holistic approach striving to achieve organizational goals through a set of activities, which manage how human resources and materials are utilized in a process and how the work is synchronized among them [5, 11].

Over the years, many methods and approaches have been developed for BP improvement. These approaches eventually evolved into an overall approach within the business process management (BPM) area, whose purpose is to establish an ongoing act of improvement through a set of supportive tools and methods for managing the organization with an emphasis on its processes [7, 22, 26, 49]. Common streams in the literature of this discipline include: Total Productive Maintenance (TPM) [18, 31],

© Springer Nature Switzerland AG 2019
I. Reinhartz-Berger et al. (Eds.): BPMDS 2019/EMMSAD 2019, LNBIP 352, pp. 3–18, 2019.
https://doi.org/10.1007/978-3-030-20618-5_1

Total Quality Management (TQM) [13, 14, 18], Six Sigma [2, 12, 40], Lean Management [8, 18, 46, 50], Benchmarking [3], Business Process Reengineering or Business Process Redesign (BPR) [11, 12, 21], and Process Innovation [5]. Methods in these streams provide guidance to system analysts during the process of improvement. However, the various methods do not replace the designers' judgment while designing a beneficial change.

The knowledge of process (re)designers is limited by their personal experiences. In order to enrich the designers of process changes, by exposing them to the experience of others, extensive knowledge sharing is required. We argue that establishing a knowledge base (KB) constructed based on past experience, can be helpful to process designers. While efforts have been made in similar directions [32, 33, 37, 38], we believe that additional work is still needed for obtaining a systematically-collected and contemporary body of empirical data. Therefore, our objective is building a repository of redesign cases in a form of a KB that will enable the following:

1. Querying improvement alternatives for a given situation based on common situation characteristics.
2. Investigating the relations between situation characteristics and improvement alternatives that may be proper to apply and yield successful outcomes.
3. Identifying improvement alternatives for unfamiliar situations.

As part of an extensive research, we pursue an iterative approach consisting of two iterations: a first iteration, which is the focus of this paper, defines the structure of the required KB, and a second iteration (in progress) seeks to populate its content. In that vein, this paper aims to answer the following question: In what structure should redesign data be arranged, in order to support revealing connections between the situations, in which process improvement is initiated, and appropriate improvement actions.

Towards the overall goal of both iterations, we will perform a systematic literature review (SLR) of cases of redesign that were documented in literature. This method was selected to gain generality over different domains and process settings. The use of past cases recorded in literature through SLR provides a means of rapidly achieving an aggregated body of empirically collected data. However, in order to systematically arrange the data when populating the KB, its structure needs to be determined at the early stages of the SLR. Therefore, the first iteration, reported in this paper, consisted of a literature review of redesign cases, in which a representational structure was established and refined so as to properly represent the reviewed case studies. This was conducted until the evolving structure of the KB became stable.

As a starting point, this work takes several well-established frameworks [31–33, 37, 38, 41] that deal with the structure and components needed for representing process improvement cases. We created a unified collection of characteristics, by which we attempted to represent the cases collected in the literature review. During this process, we continuously assessed the emerging representation, and as a result, additional building blocks of this structure were revealed, and some were refined. In addition, we determined the scales and domains of values for each of the elements. This assessment continued during the execution of the review, until saturation of the structure was achieved, namely, additional cases could be represented and did not yield changes in the structure.

This concluded the first iteration, whose outcome is presented in this paper, as a proposed template for representing and storing data about process improvement initiatives, yielding a KB that can support future improvement efforts in a generic manner. Additional research is still in process with the execution of the SLR until all reviewed cases will be documented in the KB.

The rest of the paper is organized as follows: Sect. 2 discusses the background and related work that contributed to this research. Section 3 reports on research methods. Section 4 presents the research results, and Sect. 5 discusses the results and research limitation. Finally, Sect. 6 concludes with the expected contribution of this work and our next planned steps in the full research project.

2 Background and Related Work

Using KB systems (KBS) in BP redesign is not a new idea; it has been discussed for over three decades. The purpose of KBS is to enable analysis and identification of problems in the process and offer suitable alternatives using heuristics that evolved from accumulated past knowledge [37, 38]. Over the years, many efforts have been made to define the required knowledge and its structure, and many KBS have been developed. In this section, we review existing frameworks that attempt to characterize cases in which redesign has been conducted. These frameworks serve as a baseline for this work.

When talking about KBS in BP, it is worth noting the MIT process handbook [29], which represents a fundamental work in the field of BP KBS, with findings studied and congregated over a decade. This project created a repository of business processes organized in a way that enables the retrieval and utilization of business process knowledge for future (re)designing. One of the most impressive achievements in this project is the representation of the similarity between processes through different levels of process abstraction. The methods provided in this project enable storage of multitude processes in support of designing, storing and evaluating different alternatives for the same process. However, this repository represents accumulated knowledge focusing on process design, and facilitates knowledge sharing in the context of the processes and their similarities. It does not represent and analyze the situations that lead to process redesign decisions, as our envisioned KB.

One of the most prominent early works in this field was authored by Nissen [37, 38]. Nissen characterized a redesign case through a set of measurement-driven calculations. Those measurements were subsequently mapped via if-else rule-based reasoning to a problem-class taxonomy, also known as pathologies. These problem classes, in turn, were mapped to the corresponding list of transformation-class solutions. The problem-class taxonomy and transformation-class solution matrix were built upon knowledge elicited from literature in the field of re-engineering. The author notes that although this list is incomplete, it satisfies the need for which it was created. According to Nissen, the rules' generality level enables their opportunity to be applied to different domains. Following additional studies [23, 30], different domains can affect the type of changes to be applied; for example, organizations in areas that require strict quality control or areas that require security regulations. Additionally, since the taxonomy used for improvement actions was formulated in the 1990s, it can be assumed that the development of industry and technology over the past three decades requires its expansion.

Netjes et al. [32] expand Nissen's structure from two perspectives: (1) The situation in which the redesign occurred – by formulating its measurements to more accurate workflow net-analysis definitions and additional measurements. (2) The redesign alternatives – which were updated to achieve contemporary actions of change using Reijers' [41] set of redesign "best practices". Like Nissen, Netjes et al. [32] use a rule-based engine to classify "best practices" applicable to a given situation, analyzed by a measurements-driven approach. Netjes et al. [32] based their rules on the measurements only. However, in the process of selecting and evaluating the redesign alternatives, they referred to another layer that represents the purpose of the change.

Ku et al. [23] provided an overall end-to-end case-based reasoning automated recommender. First, they formulated the problem by defining the attribute set of a case, including a limited set of redesign goals, business domain, and the redesign budget. Then they defined a method for reasoning using a K-Tree based algorithm.

Another KB structure that considers the goal and domain was suggested by Mansar et al. [30] for a case-based reasoning KB. Their hierarchal structure for knowledge representation is depicted in Fig. 1. The upper-level category of this hierarchy starts with the process domain, and the lowest level ends with the redesign practices proposed by Reijers and Mansar [41]. The case attributes, expressed by the structure layers, generally describe the environment of the case and do not express metrics pointing to the specific weakness of the case.

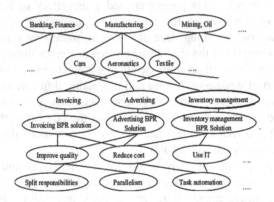

Fig. 1. Domain-dependent case hierarchy - taken from [30]

Niedermann et al. [33–36] developed a recommender tool that extracts essential behavioral information from the process management system. The tool uses a KB of redesign action practices, also known as redesign patterns, for the selection of alternatives according to the redesign goals. After the proper patterns selection, a machine learning algorithm is used for creating a process-specific design of the applied pattern. Despite the massive scope of this research, and the tool's ability to offer a solution at the design level, the components of its KB consist of the expected goal and corresponding redesign patterns only. This solution does not relate the redesign pattern to process attributes that characterize the situation prior to the redesign.

In summary, different structures have been proposed for capturing generic knowledge for process improvement, including different (partly overlapping) sets of attributes. Our aim was to use these as a basis for a unified structure, whose applicability for capturing process improvement knowledge will be grounded in an accumulated body of cases reported over the years.

3 Methods

This work presents the first iteration towards building a business process redesign KB. In order to reflect the connections between the situations in which process improvement is initiated and the appropriate act of improvement, the KB structure needs to be comprehensive and stable. In the pursuit of achieving a stable structure of KB, the following research question was defined: In what structure should redesign data be arranged to support revealing connections between initial situations and appropriate improvement actions?

We operationalized the above research question by phrasing the following concrete sub-questions:

1. What characterizes a situation that motivated a redesign action?
2. How can the redesign actions, that were carried out in order to achieve improvement, be represented?
3. How can the outcomes of the redesign be evaluated?

This research began with a literature review aimed to explore existing frameworks and constructs that are relevant to the research question. Based on this review, we developed a unified baseline framework that represents the components of the KB structure. In the consolidation phase, we examined the ability of the various attributes to provide a representative structure for mapping the characteristics of the situation to the acts of improvement. At this stage, we identified several of the baseline attributes that required refinement in order to provide more precise improvement suggestions for a given situation. In order to ensure the ability of the structure to represent a case of redesign, a collection of cases that describe redesign projects in detail was analyzed, yielding further extension, refinement, and validation of the framework.

The research method used for the full research program is systematic literature review (SLR) [19]. For the first iteration of determining the structure of the KB, a literature review was conducted, following the principles of SLR [19], until saturation of the structure was reached [9]. The review focused on cases where redesign was carried out to an existing business process. This method allowed a broad review consisting of organizations from different business areas. A search query was defined and refined to retrieve redesign implementation cases documented in literature. The final query is: ("business process") + ("redesign" OR "re-engineering" OR "improvement") + ("case study" OR "case-study" OR "case studies" OR "case-studies" OR "practice"). The relevance filtering procedure included a review of the title, abstract and the case-study sections. Articles with no redesign action or describing a general organizational change not focused on set of processes were excluded. Only articles that provide a description of "as-is" processes, which includes the description of their tasks, their synchronization and resource management, were included.

The first iteration of the literature review was conducted on the complete Springer database and a part of the AIS library. This enabled the development of a documentation strategy and the formulation of the required KB structure. The search on the Springer database retrieved 5,906 articles, from which only 37 articles were found relevant. These articles comprised of 45 cases. The AIS database was partly reviewed (100 out of 260 articles), with nine articles found relevant, resulting in 17 more cases of redesign. Each reviewed case was represented using the attributes of the evolving structural framework, assessing the ability to represent the situation, the redesign solution and its evaluation. As a result, the attributes included in the basic structure were refined, the set of attributes were expanded, and a structure that represented the connections between the various components was formed. The stability of this structure was examined using 10 additional papers that were retrieved from the IEEE database via the above described query and according to the inclusion/exclusion criteria. As the examination of those cases revealed no new information concerning required additions or modifications of the structure, we conclude that saturation has been reached [9].

4 Results

The first stage in defining the structure of the KB included the definition of its various components and their relations. For the purpose of assembling the various components and attributes that represent the structure, we explored the literature dealing with the definition of KB structures in the field of redesign, as well as the literature dealing with recommendation systems for improving BP. A prominent approach in the literature was a division to three building blocks: situation, act of improvement and output evaluation. The situation represents the "As-is" situation that raised the need for improvement. the situation can be characterized using a variety of features. The act of improvement represents redesign actions that were taken. In order to gain generality over the different cases, we will use abstract improvement patterns. Respectively, the third building block represents the evaluation measures of the applied improvement. In order to understand the relations among these components, we examined various cases of redesign in BP. In the early stages of the study, we identified that the treatment of the cases under review included a set of improvement patterns, whose contributions could not be separated. This means that the reported redesign outcome represents the combination of these patterns.

We continued to examine the literature in order to identify and understand the relevant features of the three components. We started with the feature set resolution [30, 32, 37, 38, 41] and this set was later analyzed and mapped to the sub-components.

The result of this analysis defines the framework (see Fig. 2). In this framework, three components are represented and linked:

1. Situation characteristics – features that describe the case prior to the redesign, with respect to the desired outcome. These features can be divided to:
   a. Process characteristics and measures – features that represent the nature of the process and design measures of the process under review. Examples include "process family" [30] and "value for customer" [12] (nature of the process), as well as "level of control" and "parallelism" [32] (design measures).
   b. Problems and redesign goals – The purpose for which redesign was performed, and a set of problems and constraints that are known to the organization.
   c. Organizational features – Organization or business area aspects.
2. Redesign configuration –The improvement act performed, captured as a combination of improvement patterns.
3. Output evaluation feature – Measuring the success level of the change regarding the various redesign goals.

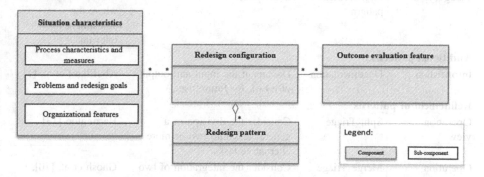

Fig. 2. Proposed KB structure

The following subsections describe in detail the set of features that represent each of the various components. First, we describe the redesign configuration, then the situational features, and finally, the output evaluation features. This order is intended to highlight the main decisions taken in a redesign project, namely, the redesign configuration. These decisions stem from the situation characteristics and thus should be understood before their possible explanation is sought.

4.1 Redesign Configuration

Since the acts of improvement reviewed were composed of sets of actions that could not be isolated in terms of output measures, we decided to represent every single case by a combination of applied patterns, which we term redesign configuration. In order to accommodate the data in a single dataset, we defined a feature for each redesign pattern. These features received a Boolean value, with "True" representing its application to the considered case and "False" otherwise.

To determine the pattern set, we examined Reijers and Mansar's "best practices" [41]. This set includes 29 redesign patterns, organized in eight higher-level categories, including: customers, operation view, behavioral view, organization: population, organization: structure, information, technology, and external environment. The justification for selecting this set as a basis lies in the way it was constructed. Since the set of patterns is based on cases that were observed or documented in the literature, and are generic in nature, we used these patterns for classifying the redesign actions in our collected dataset. After using this set as a basis while reviewing the literature, we managed to classify most of the cases accordingly. However, to accurately and consistently represent the cases under review, we had to define some additional patterns and to refine several existing ones to finer-grained ones (see Table 1). For each new or refined pattern, the table indicates references from our dataset where the adjustment was found useful.

Table 1. Redesign patterns extended and adjusted from Reijers and Mansar's [41].

Category	Improvement pattern	Description	Example papers where the adjustment is relevant
Additional patterns			
Information	Documentation	Document the input and output of a task for future use	AbdEllatif et al. [1]
Refinement of patterns			
Operation view	Split Triage	Consider the division of a general task into two or more alternative tasks	Harrington [13]
Operation view	Merge Triage	Consider the integration of two or more alternative tasks into one general task	Ghosh et al. [10], Kloos et al. [20]
Operation view	Merge Task composition	Combine small tasks into composite tasks	Ghosh et al. [10], Jansen-Vullers et al. [16]
Operation view	Split Task composition	Divide large tasks into workable smaller tasks	Ghosh et al. [10], Jansen-Vullers et al. [16]
Organization: population	Specialist	Use more specialized roles	Ghosh et al. [10], Jansen-Vullers et al. [16]
Organization: population	Generalist	Make resources more generalist over the tasks required by the process	Ghosh et al. [10], Jansen-Vullers et al. [16]

4.2 Situation Characteristics

This component represents the situation before the applied improvement as a list of features. The initial feature list was defined based on Netjes et al.'s [32] set of measurements, which was expanded from Nissen [38]. After a partial review of cases extracted from the literature and an examination of the baseline framework coverage, we refined some of the features and complemented the baseline list by features adapted from additional sources [4, 12, 30, 45]. The resulting feature list includes:

1. Features that were adopted from Netjes et al. (without modification [32]);
2. Features of Netjes et al. [32] that were refined (see Table 2);
3. Additional features adapted from a variety of sources to support the data analysis (see Table 3).

The refinement and addition of features involved two criteria:

1. When a more distinct link to redesign patterns could be established with the refined or additional feature(s).
2. At least one case in the dataset could be represented more accurately with the refined or additional feature(s).

Table 2. List of refined features based on Netjes et al. [32]

Situational feature	Justification of refinement
Internal process contacts	This feature is a refinement of the "process contacts" feature, which ties together all communication tasks: internal and external. We argue that internal and external contacts may have a different effect on the selected solution and hence we divided this feature to distinguish internal process contacts. An example which ties high assessment of internal process contacts to a specific improvement pattern can be found in [39], while [20] is an example where a high assessment of external process connections cannot be related to that specific pattern
Client process contacts	Following the division of the "process contact" feature to external and internal ones, we further divided the external contacts into those related to clients and those related to other external-entities (suppliers, law authorities, etc.). Examples which tie high assessment of client contacts and low external-entities process contacts to a specific improvement pattern can be found in [16, 47], while [20, 43] present examples where a low assessment of client contacts and high external-entities process contacts cannot be related to that specific pattern
External-entities process contacts	Examples of cases with a high external-entities contacts assessment and a low client contacts assessment resulting in a different application of patterns can be found in [43, 48]
Resource usage	The specification of this feature extends the original one to include an overall observation of the resource usage rather than a local perspective within the process itself. An example of a case where one process affects resource utilization across different processes can be found in [17]

Table 3. List of situation features added or adapted from additional sources

Situational feature	Description	Source	Justification of adaptation
Process characteristics and measures			
Variability	A measure of alternative paths within the process	–	Different variability levels may result in different redesign patterns. We found several cases of high variability which resulted in common patterns. Examples can be found in [6, 25, 42]
Waste	A measure of tasks whose output is not consumed by the following task	Conger [4]	Once a task does not consume the output of the previous task, then the previous task can be considered redundant or required only at a later stage of the process. We found cases with high "waste" indicators which resulted in similar redesign patterns. Examples can be found in [7, 43]
knowledge-intensiveness evaluation	A measure of the knowledge intensiveness of the process	Seidmann et al. [45]	We found several cases that indicate a possible connection between this feature and an associated redesign pattern. Examples can be found in [4, 6]
Value for customers	• Core – directly adds value for the customer. • Support - supports the functioning of the core processes. • Management - plans the core processes	Harmon [12]	The category of the value of the process for the customer may affect the selection of a certain pattern. Several cases revealed a possible connection between "support" value and the applied patterns. Examples can be found in [6, 22]
Process family	Process type (e.g., procurement, order fulfillment, patent intake etc.)	Mansar et al. [30]	Common improvement patterns are observed for process families irrespective of the details of the process elements. For example, all the help-desk service cases that were collected until now used similar patterns regardless of their domain (finance, telecommunications, and industrial environment). Examples can be found in [4, 15, 25]

(continued)

Table 3. (*continued*)

Granularity level	An assessment of process abstraction level: 1-high level 5-detailed	Lodhi et al. [28]	This feature was derived from our data elicitation approach. We found that information retrieved based on a scholar's report may result in different abstraction levels, focusing on certain aspects and hiding others. This may cause bias when attempting to associate situation features (that lack details or are extremely detailed about specific aspects such as tasks of process control, communication, and others) with redesign patterns Examples can be found in [15, 38, 47]
Redesign Goals			
Goals	The goals of the redesign – the desired outcome variable	Mansar et al. [30]	The goal of the improvement, whether it is time, cost, flexibility or quality, has a connection to the selected pattern. Examples can be found in [7, 20, 27]
Motivation	classification according to a taxonomy of identified problems and enablers like unskilled labor force, new regulations, overlapping of responsibilities between roles etc.	Nissen [37]	This feature was added in order to enrich the goals with contextual problems known to the organization. An example of "unskilled labor force" can be found in [24]
Organizational features			
Domain	Business area such as retail, healthcare, industrial environment, finance etc.	Mansar et al. [30]	The business area may be relevant for ruling out or supporting the need for a specific action. The review revealed a possible connection between some domains and selected redesign patterns. Finance examples: [4, 20, 32], health examples: [2, 43, 47]
Sub-domain	Sub business area – for example emergency, mental health, etc.	Mansar et al. [30]	In some domains, specific areas within the domain may be differently associated to redesign patterns. For example, in mental care some patterns are more dominant then in other healthcare sub-domains. An example can be found in [47]

Note that the features in Tables 2, 3 refer to measures, indicators, and assessments. A major concern, when developing the envisioned KB, is to set the domains of values of the features in a comparable, unbiased, and consistent way. Different ways of obtaining the values were suggested in the literature, ranging from a completely qualitative textual description to precisely-calculated metrics [32]. Our data collection, by retrieving cases from the literature, results in many approaches and granularity levels of process presentation. Therefore, a precise calculation of features following Netjes et al. [32] could not always be achieved, and introduces a risk of yielding misleading values based on incomplete and biased representation. To overcome this limitation, we decided to use a 1–5 scale assessment, which partly relies (whenever possible) on the calculated metrics suggested by Netjes et al. [32]. The conversion to this scale is based on the variability and standard scores observed in the data. This strategy was used in order to mitigate risks of bias and inaccuracies stemming from the different reporting and modeling methods observed in the literature.

4.3 Outcome Evaluation Features

In order to represent the outcome achieved in redesign projects, we started with the redesign output evaluation criteria proposed by Reijers and Mansar [41]: cost, quality, flexibility and time. Each feature could assume a value of −1(negative), 0 (neutral) or 1 (positive). Reviewing the cases in our dataset revealed additional success measurements, which were added to our list. These include: client satisfaction, capacity (in terms of the possible number of concurrent instances), and resource utilization (separately assessed for human and non-human resources). The outcomes of process redesign and their classification will enable comparison with the goals of the redesign, in order to assess the success level of the applied improvement.

5 Discussion

Building a KB structure required for the embodiment of any business process redesign project is a challenging mission. Such KB should encompass all aspects of a redesign project along its timeline: starting from the situation leading to the improvement decision, the chosen redesign actions and finally the evaluation of their outcomes. A main challenge lies in how to represent each of these components separately and their relationships. Following the SLR research method for the purpose of the data collection allowed us to systematically capture high volume and diversity over different process types and business domains. This, in turn, allowed obtaining a body of empirical evidence, which could not be accomplished in an industry field study.

This work makes extensive use of knowledge accumulated in literature, however its main contribution is in its systematic establishment of the KB structure. Another contribution is our representation of redesign configurations. This approach gives meaning to sets of patterns and the relationships among them, thereby enriching the existing approaches that address each pattern separately.

Despite the many advantages of collecting data via literature review, this method holds several limitations. First, it became apparent during our study that feature values could not be determined precisely, since the cases reported in the literature are not uniform in their reporting methods, focus, and their granularity level. In order to achieve comparability, we chose a uniform scale of values, namely, assessments on a scale of 1–5. Second, relying on reports from the past two decades, we may miss technological progress and innovations in acts of redesign which had not yet been recorded in the literature. We argue that the features of our proposed KB structure are sufficiently generic to represent additional cases in this area as well. For example, the pattern "automation" used to represent a transition of processes from manual to computerized or IS-supported in the past. Analogically, at present it can be used to represent a transition from expert-based to machine (AI)-based decision making.

Another possible limitation is a bias that may be caused by the academic literature presentation format, which constitutes a barrier for cases that could not fit into an academic paper. To address this, we added the granularity level feature, which enables relating to processes, whose granularity of representation is low, as higher-level processes. These can be associated to large processes in organizations that can be broken down into small sub-processes coordinated by the higher-level process.

To summarize, this paper presented our work, aimed to systematically and generically establish a structure for a business process redesign KB, which emphasizes generality and flexibility in order to mitigate its limitations. The next iteration of our research program will be aimed at populating the KB based on the full-scale SLR.

6 Conclusion

The objective of the study was to establish a structural basis for a business process redesign knowledge base (KB). This KB will enable process designers to explore potential solutions for problems similar to those encountered in the past, or seek solutions in situations of uncertainty. In order to create a sufficient KB, the features that represent a situation in which redesign is performed and the corresponding patterns of actions need to be determined. In this work, a structural basis for a business process redesign KB was established by combining, refining, extending and validating several existing frameworks of structural components in the field of business process decision support. These components have been assembled and tested for their ability to cover various cases in which redesign was performed.

The formed KB enbles the representation of connections between business situations and redesign actions, shedding light on the existing state-of-the-art redesign behavior, and can be used as a basis for future research in the field of automated redesign solutions. This work repersents our first iteration in a broader effort towards the creation of a redesign KB. In the current iteration we provide the KB structure and determine the capabilities of an envisioned KB in supporting redesign decision making. The next iteration will continue to populate the KB, according to its structure as determined in this study, by performing a complete SLR and investigating the relationships between each feature and each process improvement pattern in the full dataset. Future research directions also include abstract representation of similar situations components using meta model maps [44] for the purpose of building and organizing the knowledge base to enhance its querying abilities.

Acknowledgement. This research is supported by the Israel Science Foundation under grant agreement 669/17.

References

1. AbdEllatif, M., Farhan, M.S., Shehata, N.S.: Overcoming business process reengineering obstacles using ontology-based knowledge map methodology. Future Comput. Inf. J. **3**(1), 7–28 (2018)
2. Alexander, M.: Six sigma: the breakthrough management strategy revolutionizing the world's top corporations (2001)
3. Becker, J., Janiesch, C.: Restrictions in process design: a case study on workflows in healthcare. In: ter Hofstede, A., Benatallah, B., Paik, H.-Y. (eds.) BPM 2007. LNCS, vol. 4928, pp. 323–334. Springer, Heidelberg (2008). https://doi.org/10.1007/978-3-540-78238-4_34
4. Conger, S.: Six sigma and business process management. In: vom Brocke, J., Rosemann, M. (eds.) Handbook on Business Process Management 1. IHIS, pp. 127–146. Springer, Heidelberg (2015). https://doi.org/10.1007/978-3-642-45100-3_6
5. Davenport, T.H.: Process Innovation Reengineering Work through Information Technology. Harvard Business Press, Boston (1993)
6. Dias, D.: Method for Improving Healthcare Management Using Enterprise Ontology, Doctoral dissertation, Master Dissertation from Instituto Superior Técnico (2012)
7. Falk, T., Griesberger, P., Leist, S.: Patterns as an artifact for business process improvement - insights from a case study. In: vom Brocke, J., Hekkala, R., Ram, S., Rossi, M. (eds.) DESRIST 2013. LNCS, vol. 7939, pp. 88–104. Springer, Heidelberg (2013). https://doi.org/10.1007/978-3-642-38827-9_7
8. Feld, W.M.: Lean Manufacturing Tools, Techniques, and How to Use Them. CRC Press, Boca Raton (2000)
9. Fusch, P.I., Ness, L.R.: Are we there yet? Data saturation in qualitative research. The Qual. Rep. **20**(9), 1408–1416 (2015)
10. Ghosh, D., Tanniru, M.: Generating and evaluating process redesign options: a network modeling approach. Ann. Oper. Res. **71**, 293–315 (1997)
11. Hammer, M.: Reengineering work don't automate, obliterate. Harvard Bus. Rev. **68**(4), 104–112 (1990)
12. Harmon, P.: The scope and evolution of business process management. In: Brocke, J., Rosemann, M. (eds.) Handbook on Business Process Management 1, pp. 37–81. Springer, Heidelberg (2010). https://doi.org/10.1007/978-3-642-00416-2_3
13. Harrington, H.J.: Business Process Improvement: The Breakthrough Strategy for Total Quality, Productivity, and Competitiveness. McGraw Hill Professional (1991)
14. Harrington, H.J.: Business process improvement. Association for Quality and Participation (1994)
15. Hofacker, I., Vetschera, R.: Algorithmical approaches to business process design. Comput. Oper. Res. **28**(13), 1253–1275 (2001)
16. Jansen-Vullers, M.H., Netjes, M., Reijers, H.A., Stegeman, M.J.: A redesign framework for call centers. In: Dustdar, S., Fiadeiro, J.L., Sheth, Amit P. (eds.) BPM 2006. LNCS, vol. 4102, pp. 306–321. Springer, Heidelberg (2006). https://doi.org/10.1007/11841760_21
17. Jiao, Y-Y., Li, K., Jiao, R.J.: A case study of hospital patient discharge process re-engineering using RFID. In: 2008 4th IEEE International Conference on Management of Innovation and Technology. IEEE (2008)

18. Kedar, A.P., Lakhe, R.R., Deshpande, V.S., Washimkar, P.V., Wakhare, M.V.: A comparative review of TQM, TPM and related organisational performance improvement programs. In: 2008 First International Conference on Emerging Trends in Engineering and Technology, ICETET, pp. 725–730. IEEE, July 2008
19. Kitchenham, B., Charters, S.: Guidelines for performing systematic literature reviews in software engineering, Technical report, EBSE Technical report EBSE-2007–01, pp 1–57 (2007)
20. Kloos, M., Hulstijn, J., Seck, M., Janssen, M.: XBRL-driven business process improvement: a simulation study in the accounting domain. In: Counsell, S., Núñez, M. (eds.) SEFM 2013. LNCS, vol. 8368, pp. 288–305. Springer, Cham (2014). https://doi.org/10.1007/978-3-319-05032-4_21
21. Knorr, R.O.: Business process redesign key to competitiveness. J. Bus. Strateg. 12(6), 48–51 (1991)
22. Ko, R.K., Lee, S.S., Wah Lee, E.: Business process management (BPM) standards: a survey. Bus. Process Manag. J. 15(5), 744–791 (2009)
23. Ku, S., Suh, Y.H., Tecuci, G.: Building an intelligent business process reengineering system: a case-based approach. Intell. Syst. Account. Financ. Manag. 5(1), 25–39 (1996)
24. Kutucuoglu, K.Y., Hamali, J., Sharp, J.M., Irani, Z.: Enabling BPR in maintenance through a performance measurement system framework. Int. J. Flex. Manuf. Syst. 14(1), 33–52 (2002)
25. Lederer, M., Schott, P., Kurz, M.: Subject-oriented business processes meet strategic management: two case studies from the manufacturing industry. In: Fleischmann, A., Schmidt, W., Stary, C. (eds.) S-BPM in the Wild, pp. 13–34. Springer, Cham (2015). https://doi.org/10.1007/978-3-319-17542-3_2
26. Lee, R.G., Dale, B.G.: Business process management a review and evaluation. Bus. Process Manag. J. 4(3), 214–225 (1998)
27. Liu, Y., Iijima, J.: A case study of business process simulation in the context of enterprise engineering. In: Aveiro, D., Pergl, R., Valenta, M. (eds.) EEWC 2015. LNBIP, vol. 211, pp. 96–110. Springer, Cham (2015). https://doi.org/10.1007/978-3-319-19297-0_7
28. Lodhi, A., Köppen, V.: Business process modeling for post execution analysis and Improvement. In: Proceedings of the 2011 5th International Conference on Software, Knowledge Information, Industrial Management and Applications (SKIMA), pp. 1–8. IEEE (2011)
29. Malone, T.W., Crowston, K., Herman, G.A.: Organizing Business Knowledge: The MIT Process Handbook. MIT press, Cambridge (2003)
30. Mansar, S.L., Marir, F., Reijers, H.A.: Case-based reasoning as a technique for knowledge management in business process redesign. Electron. J. Knowl. Manag. 1(2), 113–124 (2003)
31. Nakajima, S.: Introduction to TPM Total Productive Maintenance (Preventative Maintenance Series). Hardcover (1988). ISBN 0-91529-923-2
32. Netjes, M., Mansar, S.L., Reijers, Hajo A., van der Aalst, W.M.P.: Performing business process redesign with best practices: an evolutionary approach. In: Filipe, J., Cordeiro, J., Cardoso, J. (eds.) ICEIS 2007. LNBIP, vol. 12, pp. 199–211. Springer, Heidelberg (2008). https://doi.org/10.1007/978-3-540-88710-2_16
33. Niedermann, F., Schwarz, H.: Deep business optimization: making business process optimization theory work in practice. In: Halpin, T., et al. (eds.) BPMDS/EMMSAD -2011. LNBIP, vol. 81, pp. 88–102. Springer, Heidelberg (2011). https://doi.org/10.1007/978-3-642-21759-3_7
34. Niedermann, F., Maier, B., Radeschütz, S., Schwarz, H., Mitschang, B.: Automated process decision making based on integrated source data. In: Abramowicz, W. (ed.) BIS 2011. LNBIP, vol. 87, pp. 160–171. Springer, Heidelberg (2011). https://doi.org/10.1007/978-3-642-21863-7_14

35. Niedermann, F., Radeschütz, S., Mitschang, B.: Business process optimization using formalized optimization patterns. In: Abramowicz, W. (ed.) BIS 2011. LNBIP, vol. 87, pp. 123–135. Springer, Heidelberg (2011). https://doi.org/10.1007/978-3-642-21863-7_11

36. Niedermann, F., Radeschütz, S., Mitschang, B.: Deep business optimization a platform for automated process optimization. In: ISSS/BPSC 2010, pp. 168–180 (2010)

37. Nissen, M.E.: An intelligent tool for process redesign manufacturing supply-chain applications. Int. J. Flex. Manuf. Syst. 12(4), 321–339 (2000)

38. Nissen, M.E.: Redesigning reengineering through measurement-driven inference. MIS Q. 22(4), 509–534 (1998)

39. Øvrelid, E., Sanner, T. Siebenherz, A.: Creating coordinative paths from admission to discharge: the role of lightweight IT in hospital digital process innovation. In: Proceedings of the 51st Hawaii International Conference on System Sciences (2018)

40. Pande, P.S., Neuman, R.P., Cavanagh, R.R.: The Six Sigma Way: How GE, Motorola, and Other Top Companies Are Honing Their Performance. McGraw-Hill, New York (2000)

41. Reijers, H.A., Mansar, S.L.: Best practices in business process redesign an overview and qualitative evaluation of successful redesign heuristics. Omega 33(4), 283–306 (2005)

42. Riempp, G.: Wide area workflow management in practical application. In: Riempp, G. (ed.) Wide Area Workflow Management, pp. 233–251. Springer, London (1998). https://doi.org/10.1007/978-1-4471-1578-6_7

43. Roberts, B., Thomas, G.: Integrating E-commerce into the retail supply chain. In: Andersen, K.V., Elliot, S., Swatman, P., Trauth, E., Bjørn-Andersen, N. (eds.) Seeking Success in E-Business. IFIP — The International Federation for Information Processing, vol. 123, pp. 365–383. Springer, Boston (2003). https://doi.org/10.1007/978-0-387-35692-1_21

44. Rolland, C., Salinesi, C., Etien, A.: Eliciting gaps in requirements change. Requirements Eng. 9(1), 1–15 (2004)

45. Seidmann, A., Sundararajan, A.: Information technology, performance control and organizational structure: effects on business process redesign. Inf. Technol. 8, 16–996 (1996)

46. Shah, R., Ward, P.T.: Lean manufacturing: context, practice bundles, and performance. J. Oper. Manag. 21(2), 129–149 (2003)

47. Smits, M.: Impact of policy and process design on the performance of intake and treatment processes in mental health care: a system dynamics case study. J. Oper. Res. Soc. 61(10), 1437–1445 (2010)

48. Van den Bergh, J., Viaene, S.: Process innovation: redesigning an enterprise backbone system. In: Poels, G. (ed.) CONFENIS 2012. LNBIP, vol. 139, pp. 1–17. Springer, Heidelberg (2013). https://doi.org/10.1007/978-3-642-36611-6_1

49. van der Aalst, W.M.P., ter Hofstede, A.H.M., Weske, M.: Business process management: a survey. In: van der Aalst, W.M.P., Weske, M. (eds.) BPM 2003. LNCS, vol. 2678, pp. 1–12. Springer, Heidelberg (2003). https://doi.org/10.1007/3-540-44895-0_1

50. Yang, M.G.M., Hong, P., Modi, S.B.: Impact of lean manufacturing and environmental management on business performance: an empirical study of manufacturing firms. Int. J. Prod. Econ. 129(2), 251–261 (2011)

Coordinating Large Distributed Process Structures

Sebastian Steinau(✉), Kevin Andrews, and Manfred Reichert

Institute of Databases and Information Systems, Ulm University, Ulm, Germany
{sebastian.steinau,kevin.andrews,manfred.reichert}@uni-ulm.de

Abstract. Representing a business process as interacting small processes has become feasible with data-centric business process management paradigms. These small processes have relations and, thereby, form a relational process structure. The interactions of processes within this relational process structure must be coordinated to arrive at a meaningful overall business goal. However, relational process structures may become arbitrarily large and, with cloud technology, they may additionally be distributed over multiple nodes. Coordination processes have been proposed to coordinate relational process structures, where processes have one-to-many and many-to-many relations at run-time. This paper shows how multiple coordination processes can be used in a decentralized fashion to coordinate large, distributed process structures. The main challenge is to effectively realize the coordinated responsibility of each coordination process. Key components of the solution are the subsidiary principle and the hierarchy of the relational process structure. Moreover, from these key components and the technical properties of coordination processes, an implementation based on microservices was developed, which allows fast and concurrent enactment of multiple, decentralized coordination processes in large, distributed process structures.

Keywords: Process interactions · Relational process structure ·
Coordination process · Distributed process execution ·
BPM in the cloud

1 Introduction

Several approaches to business process management advocate to represent business processes as collections of interacting, interdependent small processes. Examples include the artifact-centric and object-aware approaches [4,5,9], where the collaboration of artifact or object lifecycle processes forms an entire business process. Principal challenges of these approaches are to determine which processes exist and how they relate to other processes, as well as the coordination of this structure of interdependent processes. Recently, the *relational process structure* [11] and *coordination processes* [10] have been proposed to tackle these challenges. A relational process structure captures processes and their relations in a hierarchical construct, which is used by a coordination process to specify

© Springer Nature Switzerland AG 2019
I. Reinhartz-Berger et al. (Eds.): BPMDS 2019/EMMSAD 2019, LNBIP 352, pp. 19–34, 2019.
https://doi.org/10.1007/978-3-030-20618-5_2

and enforce *coordination constraints*. This allows the interactions of different processes to be guided towards a meaningful overall business process.

However, fundamental challenges still remain. A relational process structure may become arbitrarily large, i.e., it may comprise hundreds or more types of processes. At run-time, hundreds or thousands of instances of these different process types are created, as well as their interrelations, compounding the problem. Furthermore, interacting small processes are particularly suited to be employed in a distributed instead of a monolithic system. In consequence, some processes may be located on one node of the distributed system, whereas other processes are located on different nodes. Existing approaches to coordinate such large process structures propose employing a single *central coordinator* (e.g., a master artifact [13]). The term *coordinator* is hereby intended as an umbrella term for any kind of process coordination model, independent of paradigm or exact specification, e.g., choreography, coordination process, or Proclet [14]. A single, central coordinator for a vast process structure is however unsuitable. The coordinator has to incorporate all coordination requirements for all processes in its model. As a result, a central coordinator model can become overloaded, inflexible, costly to maintain, and difficult to understand. As another drawback, all distributed processes must communicate with the central coordinator, creating a huge communication overhead and, more importantly, a single point of failure. Additionally, as process structures become larger, several independent substructures may emerge, where each requires an individual coordination. For example, in the automotive industry, cars may be highly customized, requiring varying constraints on the production, assembly, and testing of the parts for each car.

As process structures may become very large and different substructures may be distributed across the nodes of a server cluster, it is beneficial to distribute and split up the coordination of processes as well. While a coordination process can serve as a central coordinator, the concept is flexible so that *multiple coordination processes* may be used to coordinate a relational process structure. Thereby, several coordination processes collaborate to achieve an overall coordination of the entire process structure. However, the challenge of *coordination responsibility* must be solved, i.e., the question which coordinator is responsible for which processes. Coordination processes are uniquely suited for a decentralized application due to leveraging the hierarchical nature of the relational process structure. This allows implementing the subsidiary principle, where a coordination process only coordinates a subset of processes, defining its coordination responsibility. The result are more flexible and smaller coordination models, a clear coordination responsibility of each coordination model, and a superior maintainability. This paper contributes the decentralized and distributed application of coordination processes and modeling guidelines to effectively model coordination processes in large, distributed relational process structures.

The remainder of the paper is organized as follows. The challenges and benefits of decentralized and distributed process coordination are elaborated in Sect. 2. Section 3 introduces background information on the relational process structure and the coordination processes. Section 4 presents the key concepts of effectively using coordination processes in a large and distributed relational process structure. Furthermore, an implementation of decentralized coordination processes is presented, based on microservices. Section 5 discusses related work before Sect. 6 concludes the paper with a summary and an outlook.

2   Challenges and Benefits

The coordination of a multitude of different, interdependent processes is a complicated and challenging endeavor. Processes and their relations have to be identified and, based on these connections, suitable *coordination constraints* have to be specified and enforced. The different processes and their relations are summarized under the term *process structure*. A coordination constraint denotes a dependency that exists between two or more processes [10]. Generally, approaches for coordinating process structures involving multiple process types advocate the use of a single entity with the purpose of coordinating all involved processes. This entity is denoted as a *central coordinator*.

Central coordinators of any kind (e.g., a master artifact) are capable of properly coordinating different processes. Their main disadvantage is poor scalability in regard to the process structure. As the number of processes in a process structure grows, central coordinators must accommodate these additional processes in their coordination description. Moreover, additional coordination constraints must be incorporated into the coordination descriptions as well. This generally leads to the central coordinator model becoming large and possibly overloaded. With increasing complexity, flexibility suffers, the central coordinator model becomes more difficult to change, and the understandability of the model is impaired as well. Furthermore, performance of the central coordinator may degrade due to the large number of processes and the resulting communication overhead. As a consequence, the central coordinator might become a bottleneck for the overall performance of the business process structure.

From a functional perspective, relying on one central coordinator for coordinating everything is neither the intuitive nor the most effective way of providing process coordination for large process structures. Consider the following example of a recruitment business process.

Example 1. (Recruitment Business Process)
In the context of recruitment, applicants may apply for job offers. The overall process goal for a company is to determine who of the many applicants is best suited for the job. Applicants must write their application for a specific job offer and send it to the company. The company employees then evaluate each application by performing reviews. To reject an application or proceed with the application, a sufficient number of reviews need to be performed, e.g., the majority of reviews determines whether or not an application is rejected. If the majority of reviews are in favor of the application, the applicant is invited for one or more interviews, after which she may be hired or ultimately rejected. In the meantime, more applications may have been sent in, for which additional reviews are required, i.e., the evaluation of different applications may be handled concurrently, as well as the conduction of interviews.

Various interdependent process types can be identified in Example 1: *Job Offer*, *Application*, *Review*, and *Interview*. Each *Job Offer* is largely independent of other *Job Offers*, having its own set of applications and reviews. Consequently, a single central coordinator is tasked with coordinating each *Job Offer* independently from others. The central coordinator must recognize and keep track of different executions states of processes, decision results made during the execution as well as enforcing the appropriate coordination constraints for the *Job Offers* and their connected processes, e.g., *Applications*. This constitutes an enormous complexity for the model of the central coordinator, especially when the run-time is concerned. Moreover, the central coordinator acts as a single point of failure, as problems that might occur with any *Job Offer* may affect all other *Job Offers* as well.

As different *Job Offers* are conceptually independent from each other, a sensible solution would be to arrange that each *Job Offer* is coordinated individually with its connected other processes such as *Applications* or *Reviews*. This means that there is one model of a coordinator that is instantiated multiple times at run-time, once for each *Job Offer*. This is denoted as *stage-1 decentralized coordination*. This shift reduces model complexity, as the logic for distinguishing different *Job Offers* may be omitted due to the coordination happening on a *per-Job Offer*-basis, which in turn benefits understandability and maintainability. The additional complexity of having to instantiate a model multiple times may generally be neglected, as this is one of the core ideas of a process-oriented system. Another advantage is that this also eliminates the single point of failure. If the coordination of one *Job Offer* fails for some reason, other *Job Offers* should remain unaffected. Stage-1 decentralized coordination is inherently supported in coordination processes (cf. [10]).

The distribution of coordinators has plenty of advantages while at the same time only small costs incur. Adding more decentralized coordinators may still yield more benefits.

Example 2. (Unsolicited Application)
Consider the recruitment scenario of an "unsolicited application", i.e. an applicant sends in an *Application* without a prior *Job Offer* from the company. In case the unsolicited *Application* is accepted, a specific *Job Offer* will be created for the application.

As the coordinator that coordinates *Applications* with *Reviews* and *Interviews* is tied to a *Job Offer*, the unsolicited *Application* cannot be processed correctly without a link to a *Job Offer*. Thus, it is reasonable to add another coordinator and transfer responsibilities to it from the *Job Offer* coordinator: The new coordinator coordinates *Applications* with *Interviews* and *Reviews*, and is tied to the respective *Application*. The existing *Job Offer* coordinator is subsequently only responsible for coordinating the *Job Offer* with its related *Applications*. As a result, an unsolicited *Application* may be handled correctly in addition to the usual recruitment procedure. This further reduces the complexity of the individual coordinator models.

Employing multiple coordinators, also denoted as *stage-2 decentralized coordination*, is also advantageous in a distributed environment. Processes may run on different *nodes* in a distributed *cluster*, e.g., servers of different departments of the same company. The nodes and their communication paths are referred to as the *layout* of the cluster. As basic premise, communication within a node is performant and cheap, whereas communication between nodes is more costly. While the primary goal is the proper coordination of all involved processes, a secondary goal is to minimize communication between nodes due to its associated cost. A single central coordinator, running on one node, is forced to communicate with processes on other nodes. By distributing coordinators among nodes, e.g., one coordinator for each node, communication between nodes can be minimized, resulting in more efficient and performant communication.

To realize the benefits from the use of decentralized coordinators in process structures, several challenges must be addressed. First, it must be determined how many coordinators are necessary for a given process structure, taking the layout of a potential cluster into account. Second, the processes that require coordination must be assigned to a suitable coordinator, i.e., the *responsibility* of the coordinator must be defined. The responsibility includes that redundancies in the coordination must be avoided. Processes should be assigned, if possible, only to one coordinator, i.e., the overlap between coordinators should be minimal. Otherwise, superfluous work would be performed, or communication costs cannot be reduced compared to a single coordinator. Dividing the responsibility among several coordinators is the primary challenge of decentralized coordinators.

Coordination processes have been designed with a decentralized application in large process structures in mind, and can therefore provide a solution to enable the discussed benefits. This paper contributes new applications of coordination processes and elicits a modeling guideline to effectively utilize the potential of coordination processes.

3   Relational Process Structures and Coordination Processes

For the purposes of this paper, a process is represented in an abstract, simplified manner, which is called a *state-based view* [12]. In a state-based view, each process model is partitioned into different states that are relevant for process coordination. This allows accommodating processes modeled in different paradigms. e.g., artifact-centric or activity-centric processes. The current execution status of a process is determined by the *active state* of the state-based view. Furthermore, process types are design-time entities, from which process instances can be created at run-time. Figure 1b shows the state-based views of the processes from Example 1.

The basis for using coordination processes is the *relational process structure*. It captures all process types relevant for the specific business process [11]. Figure 1a shows the design-time relational process structure of the Recruitment Business Process (cf. Example 1). A relational process structure not only

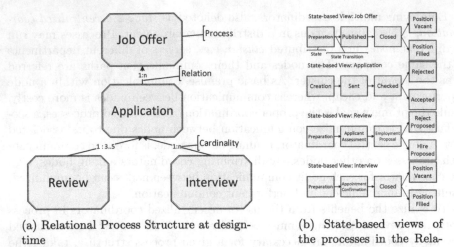

(a) Relational Process Structure at design-time

(b) State-based views of the processes in the Relational Process Structure

Fig. 1. Relational process structure and state-based views

comprises the different process types, but also includes *relations* between the process types, forming a directed acyclic graph. A relation indicates that the corresponding process types have one or more dependencies between them. A dependency may also exists transitively over a path of relations between two process types. Relations further have cardinalities, restricting how many process instances of one type at run-time may be related to an instance of another process type. Of course, this implies that processes are in one-to-many or many-to-many relationships. In order to enforce these cardinalities at run-time, the relational process structure tracks every created process instance of each process type and monitors each relation that is established between two instances. Thereby, full transparency over process instances and their relations is achieved (cf. Fig. 2), allowing a coordination approach to effectively specify constraints on process interactions at design-time and enforce them on all process instances at run-time.

Coordination processes [10] constitute an approach for managing process interactions based on the features of the relational process structure. Both coordination processes and relational process structure have their origins in the object-aware process management approach [5]. A coordination process specifies coordination constraints between process types in terms of *semantic relationships*. Semantic relationships are basic interaction patterns of processes in a one-to-many or many-to-many relationship [12]. In a coordination process, processes are represented by *coordination steps*. A semantic relationship, and consequently, a coordination constraint between two process types, is created by establishing a *coordination transition* from one coordination step to another. Figure 3 shows a coordination process that coordinates the recruitment business process (cf. Example 1).

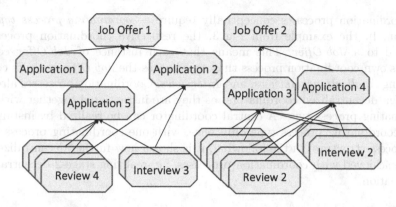

Fig. 2. Run-time relational process structure, tracking every process instance and relation (simplified view)

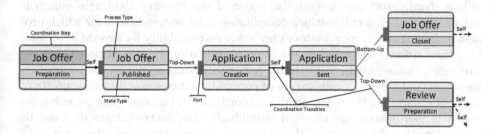

Fig. 3. Coordination process for the recruitment business process, part 1

Coordination steps specify a process type and a state of the respective process type. Each incoming semantic relationship of a coordination step represents a condition that must be fulfilled before the respective process is allowed to activate the specified state. Knowing the relations of processes from the relational process structure, fine-grained coordination of the processes becomes possible (Fig. 4).

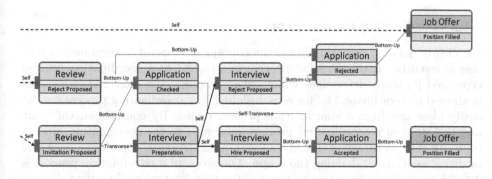

Fig. 4. Coordination process for the recruitment business process, part 2

Coordination processes conceptually require a *coordinating process type* to function. In the example from Fig. 3, the respective coordination process is attached to a *Job Offer*. This means that each instance of *Job Offer* comes with its own coordination process that coordinates the *Job Offer* with its corresponding *Applications*, *Reviews*, and *Interviews*. Coordination processes already represent decentralized coordinators, as they are instantiated together with the coordinating process type. A central coordinator can be realized by instantiating a coordinating process type only once, with one coordinating process type per process structure. In the following, it is shown how further decentralization can be achieved with coordination processes, i.e, realizing stage-2 decentralized coordination.

4   Decentralized Coordination Processes

When coordinators are decentralized, one of the primary challenges concerns *responsibility*, i.e., deciding which coordinator shall be responsible for which processes. In particular, coordinators may share responsibility for several processes, i.e., they enforce the same or different coordination constraints on the same processes. Consequently, it is crucial that coordinators do not model contradicting constraints, e.g., a combination of constraints states exactly the opposite of another constraint. With decentralized coordinators, this challenge gains importance as coordinators are modeled individually, i.e., contradictions may not be spotted easily. Consequently, the relational process structure offers a way to address this challenge, i.e., avoiding the possibility for contradictions altogether by clearly defining the responsibility of each coordinator. In particular, responsibilities must overlap as little as possible. Fundamental for the solution, the relations in a relational process structure are directed, which means that processes can be arranged hierarchically. This hierarchy is an integral part of how semantic relationships work, the cornerstone of the coordination process concept. Additionally, the hierarchy of a relational process structure offers advantages when using multiple coordination processes to coordinate a relational process structure.

4.1   Coordination Process Scope

For clearly defining responsibilities, the concept of *scope* of a coordination process is essential. A coordination process is attached to a coordinating process type, and its scope determines which other processes the coordination process is allowed to coordinate, i.e., its *responsibility*. The coordinating process can be easily identified from a coordination process model. By convention, the start and end steps of a coordination process must refer to the coordinating process type [10]. The hierarchy of the relational process structure provides an easy and intuitive solution for defining the scope. The scope of a coordination process is defined as all *lower-level process types* of the coordinating process type. Lower-level processes are all process types that have a (transitive) relation to one particular process type. Regarding the relational process structure in Fig. 1a, *Review* and *Interview* are both lower-level processes of *Application*, which in turn are all lower-level processes of *Job Offer*. Attaching a coordination process to the *Job Offer* consequently allows coordinating the entire relational process structure in Fig. 1a, i.e., *Reviews*, *Interviews*, *Job Offers* and *Applications*.

The scope of a coordination process achieves that the responsibility of a coordination process is not arbitrary, but clearly defined. This provides a great advantage when modeling decentralized coordination processes, as arbitrary responsibilities of multiple coordinators create unnecessary redundancy as well as potentially contradicting constraints, and decrease the maintainability and understandability of the overall model.

While the scope defines the responsibility of a coordination process, in a relational process structure, the scopes of multiple coordination processes may still overlap. For example, when a coordination process is attached to the top-level process in the hierarchy of the relational process structure, its scope overlaps with the scopes of coordination processes attached to lower-level processes. Consider the unsolicited application from Example 2. *Application* is a lower-level process type of *Job Offer* (cf. Fig. 1a). An unsolicited application requires its own coordination process in absence of the coordination process from a *Job Offer*. However, in the end, if an unsolicited application is accepted, a *Job Offer*, together with its associated coordination process, will be created. The *Job Offer* coordination process has the *Application* in scope.

4.2 Subsidiarity

As shown with this example, simply attaching a new coordination process to the *Application* process type creates overlapping scopes with the *Job Offer* coordination process. The required coordination constraints to coordinate *Reviews* and *Interviews* would have to be replicated in the *Application* coordination process, creating redundancy. In addition to redundancy, contradicting constraints in multiple coordination processes may, in principle, inadvertently be specified. However, the hierarchy of the relational process structure allows additional measures to remove overlap: The application of the *subsidiarity principle*. The Oxford dictionary defines subsidiarity as follows:

> **Subsidiarity** (noun)(in politics) the principle that a central authority should have a subsidiary function, performing only those tasks which cannot be performed at a more local level.[1]

Transferring this principle to both coordination processes and the relational process structure, subsidiarity means that a coordination constraint should be modeled in the lowest coordination process whose scope comprises all process types involved in the constraint. Regarding the unsolicited application, modeling any coordination constraints involving only *Application*, *Review*, and *Interview*

---

[1] https://en.oxforddictionaries.com/definition/subsidiarity.

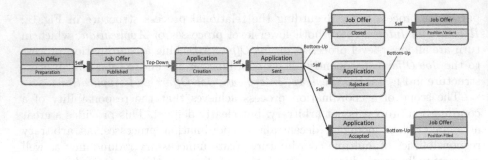

Fig. 5. Job offer coordination process

in the *Job Offer* coordination process is a clear violation of subsidiarity. By moving corresponding coordination constraints to the *Application* coordination process, subsidiarity is fulfilled. Only the coordination constraints for *Application* and *Job Offer* are kept in the *Job Offer* coordination process. Figures 5 and 6 show *Application* and *Job Offer* coordination processes after the application of the subsidiarity principle. Benefits include the proper support of the unsolicited application variant and the elimination of redundancy between coordination processes. Further, note that the correct coordination of an unsolicited application is only possible with two coordination processes. Moreover, each coordination process model is smaller, simpler and more understandable. Altogether, the subsidiarity principle and scopes enable the proper decentralized coordination of small sections of a relational process structure with coordination processes, which, in turn, collaborate as well to provide coordination for the entire relational process structure.

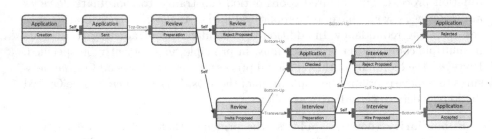

Fig. 6. Application coordination process

4.3   Coordination Processes in Distributed Environments

Distributing coordination processes across different hierarchy levels yields significant benefits for the simplicity of the coordination process models. In settings where multiple processes collaborate to achieve a business goal, it is not unreasonable to assume that these processes are not all executed on the same machine. With the advent of cloud computing, distributed applications are gaining even more momentum, as scalability is becoming an important issue [1,2]. For that matter, it is possible to distribute a relational process structure over different nodes in a distributed cluster (e.g., a cloud). Coordination processes and relational process structures originate in object-aware process management and are implemented in the PHILharmonicFlows prototype, which comprises a process execution engine based fully on microservices [1,5]. As such, the issue of distribution of processes across nodes is highly relevant not only for object-aware processes, but in the general sense as well.

Figure 7 shows an example of a feasible distribution of a relational process structure over three nodes. It assigns process types to a specific node, e.g., process A is assigned to Node 1. Each instance of A at run-time is placed onto Node 1 as well. The abstract example is chosen here instead of Example 1 due to its larger size and, therefore, a better illustration of the distribution across nodes.

In regard to process coordination in distributed environments, performance and scalability are the main challenges in addition to a correct coordination. Specifically, communication between processes, and, consequently, communication between nodes, has an important impact on the overall performance of the distributed relational process structure. In general, communication within a node is considered cheap, whereas communication between nodes is costly in terms of time and performance. This holds regardless of any specific metrics, and communication between nodes should therefore be reduced to a minimum.

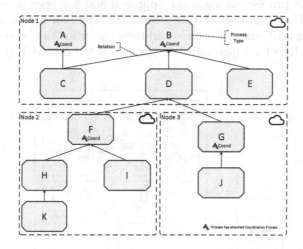

Fig. 7. Relational Process Structure distributed across different Nodes

Obviously, communication between nodes cannot be totally avoided, as processes need to be coordinated across nodes. Coordination processes, however, allow minimizing the communication between nodes significantly. By attaching coordination processes to process types where the scope encompasses the entire node, the communication is kept within a node. Note that further coordination processes within a node are still possible. In Fig. 7, process type F has a coordination process that comprises all process types of Node 2. Coordinating the process types F, H, K, and I therefore requires no communication between nodes. Process type F still requires communication with the coordination process of B on Node 1, but the communication amount of Node 2 with the coordination process of B is significantly reduced.

Altogether, coordination processes allow for the decentralized coordination of large process structures. The relational process structure hierarchy, scope, and subsidiarity principle provide clear responsibilities for each coordination process, facilitating modeling and reducing modeling errors. In particular, the coordination approach no longer contains a single point of failure. By using multiple coordination processes for the same large process structure, the individual coordination process models become smaller and simpler, resulting in greater understandability and maintainability of the models. As shown, these advantages also translate well to a distributed cluster, where a coordination process can be used for each node, significantly reducing communication overhead and, therefore, increasing performance.

4.4   Implementation

Both coordination processes and the relational process structure have been implemented in the PHILharmonicFlows prototype. This prototype is based on the object-aware process management approach and has been developed in the PHILharmonicFlows[2] project at Ulm University. The tool supports a modeling GUI, a run-time GUI where processes and their execution can be visualized, and a server with a REST-enabled interface connected to both GUIs (cf. Fig. 8).

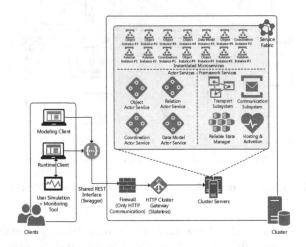

Fig. 8. PHILharmonicFlows prototype architecture

---

[2] For more details on the prototype visit https://bit.ly/2KYvyT9.

Based on this implementation, an extension of the server and GUIs has been developed to support more than one coordination process in a relational process structure. This development has been conducted based on the concepts presented in this paper. Figure 9 shows the *Application* coordination process from Fig. 6 modeled in the PHILharmonicFlows tool.

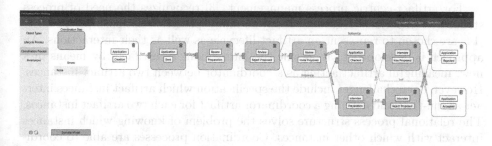

Fig. 9. Modeling the application coordination process with the PHILharmonicFlows modeling tool

The run-time engine of the server is also able to handle multiple coordination processes in a relational process structure without any adjustments. This becomes possible since the initial design of the engine considered multiple coordination processes as a future extension. Furthermore, the PHILharmonicFlows server is based on a microservice architecture [1]. Each process instance is realized as one microservice. Microservices may be organized in clusters. Therefore, a relational process structure consists of microservice processes and can be distributed in a cluster, benefiting from decentralized coordination processes as described in Sect. 4.3.

Process hierarchy and subsidiarity are simple principles, but they create challenges regarding their support *at both design and run-time*. The fact that these principles can be applied with coordination processes in a straightforward fashion to achieve decentralized process coordination in a distributed environment required extensive backing by concepts and implementations. The straightforwardness of using the principles for an intricately complex process coordination solution is the result of foresight as well as careful design and engineering. Both conceptual design and implementation in software of the relational process structure, the coordination process with its semantic relationship, and the microservice engine architecture had to converge to enable the frictionless application of decentralized coordination processes in both modeling and run-time.

5 Related Work

Artifact-centric process management [4,9] operates with artifacts that represent business entities. A business process in the artifact-centric paradigm is constituted by the interactions of the involved artifacts. As such, artifact-centric process management has been dealing with the same challenges as coordination processes in object-aware process management. Traditional activity-centric process management paradigms have investigated the interactions of different processes in one-to-one relationships, where no process structures emerge at run-time. Therefore, activity-centric process coordination is not considered close related work and is therefore not discussed here.

For artifact-centric process management, [3] recognizes the need of process structures, especially regarding many-to-many process relationships. Proclets [14] are chosen to represent an artifact lifecycle as well as their interactions. An approach is developed to represent the interactions of artifacts by means of a new, meaningful artifact acting as a coordinator between two artifact instances. However, open challenges include the specification which artifact instances interact at run-time and defining a coordinator artifact for each two artifact instances. The relational process structure solves the problem of knowing which instances interact with which other instances. Coordination processes are able to coordinate processes in any relationship, reducing the complexity compared to having a coordinator between any two processes.

Again in the context of artifact-centric process management, [13] proposes declarative artifact choreographies to coordinate the interactions of different artifacts. The declarative choreographies operate on a type-instance schema and involve many-to-many relationships between artifacts, sharing similarities with the coordination process approach. The artifact instances and their relations are captured in a correlation graph, which shares the same responsibility as a relational process structure, but is not hierarchically organized. Based on this correlation graph, declarative rules and constraints may be specified, implementing the declarative choreography. It is however unclear whether a declarative choreography acts only as a central coordinator or is capable of decentralized coordination of a correlation graph.

Finally, [6] introduces the concept of agents and location-aware artifacts. More precisely, an artifact knows which agent it (currently) belongs to. The general idea consists of agents acting upon artifacts and eventually passing artifacts on to other agents. This approach requires an interaction model between agents, i.e., a choreography. The approach synthesizes this interaction model from the lifecycles of all artifacts, which, in essence, represents a central coordinator. The approach is tailored towards artifact-based inter-organizational processes.

The coordination of large process structures not rooted in artifact-centric process management, but with focus on the engineering domain, is considered in [7,8]. The COREPRO approach explicitly considers process relations with one-to-many cardinality, thereby exhibiting the concept of a process structure. A Lifecycle Coordination Model acts as a central coordinator of a process structure. Decentralized lifecycle coordination models are not considered in this approach.

Finally, for an overview and a discussion of coordination approaches in general, that do not necessarily act on process structures, please refer to [10].

6   Summary and Outlook

With coordination processes, the conceptual, technical and methodological capabilities exist to successfully implement decentralized process coordination in large process structures. The concepts of scope, hierarchy of the relational process structure, and the principle of subsidiarity make the complexity of it all manageable and, therefore, the whole approach feasible. On the benefits side, large-scale coordination of large process structures becomes feasible, while at the same time, the complexity and size of individual coordination process models is reduced compared to a central coordinator. As has been shown, this also applies to distributed relational process structures. However, in a different sense multiple coordination processes are more complex than a central coordinator. Again, subsidiarity and hierarchy are central to managing this complexity, enabling modelers to model the coordination of large process structures.

In future work, a thorough empirical investigation and evaluation of the coordination process concept, including large relational process structures, will be conducted. This investigation is challenging due to the inter-linked nature of the concepts of coordination process, semantic relationships and relational process structure. Individual evaluations of each concept are therefore rather pointless, as they must be seen and evaluated in a broader context.

Acknowledgments. This work is part of the ZAFH Intralogistik, funded by the European Regional Development Fund and the Ministry of Science, Research and the Arts of Baden-Württemberg, Germany (F. No. 32-7545.24-17/3/1).

References

1. Andrews, K., Steinau, S., Reichert, M.: Engineering a highly scalable object-aware process management engine using distributed microservices. In: Panetto, H., Debruyne, C., Proper, H., Ardagna, C., Roman, D., Meersman, R. (eds.) CoopIS 2018, Part II. LNCS, vol. 11230, pp. 80–97. Springer, Cham (2018). https://doi.org/10.1007/978-3-030-02671-4_5

2. Baeyens, T.: BPM in the cloud. In: Daniel, F., Wang, J., Weber, B. (eds.) BPM 2013. LNCS, vol. 8094, pp. 10–16. Springer, Heidelberg (2013). https://doi.org/10.1007/978-3-642-40176-3_3

3. Fahland, D., de Leoni, M., van Dongen, B.F., van der Aalst, W.M.P.: Many-to-many: some observations on interactions in artifact choreographies. In: 3rd Central-European Workshop on Services and their Composition (ZEUS). CEUR Workshop Proceedings, vol. 705, pp. 9–15. CEUR-WS.org (2011)

4. Hull, R., Damaggio, E., de Masellis, R., Fournier, F., et al.: Business artifacts with guard-stage-milestone lifecycles: managing artifact interactions with conditions and events. In: DEBS 2011, pp. 51–62. ACM (2011)

5. Künzle, V., Weber, B., Reichert, M.: Object-aware business processes: fundamental requirements and their support in existing approaches. Int. J. Inf. Syst. Model. Des. (IJISMD) **2**(2), 19–46 (2011)

6. Lohmann, N., Wolf, K.: Artifact-centric choreographies. In: Maglio, P.P., Weske, M., Yang, J., Fantinato, M. (eds.) ICSOC 2010. LNCS, vol. 6470, pp. 32–46. Springer, Heidelberg (2010). https://doi.org/10.1007/978-3-642-17358-5_3

7. Müller, D., Reichert, M., Herbst, J.: Data-driven modeling and coordination of large process structures. In: Meersman, R., Tari, Z. (eds.) OTM 2007. LNCS, vol. 4803, pp. 131–149. Springer, Heidelberg (2007). https://doi.org/10.1007/978-3-540-76848-7_10

8. Müller, D., Reichert, M., Herbst, J.: A new paradigm for the enactment and dynamic adaptation of data-driven process structures. In: Bellahsène, Z., Léonard, M. (eds.) CAiSE 2008. LNCS, vol. 5074, pp. 48–63. Springer, Heidelberg (2008). https://doi.org/10.1007/978-3-540-69534-9_4

9. Nandi, P., Kumaran, S.: Adaptive business objects-a new component model for business integration. In: ICEIS (3), pp. 179–188 (2005)

10. Steinau, S., Andrews, K., Reichert, M.: Modeling process interactions with coordination processes. In: Panetto, H., Debruyne, C., Proper, H., Ardagna, C., Roman, D., Meersman, R. (eds.) OTM 2018. LNCS, vol. 11229, pp. 21–39. Springer, Cham (2018). https://doi.org/10.1007/978-3-030-02610-3_2

11. Steinau, S., Andrews, K., Reichert, M.: The relational process structure. In: Krogstie, J., Reijers, H.A. (eds.) CAiSE 2018. LNCS, vol. 10816, pp. 53–67. Springer, Cham (2018). https://doi.org/10.1007/978-3-319-91563-0_4

12. Steinau, S., Künzle, V., Andrews, K., Reichert, M.: Coordinating business processes using semantic relationships. In: CBI 2017, pp. 33–43. IEEE Computer Society Press (2017)

13. Sun, Y., Xu, W., Su, J.: Declarative choreographies for artifacts. In: Liu, C., Ludwig, H., Toumani, F., Yu, Q. (eds.) ICSOC 2012. LNCS, vol. 7636, pp. 420–434. Springer, Heidelberg (2012). https://doi.org/10.1007/978-3-642-34321-6_28

14. van der Aalst, W.M.P., Barthelmess, P., Ellis, C.A., Wainer, J.: Proclets: a framework for lightweight interacting workflow processes. Int. J. Coop. Inf. Syst. **10**(04), 443–481 (2001)

Early Validation Framework for Critical and Complex Process-Centric Systems

Fahad Rafique Golra[✉], Joël Champeau, and Ciprian Teodorov

Lab STICC UMR6285, ENSTA Bretagne, Brest, France
{fahad.golra,joel.champeau,ciprian.teodorov}@ensta-bretagne.fr

Abstract. Guaranteeing the correctness of the future system is of vital importance for the development of critical and complex systems. Rigorous software development methodologies are used for such systems, where formal methods for the verification of properties guarantee the required level of correctness. For process-centric, critical and complex systems, one needs continuous observation of the process (through simulation and visualization) both during the development for correctness and afterwards for process improvement. We present a framework with associated methodology and tools, for the development of process-centric critical and complex systems. This early validation methodology promotes formal verification of the process model alongside agent-oriented simulation and visualization of the process models in a distributed context. Moreover, the process simulation technique proposed in the methodology allows step-wise replacement of the simulated components with the actual system services. We explain the proposed methodology using an adaptation of a real-life case-study from the military sector.

Keywords: Business process · Modeling · Simulation · Visualization

1 Introduction

As the demand for web based solutions and services is rising, we witness an increased focus on business services and componentization of business functionalities. Many organizations have shifted their focus from a data-centric approach to a process-centric one for information system technology and solutions [15]. Initially, the focus remained on workflow technology and was limited to the automation of routine processes and the execution of relatively simple activities. Gradually process-centric systems have moved towards coordination and collaboration management and information based decision making activities that can manage complex, dynamic and higher value mission critical processes [15]. When process definitions serve as the main controller of the enterprise systems, we need to use a development methodology that ensures that the defined processes exhibit the necessary properties for running the system. This promotes early validation of the processes used in such systems. In case of critical and complex systems, one needs to guarantee that the process, around which the complete system is

© Springer Nature Switzerland AG 2019
I. Reinhartz-Berger et al. (Eds.): BPMDS 2019/EMMSAD 2019, LNBIP 352, pp. 35–50, 2019.
https://doi.org/10.1007/978-3-030-20618-5_3

developed, is rigorously tested for correctness using formal methods. Apart from model checking approaches, one also needs to simulate and visualize the process, when the system under development is safety/mission-critical. In such systems it is important to simulate the impact of individual components on the collective behavior of the system. Simulation of scenarios generates accurate information about the utilization, performance and overall effect. Visualizations can then be used for analysis, discovering sensitivities, optimization and monitoring [12].

In the context of process-centric critical and complex systems, we suggest using iterative development and incorporating model checking techniques alongside process simulation and visualization approaches. However, such a methodology will have to face the challenges of seamless integration of these varying approaches that have different point of views over the same components of the system. The novelty of our approach lies in the integration of these approaches under a holistic methodology. The goal is to tackle the challenges that we face in the integration of an evolutionary development process using a model checking technique and agent-based simulation. Our research objectives are:

- *Objective 1: Simulating and visualizing the higher abstraction level business processes.* Process simulations for software systems require low level implementation details which can be considered as noise by a business user. We focus on a methodology to hide this complexity under multiple abstraction levels that are linked together through mappings.
- *Objective 2: Formal verification of a process model according to the operational semantics defined in the process interpreter.* Traditionally translation of a model into a specific formal language for verification guarantees the correctness of the model in that particular language. It raises the problem of ensuring the equivalence between the semantics of the (generated) implementation from the model and the semantics defined in the formal language *e.g.* Promela [11]. The goal is to verify the process with the semantics defined in the interpreter that would later become the process engine of a deployed process-centric system.
- *Objective 3: Guaranteeing the correctness for both the individual activities and the complete process model containing them.* To ensure the correctness of a process model, we argue that one needs to decompose the verification problem into: the verification of the actions described within an individual activity and the verification of the control flow specified in the process model containing these individual activities. Simulation and visualization of the process activities helps in the verification of actions defined in an individual activity. Model checking techniques focus on the verification of certain properties in a control-intensive process model.
- *Objective 4: Allowing seamless transfer from simulation to the actual system services.* The transition of a system from a simulation to an actual system should be seamless. We focus on a framework (methodology, architecture and associated tools) that allows the transition from simulated components to actual components for the development of a critical and complex system.

With these objectives in mind, we propose a framework for process development and early validation that offers an architecture, a methodology and associated tools developed for putting this methodology into practice. The rest of the paper is organized as follows: In Sect. 2, we explain the existing technologies used in the framework and present the proposed framework. In Sect. 3, we present an adaptation of a real-life case study to explain this framework. We discuss the related works in Sect. 4 and finally conclude the paper in Sect. 5.

2 Process-Centric Critical and Complex Systems

We propose a framework that relies on the use and integration of some existing technologies, coupled with dedicated components and tools. The most notable of these technologies are the NATO Architecture Framework (NAFv4) for enterprise modeling and the DirectSim framework for simulations.

NATO Architecture Framework (NAFv4): It provides a standardized way to develop and describe architectures for both military and business use [3]. The framework is defined through multiple viewpoints distributed across five layers: Concepts, Service, Logical, Physical Resource and Architecture Meta-Data. NAFv4 suggests using ArchiMate specification [2] as the standard metamodel. The behavior in NAFv4 is captured by the following viewpoints around processes, states and sequences.

- *C4: Standard Processes* viewpoint identifies the business activities and links them to corresponding capabilities.
- *S4: Service Functions* viewpoint identifies the functions performed by each service.
- *L4: Logical Activities* viewpoint identifies the logical activities, their grouping and composition and the logical flow between them. It forms the business level process model.
- *P4: Resource Functions* viewpoint specifies the functionality of resources in the architecture. These functions and the flow (of data and control) between them form the application process model.
- *L4-P4: Activity to Function Mapping* viewpoint specifies the mapping between the activities of the business process and the functions of the application process. It also addresses the relation between the functions of the application process and that of business services.

DirectSim: DirectSim[1] is an open source framework, developed by the French ministry of armed forces, that allows the development of simulation applications. It has mostly been used for military simulations [4], but being open source, it is increasingly being used for other civilian projects as well. The simulation engine at the core of the framework is based on a timed agent-based event simulation.

---

[1] https://www.directsim.fr.

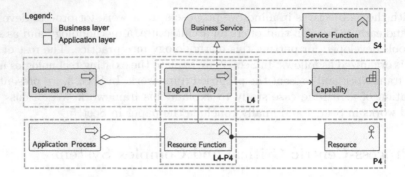

Fig. 1. Archimate diagram of the process related viewpoints of NAFv4

A monitor and a set of plug-ins allow the edition and visualization of scenarios in 2D and 3D spaces. Multiple views of the tool allow the interaction with the simulation *e.g. scenario editor view* to edit the scenarios, *default view* for the visualization, *etc.* It also offers a test toolkit for testing the scenarios. A compilation of the simulation may be necessary, in case one wants to modify the behavior of the simulation. The core simulation framework is based on .Net framework and the development is done in C#.

2.1   Proposed Framework

We propose a framework for the development and early validation of processes in critical and complex systems through formal verification, simulation and visualization of the process models. Apart from the existing technologies that we used, all other tools that we developed for this framework are accessible online[2].

Process Modeling: We follow NATO architecture framework (NAFv4) for enterprise modeling, where processes are described at different levels of abstraction. In an ArchiMate model presented in Fig. 1, we extract the process relevant viewpoints and show their interrelation using the concerned NAFv4 concepts. The *C4: Standard Processes* viewpoint of NAFv4 identifies the list of business activities that are eventually modeled in the Business layer. The functions perform by each business service are also defined in the same Business layer through the *S4: Service Functions* viewpoint. Hence, taking *L4: Logical Activities* viewpoint into account gives us access to the complete business process. The *P4: Resource Functions* viewpoint is used to capture the application processes. We use the *L4-P4: Activity to Function Mapping* viewpoint of NAFv4 to map the application process activities to the corresponding business process activities. This mapping between the two levels of abstraction can be used either to create a holistic process view that contains the activities from both the abstraction

---

[2] https://github.com/plug-obp.

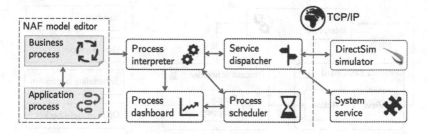

Fig. 2. Architecture of the proposed framework

levels, or to trace back to the business level activities from the application level activities. In accordance with the first objective outlined in Sect. 1, we use the latter approach, where we interpret the application process in way that individual activities can be traced back to the business process. This allows us to simulate business processes by passing through the application processes that carry the details needed for the simulation.

Process Interpretation: Our approach is to interpret the process model before model checking and simulation activities, as shown in Fig. 2. We have developed a process interpreter than takes the serialized version of the process model (*.bpmn) as input. Similar to other proposals in the literature (*e.g.* [5]), our process interpreter uses direct semantics, given in terms of features and constructs of the process model, rather than in terms of their low-level encoding into another formalism. It takes into account the core elements like activity nodes and other control nodes *i.e.* initial, final, decision, merge, fork and join nodes. This process interpreter also takes into account multiple pools with participants, each having a separate process. The collaboration between multiple pools is handled by interpreting the message flows between them. The interpreter develops an automaton for each process by relying on the notion of Labeled Transition System (LTS). The semantics of the interpreter are defined using the notion of tokens. Tokens are used in the automaton to mark the active places of the process. The location of all the tokens in a given automaton describes a configuration. The structure of the interpreter is developed around three main functions:

- `initialConfigurations` returns the set of all possible configurations for the process.
- `fireableTransitions` returns the collection of all possible transitions that can be fired from a given configuration.
- `fireTransition`: fires a given transition and returns the target configuration reached as a result of firing the transition.

These functions of the interpreter are used for the development of the LTS graph for a given process and the possibility to traverse it using `fireTransition`.

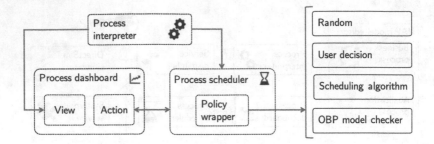

Fig. 3. Process scheduling architecture through policies

The semantics[3] defined in the process interpreter are local to it. Other components use these functions to access the current state of the process model and to see what states of the process model can be attained next. It is important to note here that the process interpreter develops a single LTS graph for all the collaborations and the parallel processes executing in different pools.

Where the process interpreter is responsible for interpreting each individual activity and enacting it, the process scheduler chooses the control flow between these activities. This choice of activities is forwarded to the interpreter, which is then capable of enacting the complete process model. For every non-deterministic choice, the process scheduler chooses a control flow branch according to the policy selected in the policy wrapper. Figure 3 shows the role of policy wrapping for the process scheduler. Under the current implementation, the policy wrapper can choose one of the following policies for scheduling the process:

- *Random:* This policy deals with the non-determinism in the process in a random fashion. It does not evaluate any guard conditions for choosing one of the LTS graph branches and randomly selects any one of them.
- *User decision:* This policy delegates the responsibility of choosing one of the branches to the user. This responsibility is delegated using the Process dashboard. It is used when the system is enacted with a human in the loop.
- *Scheduling algorithm:* This policy allows the use of a user-defined algorithm for choosing between two branches of the LTS graph. Such algorithms can also evaluate the condition expressions associated with the outgoing sequence flows from the decision node by using Decision Model and Notation (DMN) tables. This policy also adds the possibility to use complex user-defined algorithms from decision support systems, artificial intelligence, *etc.*
- *OBP model checker:* This policy is specifically defined for connecting the process interpreter with the model checker through the process scheduler. The objective is to capture all possible control flows of a process without restricting the interpreter to only those triggered by specific input choices. Hence, this policy passes a holistic graph of all possible states to the model checker for formal verification.

---

[3] The objective of this article is not to present the in-depth semantics of the process model, instead we focus on presenting the global methodology of the framework.

Process Verification: OBP model checker[4] is responsible for process verification in our framework. It relies on the identification of contexts and their exploitation during the exploration of the models. Observer-Based Prover (OBP) uses Context Description Language (CDL) for formally describing the context of the system [6]. It reduces the state space for proving/disproving the correctness of the system with respect to the relevant properties. The principle is to lead the explorer in a way that it does not concentrate its efforts on the exploration of the complete space of the behaviors, but on a relevant restriction of the latter for the verification of specific properties. Once the state space is reduced, it becomes easier to verify the properties. These properties are defined as part of the context description using the CDL language. *OBP model checker* component is connected to the process interpreter through a *process scheduler*, allowing it to the construct and traverse the LTS graph of all the possible configurations for a process model. A configuration for OBP model checker is a unique state of the process, where a subset of activities from the process (including all or none) have been executed. Each activity in the process model is considered as a transition that moves the process from one configuration to another in this directed graph. Using this connection to process interpreter, the OBP model checker component can focus on the formal verification of the temporal properties of a given process.

Considering critical and complex nature of the systems, we focused on the safety properties of the process. The architectural choice of linking the process model to the model checker through the process interpreter and process scheduler is motivated by the second research objective. Traditionally, an *original* model to be verified is rewritten in a chosen formal language. After the formal verification, it becomes hard to verify (and maintain) the equivalence between the model defined in the formal language and the code/application generated from the *original* model. This architectural choice allows us to carry out model checking on the process models based on the semantics defined in the process interpreter. The same process interpreter is later used as the core of the process-centric critical and complex system. Hence, this issue of verifying and maintaining the equivalence does not apply in our framework.

A process dashboard component serves as an interface to manage the enactment of a process model. The execution of the activities is triggered by the interface provided by the process dashboard. The process dashboard is mainly composed of two components: *view* and *action*. The *view* component gives information about the current state of activities in the process model in order to allow process monitoring. This component takes the information about the enacted process from the process interpreter. The *action* component provides an interface to process dashboard for taking user inputs. These actions depend on the type of policy chosen by the process scheduler. For example, in case of the *random* policy, a user can simply choose start, next, stop, pause and resume actions, however the *user decision* policy allows the user to choose specific activities for the control flow.

---

[4] http://www.obpcdl.org.

Process Simulation: When process models are used to define the behavior in critical and complex systems, they need to be accompanied by methods that can analyze the processes. Model checking techniques analyze the structure and behavior of the process model by focusing on the flow of control. In order to respond to the third objective, we introduced a mechanism to separate the control flow analysis of the process from the analysis of the actions defined in individual activities. In order to analyze individual activities and their impact on the global behavior of the process, we use agent-based simulation and visualization approach. Like traditional formal verification approaches, existing simulation techniques are based on the static description of the process without taking into account the semantics defined in the process interpreter. Our objective is to propose a methodology to remotely simulate the process models according to the semantics defined in the process interpreter. Through remote simulation, the idea is not to orchestrate between multiple simulations (*e.g.* federates in a federation of HLA [1]), rather it is to control the execution of the scenarios, for both simulation and visualization, through the defined process models.

Similar to the approach followed for model checking, we linked the simulator to the process interpreter instead of analyzing the serialized process model. Instead of connecting the process interpreter directly with the process simulator, we developed a *service dispatcher* component that allows to access the functions of the process interpreter remotely. Directly linking a process model to the simulation framework enforces the predefined control flow on the agent-based system. However, putting a process interpreter in between the both, allows autonomous agents to develop localized process behaviors. Then the coordination of these localized process behaviors helps to emerge the global behavior of the complete system. One way of validating the process model is to analyze if the emerged behavior of the agent-based simulation conforms to the process specifications and is aligned with user expectations.

We used an open-source agent-based simulator, DirectSim, for the simulation of process models. The simulator itself is extensible using a plugin mechanism. In our implementation, we developed a plugin for the DirectSim simulator that adds a TCP/IP client to the simulator. This way, the simulator is able to communicate with the process interpreter through the service dispatcher. Once the simulation is launched from DirectSim, the user can control the simulation using the process dashboard. Currently, we are using the *user decision* policy to control the simulation of process model, but in future we plan to develop advanced scheduling algorithms for process simulation.

2.2   Proposed Methodology

In the proposed framework, the architecture for the process-centric system is based around a methodology that seeks early validation of critical and complex systems. The proposed methodology, as shown in Fig. 4, exploits this architecture

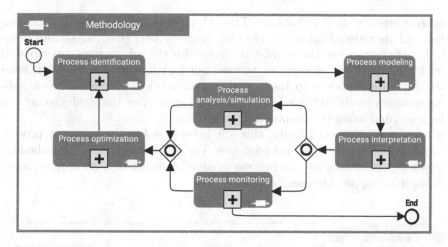

Fig. 4. Process modeling methodology in the proposed framework

to reinforce the objectives outlined in Sect. 1. This methodology involves the following sub-processes:

- *process identification:* Process identification is handled through the *C4: Standard Processes* viewpoint of the NATO architecture framework. This viewpoint also establishes the traceability of the identified processes to the capabilities supporting them. The tools needed for developing a hierarchical table of processes are simple word processors or spreadsheets.
- *process modeling:* This sub-process focuses on modeling the processes identified in the first sub-process. In order to keep Fig. 4 simple, we did not show the iteration between process identification and process modeling. An alternating cycle between process modeling and identification is used for the refinement of processes. Another important activity within this sub-process is the development of multi-layered process model, where the logical activities describe the business process at one level and the resource functions describe the application process at the other level. The tools used for this activity are process modeling editors e.g. we use Mega HOPEX.
- *process interpretation:* This sub-process focuses on the interpretation of the process model in a way that all the activities of a given process can be executed with a well defined flow between them. The interpretation of a process model locks the operational semantics defined for a given process. Both the process model and the operational semantics defined in the interpreter together are responsible for the execution of the process-centric system.
- *process analysis & simulation:* This sub-process aims at the analysis of the process using two methods. Model checking techniques are used for the verification of properties concerning the control flow of the process. The second method is to simulate the process for strategic management, planning, understanding, training and improvement. The simulation of the process model is mostly focused on the analysis of the actions inside individual activities.

– *process monitoring & enactment:* This sub-process is responsible for the control and operational management of the process. After the analysis and simulation of the process, the simulated services for the sub-systems are replaced with the actual system services, to meet our fourth objective. The shift from the simulated services to the actual system services is gradual. New sub-components modified/added to the system, even after the deployment, can be simulated using the proposed framework.

– *process optimization:* Finally, this sub-process ensures a constant process improvement for the specified processes. The recommendations from the process analysis/simulation and process monitoring/enactment serve as an input for optimizing process specifications.

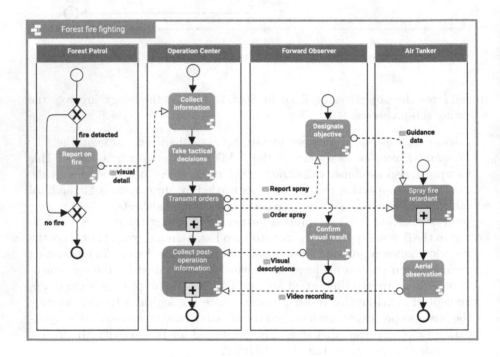

Fig. 5. Application process for the case study

3   Case Study

The methodology proposed in this article has been applied to real-life case-studies in the military context. Bound by the non-disclosure agreement, we are obliged to adapt the actual military case study to secure some sensitive information and processes. This adapted case study, shown in Fig. 5, illustrates the process of launching/spraying fire retardant at a wild fire identified in a forest. Four participants that coordinate to realize this process are air tanker, operation center, forward observer and forest patrol. The forest patrol identifies the fire and reports it to the operation center, which then transmits the orders to the air tanker. The air tanker then follows the coordinates given by the forward observer and sprays the fire retardant. The forward observer visually observes the results and reports back to the operation center.

Process Development: The *C4: Standard Processes* viewpoint of NATO architecture framework (NAFv4) is used to identify the activities involved in the process. This viewpoint used a tabular representation with a hierarchy of activities with corresponding links to capabilities. Then, the identified activities were modeled as business process model in the *L4: Logical Activities* viewpoint. In our case study, we used the HOPEX tool[5], which supports the development of NAF models. The business process model developed with this tool categorizes the activities in swimlanes and provides the control-flow semantics that are fairly close to that of BPMN Collaboration Diagrams.

Once the business process is defined, it needs to be refined to an application process to get low-level enactable/executable activities. The application process in our case study was captured by the *P4: Resource Functions* viewpoint. The same tool, HOPEX, was used for the development of the application process. The adapted version of this case study, shown in Fig. 5 presents 9 activities/sub-processes (instead of 24 in the actual case study). A mapping between the business and application processes was assured using *L4-P4: Activity to Function Mapping* viewpoint. HOPEX allowed us to serialize the process model in *.bpmn format.

Process Control Flow Analysis: Our process interpreter took the serialized process as input to enact the process according to the defined semantics. Once the process model was loaded into the process interpreter, the process scheduler could access the initial configuration using the `initialConfiguration` interface and traverse the complete model using `fireableTransitions()` and `fireTransition` interfaces. We initially chose the OBP model checker as the scheduling policy, allowing us to continue with the formal verification of the control-flow of the process model. Context models and properties were expressed in a Context Description Language (CDL) so that the model checker, OBP (Observer-Based Prover), can construct its exploration space with all the possible configurations for the given process. It is important to note here that the complete process had four parallel collaborating processes, defined in four different pools. OBP model checker follows the technique of exploration space reduction by focusing only on the configurations that are relevant for the verification of chosen properties. In the process of the adapted case study, OBP reduced the exploration space to 13 states and 12 transitions (considering each collapsed sub-process as single activity). This tool allows one to visualize the state space and analyze the variable values inside each state. Figure 6 depicts a fragment of the exploration space developed by the OBP Explorer.

---

[5] https://www.mega.com/en/product/hopex.

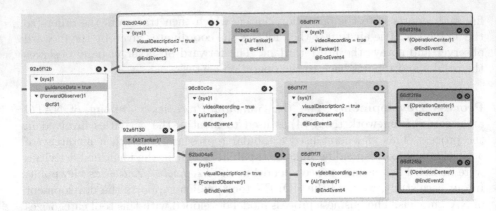

Fig. 6. Fragment of the configurations produced by OBP model checker

The analysis of the adapted case study process model gave insights into the collective behavior of the four collaborating sub-processes. Once the *Designate objective* activity of the forward observer is executed, it sends a message to the *Spray fire retardant* activity of the air tanker with *Guidance data*. Note that the semantics defined for the *send task* in BPMN collaboration are non-blocking *i.e.* once the send task has been completed, this activity can continue its normal execution. Thus, after sending the message, the forward observer can continue with the next activity, *Confirm visual result*. At this point in time, there is a non-determinism between the *Confirm visual result* activity of the forward observer and *Spray fire retardant* activity of the air tanker, as shown in the Fig. 6. In this case, if the former activity is executed before the later (the branch depicted in the red box in Fig. 6), it does not make a logical sense to witness the result before the action is performed. In this case, the formal verification of this process model through our model checker suggests us to add a construct between these activities in a way that the *Confirm visual result* activity is always executed after the *Spray fire retardant* activity has been completed.

Process Simulation: Once the process model has been verified through the model checking activities, one can guarantee that the model carries the tested properties. However, in our case, we had an added guarantee that the model as defined and *the way interpreted by our process interpreter* carries the verified (safety) properties. The next part of the methodology was to connect the process interpreter with the DirectSim Simulator. In order to carry this out, first we changed the policy to *User decision* in the *policy wrapper*. This puts the user in command for controlling the execution of the process. The view of the dashboard changes according to the policy and the user can chose to start and stop individual activities. In this case, whenever a branching in the LTS graph is approached, the system relies on the user input for deciding between the choices.

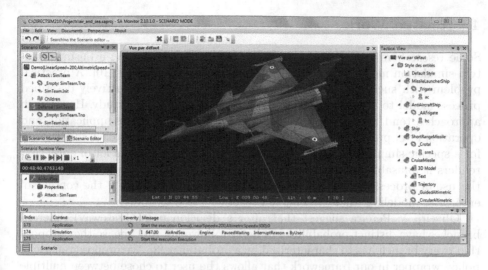

Fig. 7. DirectSim simulation and visualization

For the DirectSim simulation of the process model, we developed the simulation of the process activities using the Visual Studio Editor as suggested by the simulator specification. DirectSim offers a domain specific language for the development of simulations. These simulations are developed around the concepts of agents. In this case study, all the participants of the process were considered as individual agents. DirectSim also serves for the visualization of the 2D/3D simulations. In this case, each of the agents was given a 3D decorator to be used in the simulation. The visualizations developed in DirectSim are multilayered. The background layer was chosen using the latitude/longitude coordinates for the 3D model of the world. The implementation of each individual activity was programmed in the DSML e.g. the flight of the air tanker from the runway to the point of action. Once the simulation was developed in the DSML, it was used to generate the C# code for the simulator. The plugin extension that we have developed for the DirectSim simulator allowed us to control the simulation from the process dashboard. This remote simulation was realized through a TCP connection between the *Service dispatcher* component and the DirectSim plugin.

In this case study, we developed the simulation of the actual system on an agent-based simulator, as shown in Fig. 7. As a process-centric system, the process interpreter was placed at the core of the system to control the execution of the simulation. We did not replace the simulated activities with the actual activities in this adapted case study. However, we can imagine a communication interface with the forest patrol participant of the case study. In this case, when the forest patrol sends a visual detail of the event through the communication interface, the *Report on fire* activity of the process will be consider as executed.

4   Related Work

Some researchers have looked into the possibility of generating a business system simulation model using a set of executable BPMN models [10]. A practical problem with such approaches is that they suppose an exhaustively described process model to a very low level detail of the system under study. Hence such approaches tend to mix the business level processes with the application and operation level processes in a single model. Using such an approach might work for a specific simulation but plagues the business process with a lot of noise that renders it unusable for other strategic activities. For these reasons, we suggest the use of process models with varying level of abstraction, in the context of enterprise modeling, that are mapped together for traceability.

Oliveira & Pereira suggest that after a decision point (gateway) different branches have distinct probabilities of being followed in runtime, so they propose that every branch has to characterized by a probability [8]. We propose the use of policy wrapper in our framework that allows the user to chose between multiple options to deal with non-determinism. For example, the *scheduling algorithm* policy allows us to couple the decision points of a process model with genetic algorithms or machine learning for decision support systems.

Mappings between business processes and agent based simulation have already been proposed for the validation of processes [14] and description of agent-based conceptual models [13]. These approaches focus on the simulation of the process models for their verification. We decomposed process model verification into action verification and process verification, where the former focuses on the verification of individual activities and the later for the verification of the control flow between them. We propose using process simulation for action verification and model checking for the process verification. For the simulation of process models, we chose an architecture that links the process interpretation and simulation through a service dispatcher. Some approaches suggest a distributed simulation of BPMN models using HLA [1] framework [7,9]. Their focus is mostly on dividing a simulation in multiple sub-functions and executing each (federate) on a different (possibly geographically distributed) system [9]. As for now, we did not focus on federating multiple simulating components on different machines, but this remains a perspective for us. We also plan on carrying out experimentation and sharing the results when the original sub-components of the system are replaced with the simulated functions of the process.

5   Conclusion

We present a framework with architecture, methodology and associated tools for the development of processes in the context of process-centric critical and complex systems. The proposed architecture uses the business and application level process models from NATO architecture framework and interprets them for model checking, simulation and process monitoring. The framework keeps the process interpreter at its core, where the scheduling approach for the activities is chosen by a policy. These scheduling policies allow using the same interpreter for model checking, simulation and the final system implementation. Model checking is performed using an observer-based prover that is linked directly to the process interpreter. Instead of taking a static serialized process model as input, it takes the dynamic interpretation of the process model as input. We present an approach for simulating the activities of a process model using process dashboard to control the simulation. Our approach is explained through an adapted case study of a real life military project.

Acknowledgment. We thank French ministry of the armed forces and specifically the Directorate General of Armaments for funding this research work.

References

1. IEEE Standard for Modeling and Simulation (M&S) High Level Architecture (HLA) - Framework and Rules. IEEE Std. 1516-2010, August 2010
2. ArchiMate 3.0.1 Specification. Open Group Standard, August 2017
3. NATO Architecture Framework version 4.0. NATO Std. NAFv4, January 2018
4. Cornu, F., Garnier, A., Audoly, C.: Simulation of the efficiency of a system of drones in a mine warfare scenario. In: Undersea Defence Technology, pp. 1–8 (2008)
5. Corradini, F., Fornari, F., Polini, A., Re, B., Tiezzi, F.: A formal approach to modeling and verification of business process collaborations. Sci. Comput. Program. **166**, 35–70 (2018)
6. Dhaussy, P., Boniol, F., Roger, J.C., Leroux, L.: Improving model checking with context modelling. Adv. Softw. Eng. **2012**, 9 (2012)
7. Falcone, A., Garro, A., D'Ambrogio, A., Giglio, A.: Engineering systems by combining BPMN and HLA-based distributed simulation. In: 2017 IEEE International Systems Engineering Symposium (ISSE), pp. 1–6. IEEE (2017)
8. Freitas, A.P., Pereira, J.L.M.: Process simulation support in BPM tools: the case of BPMN. In: 5th International Conference on Business Sustainability: Management, Technology and Learning for Individuals, Organisations and Society in Turbulent Environments (BS 2015) (2015)
9. Gorecki, S., Bouanan, Y., Zacharewicz, G., Perry, N.: BPMN modeling for HLA based simulation and visualization. In: Proceedings of the Model-driven Approaches for Simulation Engineering Symposium, p. 11. Society for Computer Simulation International (2018)
10. Guizzardi, G., Wagner, G.: Can BPMN be used for making simulation models? In: Barjis, J., Eldabi, T., Gupta, A. (eds.) EOMAS 2011. LNBIP, vol. 88, pp. 100–115. Springer, Heidelberg (2011). https://doi.org/10.1007/978-3-642-24175-8_8
11. Holzmann, G.J.: The model checker SPIN. IEEE Trans. Softw. Eng. **23**(5), 279–295 (1997)
12. Inselberg, A.: Multidimensional detective. In: Proceedings of the 1997 IEEE Symposium on Information Visualization. IEEE Computer Society (1997)
13. Onggo, B.S.: Agent-based simulation model representation using BPMN. In: Formal Languages for Computer Simulation: Transdisciplinary Models and Applications, pp. 378–400. IGI Global (2014)

14. Pascalau, E., Giurca, A., Wagner, G.: Validating auction business processes using agent-based simulations. BPSC **147**, 95–109 (2009)
15. Sheth, A.: From contemporary workflow process automation to adaptive and dynamic work activity coordination and collaboration. In: International Conference of Database and Expert Systems Applications, DEXA 1997, pp. 24–27. IEEE (1997)

Execution and Understandability of Declarative Process Models (BPMDS 2019)

Logic Based Look-Ahead
for the Execution of Multi-perspective
Declarative Processes

Martin Käppel, Nicolai Schützenmeier(✉), Stefan Schönig, Lars Ackermann,
and Stefan Jablonski

Institute for Computer Science, University of Bayreuth, Bayreuth, Germany
{martin.kaeppel,nicolai.schuetzenmeier,stefan.schoenig,lars.ackermann,
stefan.jablonski}@uni-bayreuth.de

Abstract. In declarative process models all the activities which do not
violate a constraint of the process model can be executed. Consequently,
the number of viable paths is large. In turn, when considering multiple perspectives during execution, i.e., constraints on resources and data
values, it may happen that the execution of activities or the change
of data values may result in the non-executability of crucial activities. Execution engines for single-perspective declarative process models have been extensively discussed in research where, among others
look-ahead functionality has been investigated. Execution approaches
for multi-perspective declarative models that involve constraints on data
and resources, however, are less mature. In this paper, we introduce a
logic based look-ahead approach for the execution of multi-perspective
declarative processes. We use the look-ahead for simulating a fixed number of execution steps with regard to the existing trace and the choice
of the next step. The look-ahead allows for estimating all consequences
and effects of certain decisions at any time of process execution. We
develop an algorithm for trace generation and checking traces using the
logic language Alloy. We extensively evaluate our approach by means of
a practical example and give some advice for further optimizations.

Keywords: Declarative processes · Multi-perspective · Look-ahead

1 Introduction

A Process-Aware Information System is a collaborative system that executes
processes involving people, applications, and data on the basis of process
models [1]. Two different paradigms can be distinguished: (i) procedural models
describe the execution paths in a graph-based structure, (ii) declarative models
consist of temporal constraints that a process must satisfy. Declarative languages
like Declare [2], DCR graphs [3] and Declarative Process Intermediate Language
(DPIL) [4,5] have been proposed to define the latter.

© Springer Nature Switzerland AG 2019
I. Reinhartz-Berger et al. (Eds.): BPMDS 2019/EMMSAD 2019, LNBIP 352, pp. 53–68, 2019.
https://doi.org/10.1007/978-3-030-20618-5_4

Declarative models represent processes by restrictions over the permissible behaviour. The restricting rules are named constraints, which express those conditions that must be satisfied throughout process execution. Modeling languages like Declare [2] provide a repertoire of templates, i.e., constraints parametrized over activities. A central shortcoming of languages like Declare is the fact that constraints are not capable of expressing the connection between the behaviour and other perspectives of the process. Behaviour can be intertwined with dependencies upon value ranges of data parameters and resource characteristics [6–8]. Therefore, Declare has been extended towards Multi-Perspective Declare (*MP-Declare*) [9]. In declarative process models all the activities which do not violate a constraint of the model can be executed such that a big amount of different paths are considered viable. In turn, when considering multiple perspectives during execution, i.e., constraints on resources and data values, it may happen that the execution of activities or the change of data values may result in the non-executability of crucial activities. In this case, the process cannot be completed or the execution takes more time or further resources. A process can be completed if the corresponding trace is valid.

In such cases it is beneficial to know the consequences of decisions on the further course of execution, i.e., a look-ahead functionality for multi-perspective declarative processes is crucial. We further want to motivate the necessity of our approach by means of a simple example. Let us consider the process *hidden-CoExistence*, shown in Fig. 1 with five different activities. In the following, we call these activities a, b, c, d and e. The activities d and e such as a and b are connected with a *response* template which means if activity d or a is executed, the activity e or b must follow. The *notCoExistence* template between e and b forbids the common occurrence of both activities. The activity c can only be executed if activity b was executed sometimes before. It follows that this process has some implicit dependencies. For example, if activity d is executed, neither b nor c can be executed afterwards. Analogously activity e can never be executed if a was executed before.

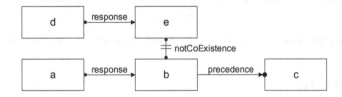

Fig. 1. *hiddenCoExistence* example process in graphical Declare notation

Execution engines for single-perspective declarative processes have been extensively discussed in research where, among others look-ahead functionality has been investigated [10,11]. Execution approaches for multi-perspective declarative models that involve constraints on data and resources are less mature and do not consider preventive look-ahead strategies [12]. In this paper, we introduce a logic based look-ahead approach for the execution of multi-perspective declarative processes. We use a look-ahead strategy for simulating a fixed number of execution steps in dependency of the existing trace and the choice of the next step. The look-ahead allows for estimating all consequences and effects of certain decisions at any time of execution. We develop an algorithm for trace generation and checking traces using the logic language Alloy. We extensively evaluate our approach by means of a practical example and give some advice for optimizations. In summary the work at hand tackles the following research questions: Which activities, identities or data objects can be used in the next n steps? Is it possible to complete the process instance within n steps?

The remainder of the paper is structured as follows: Sect. 2 provides an introduction into the declarative modeling paradigm, the language Alloy and the underlying meta model. Section 4 explains the logic based look-ahead approach. In Sect. 6 we extensively evaluate our approach by means of two practical examples. In the last section we give some advice for further optimizations.

2 Preliminaries

In this section we introduce the foundations of our approach, i.e., Process Event Chain Metamodel, multi-perspective Declare and the logic language Alloy.

2.1 MP-Declare

Declarative constraints are well-suited for representing the permissible behaviour of business processes. Modeling languages like Declare [13] describe a set of *constraints* that must be satisfied throughout the process execution. Constraints, in turn, are instances of predefined *templates*. Templates, in turn, are patterns that define parameterized classes of properties. Their semantics can be formalized using formal logics such as Linear Temporal Logic over finite traces (LTL_f) [14].

A central shortcoming of languages like Declare is the fact that templates are not directly capable of expressing the connection between the behaviour and other perspectives of the process. Consider the example of a loan application process. The process modeler would like to define constraints such as the following:

1. Activation conditions: When a loan is requested and *account balance > 4,000 EUR*, the loan must subsequently be granted.
2. Correlation conditions: When a loan is requested, the loan must subsequently be granted and *amount requested = amount granted*.
3. Target conditions: When a loan is requested, the loan must subsequently be granted by a specific member of the financial board.
4. Temporal conditions: When a loan is requested, the loan must subsequently be granted *within the next 30 days*.

Standard Declare only supports constraints that relates activities without considering other process perspectives. Here, the $\mathbf{F}$, $\mathbf{X}$, $\mathbf{G}$, and $\mathbf{U}$ LTL$_f$ future operators have the following meanings: formula $\mathbf{F}\psi_1$ means that ψ_1 holds sometime in the future, $\mathbf{X}\psi_1$ means that ψ_1 holds in the next position, $\mathbf{G}\psi_1$ says that ψ_1 holds forever in the future, and, lastly, $\psi_1\mathbf{U}\psi_2$ means that sometime in the future ψ_2 will hold and until that moment ψ_1 holds (with ψ_1 and ψ_2 LTL$_f$ formulas). The $\mathbf{O}$, $\mathbf{Y}$ and $\mathbf{S}$ LTL$_f$ past operators have the following meaning: $\mathbf{O}\psi_1$ means that ψ_1 holds sometime in the past, $\mathbf{Y}\psi_1$ means that ψ_1 holds in the previous position, and $\psi_1\mathbf{S}\psi_2$ means that ψ_1 has held sometime in the past and since that moment ψ_2 holds.

Consider, e.g., the *response* constraint $\mathbf{G}(A \to \mathbf{F}B)$. It indicates that if A *occurs*, B must eventually *follow*. Therefore, this constraint is fully satisfied in traces such as $\mathbf{t}_1 = \langle A, A, B, C \rangle$, $\mathbf{t}_2 = \langle B, B, C, D \rangle$, and $\mathbf{t}_3 = \langle A, B, C, B \rangle$, but not for $\mathbf{t}_4 = \langle A, B, A, C \rangle$ because the second occurrence of A is not followed by a B. In $\mathbf{t}_2$, it is *vacuously satisfied* [15], in a trivial way, because A never occurs.

An *activation activity* of a constraint in a trace is an activity whose execution imposes, because of that constraint, some obligations on the execution of other activities (target activities) in the same trace (see Table 1). For example, A is an activation activity for the *response* constraint $\mathbf{G}(A \to \mathbf{F}B)$ and B is a target, because the execution of A forces B to be executed, eventually. An activation of a constraint leads to a *fulfillment* or to a *violation*. Consider, again, $\mathbf{G}(A \to \mathbf{F}B)$. In trace $\mathbf{t}_1$, the constraint is activated and fulfilled twice, whereas, in trace $\mathbf{t}_3$, it is activated and fulfilled only once. In trace $\mathbf{t}_4$, it is activated twice and the second activation leads to a violation (B does not occur subsequently).

The importance of multi-perspective dependencies led to the definition of a multi-perspective version of Declare (MP-Declare) [9]. Its semantics build on the notion of *payload* of an event. $e(activity)$ identifies the occurrence of an event in order to distinguish it from the activity name. At the time of a certain event e, its attributes $x_1, \ldots, x_m$ have certain values. $p^e_{activity} = (val_{x1}, \ldots, val_{xn})$ represents its payload. To denote the projection of the payload $p^e_A = (x_1, \ldots, x_n)$ over attributes $x_1, \ldots, x_m$ with $m \leqslant n$, the notation $p^e_A[x_1, \ldots, x_m]$ is used. For instance, $p^e_{ApplyForTrip}[Resource]$=SS is the projection of the attribute *Resource* in the event description. Furthermore, the n-tuples of attributes x_i are represented as $\boldsymbol{x}$. Therefore, the templates in MP-Declare extend standard Declare with additional conditions on event attributes. Specifically, given the events $e(A)$ and $e(B)$ with payloads $p^e_A = (x_1, \ldots, x_n)$ and $p^e_B = (y_1, \ldots, y_n)$, the *activation condition* φ_a, the *correlation condition* φ_c, and the *target condition* φ_t are defined. The activation condition is part of the activation ϕ_a, whilst correlation and target conditions are part of the target ϕ_t, according to their respective time of evaluation. The *activation* condition is a statement that must be valid when the activation occurs. In the case of the *response* template, the activation condition has the form $\varphi_a(x_1, \ldots, x_n)$, meaning that the proposition φ_a over $(x_1, \ldots, x_n)$ must hold true. The *correlation* condition is a statement that must be valid when the target occurs, and it relates the values of the attributes in the payloads of the activation and the target event. It has the form

Table 1. Semantics for MP-Declare constraints in LTL_f.

Template	LTL_f Semantics
existence	$\top \to \mathbf{F}(e(A) \wedge \varphi_a(x)) \vee \mathbf{O}(e(A) \wedge \varphi_a(x))$
respondedExistence	$\mathbf{G}((A \wedge \varphi_a(x)) \to$ $(\mathbf{O}(B \wedge \varphi_c(x,y) \wedge \varphi_t(y)) \vee \mathbf{F}(B \wedge \varphi_c(x,y) \wedge \varphi_t(y))))$
response	$\mathbf{G}((A \wedge \varphi_a(x)) \to \mathbf{F}(B \wedge \varphi_c(x,y) \wedge \varphi_t(y)))$
alternateResponse	$\mathbf{G}((A \wedge \varphi_a(x)) \to$ $\mathbf{X}(\neg(A \wedge \varphi_a(x))\mathbf{U}(B \wedge \varphi_c(x,y) \wedge \varphi_t(y)))$
chainResponse	$\mathbf{G}((A \wedge \varphi_a(x)) \to \mathbf{X}(B \wedge \varphi_c(x,y) \wedge \varphi_t(y)))$
precedence	$\mathbf{G}((B \wedge \varphi_a(x)) \to \mathbf{O}(A \wedge \varphi_c(x,y) \wedge \varphi_t(y)))$
alternatePrecedence	$\mathbf{G}((B \wedge \varphi_a(x)) \to$ $\mathbf{Y}(\neg(B \wedge \varphi_a(x))\mathbf{S}(A \wedge \varphi_c(x,y) \wedge \varphi_t(y)))$
chainPrecedence	$\mathbf{G}((B \wedge \varphi_a(x)) \to \mathbf{Y}(A \wedge \varphi_c(x,y) \wedge \varphi_t(y)))$
notRespondedExistence	$\mathbf{G}((A \wedge \varphi_a(x)) \to$ $\neg(\mathbf{O}(B \wedge \varphi_c(x,y) \wedge \varphi_t(y)) \vee \mathbf{F}(B \wedge \varphi_c(x,y) \wedge \varphi_t(y))))$
notResponse	$\mathbf{G}((A \wedge \varphi_a(x)) \to \neg\mathbf{F}(B \wedge \varphi_c(x,y) \wedge \varphi_t(y)))$
notPrecedence	$\mathbf{G}((B \wedge \varphi_a(x)) \to \neg\mathbf{O}(A \wedge \varphi_c(x,y) \wedge \varphi_t(y)))$
notChainResponse	$\mathbf{G}((A \wedge \varphi_a(x)) \to \neg\mathbf{X}(B \wedge \varphi_c(x,y) \wedge \varphi_t(y)))$
notChainPrecedence	$\mathbf{G}((B \wedge \varphi_a(x)) \to \neg\mathbf{Y}(A \wedge \varphi_c(x,y) \wedge \varphi_t(y)))$

$\varphi_c(x_1, \ldots, x_m, y_1, \ldots, y_m)$ with $m \leqslant n$, where φ_c is a propositional formula on the variables of both the payload of $e(A)$ and the payload of $e(B)$. *Target* conditions exert limitations on the values of the attributes that are registered at the moment wherein the target activity occurs. They have the form $\varphi_t(y_1, \ldots, y_m)$ with $m \leqslant n$, where φ_t is a propositional formula involving variables in the payload of $e(B)$.

2.2 Process Event Chain Metamodel

Our approach covers the five most important process perspectives, namely the data oriented, operational, functional, organizational and behavioural perspective. The approach based on the well known Process Event Chain Metamodel introduced in [16] which fulfills with exception of the operational perspective all of the above mentioned perspectives. The behavioural perspective is expressed by the position attribute in the abstract signature *Task*. The organizational perspective is mapped by the interaction of *Relation*, *RelationType*, *Group* and *Identity*. The data oriented perspective is modeled by the *WriteAccess*, *Value* and *VariableObject*. For the implementation of the operational perspective the meta model is expanded by the class *Tool* as a subclass of *Element*. Note that you ensure in the implementation that there is no relationship between two different types, i.e. between a tool and an identity. In the following we shortly describe for understanding the most important parts of the meta model.

A *WriteAccess* is needed to assign a value to a data object. A *WriteAccess* capsules the *VariableObject* and the associated *Value*. For every change of the *Value* a new *WriteAccess* is needed. Our approach only supports integers and strings as domain of the values. This is a result of the non-support of floating-point numbers by the Alloy language. Theoretically it would be possible to simulate a floating-point number by two integers at the cost of a significantly larger bit width. An implementation of the meta model is given in [17].

2.3   Alloy

Alloy is a declarative logic language for building process models that describe structures with respect to desired restrictions which was invented by Daniel Jackson at the MIT [17]. In this section we provide a concise and short description of the main Alloy language features. For understanding the Alloy language it is useful to compare it with object oriented programming languages (OOPLs). So a signature (sig) is similiar to a class and the fields inside of a signature are comparable to attributes in the OOP. Alloy uses fact blocks similiar to invariants in the Object Constraint Language (OCL) for the specification of non-structural constraints. It is possible to define functions (fun) that act as parameterizable snippets of re-usable code. A predicate is a special type of function with the limitation that the return type is always a boolean expression. With the run command you can run a predicate, which means that the Alloy analyzer tries to find models for which this predicate holds. For further information about the general Alloy syntax we refer to the dedicated literature [18].

3   Related Work

This work relates to the stream of research on (multi-perspective) declarative process management. The *Declare* framework was designed for modeling and executing declarative business processes. In its most publicized variant, a Declare process model is built from a set of rule templates each of which is mapped to an expression in Linear Temporal Logic (LTL). The resulting LTL formula is then converted to an automaton for execution [2]. Declare only constrains the starts of activities and interrelates them temporally. Data oriented aspects and the organizational perspective are completely missing in traditional Declare. The approaches proposed in [19,20] allow for the specification of constraints that go beyond the traditional Declare templates. In [21], the authors define *Timed Declare*, an extension of Declare that relies on timed automata. In [22], the authors introduce for the first time a data aware semantics for Declare. In [9] a general multi perspective LTL semantics for Declare (*MP-Declare*) has been presented. Here, Declare is extented with elements of first order logic to refer to data values in constraints. Data aware as well as generalized MP-Declare models are supported in the context of conformance checking [9], process discovery [23] and trace generation [17,24]. Recently, the authors presented an approach for executing MP-Declare specifications. The execution engine builds on a classification strategy for different constraint types and a transformation component into the execution language Alloy that is used to solve SAT problems. Here, a modeling and execution prototype has been implemented as well. Similar to the Declare specification language, further frameworks for defining declarative processes exist. *CLIMB* [25] is a first-order logic declarative language for the specification of interaction models. However, there is no system support for modeling and execution of CLIMB models. The *DCR Graph* framework [3,26] and graphical representation is similar to Declare. The DCR Graph model directly supports execution of the process model based on the notion of markings of the graph. An algorithm for discovering DCR graphs has been proposed in [27]. The declarative process modeling and execution framework *DPIL* [4,5] covers resource and data modeling as well. The *EM-BrA^{2}CE* project [28] represents a first step towards the unification of business rules and processes. It extends the Semantics of Business Vocabulary and Business Rules (SBVR) framework by concepts like activities, states and participants. For execution, the SBVR rules are translated to event-condition-action (ECA) rules using templates. Both frameworks lack system support for data and resource oriented aspects. Several approaches for executing case models and artifact-centric processes that are similar but not equal to declarative processes have been proposed.

The research endeavors in [10,11] present a technique for discovering hidden dependencies in (control-flow oriented) Declare specification and making them explicit by means of dependency structures. Experiments show that the proposed technique lowers the cognitive effort necessary to comprehend the given declarative process model. In [29] the authors discuss how hidden dependencies affect human understanding and reasoning of declarative models. Furthermore, [30] proposes a technique that automatically resolves conflicts in (control-flow oriented) Declare models to eliminate redundancies. The approach at hand presents a next step towards the incorporation of multiple perspectives.

4 Logic Based Look-Ahead

In this chapter we introduce our main idea, a logic based look-ahead algorithm for multi-perspective process models. Our look-ahead will answer the questions which activities and resources are allowed to be used in the next n steps if in the next step a specific activity is performed by using one or more resources. Therefore all possible traces of a fixed length are simulated and validated. The validity of a trace depends not only on the next step activity but rather on the previous trace. For example if our process model contains a *precedence* constraint, it is important to check whether the corresponding activity occurred before. Based on the set of all valid traces, activities can be classified into *executable* and *nonexecutable activities*. If no valid trace is found we can determine that the process instance cannot be completed within the next n steps. We call n *length of the look-ahead* or *look-ahead length*. In general, there is a big amount of valid traces for a process model but not all traces are as good as others. So we use a filter with some conditions to get the best traces for a specific situation. The specific situation depends on individual preferences like using as few resources as possible. We are not only interested in valid traces but also in activities or resources

---

Algorithm 1. Procedure for trace generation.

Data: Trace Tr, activity a, tools T_a, identities I_a, data objects D_a
Result: by a expanded trace
1 a.tools $\leftarrow T_a$
2 a.identities $\leftarrow I_a$
3 a.dataObjects $\leftarrow D_a$
4 $Tr(\text{length}(Tr) + 1) \leftarrow a$
5 **return** Tr

Algorithm 2. Procedure for generating all possible assignments of a set of data objects.

Data: data objects D
Result: all possible assignments of D
1 result $\leftarrow \emptyset$
2 **for** $x \in D$ **do**
3 | $B_x \leftarrow$ all assignments of x
4 **end**
5 $B \leftarrow \mathcal{P}(\{B_x \mid x \in D\})$
6 **for** $b \in B$ **do**
7 | transform b into a set $\tilde{B}$ of the corresponding data objects
8 | result.add($\tilde{B}$)
9 **end**
10 **return** result

---

which are forbidden in the further course of execution. Sometimes this kind of information makes it easier to choose an activity for the next step because all of the denied activities may be unnecessary for the intended execution.

In the following we denote for an activity a by T_a the set of tools, by I_a the set of identities and by D_a the set of data objects that occur in a. A data object has always got a certain value. By abuse of notation of the Process Event Chain Metamodel we describe a data object only by its value and do not note the corresponding write accesses. A trace is a temporal sequence of activities and the used tools, identities and data objects. In the first step we want to reconstruct traces and be able to generate new traces. In Algorithm 1 we attach to a given trace Tr an activity a and the in the execution used tools T_a, identities I_a and data objects D_a.

In this paper we assume that the value of a data object has a given finite domain. Let us discuss a small example with an activity a and two variables x and y that are allowed to be used in a and may have the values b and 1. We denote by $a_{\{x=1\}}$ that activity a is executed with data object x and associated value 1. Hence in a there might appear none, one ore both variables we have the eight possibilities $a_{\{x=1\}}, a_{\{x=b\}}, a_{\{y=1\}}, a_{\{y=b\}}, a_{\{x=b\}\wedge\{y=1\}}, a_{\{x=b\}\wedge\{y=b\}}, a_{\{x=1\}\wedge\{y=1\}}, a_{\{x=1\}\wedge\{y=b\}}.$

Algorithm 3. Procedure to generate all possible traces of length $n + 1$

Data: Trace Tr of length n, activities A_P, tools T_P, identities I_P, data objects
D_P
Result: all possible traces of length $n + 1$

```
1  traces ← ∅
2  for a ∈ A do
3  │   for M₁ ∈ P(T_P) do
4  │   │   for M₂ ∈ P(I_P) do
5  │   │   │   for M₃ ∈ alg2(D_P) do
6  │   │   │   │   traces.add(alg1(Tr, a, M₁, M₂, M₃))
7  │   │   │   end
8  │   │   end
9  │   end
10 end
11 return traces
```

In Algorithm 2 we create a set B_x for each data object x which contains all the different assignments of x. After that we determine the power set of all these sets B_x. Note that $\mathcal{P}(\{B_x \mid x \in D\})$ is a set of sets of sets(!). The elements of the power set are transformed into a set of assignments. The next step is to create for a given trace of length n all theoretically possible traces of length $n+1$ (without taking care of the validity of the created traces). For a process P let A_P be the activities, T_P the tools, I_P the identities and D_P the data objects which are allowed in the process. Since we are interested in all possible traces, we have to loop over the power set of all the sets that are involved in the process. Algorithm 3 creates all the traces via combining all possible assignments.

We want to improve Algorithm 3 by expanding traces of length n by l positions for $l > 1$. That means that we are interested in all possible traces of length $n + 1, \ldots, n + l$. In Algorithm 4 we create all these traces by adding recursively all possible events and save these results.

Finally we can formulate the look-ahead algorithm. For a given trace Tr of length n we want to check if the process can be successfully completed in $n+l+1$ steps if we execute activity a with tools T_a, identities I_a and data objects D_a at position $n + 1$. We first calculate all possible traces with Algorithm 5. After that we create the corresponding activities, tools etc. in Alloy and check if the single traces are valid using the Alloy Analyzer. Our result is a list of valid traces.

5   Implementation

Alloy offers a JavaAPI which makes it possible to use the Alloy Analyzer in a Java application. So we can implement the trace generation with Java and only leave the task of trace validation to the Alloy Analyzer. Therefore we automatically generate an Alloy code which contains all possible activities such as resources as signatures, the process model itself (that means MP-Declare templates) and the generated trace. We followed the method described in [12] to

---

Algorithm 4. Procedure for generating all possible traces of length $n + 1, \ldots n + l$

Data: Trace Tr, activities A_P, tools T_P, identities I_P, data objects D_P, look-ahead length l

Result: all possible traces of length $n + 1, \ldots, n + l$

1 tempTraces $\leftarrow \emptyset$
2 stepTraces $\leftarrow$ alg3(Tr, A_P, T_P, I_P, D_P)
3 **while** $l > 1$ **do**
4 $\quad$ tempSet $\leftarrow \emptyset$
5 $\quad$ **for** $tr \in$ stepTraces **do**
6 $\quad\quad$ temp $\leftarrow$ alg3(tr, A_P, T_P, I_P, D_P)
7 $\quad\quad$ **for** $e \in$ temp **do**
8 $\quad\quad\quad$ tempSet.add(e)
9 $\quad\quad$ **end**
10 $\quad\quad$ **for** $t \in$ tempSet **do**
11 $\quad\quad\quad$ tempTraces.add(t)
12 $\quad\quad$ **end**
13 $\quad\quad$ tempSet $\leftarrow \emptyset$
14 $\quad$ **end**
15 $\quad$ stepTraces $\leftarrow \emptyset$
16 $\quad$ stepTraces $\leftarrow$ tempTraces
17 $\quad$ $l \leftarrow l - 1$
18 **end**
19 **return** stepTraces

---

transform a declarative process model into Alloy. The generated trace consists of the previous trace, the next step activity and the next simulated positions in the trace according to the look-ahead length. To represent the trace in Alloy it is necessary to restrict the usage of tools, identities and data objects so that the trace cannot be edited by the Alloy Analyzer. That means that the Alloy Analyzer finds no possibility to add a resource to a trace position. It is possible to forbid the use of certain resources at a specific position by setting the number of their occurrence to zero. Furthermore, we limit with the run command the trace length so that the Alloy Analyzer cannot append a further activity. In other words, we force the Alloy Analyzer to generate – apart from symmetric solutions – either exactly one or zero solutions. Symmetric solutions mean that two solutions are equal apart from the designation of the objects. This means that the solutions can be transferred into each other by renaming the objects. If our trace is valid the Alloy Analyzer finds exactly one solution, namely the specific generated trace, otherwise there is no solution, so our trace violates a constraint of the process model.

6   Evaluation

In this section we want to run the developed algorithms on two different processes and give further remarks of how to improve performance.

Algorithm 5. Procedure for look-ahead algorithm

    Data: Trace Tr, activity a, tools T_a, identities I_a, data objects D_a, activities
           A_P, identities I_P, data objects D_P, look-ahead length l

    Result: valid traces between length $n + 1$ and $n + l + 1$

1 currentTrace $\leftarrow$ alg1(Tr, a, T_a, I_a, D_a)
2 allTraces $\leftarrow$ alg4(Tr, A, T_P, I_P, D_P)
3 validTraces $\leftarrow \emptyset$
4 **for** $t \in$ allTraces **do**
5   generateAlloyCode(t)
6   ans $\leftarrow$ check t with Alloy
7   **if** $ans.satisfiable()$ **then**
8 | validTraces.add(t)
9   **end**
10 **end**
11 **return** validTraces

6.1 Performance Evaluation

We first run the *hiddenCoExistence* process introduced in Sect. 1. At the beginning we start with an empty trace and want to execute activity a first.

Table 2. Run-time evaluation with respect to look-ahead length

	1	2	3	4	5
hiddenCoExistence	$1,67$ s	$4,88$ s	$34,94$ s	2.1 m	21.89 m
publishPaper with first activity *WriteAbstract*	$54,2$ s	3.45 h	11.24 h	–	–
publishPaper with first activity *WritePaper*	$58,234$ s	3.42 h	11.20 h	–	–

Our second process *publishPaper* is shown in Fig. 2. This process has got seven activities: *writeAbstract, submitAbstract, writePaper, submitPaper, checkPaper, acceptPaper* and *rejectPaper*. Of course an abstract has to be written before it can be submitted. So we have the *precedence* constraint between these two activities. Same holds for the activities *writePaper* and *submitPaper*. Furthermore we have another *precedence* constraint between *submitAbstract* and *submitPaper* which means that the abstract has to be submitted before the paper. We also add a *chainResponse* constraint between the two activities *submitPaper* and *checkPaper*. This means that a paper has to be checked instantly after its submission. There is also a *chainPrecedence* constraint between these activities which presupposes the submission of a paper before it can be checked. No paper can be accepted or rejected without having been checked before. This leads to a *chainPrecedence* constraint as well between check paper and accept paper as between *checkPaper* and *rejectPaper*. No paper can be accepted and rejected simultaneously. That is why we have a *notCoExistence* constraint between these two activities. A rejected paper cannot be submitted twice. This fact is guaranteed by the *notPrecedence* and the *notResponse* constraint between the activities *rejectPaper* and *submitPaper*.

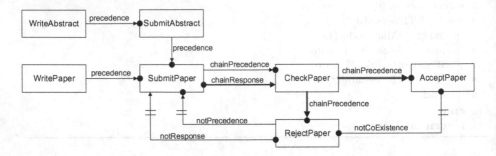

Fig. 2. *publishPaper* example process in Declare notation

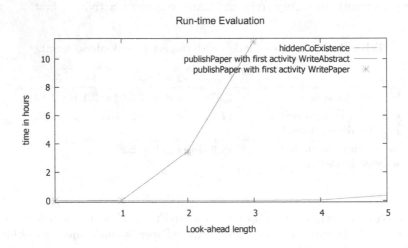

Fig. 3. Performance evaluation of the approach at hand

We want some more constraints to be observed during the process that refer to other perspectives as well. An abstract may not contain more than eight lines. Otherwise the corresponding paper is rejected instantly. Analogously a paper must consist at least of five pages. We limit the two data objects on the values $\{1, \ldots, 10\}$. These two facts are observed by using a *response* template including the respective condition. An additional constraint is that a paper may not be checked by the same person who has written the paper, i.e., a *Separation of Duties* constraint that can be expressed as a correlation condition

$\mathbf{G}(A \rightarrow \mathbf{X}(B \wedge \varphi_c(x, y)))$ with $\varphi_c(\boldsymbol{x}, \boldsymbol{y}) = (p_A^e[Resource] \neq p_B^e[Resource])$ on the corresponding *chainResponse* constraint. In our example we used three different tools and identities. We run the process twice. At first we start with the activity *writeAbstract*. After that we run the process starting with *writePaper*. In Table 2 we record the time of execution in respect to the look-ahead length. For these benchmarks we used a Windows 10 system equipped with an Intel Core i7-7600U CPU @2.80GHz and 24 GB RAM. Furthermore, the performance evaluation is visualized in Fig. 3. It is obvious that with increasing look-ahead length the time of execution really grows exponentially so that it is not practicable for realtime look-ahead applications. In comparison to the *hiddenCoExistence* process, the time of execution of the process *submitPaper* is even more time consuming because of the additional tools, identities and data objects. A deeper analyzis of the results shows that especially the data objects with the ten different values are responsible for the bad performance.

Table 3. Classification of MP-Declare templates

	Impact global concurrency	Impact global timing	Permanently disabling
existence		x	
respondedExistence		x	
response		x	
precedence			
alternateResponse		x	
alternatePrecedence			
chainResponse	x	x	
chainPrecedence	x		
notResponse			x
notRespondedExistence			x
notChainResponse	x		
notPrecedence			x
notChainPrecedence		x	
notCoExistence			x

6.2 Possibilities for Optimization

There are several possibilities to speed up the execution of our algorithm. The best option is to reduce the amount of possible traces. A deeper study of the multi-perspective constraints shows that a few of them guarantee the permanent or temporal non-executability of one or more activities. If we know the state of each process constraint (that means that we can say if a constraint is violated or not), we only have to prove traces which consist exclusively of executable activities. According to [31] we classify the multi-perspective declare templates of this paper into three categories: impact global concurrency, impact global timing and permanently disabling. Permanently disabling means that one activity is disabled for the rest of the execution. Impact global concurrency means that all activities except of one are temporally disabled. For example an activated *chainResponse* template means that in the next step only one activity is possible. Impact global timing means that one specific activity is not executable in the next step. The classification of the used MP-Declare templates in the work at hand is shown in Table 3.

Using the fact that different traces do not depend on each other, we can easily use parallel programming to check all possible traces to get a better performance. In practical use the majority of valid traces are of no interest. So we can use the above mentioned filter condition in this way that only traces which fullfil our filter conditions are generated. A further important matter for the bad performance is the domain of the values of the data objects. In many cases a great amount of possible values have the same effect because the conditions which use this value only compare it with a threshold. So we can minimize the domain on up to three values. One value representing the threshold, one for the values lower and one value for all the values greater than the threshold. We call this preprocessing of the domain. In the example of the previous section we would have a threshold for the number of pages and one for the number of lines. Another optimization would be a scoring system. This works like the above mentioned filter. At first activities and resources are labeled with different scores. A score represents the complexity or costs of using the activity or resource. The scores of all activities and resources used in the generated trace were added up. If this sum surpasses a chosen threshold, the trace is ignored and not checked.

7 Conclusion

In this paper, we introduced a logic based look-ahead approach for the execution of multi-perspective declarative processes. The look-ahead allows for estimating all consequences and effects of certain decisions at any time of process execution. We develop an algorithm for trace generation and checking traces using the logic language Alloy and extensively evaluate our approach by means of several example models. For future work, we plan to improve the applicability and performance of our approach, in particular, by implementing the proposed optimization possibilities described in Sect. 6.2.

References

1. Dumas, M., Rosa, M.L., Mendling, M.L., Reijers, H.A.: Fundamentals of Business Process Management, 2nd edn. Springer, Heidelberg (2018). https://doi.org/10.1007/978-3-662-56509-4
2. Pesic, M., Schonenberg, H., van der Aalst, W.M.P.: Declare: full supportfor loosely-structured processes. In: IEEE EDOC Conference 2007, pp. 287–300 (2007)
3. Hildebrandt, T.T., Mukkamala, R.R., Slaats, T., Zanitti, T.: Contracts for cross-organizational workflows as timed dynamic condition response graphs. J. Log. Algebr. Program. **82**(5–7), 164–185 (2013)
4. Zeising, M., Schönig, S., Jablonski, S.: Towards a common platform for the support of routine and agile business processes. In: Collaborative Computing: Networking, Applications and Worksharing (2014)
5. Schönig, S., Ackermann, L., Jablonski, S.: Towards an implementation of data and resource patterns in constraint-based process models. In: Modelsward, pp. 271–278 (2018)
6. Rozinat, A., Mans, R.S., Song, M., van der Aalst, W.M.P.: Discovering simulation models. Inf. Syst. **34**(3), 305–327 (2009)
7. de Leoni, M., van der Aalst, W.M.P., Dees, M.: A general process mining framework for correlating, predicting and clustering dynamic behavior based on event logs. Inf. Syst. **56**, 235–257 (2016)
8. Baumann, M., Baumann, M.H., Schönig, S., Jablonski, S.: Resource-aware process model similarity matching. In: Toumani, F., et al. (eds.) ICSOC 2014. LNCS, vol. 8954, pp. 96–107. Springer, Cham (2015). https://doi.org/10.1007/978-3-319-22885-3_9
9. Burattin, A., Maggi, F.M., Sperduti, A.: Conformance checking based on multi-perspective declarative process models. Expert Syst. Appl. **65**, 194–211 (2016)
10. Smedt, J.D., Weerdt, J.D., Serral, E., Vanthienen, J.: Improving understandability of declarative process models by revealing hidden dependencies. CAiSE **2016**, 83–98 (2016)
11. Smedt, J.D., Weerdt, J.D., Serral, E., Vanthienen, J.: Discovering hidden dependencies in constraint-based declarative process models for improving understandability. Inf. Syst. **74**(Part), 40–52 (2018)
12. Ackermann, L., Schönig, S., Petter, S., Schützenmeier, N., Jablonski, S.: Execution of multi-perspective declarative process models. In: Panetto, H., Debruyne, C., Proper, H., Ardagna, C., Roman, D., Meersman, R. (eds.) OTM 2018. LNCS, vol. 11230, pp. 154–172. Springer, Cham (2018). https://doi.org/10.1007/978-3-030-02671-4_9
13. van der Aalst, W., Pesic, M., Schonenberg, H.: Declarative workflows: balancing between flexibility and support. CSRD **23**, 99–113 (2009)
14. Montali, M., Pesic, M., van der Aalst, W.M.P., Chesani, F., Mello, P., Storari, S.: Declarative specification and verification of service choreographies. ACM Trans. Web **4**(1), 3 (2010)
15. Burattin, A., Maggi, F.M., van der Aalst, W.M., Sperduti, A.: Techniques for a posteriori analysis of declarative processes. In: EDOC, Beijing, pp. 41–50. IEEE, September 2012
16. Bussler, C.: Analysis of the organization modeling capability of workflow-management-systems. In: PRIISM 1996 Conference Proceedings, pp. 438–455 (1996)

17. Ackermann, L., Schönig, S., Jablonski, S.: Simulation of multi-perspective declarative process models. In: Dumas, M., Fantinato, M. (eds.) BPM 2016. LNBIP, vol. 281, pp. 61–73. Springer, Cham (2017). https://doi.org/10.1007/978-3-319-58457-7_5

18. Jackson, D.: Software Abstractions: logic, language, and analysis. MIT press, Cambridge (2012)

19. Lamma, E., Mello, P., Riguzzi, F., Storari, S.: Applying inductive logic programming to process mining. In: Blockeel, H., Ramon, J., Shavlik, J., Tadepalli, P. (eds.) ILP 2007. LNCS (LNAI), vol. 4894, pp. 132–146. Springer, Heidelberg (2008). https://doi.org/10.1007/978-3-540-78469-2_16

20. Chesani, F., Lamma, E., Mello, P., Montali, M., Riguzzi, F., Storari, S.: Exploiting inductive logic programming techniques for declarative process mining. In: Jensen, K., van der Aalst, W.M.P. (eds.) Transactions on Petri Nets and Other Models of Concurrency II. LNCS, vol. 5460, pp. 278–295. Springer, Heidelberg (2009). https://doi.org/10.1007/978-3-642-00899-3_16

21. Westergaard, M., Maggi, F.M.: Looking into the future. In: Meersman, R., et al. (eds.) OTM 2012. LNCS, vol. 7565, pp. 250–267. Springer, Heidelberg (2012). https://doi.org/10.1007/978-3-642-33606-5_16

22. Montali, M., Chesani, F., Mello, P., Maggi, F.M.: Towards data-aware constraints in declare. In: SAC, pp. 1391–1396. ACM (2013)

23. Schönig, S., Di Ciccio, C., Maggi, F.M., Mendling, J.: Discovery of multi-perspective declarative process models. In: Sheng, Q.Z., Stroulia, E., Tata, S., Bhiri, S. (eds.) ICSOC 2016. LNCS, vol. 9936, pp. 87–103. Springer, Cham (2016). https://doi.org/10.1007/978-3-319-46295-0_6

24. Skydanienko, V., Francescomarino, C.D., Maggi, F.: A tool for generating event logs from multi-perspective declare models. In: BPM, Demos (2018)

25. Montali, M.: Specification and Verification of Declarative Open Interaction Models: A Logic-Based Approach, vol. 56. Springer, Heidelberg (2010). https://doi.org/10.1007/978-3-642-14538-4

26. Slaats, T., Mukkamala, R.R., Hildebrandt, T., Marquard, M.: Exformatics declarative case management workflows as DCR graphs. In: Daniel, F., Wang, J., Weber, B. (eds.) BPM 2013. LNCS, vol. 8094, pp. 339–354. Springer, Heidelberg (2013). https://doi.org/10.1007/978-3-642-40176-3_28

27. Debois, S., Hildebrandt, T.T., Laursen, P.H., Ulrik, K.R.: Declarative process mining for DCR graphs. In: SAC, pp. 759–764 (2017)

28. Goedertier, S., Haesen, R., Vanthienen, J.: Rule-based business process modelling and enactment. Int. J. Bus. Process Integr. Manag. 3(3), 194–207 (2008)

29. Haisjackl, C., et al.: Understanding declare models: strategies, pitfalls, empirical results. Software Syst. Model. 15, 325–352 (2016)

30. Ciccio, C.D., Maggi, F.M., Montali, M., Mendling, J.: Resolving inconsistencies and redundancies in declarative process models. Inf. Syst. 64, 425–446 (2017)

31. Smedt, J.D., Weerdt, J.D., Vanthienen, J., Poels, G.: Mixed-paradigm process modeling with intertwined state spaces. Bus. Inf. Syst. Eng. 58(1), 19–29 (2016)

Exploring the Understandability of a Hybrid Process Design Artifact Based on DCR Graphs

Amine Abbad Andaloussi[1]([✉]), Andrea Burattin[1], Tijs Slaats[2],
Anette Chelina Møller Petersen[3], Thomas T. Hildebrandt[2],
and Barbara Weber[1,4]

[1] Software and Process Engineering, Technical University of Denmark,
2800 Kgs., Lyngby, Denmark
amab@dtu.dk
[2] Department of Computer Science, University of Copenhagen,
2100 København Ø, Denmark
[3] Business IT Department, IT University of Copenhagen,
2300 København S, Denmark
[4] Institue of Computer Science, University of St. Gallen,
9000 St., Gallen, Switzerland

Abstract. Process design artifacts (e.g., process models, textual process descriptions and simulations) are increasingly used to provide input for requirements elicitation and to facilitate the design of business processes. To support the understandability of process models and make them accessible for end-users with different backgrounds, several hybrid representations combining different design artifacts have been proposed in the literature. This paper investigates the understandability of DCR-HR, a new hybrid process design artifact based on DCR graphs. Using eye-tracking and think-aloud techniques, this paper explores the benefits and challenges associated with the use of different design artifacts and investigates the way end-users engage with them. The results motivate the use of DCR-HR and provide insights about the support it provides to end-users with different backgrounds.

1 Introduction

In the development of today's Process-Aware Information Systems (PAIS), process design artifacts (shortly process artifacts) play a central role both in the enactment and the management of business processes. Besides providing a blueprint for process execution and enabling simulation and model checking, process artifacts provide input for requirements elicitation and allow a shared understanding of the business process [6, pp. 66–67]. Depending on the target

Work supported by the Innovation Fund Denmark project *EcoKnow* (7050-00034A); the third author additionally by the Danish Council for Independent Research project *Hybrid Business Process Management Technologies* (DFF-6111-00337).

© Springer Nature Switzerland AG 2019
I. Reinhartz-Berger et al. (Eds.): BPMDS 2019/EMMSAD 2019, LNBIP 352, pp. 69–84, 2019.
https://doi.org/10.1007/978-3-030-20618-5_5

audience and the nature of the task to be fulfilled, different process artifacts (e.g., process models, textual process descriptions and interactive simulations) can be more or less beneficial [18]. The background of the process stakeholders (i.e., domain experts and IT specialists) influences the degree of formality required to describe the business process specifications. Domain experts often lack the skills to derive knowledge from formal process models; thus, they tend to rely on informal process artifacts to describe and communicate their knowledge of the domain. Conversely, IT specialists are more familiar with formal representations; thus they tend to use process models to derive a fine-grained understanding of the business process [13]. As the development of PAIS involves the collaboration of both process stakeholders, the deployment of a single type of process artifact is usually not sufficient to support knowledge transfer and provide an overarching understanding. Moreover, a process artifact can be used in several contexts to fulfill different tasks. For instance, it can be used *(a)* to check the constraints governing the execution of the business process activities, *(b)* to extract contextual information about the business process *(c)* to determine the behavior of a specific process execution based on the case history. Depending on the task, one artifact might be better suited than the others. In addition, the use of a single language to describe the business process can negatively impact its understandability. This is clearly the case with declarative languages, which despite their enhanced flexibility (compared to imperative languages), they are still controversial in terms of understandability especially with regards to novice end-users [7]. This, in turn, suggests the need to support declarative process models with other representations in different languages to improve their understandability.

In order to overcome the limitations of single process artifacts, a set of hybrid process artifacts have been proposed in the literature (e.g., [4,5,10,14,15,20]). These approaches combine different types of process artifacts and claim an enhanced user understanding of the process model. However, none of these approaches has explored the reading patterns of stakeholders with different backgrounds when dealing with all the previously mentioned tasks. This work reports the results of an exploratory study investigating the understandability of a hybrid process artifact (called "DCR Hybrid Representation" or DCR-HR shortly) combining a declarative DCR (Dynamic Conditional Response) graph model [8] with textual annotations depicting the law and an interactive simulation. The study investigates the usefulness of hybrid process artifacts by *(a)* identifying the benefits and challenges associated with each of the DCR-HR artifacts, *(b)* observing the way end-users with different backgrounds engage with the different artifacts proposed by DCR-HR, and *(c)* exploring the way the different DCR-HR artifacts can be used to fulfill different tasks. To support the findings, this work deploys a novel approach to investigate the reading patterns of end-users and uses concepts from grounded theory [3] to extract subjective insights from the participants who took part in the study.

The remaining of this paper is structured as follows. Section 2 provides an overview of hybrid process artifacts and describes the related work. Section 3 presents the research method followed to plan and conduct the exploratory study.

Section 4 reports the results of the analysis. Section 5 discusses the analyzed findings and highlights the circumstances when the use of a hybrid process artifact can be beneficial. Finally, Sect. 6 wraps up the main findings of the study and highlights the directions for future work.

2 Background and Related Work

Hybrid process representations have been introduced in the literature to designate (a) hybrid languages or (b) hybrid process artifacts. Hybrid languages (e.g., [17]) combine existing languages in order to enable a concise and precise representation of business processes. Hybrid process artifacts, in turn, combine two or more process artifacts overlapping in the description of some business process aspects. DCR-HR is a hybrid process artifact combining two *static* process artifacts (i.e., a declarative process model and a textual description of the process) with an *interactive* process artifact (i.e., an interactive simulation showing the possible outcomes depending on the user input). DCR-HR (cf. Fig. 1) aims at improving the understandability of DCR process models and helping end-users with different backgrounds to make sense of law's digitized models [1,2].

The literature proposes similar hybrid process artifacts. These representations can be categorized into the following sets: (a) process artifacts combining a process model with textual process descriptions and (b) process artifacts combining a process model with an interactive simulation. In the former set, several approaches (e.g., [10,14]) combining an imperative process model in BPMN (Business Process Modeling Notation)[1] with business rules described textually have emerged. These approaches have been evaluated in [15] where the authors have investigated the effect of using linked rules (i.e., a type of business rules) on the understandability of process models. The findings of the study show that the combination of BPMN and business rules is associated with higher performance and reduced mental effort. Similarly in [4], the authors evaluated the understandability of a hybrid process artifact combining a declarative process model and a textual artifact revealing the hidden dependencies in the model. The results demonstrate a lower response time and reduced mental effort when using the proposed hybrid representation. In the latter set, two approaches combining a process model with an interactive simulation (i.e., [5,20]) have been proposed. The former approach combines a declare process model with test cases to support the maintainability and modeling of process models. This approach was evaluated in [18] where the authors have analyzed the verbal data transcribed from a set of modeling sessions. The results show that the proposed process artifact helped to increase the perceived model quality. The latter approach (i.e., [5]) proposes a hybrid process artifact combining a process model in DCR with an interactive simulation. A similar representation is used as a basis to derive the hybrid process artifact scrutinized in this work.

The evaluation presented in this work differs from the existing ones in different aspects. In term of experimental subjects (cf. Sect. 3), unlike the existing

---

[1] See https://www.omg.org/spec/BPMN/2.0/About-BPMN/.

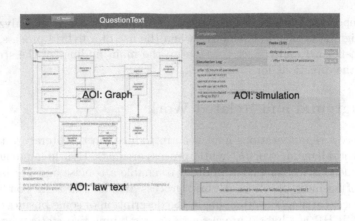

Fig. 1. A view showing the DCR-HR layout. At the analysis, this view is divided into 3 AOIs referring to the different artifacts. A higher resolution of this figure is available at http://andaloussi.org/papers/BPMDS2019/DCRHRLayout.pdf

evaluations which have mainly covered university students, this study recruits participants with different backgrounds (i.e municipality case-workers and people from academia), which in turn allows evaluating the usefulness of DCR-HR in a wider scope. In term of experimental material (cf. Sect. 3), while the existing evaluations have usually used made-up process descriptions or domain-free process models (where activities are labeled with single characters e.g., A, B ...), this work deploys digitized models of the law meant to be used by case-workers to handle citizens' requests. In addition, the experimental tasks used in the proposed evaluation are crafted to cover different contexts (i.e., checking constraints, checking contextual information or determining the behavior of a process instance based on a given case history, cf. Sect. 3). In term of analysis approach (cf. Sect. 3), this work extends the findings of the existing evaluations by investigating the reading patterns obtained from the eye-tracking gaze recordings and triangulating them with subjective insights obtained from think-aloud sessions. Hence, the proposed approach provides novel insights into the usefulness of hybrid process artifacts.

3   Research Method

This section presents the research method deployed to plan and conduct this exploratory study. The following paragraphs introduce the research questions addressed in this work, highlight the key design aspects and provide insights about the measurements used during the analysis.

Research Questions. This work considers three types of process artifacts (i.e., process models, textual process descriptions, and interactive simulations) which are commonly used to represent business processes. In order to support end-users when dealing with business process representations, it is necessary to understand the benefits and challenges associated with their use. The first research question is formulated as follows: **RQ1: What are the benefits and challenges associated with each of the artifacts proposed by DCR-HR?**

Process artifacts are used by domain experts and IT specialists. The two groups have different backgrounds which raise the question of whether the disparity of backgrounds is reflected in the way they use the different artifacts. The second research question is formulated as follows: **RQ2: How do end-users engage with the different DCR-HR artifacts?**

Finally, as process artifacts can be used to fulfill different tasks, it is also essential to investigate whether a single process artifact or a specific combination of process artifacts can provide global support in solving different types of tasks. The third research question is formulated as follows: **RQ3: How are the different DCR-HR artifacts used to fulfill different task types?)**

Participants. To investigate the above research questions, an exploratory study is conducted. In this study data is collected from 5 case-workers from Syddjurs municipality in Denmark and 10 academics (i.e., students, faculty) from the Technical University of Denmark and the IT University of Copenhagen. Case-workers serve as proxies for domain experts. They have proficiency in reading law texts but lack knowledge in process modeling. Academics serve as proxies for IT specialists. They have knowledge in process modeling, but lack proficiency in law.

Material. As part of this exploratory study, participants had to perform several model comprehension tasks. The process deployed for this study originates from Section §45 of the "Consolidation Act on Social Services"[2]. The material was provided in both English and Danish depending on the participant's preference. The designed artifacts are intended to be complementary to each other. Nevertheless, a considerable overlap exists between all of them. Following the modeling of an expert in DCR graphs, the graph captures the requirements of the law text, while the simulation represents a concrete implementation of the DCR graph. The experiment comprises a familiarization and 6 tasks. It is possible to categorize these tasks into *constraint tasks*, *decision tasks* and *scenario tasks*. Constraint tasks comprise questions about the relationships between pairs of activities in the process model. These questions reflect the circumstance where an end-user has to maintain a process model (e.g., update a constraint between two activities). In this context, it is necessary for the end-user to identify the specific constraint that should be changed in the model. Decision tasks comprise questions where the system is prompting the end-user to decide among several options. In that regard, the end-user should be able to identify the contextual information required to guide her/his decision-making process in order to achieve the desired outcome. Finally, scenario tasks illustrate the follow-up on customer

---

[2] http://english.sm.dk/media/14900/consolidation-act-on-social-services.pdf (Eng), https://www.retsinformation.dk/Forms/R0710.aspx?id=197036 (Dan).

cases. Namely, this type of tasks provide the end-user with a case history and ask her/him to determine the allowed behavior based on the given history. For each of these types, 2 tasks were designed. The experiment material can be found online at http://andaloussi.org/papers/BPMDS2019/Material.pdf.

Procedure. Prior to the experiment, the participants were given a screening form to check their physical ability to participate in an eye-tracking experiment, afterward, they were given a pre-experiment questionnaire to collect their background information. At the beginning of the experiment, each participant has received an introduction to DCR-HR where the semantics of the different DCR relations have been presented and the features of the DCR platform have been demonstrated. During the eye-tracking experiment, the 6 understandability tasks were sequentially displayed. At the end, a retrospective think-aloud session [9, pp. 104–108] was held to collect insights about the use of DCR-HR.

Settings. The experiment material was designed and presented in the DCR platform[3]. A view showing the presented layout in depicted in Fig. 1. Prior to each eye-tracking session, a calibration procedure was conducted to ensure a good data quality. The gaze data were collected using Tobii X3-120[4]. Fixation data [9, p. 22]) were derived using the I-VT Algorithm [11] in Tobii Pro Studio 3.4.8. Finally, all the subjective insights provided verbally by the participants were recorded with their consent.

Analysis Approach. To answer our research questions, two different types of analysis are proposed. Namely, we use concepts from grounded theory [3] to extract subjective insights from think-aloud data and process mining techniques to explore the participants' reading patterns through attention maps. The subjective insights are extracted with the support of Atlas.ti[5]. During this process, the most reoccurring aspects related to the use of the different DCR-HR artifacts are identified and then grouped into categories based on their common traits.

The attention maps are obtained from the fixation data provided by the eye-tracking software. After dividing the stimulus into three areas of interest (AOIs) [9, pp. 187–230] (each referring to a distinct DCR-HR artifact, cf. Fig. 1), a time-stamped fixation data-set comprising a set of scan-paths (i.e., distinct sequences of fixations illustrating the reading paths participants) is exported and transformed into an XES event log[6]. After identifying the direct relationships in the log [16], a descriptive process model (referred as attention map in the context of this work) illustrating the participants' reading pattern is generated. Examples of such attention maps are shown in Figs. 2 and 3. The different AOIs are represented as activities in the attention maps, while the transitions

---

[3] see http://dcrgraphs.net/ and http://wiki.dcrgraphs.net/.

[4] See https://www.tobiipro.com/product-listing/tobii-pro-x3-120/.

[5] A qualitative data analysis tool. See https://atlasti.com.

[6] See http://www.xes-standard.org/start.

between the different AOIs are represented as edges. In order to analyze the different reading patterns, the total fixation duration on each AOI (i.e., the sum of the duration of all fixation landing on a particular area of the stimulus [9, pp. 377–386]) and the frequency of transition between each pair of AOIs are extracted from the fixation data-set. Afterward the mean fixation duration *(D)* and mean transition frequency *(F)* are derived by dividing each measure by the number of traces (i.e., scan-paths) used to discover the attention map. These two measurements are projected respectively on activities and edges in the attention map to allow comparing the reading patterns in different attention maps.

4   Findings

This section reports the finding of the study answering the research questions presented in Sect. 3. Section 4.1 identifies the benefits and challenges associated with each of the DCR-HR artifacts. Section 4.2 investigates the way end-users with different backgrounds engage with DCR-HR. Section 4.3 scrutinizes the end-users' reading patterns when dealing with different types of tasks.

4.1   What Are the Benefits and Challenges Associated with Each of the Artifacts Proposed by DCR-HR? (RQ1)

The individual think-aloud sessions held with the participants after the experiment provide rich insights about the usability of DCR-HR as well as the support provided by the different artifacts. As explained in Sect. 3, think-aloud audio recordings were transcribed, then following a qualitative coding approach different labels were assigned to distinguish the different aspects emphasized by the participants during the think-aloud sessions. This section investigates the codes associated with the benefits and challenges of the DCR graph, the law text and the simulation.

The results show that the DCR graph helped several participants to get a good overview about the business process (e.g., *"The model I mainly used it to identify like how the overall process works"*). As each activity in the DCR graph is linked to its corresponding law fragment, the DCR graph allowed the participants to identify and navigate through the different sub-sections of the law (e.g., *"You can highlight different sections of law through [the] model"*). Some academics mentioned that the DCR graph helped them to understand the interplay between the different process activities (e.g., *"I use the model to see [the] interaction between the four different activities"*), whereas some case-workers were challenged by the semantics of the DCR relations. These challenges were inferred from their quotes during the think-aloud, as several participants were unable to identify the appropriate DCR relation specifying a certain behavior. In addition, some participants found the DCR graph very abstract and pointed out that the model was sometimes missing the details of the law text (e.g., *"If you only have the model it's very abstract"*, *"The strange thing is that many things which the law is talking about the model did not talk about"*).

The law text, in turn, provided the participant with details which were missing in the DCR graph (e.g., *"I mean I guess it provided more details in some cases than the model"*, *"The law text might be able to add some details that can't be in the model "*, *"If I didn't think that model accurately captured enough for me to answer the question then I would read the whole text instead"*). The participants also mentioned that the law text supported their decision-making process when the DCR graph allows for more than one choice (e.g., *"When I had to use the law text was for questions about'should I do this' at all, for example should I give personal permission should I take the accept or should I take the reject button on an activity."*). In addition, several case-workers have shown a preference for the law text as they were already familiar with reading and interpreting law paragraphs (e.g., *"I mostly used the law text because that's what I'm used to looking at"*[7]). In turn, many of the academics had difficulties to understand the legal terms and the linguistic patterns used in the law text (e.g., *"I think understanding this law jargon was kind of difficult"*, *"I tried to read the law text to understand the law but it actually didn't help at all because the language that is used is pretty formal"*). Therefore, some academics were avoiding referring to the law text to extract knowledge about the business process (e.g., *"It is not so easy to read the law text . . . I have totally ignore it"*).

Finally, the interactive simulation, allowed the participants to check the viability of different process executions (e.g., *"The simulation is helpful to see the possible paths"*, *"You can actually see if you have a viable execution"*). Moreover, some academics have affirmed that using the simulator helped to reduce the mental effort required to keep track of the dependencies between the different DCR relations (e.g., *"It's a little much to have all the steps in your mind while you're going . . . "*, *"It is easier to see it simulated instead of manually analyze the model"*). These comments fall in line with the previous claims about the role of interactive simulations in improving the understandability of declarative process models [19]. The analysis of the transcripts shows also that the simulation helped participants to validate the insights retrieved from the DCR graph (e.g., *"You can like simulate the process then you like get a clear understanding of how the process works . . . if you're in doubt of like relations or anything in the graph then you can use the simulation to like confirm what you actually think about the model "*], *". . . checking if it is exactly what I thought the model is doing it's actually doing it"*). Yet, other participants have pointed out some drawbacks associated with the use of the simulation. In particular, some academics thought it was inefficient to restart the simulation all the way back at the beginning every time an undesired state is reached (e.g., *"Actually this was not very convenient because you click the all way through and if you miss click, which I actually did, you need to do it again"*). In addition, some academics have abstained from using the simulation because they were able to mentally simulate the process (e.g., *"Primarily, I didn't use the simulator at all because I pretty much simulated in my head"*). Other case-workers were not used to such an approach in their work practice and thought that the use of the simulation

---

[7] Quote translated from Danish.

could be time-consuming for them (e.g., *"I'm used to working under very high work pressure, so getting in and checking such things through that way is not in my habits"*[11], *"You would spend too long to press and read all four options, then press again and read three new options, then press again and there will be five new options"*[11]).

These insights show that each artifact has some strengths – but has also some weaknesses. Although the participants have been exposed to the three process artifacts during all the experiment trials, it can be seen that they have shown a preference for different process artifacts based on their perceived usefulness and the context in which they have been deployed. In the meantime, the participants have also reported a set of challenges they faced when interacting with these artifacts. This suggests that no single artifact can be enough to provide an overarching understanding of the business process for end-users with different backgrounds, which supports the idea of combining all these artifacts into a hybrid representation to complement each other and make up for their individual weaknesses.

4.2 How Do End-Users Engage with the Different Artifacts Proposed by DCR-HR? (RQ2)

This section investigates the reading patterns of case-workers and academics in order to obtain more insights about their use of DCR-HR. We differentiate in our analysis between case-workers and academics because of their different backgrounds. As mentioned in Sect. 3, case-workers have proficiency in reading law texts, but lack knowledge in process modeling. Academics, in turn, have a background in process modeling, but lack proficiency in reading law texts. Based on their different backgrounds, we expect that case-workers and academics might use different artifacts (in line with their background) to answer the given tasks. We use attention maps and the insights obtained from think-aloud to explore this assumption. Hereby, activities represent the different artifacts and the mean dwell time measure and the corresponding proportions show the distribution of attention between the different artifacts, while the mean transition frequency and the corresponding proportions provide insights about the interactions between the different artifacts (cf. Sect. 3).

Figures 2a and b show the attention maps comparing the reading patterns of case-workers and academics when answering the given tasks. These visualizations show that both groups typically started by reading the DCR graph, which is reasonable since the DCR graph is placed in the center of the screen and occupies a large portion of it (cf. Fig. 1). Furthermore, it can be observed that academics spent substantially more time looking at the different artifacts compared to case-workers (cf. mean fixation duration D in Figs. 2a and b). This observation is supported by the subjective insights obtained from the transcripts. Indeed case-workers have affirmed using sometimes common sense or relating to knowledge acquired through experience when answering to some tasks (e.g., *"If the recipient is unsatisfied, then, of course, you can change the decision [while the DCR graph shows clearly that such a decision cannot be reversed]"*[11]). However, academics, when asked whether they have used common sense, they all affirmed restricting themselves only to the provided artifacts.

The attention map depicted in Fig. 2a indicates that case-workers have split their attention mainly between the DCR graph and the law text. This is also supported by the think-aloud data where the majority of case-workers pointed out that they did not use the simulator, but only the graph and the law text (e.g., *"I have either read through the law text or the model but I have not used the simulation."*[11]). Other case-workers combined all the three artifacts when solving the given tasks. In particular, a case-worker affirmed to rely on the law text but still using the simulation as a means for validation, while another case-worker mentioned using the simulation but only twice during the experiment. These insights line up also with the proportions of transitions between the artifacts. Indeed as shown in Fig. 2a, case-workers did roughly the same number of transitions between the graph and the simulation and between the graph and the law text. This suggests that case-workers have generally interacted with all the different artifacts when answering the given tasks.

When looking at the attention map of academics in Fig. 2b, a different reading pattern can be observed. Indeed, the distribution of attention shows that academics gave most attention to the DCR graph and split the rest of their attention between the law text and the simulation. As mentioned in Sect. 4.1 academics were challenged by the legal terms and the linguistic patterns used in the law text which can be a possible explanation for the limited attention on the law text (compared to case-workers). The proportion of transitions between the different artifacts show that academics did almost twice more transitions between the graph and the simulation than between the graph and the law text. These insights show that academics have not only spent a limited time on the law text but also switched less often between the DCR graph and the law text. In addition, one can argue that the academics interacted more with the DCR

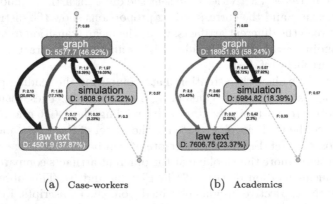

(a) Case-workers   (b) Academics

Fig. 2. Attention maps comparing the reading patterns of case-workers and academics. D refers to the mean fixation duration and F refers to the mean transition frequency between two AOIs (cf. Sect. 3).

graph and the simulation than with the law text, which can be justified when looking at the insights obtained from the think-aloud (e.g., *"I could actually solve the questions by not looking at the law but the model and the simulator"*).

Overall, the attention maps (cf. Fig. 2) suggest that end-users with different backgrounds use different artifacts to understand the model. Hereby, the hybrid nature of DCR-HR can provide a unified representation that can make process models accessible for end-users with different backgrounds.

4.3   How Are the Different DCR-HR Artifacts Used to Fulfill Different Task Types? (RQ3)

This section investigates the way end-users change their reading patterns when dealing with different tasks. As explained in Sect. 3, the participants were given different types of tasks (i.e., constraint, decision and scenario tasks) to illustrate the different contexts where process artifacts are used in real-life. On that matter, it is assumed that each task type would be efficiently accomplished using a certain combination of artifacts (cf. Sect. 3). To explore this idea, attention maps are used to scrutinize the attention distribution and transition patterns of the participants.

Figures 3a, b and c depicts the attention maps associated with the reading patterns of participants solving constraint, decision and scenario tasks respectively. These visualizations reveal a different reading pattern for each type of task. Figure 3a shows that in constraint tasks (i.e., questions about the relationships between pairs of activities in the process model, cf. Sect. 3), the participants gave most attention to the DCR graph, and split the rest of their attention between the simulation and the law text. This pattern can be explained by the nature of constraint tasks and the subjective insights obtained from the think-aloud. In fact, several participants highlighted the ability of the DCR graph to show the interplay between the different process activities (cf. Sect. 4.1). However, the think-aloud shows also that some other participants were challenged by the semantics of the DCR relations and were constantly using the simulation to clarify the implications of the different relations on the model behavior (e.g., *"The simulator, I used when I was in doubt because, the different arrows I wasn't always sure what they did, so then I rendered simulator ... then you could actually know for sure if you could do this after this or not"*). These subjective insights can be also seen from the high number of transitions between the DCR graph and the simulation. Indeed, the participants did twice more transitions between these two artifacts compared to between the graph and the law text.

When looking at decision questions (i.e., questions about contextual information intended to guide the decision-making process of the end-user, cf. Sect. 3) a different reading pattern can be observed (cf. Fig. 3b). Indeed, the participants split their attention mainly between the DCR graph and the law text. This pattern suggests that, when asked to choose among several options (cf. Sect. 3), participants have referred to the law text to support their decision-making process. Nevertheless, as mentioned in Sect. 4.1, the DCR graph was also used by the participants to navigate between the different law fragments. This subjective

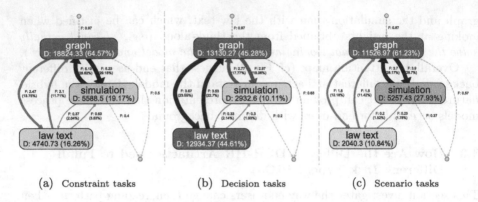

(a) Constraint tasks   (b) Decision tasks   (c) Scenario tasks

Fig. 3. Attention maps comparing the reading patterns of the participants when dealing with different types of tasks. D refers to the mean fixation duration and F refers to the mean transition frequency between two AOIs (cf. Sect. 3).

insight explains also the high number of transitions between the graph and the law text in decision tasks.

The reading pattern in scenario tasks (i.e., questions about the allowed model behavior based on a given history, cf. Sect. 3) differ from both constraint and decision tasks (cf. Fig. 3c). First, it is clear that the participants spent relatively less time on the law text while switching their attention mainly between the DCR graph and the simulation. This observation is inferred from both the distribution of attention between the different artifacts and the transition patterns. Hereby, one can argue that the participants have mainly combined the DCR graph and the simulation to answer scenario tasks. This assumption is supported by the think-aloud data where participants affirmed combining the DCR graph and the simulation when given questions comprising a sequence of activities and being asked to determine the model behavior from the set of next enabled activities (e.g., *"When the question is in a scenario then I use the simulator, because it's easy to see what happens after"*).

The reading patterns in constraint, decision and scenario tasks share one common trait that is the limited number of transitions between the law text and the simulation. The think-aloud data support this trait as the participants could not see any circumstance where the combination of law text and simulation is beneficial (e.g., *"Simulation and law text doesn't go well together because that if you can actually solve it with the simulator, you don't need the law text"*).

Overall, the insights provided by the attention maps show that the participants combined different artifacts when answering different tasks, which was manifested in the different reading patterns depicted in Fig. 3. On those grounds, we suggest that different type of tasks require combining different artifacts. Therefore, the deployment of hybrid process artifacts such as DCR-HR can support end-users when dealing with different tasks in a situation-specific manner.

5   Discussion

The disparity of the participants' background and the diversity of the given tasks provide important insights about the understandability of DCR-HR. The analysis of the transcripts revealed that each artifact is associated with a set of benefits and challenges. As presented in Sect. 4.1, the DCR graph allowed the participants to familiarize with the process scope and provided insights about the constraints governing the execution of the different process activities. Yet, some participants were challenged by the semantics of the different DCR relations. The interactive simulation proposed as part of DCR-HR can help to complement the understanding of the DCR graph by allowing end-users to offload their memory and gradually track the dependencies between the different constraints. Nonetheless, its usage was still inefficient and time consuming for some participants. The law text, in turn, was used to complement the information of the DCR graph and provided support in the participants' decision-making process. However, most academics were challenged by reading the law. These insights suggest that a single artifact may not be capable of providing a clear and overarching understanding of the business process. Alternatively, the deployment of a hybrid representation (e.g., DCR-HR) can help to make up for the weakness of individual artifacts. This idea is also supported by the dual coding theory [12] which motivates the combination of graphical and textual artifacts to covey information more effectively.

The reading patterns explored in Sect. 4.2 come to support the subjective insights provided by the participants. Indeed, case-workers and academics showed different reading patterns when interacting with DCR-HR. Although the majority of case-workers relied on the law text to answer the given tasks, they have additionally been guided by the DCR activities and some of them used the simulation. Academics, in turn, were highly challenged by the law and interacted mainly with the DCR graph and the simulation. This difference of reading patterns can be associated with the disparity of the background of case-workers and academics, which also reflects the circumstance where both domain experts (represented by case-workers) and IT specialists (represented by academics) are challenged when being exposed to unfamiliar process artifacts [13]. The deployment of a hybrid process artifact (e.g., DCR graph) in turn, will help to overcome this issue by providing a hybrid representation that is understandable to both stakeholders. Moreover, several authors in the literature have linked the understandability of the business process with the effectiveness of communication between the different stakeholders [6, pp. 104–108] and [7,13]. As a good understanding of the process would help to clarify the terms and relationships in the domain and prevent miss-interpretations of the process, the deployment of a hybrid process artifact is also expected to foster the communication during the development of PAIS.

The differentiation between different tasks has been clearly reflected in the end-users' reading patterns. The attention maps and the think-aloud output analyzed in Sect. 4.3 show that the participants have adapted their reading pattern in line with the different task types they have been given. Indeed, the participants gave most attention to the DCR graph in constraint tasks and used the support of the simulation to clarify the information extracted from the DCR graph, whereas in decision tasks the participants have switched their attention to the law text and used the DCR graph as a navigation tool to identify the law fragment in question. In scenario tasks, the participants have combined the simulation and the DCR graph to infer the model behavior at different stages of execution. These indications raise another aspect to be taken into consideration when offering tool support to end-users. Indeed besides the disparity of stake-holders' backgrounds, different types of tasks may require the use of different combination of artifacts.

The outcome of this study is twofold. On the one hand, it motives the deploy-ment of hybrid process artifacts and emphasizes the importance of enriching process models with textual artifacts and tool supports (e.g., interactive simula-tions). On the other hand, as the majority of hybrid process artifacts proposed in the literature combine either a textual artifact or an interactive simulation with a process model (cf. Sect. 2), this work gives empirical insights allowing to enhance the support offered by existing approaches. In this context, we encour-age customizing the tool support based on the background of end-users and the nature of the tasks at hand. This support can, for instance, be implemented by learning from the end-users' behavior and context of use in order to bring the artifact with the most value to their attention, while at the same time ensuring that the end-users can freely switch between the different artifacts.

Finally, it has to be noted that the outcome of this study is subject to limi-tations with regards to the limited number of participants and the exploratory nature of the study. In this sense, it is difficult to generalize the reported find-ings. Nevertheless, the results provide good insights about the understandability of DCR-HR and can serve a basis for the upcoming studies.

6   Conclusion and Future Work

This work summarizes the findings of an exploratory study investigating the understandability of DCR-HR. The results of the analysis suggest that *(a)* no single artifact is capable of providing a clear understanding of the process, *(b)* participants with different backgrounds use different combinations of artifacts, *(c)* different task types require combining different artifacts. All these findings motivate the use of DCR-HR and support its ability to help end-users with different backgrounds to perform different types of tasks.

As future work, we consider the following: *(1)* First and foremost, we are planning to conduct a follow-up study to further investigate and validate the insights reported in this work. Following a controlled experimental design, we will deploy a control group and treatment group to compare the understandability of process models with and without the support of a hybrid representation. *(2)* Secondly, we are planning to link the understandability of DCR-HR with the performance of the participants. To this end, the performance of the control and treatment groups will be analyzed and compared when dealing with different types of tasks. *(3)* Finally, with the availability of more data, we are planning to explore the machine learning capabilities to predict end-users' performance based on the gathered behavioral features. This, in turn, will empower end-users by adapting at run-time the support provided by DCR-HR.

References

1. Abbad Andaloussi, A., Slaats, T., Burattin, A., Hildebrandt, T.T., Weber, B.: Evaluating the understandability of hybrid process model representations using eye tracking: first insights. In: Daniel, F., Sheng, Q.Z., Motahari, H. (eds.) BPM 2018. LNBIP, vol. 342, pp. 475–481. Springer, Cham (2019). https://doi.org/10.1007/978-3-030-11641-5_37
2. Andaloussi, A.A., Slaats, T., Burattin, A., Hildebrandt, T.T., Weber, B.: A research model to test the understandability of hybrid process models using DCR graphs. In: 30th International Conference on Advanced Information Systems Engineering, EcoKnow Workshop, pp. 1–7, 2018
3. Corbin, J., Strauss, A.: Basics of Qualitative Research: Techniques and Procedures for Developing Grounded Theory. SAGE Publications, Thousand Oaks (2014)
4. De Smedt, J., De Weerdt, J., Serral, E., Vanthienen, J.: Discovering hidden dependencies in constraint-based declarative process models for improving understandability. Inf. Syst. **74**, 40–52 (2018)
5. Debois, S., Hildebrandt, T., Marquard, M., Slaats, T.: Hybrid process technologies in the financial sector. In: Proceedings of the Industry Track at the 13th International Conference on Business Process Management, pp. 4:107–119 (2015)
6. Dumas, M., La Rosa, M., Mendling, J., Reijers, H.A.: Fundamentals of Business Process Management. Springer, Heidelberg (2018). https://doi.org/10.1007/978-3-662-56509-4
7. Fahland, D., et al.: Declarative versus imperative process modeling languages: the issue of understandability. In: Halpin, T., et al. (eds.) BPMDS/EMMSAD -2009. LNBIP, vol. 29, pp. 353–366. Springer, Heidelberg (2009). https://doi.org/10.1007/978-3-642-01862-6_29
8. Hildebrandt, T.T., Mukkamala, R.R.: Declarative event-based workflow as distributed dynamic condition response graphs. Electron. Proc. Theoret. Comput. Sci. **69**, 59–73 (2011)
9. Holmqvist, K., Nyström, M., Andersson, R., Dewhurst, R., Jarodzka, H., van de Weijer, J.: Eye tracking: a comprehensive guide to methods and measures. OUP Oxford, Lund (2011)
10. Kluza, K., Kaczor, K., Nalepa, G.J.: Enriching business processes with rules using the Oryx BPMN editor. In: Rutkowski, L., Korytkowski, M., Scherer, R., Tadeusiewicz, R., Zadeh, L.A., Zurada, J.M. (eds.) ICAISC 2012. LNCS (LNAI), vol. 7268, pp. 573–581. Springer, Heidelberg (2012). https://doi.org/10.1007/978-3-642-29350-4_68
11. Olsen, A.: The Tobii I-VT Fixation Filter. Tobii Technology, Danderyd (2012)
12. Paivio, A.: Mental Representations: A Dual Coding Approach. OUP, New York (1990)
13. Pinggera, J., Porcham, T., Zugal, S., Weber, B.: LiProMo-Literate process modeling. In: CEUR Workshop Proceedings, vol. 855, pp. 163–170 (2012)
14. Sapkota, B., Sinderen, M.V.: Exploiting rules and processes for increasing flexibility in service composition. In: 2010 14th IEEE International Enterprise Distributed Object Computing Conference Workshops, pp. 177–185, October 2010

15. Wang, W., Indulska, M., Sadiq, S., Weber, B.: Effect of linked rules on business process model understanding. In: Carmona, J., Engels, G., Kumar, A. (eds.) BPM 2017. LNCS, vol. 10445, pp. 200–215. Springer, Cham (2017). https://doi.org/10. 1007/978-3-319-65000-5_12
16. Weijters, A.J.M.M., van der Aalst, W.M.P., Medeiros, A.K.A.D.: Process Mining with the Heuristics Miner Algorithm. TU/e Tech. Report 166:1–34 (2006)
17. Westergaard, M., Slaats, T.: Mixing paradigms for more comprehensible models. In: Daniel, F., Wang, J., Weber, B. (eds.) BPM 2013. LNCS, vol. 8094, pp. 283–290. Springer, Heidelberg (2013). https://doi.org/10.1007/978-3-642-40176-3_24
18. Zugal, S., Haisjackl, C., Pinggera, J., Weber, B.: Empirical evaluation of test driven modeling. Int. J. Inf. Syst. Model. Des. 4(2), 23–43 (2013)
19. Zugal, S., Pinggera, J., Weber, B.: Creating declarative process models using test driven modeling suite. In: Nurcan, S. (ed.) CAiSE Forum 2011. LNBIP, vol. 107, pp. 16–32. Springer, Heidelberg (2012). https://doi.org/10.1007/978-3-642-29749-6_2
20. Zugal, S., Pinggera, J., Weber, B.: Toward enhanced life-cycle support for declarative processes. J. Software Evol. Process 24(3), 285–302 (2012)

Novel Approaches in Enterprise Modeling (BPMDS 2019)

A Landscape for Case Models

Fernanda Gonzalez-Lopez[1](✉) and Luise Pufahl[2]

[1] Pontificia Universidad Catolica Valparaiso, Valparaiso, Chile
m.fernanda.gonzalez@gmail.com
[2] Hasso Plattner Institut, University of Potsdam, Potsdam, Germany
luise.pufahl@hpi.de

Abstract. Case Management is a paradigm to support knowledge-intensive processes. The different approaches developed for modeling these types of processes tend to result in scattered models due to the low abstraction level at which the inherently complex processes are therein represented. Thus, readability and understandability is more challenging than that of traditional process models. By reviewing existing proposals in the field of process overviews and case models, this paper extends a case modeling language – the fragment-based Case Management (fCM) language – with the goal of modeling knowledge-intensive processes from a higher abstraction level – to generate a so-called fCM landscape. This proposal is empirically evaluated via an online experiment. Results indicate that interpreting an fCM landscape might be more effective and efficient than interpreting an informationally equivalent case model.

Keywords: Case Management · Process landscape · Process map · Process architecture · Process model

1 Introduction

Case Management (CM) is a paradigm to support the design, execution, monitoring, and evaluation of knowledge-intensive processes [20]. These types of processes are often found in domains where highly trained workers (i.e. *knowledge workers*) deal with very diverse units of work (i.e. *cases*). In fact, the term CM originated in the healthcare domain, where *medical personnel* – knowledge workers – deal with *patients* – cases – and the end-to-end process is not clear beforehand, but is rather tailored on-the-go based on aspects, such as examination results and medical team expertise.

In CM and analogous to a traditional *process model*, a *case model* represents all possible courses of action for handling cases in a given scenario. Different approaches have been developed for CM, most of them with a strong data-orientation. Business artifacts [23] and their Guard-Stage-Milestone (GSM) lifecycles [14] put data in the center of the approach. Based on GSM, the industry-standard CMMN (Case Management Modeling and Notation) [25] was designed. The *fragment-based Case Management* (fCM) [12] understands

© Springer Nature Switzerland AG 2019
I. Reinhartz-Berger et al. (Eds.): BPMDS 2019/EMMSAD 2019, LNBIP 352, pp. 87–102, 2019.
https://doi.org/10.1007/978-3-030-20618-5_6

knowledge-intensive processes as having structured parts – i.e. *process frag-ments* – that are flexibly combined at run-time based on data handled by the process. Regarding its notation, fCM reuses concepts from BPMN (Business Process Model and Notation) [24]; we call this the fCM-language. As the CM approaches capture complex behaviour of knowledge-intensive processes – includ-ing processed data artifacts, possible operations on them, and their interrelation – case models tend to include more concepts and are more scattered than tradi-tional workflow-like process models. For capturing flexibility, the routing and the control flow might be more difficult to understand compared to an imperative sequence flow [31], such that Lantow [16] reports a lack of understandability of CMMN models.

Several works have been developed to provide accessibility to a comprehen-sive functional description of a business [17]. In such level of abstraction, indi-vidual processes are depicted as black boxes and, therefore, the focus of the model is on the structure of the collection of processes [8]. By analogy, this view could be used to depict process fragments within a case model. In this paper, we use the term *process overviews* to refer either to *process maps* [17,18], *pro-cess landscapes* [3,10], or *process architectures* [6,9]. In the range of possibilities of process overviews, process landscapes stand as the middle ground between the less-technical process maps and the more-technical process architectures [8]. Compared to detailed process models, process overviews allow to represent in a more straightforward way: (a) high-level concepts regarding to a single pro-cess, such as inputs/outputs; as well as (b) concepts regarding the relationships between processes, such as trigger and data flow. These concepts are either not available or indirectly represented in current approaches for case modeling.

This paper extends the fCM-language for modeling overviews of knowledge-intensive processes. The goal is making case models more accessible and under-standable, and thus easier to analyze by their users. We classify these models as *case model landscapes* (CMLs) since we expect the proposal to be, on one side understandable by non-technical users, but also useful for technical ones. We focus on the fCM approach [12]; still we will discuss its application to other approaches. Existing languages for modeling cases and process overviews are reviewed and their usefulness for CMLs is discussed. Based on the found lim-itations, we develop a language[1] for CMLs as extension of the fCM-language. The proposal is evaluated in comparison to the non-extended fCM-language in an online experiment where the participants are asked to answer questions on two business scenarios represented in these two languages The correctness of the answers as well as the time needed is measured to assess *interpretation efficiency* and *effectiveness* as proposed by [4,18].

In the remainder, related work on case management and process overviews is discussed in Sect. 2. Then, requirements for a CML and different alternatives are

---

[1] A *language* is a structured set of symbols whose combination represents concepts which carry a certain meaning. A language is specified using a meta-model describing its *abstract syntax* (i.e. constituting concepts and their relations) and its *semantics* (i.e. meaning of the concepts).

presented in Sect. 3. The extension of the fCM-language for CML is presented in Sect. 4 and its empirical evaluation is discussed in Sect. 5, followed by conclusions in Sect. 6.

2 Related Work

In this section, related work regarding case management and attempts to ease the case model understanding, and approaches for process overviews are presented.

Case Management. A first approach for capturing case models has been introduced as *Case Handling* in [1,2], which led to shifting the focus from activities to data. *Business Artifacts* [23] with the Guard-Stage-Milestone (GSM) approach [14] focus on the high-level data artifacts handled during case processing. This was used as the basis for the CMMN (Case Management Modeling and Notation) [25] standard which allows to specify, for example, optional and non-optional parts of a case and milestones that need to be reached. However, some aspects of data – essential for case management (CM) – cannot be represented using CMMN. Despite an existing standard, other CM approaches were still continued or newly developed, most prominently PHILharmonicFlows [15], fragment-based Case Management (fCM) [12], and the declarative approach [27]. PHILharmonicFlows [15] splits a process into micro processes describing how a data artifact can be changed and macro processes handling micro processes relations. To deal with complexity, Steinau et al. [29] propose relational process structures representing the relationships between processes with cardinalities. However, aspects, such as the results exchanged by the process fragments or the trigger relations are not captured, limiting the understanding and the analysis of such a case model. fCM by Hewelt and Weske [12] combines process fragments at runtime according to data conditions. In [11], Hewelt et al. provide a method for supporting the case model elicitation. Still, it is an open challenge that the resulting case model is difficult to read for people not involved in the case model design. The declarative approach [27] tries to avoid the disadvantages of imperative process models and allows more flexibility by defining constraints and rules between activities, whereby produced and consumed data of the activities is not considered. However, experiments showed that declarative process models seem to be more difficult to comprehend [28]. Therefore, De Smed et al. [5] propose dependencies diagrams to visualize implicit dependencies between actions in declarative models. It has a quite low abstraction level which might lead to understandability issues in case of more complex models. Furthermore, it builds upon on the constraint concepts of declarative models with no graphical elements targeting more declarative modeling experts.

Process Overviews. Process overviews – a term used in this paper for referring either to a process map, landscape, or architecture – support reasoning and analysis of the structure of the process collection, leaving aside much detail of individual processes [8]. Commonly, process overviews address the concerns of business-oriented users but they can also address the concerns of technical-oriented ones. Consequently, a language to express such a model aims to be easily understood by a non-technical audience [9]. Process maps are usually easily readable by non-technical users due to being modeled with a small set of concepts with a lax semantics. It might consists solely of a hierarchical classifications of processes, or also that inputs/outputs of the constituting processes are specified [19]. Process architectures are more technically oriented and each represented concept has a precise semantics. For example, the approach by Eid-Sabbagh et al. [6] provides information, about trigger and resource flow relationships between processes based on events. In the extension of this work, exclusive, sequential, and interaction relations between processes are discovered based on the data they handle, however data is not explicitly represented in the architecture model [7]. Process landscapes could be seen as the middle ground between process maps and architectures. Proposals in this area also struggle with the issue of ensuring an adequate level of understandability, e.g. [3,10]. Altogether, multiple approaches have been proposed to convey overviews for collections of processes. We argue that the therein used concepts could be adapted for building overviews for case models. In order to do so, it would be necessary to abstract from the details of process fragments and rather focus on the way they relate to each other. This is similar to the dependencies diagrams proposed by De Smed et al. [5]. However, our proposal places the emphasis on data-based relationships and a intuitively understandable graphical language.

3   Requirements for a Case Model Landscape

Section 3.1 introduces the fCM-language using the meta-model in Fig. 1 and the health-care example in Fig. 2. Then, requirements for a fCM landscape are defined in Sect. 3.2. Finally, alternative landscape approaches and their limitations are discussed in Sect. 3.3. In the remainder of the paper, we use a *medical consultation* business scenario to illustrate the discussed concepts. In the example, when a patient arrives to the hospital, she will be attended by a medical team for providing diagnosis and treatment and also by personnel for administrative matters, all with the goal of sending her healthy back home.

3.1   Fragment-Based Case Management Language

Figure 1 shows the meta-model that specifies the fCM-language, based on the specifications in [12]. In fCM, a case model consists of four artifacts to be detailed in the following: (a) a *domain model*, (b) a set of *object lifecycles*, (c) a *goal state*, and (d) a set of *process fragments*.

Domain Model. The domain model represents the static view of the data that is relevant to the scenario. As portrayed in Fig. 1 (upper section), it is composed of a collection of data classes defining relevant data types and their data attributes. In the example in Fig. 2a, the relevant data types are Biopsy, Patient File, X-ray, and Tomography.

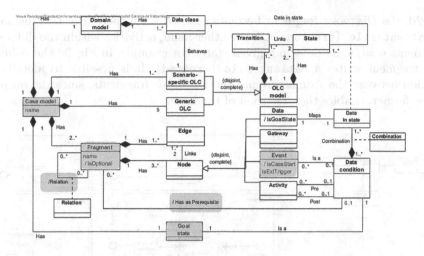

Fig. 1. Meta-model for fCM-language (fCML requirements highlighted)

Object Lifecycles. As showed in Fig. 1 (middle upper section), every class of the domain model behaves according to a scenario-specific object lifecycle (OLC). An OLC depicts possible states and transitions that an instance of a certain data type may undergo during the handling of a case. Figure 2b shows the OLC of the **Patient file** as a finite state machine with the following possible states: *created, furtherDiagnosis, diagnosed, medicationNeeded, surgeryNeeded,* and *finished*. Additionally, a set of *generic OLCs* is pre-defined in fCM for the execution semantics of cases, fragments, activities, gateways, and events.

Goal State. The goal state defines when a case model instance may terminate in terms of a logical combination of a subset of all possible classes in their OLC-defined states, as showed in Fig. 1 (bottom section). Figure 2c shows the goal state for our running example: a **Patient File** in state *finished*.

Process Fragments. A case model contains multiple process fragments as showed in Fig. 1 (middle lower section). In the example, the fragments are *Admission, Diagnosis, Surgery, Medication, Biopsy, Tomography,* and *Cardiorespiratory Resuscitation (CPR)*, as depicted in Fig. 2d. As showed in the meta-model, each process fragment is composed by a set of data, gateway, event, and activity nodes linked by flow edges, as in traditional process models. Fragment modeling requires consistency in labeling data objects to capture the relations between fragments. In Fig. 2d data types and their states are depicted using BPMN data-object notation: **Object type [state]**. As in many CM approaches, data is the key element around which fCM process fragments are organized. Figure 1 (right section) shows that data conditions are defined as the combination of data class type in some state of their OLCs. On one hand, a start event of a fragment could be itself a data condition, which means that such fragment is only enabled to start once a given data condition is true. For example, and as showed in

Fig. 2d, the *Diagnosis* fragment becomes enabled when there is a data instance of `Patient file [created]`. On the other hand, activities within the different fragments read/write data in a given state. For example, in Fig. 2d the *Admission* fragment writes a `Patient file [created]`. It is possible to identify a relation between the *Admission* and the *Diagnosis* fragments, since the output of the former, enables the execution of the latter.

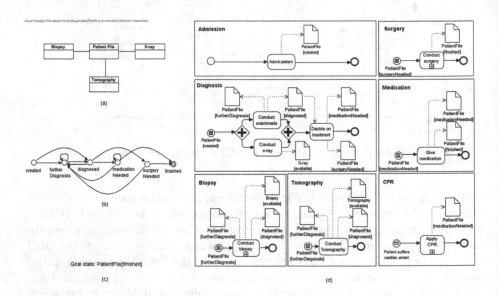

Fig. 2. Partial fCM case model for medical consultation: (a) domain model, (b) object lifecycle for the `Patient File`, (c) goal state, and (d) process fragments.

3.2 Requirements

As showed in our running example (see Fig. 2), the information within an fCM case model is scattered between various sub-models. In our experience (e.g. [11]), this poses a challenge for the readers using the model to answer simple high-level questions, such as *Where does the knowledge-intensive process start?* This issue can be tackled by creating a more abstract view, where some information from the case model is hidden and some information is made more straightforward/accessible. For fCM, we name such a view an fCM-landscape (fCML). We define requirements for fCML based on: (i) particularities of CM and knowledge-intensive processes as modeled using fCM, (ii) research on Process Overviews, and (iii) available standards in the fields of CM and Process Overviews. Requirements are described in the following and are showed as highlighted elements in the fCM-language meta-model in Fig. 1:

– **Business scenario.** Approaches for CM and Process Overviews consider often a – sometimes implicit – container specifying the limits of what lies within the business scenario (e.g. [25]) or process collection (e.g. [18]), respectively. This concept is also important for fCML as it defines a case model as a container for a set of fragments and data objects to reach a certain goal. This is showed in the *name* attribute of the `Case model` class in Fig. 1.

- **Case start.** In fCM, the start of a knowledge-intensive process is represented as a BPMN blank start event in the first fragment that can be executed. Neither in CMMN nor in Process Overviews is this distinction required, though it might be represented explicitly as an event listener [25], or implicitly by the sequence of processes [6] or the input for a process map [18]. However, we define it as a requirement for fCML due to being relevant for fCM. This is expressed by the derived attribute *isCaseStart* of the `Event` class in Fig. 1.
- **Goal state.** Another key feature of fCM to be included in the fCML, is the definition of a data condition for ending the case, represented by the `Goal state` class in Fig. 1. This concept relates to process map outputs [18].
- **Fragment.** The central concept of a Process Overview is the process depicted as a labeled black box [6,19]. By analogy, the process fragment should be defined as the central concept of a fCML. This requirement is showed in the *name* attribute of the `Fragment` class in Fig. 1.
- **External trigger.** Process Overviews consider that processes might be triggered by events [6]. Analogously, we then define that a fCML should provide information regarding triggering of fragments via external events. This is showed in the *isExtTrigger* attribute of the `Event` class in Fig. 1.
- **Pre-requisite.** The fact that some fCM fragments need to be data-enabled to be executed is similar to the concept of processes needing an input in a Process Overview (e.g. [18]). This fCML requirement is considered in the *Has as Prerequisite* derived association in Fig. 1.
- **Fragment relations.** *Data-flow relations* between processes are data-related aspects usually visualized in Process Overviews [19]. A key aspect of fCM is that the relations between fragments are based on data. Therefore, this concept is considered as an fCML requirement as showed on the *Relation* derived association in Fig. 1. Concepts like exclusiveness, sequential dependency, and interaction proposed by Eid-Sabbagh et al. [7] are of high relevance.
- **Fragment optionality.** A central aspect of CM are process fragments combination depending on the case at hand. Accordingly, CMMN defines that some parts of the case model can be discretionary. We rank this concept as important for end users to highlight the optional fragments which do not need to be executed for all possible cases. This fCML requirement is showed as the *isOptional* derived attribute of class `Fragment` in Fig. 1.

3.3   Alternatives

Together with fCM [12], a set of languages for Process Overviews and CM approaches was assessed to find out whether they provided the means to fulfill the requirements for an fCML previously discussed in Sect. 3. The justification for selecting these works, is that they are either the industry standards in their fields – ArchiMate [30] and CMMN [25] –, or they are representative and well documented proposals from the research community – Process Architecture by Eid-Sabbagh [6,7] and Process Maps by Malinova [18]. A summary of the results is presented in Table 1 and discussed in detail in the following.

Table 1. Alternatives, where ✓: full support, -: partial support, and X: no support.

	ArchiMate [30]	CMMN [25]	fCM [12]	Process architecture [6,7]	Process map [18]
Business scenario	-	✓	-	-	-
Case start	-	✓	✓	-	-
Goal state	-	X	✓	X	-
Fragment	-	✓	✓	-	-
External trigger	-	✓	✓	-	-
Pre-requisite	X	-	✓	-	-
Fragment relations	-	-	-	✓	-
Fragment optionality	-	✓	-	-	X

ArchiMate. ArchiMate is an architecture description language for enabling unambiguous description, analysis, and visualization of the relationships among business domains [30]. This language has become an industry standard for modeling enterprise architectures, and therefore, can be used to model Process Architectures. As showed in Table 1, ArchiMate supports most of the requirements for fCML, but only in a partial way due to being a general purpose language.

CMMN. As a modeling standard for CM, CMMN [25] fulfills many of the fCML requirements, as showed in Table 1. The weak points of CMMN are, however, those related to data, namely goal state, data pre-requisites, and data-aspects of fragments relations. An interesting aspect of CMMN is the concept of *sentries* (cf. [14]), which stand for entry and exit conditions of fragments.

fCM. The fCM approach [12] has been already described in detail in previous sections. As showed in Table 1, fCM supports the fCML requirements either fully or partially. In line with what we have previously discussed, the limitation of fCM is the scattered information among its various models.

Process Architecture. The approach to Process Architecture by Eid-Sabbagh [6,7] provides a language for describing process architectures. This language, however, does not consider goal states, as showed in Table 1. Data considerations are rather implicit in the architecture model: they provide a conceptual ground for defining some inter-process relations in [7]. Two particularities of this approach are the strong focus on events and the fact that it defines exclusiveness, sequential dependency, and interaction between processes.

Process Map. The Process Map approach by Malinova [18] provides partial support of most of the fCML requirements, as showed in Table 1. The main limitation of this language for modeling fCML is, again, related to data. Being a business-oriented model, data-flow between processes is considered at a very high level of abstraction, leaving outside details regarding data handling. The language provides the concept of condition, which semantic is not described in detail, but that somehow relates to the CMMN notion of sentries.

Results of the analysis proved none of the approaches was entirely suitable for the task of modeling a fCML. However, they ground our proposal (see Sect. 4).

4 Extension of fCM-Language for Modeling Landscapes

After identifying its requirements, this section introduces the extension of the fCM-language for modeling a fCML. We decided to re-use notational elements from BPMN and CMMN – both standards of the Object Management Group – due to having a high recognition factor by business people working with process models. We mostly reuse the notational elements of BPMN and CMMN in such a way that they still have the original meaning. The elements of the proposal, their semantic meaning, and the notation is given in Table 2. We will introduce the language extension based on the running example of the *medical consultation*: Fig. 3 shows the equivalent fCML for the case model in Fig. 2.

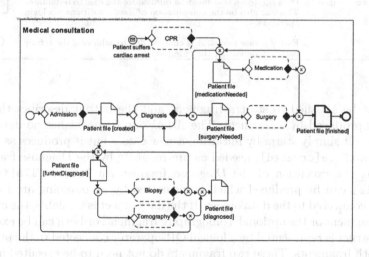

Fig. 3. Case Model Landscape for the medical consultation scenario.

The case model always starts with the *Admission* fragment, which follows the blank start event. Each fragment can have a pre-requisit and an output which are shown as unfilled and filled diamonds at the boarders of the fragments similar to the entry and exit criteria in CMMN. The pre-requisit describes the condition

Table 2. Modeling elements of the fCM-language extension for fCML.

Element	Description	Notation
Business scenario	Container of a landscape for a specific case model.	
Blank start event	Start of a case model. If a new case of the model is instantiated then it is started with the succeeding process fragment.	
Message start event	External occurrence of an event, which is relevant for the case. It enables the start of the succeeding process fragment.	
Process fragment, non-optional	Non-optional process fragment that needs to be executed in every possible execution of a case model.	
Process fragment, optional	Optional process fragment that is not necessarily executed in every possible execution of a case model.	
Pre-requisite	Data pre-condition or an event that enables the start of a process fragment.	
Output	Output produced by a process fragment, in terms of data. It is optional to include it if it is not required by another process fragment.	
Connector	Causal relation between the elements of the case model.	
Logic operator, AND	Forking or merging of paths following the logic of a logical AND-operator.	
Logic operator, OR	Forking or merging of paths following the logic of a logical OR-operator.	
Data object	Data type holding a particular state in which it is available as an input or an output of a process fragment.	
Data object, goal state	Data condition that must be fulfilled for the case to terminate. This can also be the combination of data conditions via logic operators.	
End event	End of a case model, it is enabled due to achieving the termination condition of the case model.	

that must be satisfied to start a fragment and the output describes the data outcomes produced by a fragment. The *Admission* fragment has no data input condition – it simply starts by initiating a new case – but it produces as output the `PatientFile[created]`, needed as pre-requisite by the *Diagnose* fragment.

During the execution of the *Diagnose* fragment, a `PatientFile[further Diagnosis]` can be produced which is visualized by an outgoing arc from the fragment connected to the data object. If the data object is available, the optional *Biopsy* fragment or the optional *Tomography* fragment, or both can be executed. This construct is represented by a logical OR-operator connected to the prerequisite of both fragments. These two fragments do not need to be executed in every case, they are optional which is shown by a dotted boarder line similar to the discretionary tasks/states in CMMN. The output of both fragments can be the `PatientFile` in *furtherDiagnosis* or *diagnosed* also represented with the help of a logical OR operator. In case of *furtherDiagnosis*, the two just discussed fragments can be restarted. In the other case, the *Diagnose* fragment is continued, which is shown by the incoming connector into the fragment box.

This fragment produces as output either the `PatientFile` in *surgeryNeeded* or *medicationNeeded* triggering the optional fragments *Surgery* or *Medication*, respectively. Both the fragments can produce `PatientFile[finished]` representing the goal state of the case model and leading to the end event, the end of the case model. The *Medication* fragment can also result in `PatientFile` `[medicationNeeded]` as alternative, re-triggering this fragment.

During the case execution, also a relevant event for this business scenario can occur – *Patient suffers from cardiac arrest*. Represented by a message start event, this event triggers the *CPR* fragment. It also results in the `PatientFile` `[medicationNeeded]` object. The logical OR connector above this data object implies that `PatientFile[medicationNeeded]` can be result of three fragments: the *Diagnose*, the *Medication*, or the *CPR* fragment. Here, the AND connector was not applied. This can be used to represent the need of several data objects to trigger a fragment, or different data objects are produced as output.

5   Evaluation

An experiment was design to assess our proposal. The experimental design is described in Sect. 5.1, and results are presented and discussed in Sect. 5.2.

5.1   Experimental Design

The independent variable of the experiment is the case modeling language: the proposed extension vs. the fCM-language (as discusses in Sect. 3.2, no other analyzed approach supports all requirements). Following [4], the experiment dependent variables are *interpretation effectiveness* – i.e. how faithfully does the interpretation of the model represents the semantics of the model –, *interpretation effort* – i.e. amount of resources needed to interpret the model –, and *interpretation efficiency* – quotient of them both. In this regard, the hypotheses we aimed to test were whether interpretation of case models is less effective ($H1_0$), requires more effort ($H2_0$), and is less efficient ($H3_0$) when using the fCM-language than when using the proposed extension. For testing these three hypotheses, we used paired Wilcoxon signed rank test, the non-parametric version of the paired t-test (see [13]). The grounds for using non-parametric statistics for data analysis is that, as showed in Fig. 4, no assumption of normality could be made about the collected data. Statistical analysis in this study considered a 95% confidence.

The subjects were students from the Hasso Plattner Institute, University of Potsdam, who were invited to voluntarily join the experiment. These students are easy accessible representatives of the target audience of case models. To maximize data collection, the experiment followed a crossover design in which each subject read a case model of one business scenario in fCM-language (control treatment or C) followed/preceded by reading a case model of another business scenario in the proposed extension (experimental treatment or E). The business scenarios used were *traumatology emergency* [22] (H) and *organization of a business trip* [11] (B), and their control and treatment model variants were designed to be informationally equivalent and were available during the whole experiment as recommended by Parson and Cole [26]. Altogether, this resulted in the following four treatments: EH/CB (treatment A), CB/EH (treatment B), EB/CH (treatment C), and CH/EB (treatment D). For example, treatment A corresponds to exposure to, firstly, the experimental treatment using the traumatology emergency scenario and, secondly, to the control treatment using the business trip organization scenario. We used block random assignment of the subjects according to the initial letter of their last name.

The experiment was conducted online using *Google Forms*[2]. We first defined a set of design-time and run-time aspects of case models (e.g. *case start, fragment repetition*), and then a set of 20 true or false statements addressing those aspects. For example, to address the *case start* aspect we formulated the following question: *In all cases, fragment X is the first to be executed*, where X is the name of a fragment in a given case model. For each respondent, she was firstly asked demographic questions. Before reading each model, the respective language was explained to her, and afterwards she was asked to answer the set of questions regarding a model of one of the business scenarios. Then this was repeated for the other business scenario using the other language. Interpretation effectiveness was measured as the total score of the set of questions (1 point per correct answer), interpretation effort was measures as the total time (in minutes) she used to complete the task, and interpretation efficiency was measured as the quotient of the previous variables.

5.2   Results and Discussion

The 24 subjects of the study were classified as novice or experienced, according to the modeling courses they had undertaken: one or more. Compared to the experienced subjects (8 in total), the novice subjects (16 in total) self-reported lower BPMN and CM experience but higher domain knowledge on the traumatology emergency and business trip scenarios. The overall low self-reported domain knowledge is desirable since it prevents subjects from answering questions based on prior domain knowledge rather than on model interpretation [4].

Figure 4 summarizes data gathered in the experiment after discarding two problematic observations. Overall and leaving outside out-layer observations, data in Fig. 4 for interpretation effectiveness and effort is shifted towards better performance for our proposal. Regarding average interpretation effectiveness, its value was slightly higher for the extension (15.8/20 points) than for the fCM-language (15.5/20 points). Again in average, interpretation effort led to slightly better results when using the proposal (12 min) in comparison to the fCM-language (13.3 min). Average interpretation efficiency, consequently, follows the same pattern of the proposal (1.6 points/min) slightly outperforming the fCM-language (1.3 points/min). As showed in Fig. 4, it is also possible to observe a higher dispersion of both scores and time is found for the fCM-language.

---

[2] Forms and raw data available at: https://drive.google.com/drive/folders/1c-ZZ6HA6H7d7yOgthcoVANLt-wnRfOhS?usp=sharing.

This might indicate a desirable feature of the proposal: leading to more consistent interpretation of case models in terms of effectiveness and effort.

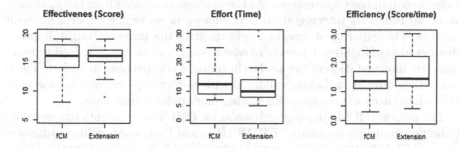

Fig. 4. Descriptive statistics of the experimental dependent variables.

Hypothesis testing provided no significant evidence to reject H1$_0$ (p = 0.2605), H2$_0$ (p = 0.9327), nor H3$_0$ (p = 0.7537). This means that the data in our experiment weakly supports the thesis that the proposed extension outperforms the fCM-language in effectiveness, effort, or efficiency. We conducted additional tests to verify aspects that might have influenced the results using the Spearman rank-order correlation test [13]. By this, we were able to ruled out the influence of treatment order (first C or E), lecture-based and self-reported BPMN/CM modeling experience, and self-reported prior domain knowledge. A limitation of our work is that we ensured similar complexity between the models used for the experiment – measured as the number of nodes [21] – based only on control models. However, the experimental versions of the models did not have a similar number of nodes due to fragment inter-relations leading to having treatments with different difficulty levels. A Spearman correlation test then indicated a significant direct relation between treatment difficulty – valuated as 0 for treatments A and B, and as 1 to treatments C and D – and interpretation effort (p = 0.0041). We believe that this is an issue that might have negatively impacted our results and that, avoiding it, might lead to improving significance of the evidence supporting the benefits of our proposal. An additional aspect that might contribute to improving our results in future versions of the experiment would be to conduct it in a laboratory setting such that, for example, time measures are more accurate.

6   Conclusions

This paper provided a new concept for case management by presenting a means for modeling case model landscapes. This contribution is built upon the creation of a meta-model for extending the fragment-based Case Management (fCM) language. A case model landscape (CML) gives end users an integrated, comprehensive overview of the high-level activities and the processed data during the execution of a knowledge-intensive process instead of the detailed case models with often scattered information about actions and data in different models. It can be used to get an understanding, but also to analyze case models, redesign, or check compliance requirements. As the landscapes builds up on the fCM app-roach, we tested its interpretation performance in an online experiment with students. The experiment results implicate that the proposal might improve interpretation of high-level aspects of case models, and that it may lead to more consistent interpretation of the models in terms of effectiveness and effort. These results should be, nonetheless, validated with further experimentation and con-sider a laboratory environment for having more reliable time data.

The proposed fCM-language extension for CML re-uses notational elements of the two modeling standards, BPMN (Business Process Modeling and Nota-tion) and CMMN (Case Management Modeling and Notation), having the advan-tage that it might be easier understandable by business people working with pro-cess models. Still, it has the risk of some minor miss-interpretation which need to be further tested. The proposal could be also used for CMMN models, whereby stages and their relation could be shown on an abstract level. CMMN repre-sents data mainly implicitly, our language represents data and data relations explicitly. Furthermore, the approach might be also interesting for PHILharmon-icFlows, another relevant case management approach, to represent the relation between the micro processes. An important concept for PHILharmonicFlows are the cardinalities between the generated objects. These are only implicitly given in the proposed landscape by distinguishing between optional and mandatory fragments, and the possibility to trigger certain fragments more than once. An explicit representation might be a useful extension. In this work, so far the lan-guage for CML was presented, but not how to design or automatically derive it. On this, we want to focus in our future research.

References

1. van der Aalst, W., Berens, P.: Beyond workflow management: product-driven case handling. In: 2001 International ACM SIGGROUP Conference on Supporting Group Work, pp. 42–51. ACM (2001)
2. van der Aalst, W., Weske, M., Grünbauer, D.: Case handling: a new paradigm for business process support. Data Knowl. Eng. **53**(2), 129–162 (2005)
3. Becker, J., Pfeiffer, D., Räckers, M., Fuchs, P.: Business Process Management in Public Administrations - The PICTURE Approach. In: PACIS 2007, Auckland, New Zeland, July 3–6, pp. 1–14 (2007)
4. Burton-Jones, A., Wand, Y., Weber, R.: Guidelines for empirical evaluations of conceptual modeling grammars. J. Assoc. Inf. Syst. **10**(6), 495–532 (2009)
5. De Smedt, J., De Weerdt, J., Serral, E., Vanthienen, J.: Discovering hidden depen-dencies in constraint-based declarative process models for improving understand-ability. Inf. Syst. **74**, 40–52 (2018)
6. Eid-Sabbagh, R.-H., Dijkman, R., Weske, M.: Business process architecture: use and correctness. In: Barros, A., Gal, A., Kindler, E. (eds.) BPM 2012. LNCS, vol. 7481, pp. 65–81. Springer, Heidelberg (2012). https://doi.org/10.1007/978-3-642-32885-5_5

7. Eid-Sabbagh, R.-H., Hewelt, M., Meyer, A., Weske, M.: Deriving business process data architecturesfrom process model collections. In: Basu, S., Pautasso, C., Zhang, L., Fu, X. (eds.) ICSOC 2013. LNCS, vol. 8274, pp. 533–540. Springer, Heidelberg (2013). https://doi.org/10.1007/978-3-642-45005-1_43

8. Gonzalez-Lopez, F., Bustos, G.: Business process architecture design methodologies - a literature review. Bus. Process Manag. J. (2019). https://doi.org/10.1108/BPMJ-09-2017-0258

9. Green, S., Ould, M.: The primacy of process architecture. In: CAiSE Workshops (2), pp. 154–159 (2004)

10. Gruhn, V., Wellen, U.: Analysing a process landscape by simulation. J. Syst. Software **59**(3), 333–342 (2001)

11. Hewelt, M., Wolff, F., Mandal, S., Pufahl, L., Weske, M.: Towards a methodology for case model elicitation. In: Gulden, J., Reinhartz-Berger, I., Schmidt, R., Guerreiro, S., Guédria, W., Bera, P. (eds.) BPMDS/EMMSAD -2018. LNBIP, vol. 318, pp. 181–195. Springer, Cham (2018). https://doi.org/10.1007/978-3-319-91704-7_12

12. Hewelt, M., Weske, M.: A hybrid approach for flexible case modeling and execution. In: La Rosa, M., Loos, P., Pastor, O. (eds.) BPM 2016. LNBIP, vol. 260, pp. 38–54. Springer, Cham (2016). https://doi.org/10.1007/978-3-319-45468-9_3

13. Hollander, M., Wolfe, D.A., Chicken, E.: Nonparametric Statistical Methods, 3rd edn. Wiley, Hoboken (2014)

14. Hull, R., et al.: Business artifacts with guard-stage-milestone lifecycles: managing artifact interactions with conditions and events. In: DEBS 2011, pp. 51–62. ACM (2011)

15. Künzle, V., Reichert, M.: PHILharmonicFlows: towards a framework for object-aware process management. J. Software Maintenance Evol. Res. Pract. **23**, 205–244 (2011)

16. Lantow, B.: Adaptive case management - a review of method support. In: Buchmann, R.A., Karagiannis, D., Kirikova, M. (eds.) PoEM 2018. LNBIP, vol. 335, pp. 157–171. Springer, Cham (2018). https://doi.org/10.1007/978-3-030-02302-7_10

17. Lunn, K., Sixsmith, A., Lindsay, A., Vaarama, M.: Traceability in requirements through process modelling, applied to social care applications. Inf. Software Technol. **45**(15), 1045–1052 (2003)

18. Malinova, M.: A Language for Designing Process Maps. Ph.D. thesis, Vienna University of Economics and Business (2016)

19. Malinova, M., Leopold, H., Mendling, J.: An explorative study for process map design. In: Nurcan, S., Pimenidis, E. (eds.) CAiSE Forum 2014. LNBIP, vol. 204, pp. 36–51. Springer, Cham (2015). https://doi.org/10.1007/978-3-319-19270-3_3

20. Marin, M.A., Hauder, M., Matthes, F.: Case management: an evaluation of existing approaches for knowledge-intensive processes. In: Reichert, M., Reijers, H.A. (eds.) BPM 2015. LNBIP, vol. 256, pp. 5–16. Springer, Cham (2016). https://doi.org/10.1007/978-3-319-42887-1_1

21. Mendling, J., Reijers, H.A., Cardoso, J.: What makes process models understandable? In: Alonso, G., Dadam, P., Rosemann, M. (eds.) BPM 2007. LNCS, vol. 4714, pp. 48–63. Springer, Heidelberg (2007). https://doi.org/10.1007/978-3-540-75183-0_4

22. Mertens, S., Gailly, F., Poels, G.: Enhancing declarative process models with DMN decision logic. In: Gaaloul, K., Schmidt, R., Nurcan, S., Guerreiro, S., Ma, Q. (eds.) CAISE 2015. LNBIP, vol. 214, pp. 151–165. Springer, Cham (2015). https://doi.org/10.1007/978-3-319-19237-6_10

23. Nigam, A., Caswell, N.S.: Business artifacts: an approach to operational specification. IBM Syst. J. **42**(3), 428–445 (2003)
24. OMG: Business Process Model and Notation (BPMN), V. 2.0 (2011)
25. OMG: Case Management Model and Notation (CMMN) V. 1.1 (2016)
26. Parsons, J., Cole, L.: What do the pictures mean? guidelines for experimental evaluation of representation fidelity in diagrammatical conceptual modeling techniques. Data Knowl. Eng. **55**(3), 327–342 (2005)
27. Pesic, M., van der Aalst, W.M.P.: A declarative approach for flexible business processes management. In: Eder, J., Dustdar, S. (eds.) BPM 2006. LNCS, vol. 4103, pp. 169–180. Springer, Heidelberg (2006). https://doi.org/10.1007/11837862_18
28. Pichler, P., Weber, B., Zugal, S., Pinggera, J., Mendling, J., Reijers, H.A.: Imperative versus declarative process modeling languages: an empirical investigation. In: Daniel, F., Barkaoui, K., Dustdar, S. (eds.) BPM 2011. LNBIP, vol. 99, pp. 383–394. Springer, Heidelberg (2012). https://doi.org/10.1007/978-3-642-28108-2_37
29. Steinau, S., Andrews, K., Reichert, M.: The relational process structure. In: Krogstie, J., Reijers, H.A. (eds.) CAiSE 2018. LNCS, vol. 10816, pp. 53–67. Springer, Cham (2018). https://doi.org/10.1007/978-3-319-91563-0_4
30. The Open Group: ArchiMate 3.0.1 Specification (2017)
31. Zensen, A., Küster, J.: A comparison of flexible BPMN and CMMN in practice. In: EDOC 2018, pp. 105–114. IEEE (2018)

Testing the Fractal Enterprise Model in Practice

Experience Report

Toomas Saarsen[1]($\boxtimes$), Ilia Bider[2], and Erik Perjons[2]

[1] University of Tartu, Tartu, Estonia
toomas.saarsen@ut.ee
[2] DSV - Stockholm University, Stockholm, Sweden
{ilia, perjons}@dsv.su.se

Abstract. This paper is devoted to testing in practice a new kind of enterprise model, called the Fractal Enterprise Model (FEM), that connects enterprise processes via assets used for running these processes. The case study was implemented for a larger manufacturing company that has a large repository of process models. FEM was generated from the existing repository data, elaborated and used for analysis. This paper presents the lessons learned from the case study and could be useful for a novice FEM modeler.

Keywords: Fractal Enterprise Model · Business process · Business process modeling · Process architecture

1 Introduction

The Fractal Enterprise Model (FEM) [1] presents an enterprise/organization as a network of interconnected processes and assets [1] suggests several areas where the FEM can be used in practice, most of them being related to organizational change, including a radical one, such as business model transformation. Some examples of using the FEM for different purposes are presented in the literature [2, 3]. However, these examples are limited, and all of them were completed by the group that has developed the FEM modeling technique. It is necessary to gather more experience of using FEM for practical tasks, including its usage by experts not included among the original FEM developers. Such experience can help to disseminate as well as to develop the FEM technique further.

In our case study, the FEM model was built for a larger company having a large repository that includes more than a hundred models of their process. In this case, an idea of deriving a FEM based on such a repository has been tested. A group of interconnected processes has been chosen and a procedure of building a FEM from models of these processes has been designed. The FEM was created on the basis of a procedure that visually revealed the interconnection between the process in the group that was implicitly present, but not revealed for the company's staff. The employees of the company found this visualization quite useful as it gave a more holistic picture of this particular part of their business.

I. Reinhartz-Berger et al. (Eds.): BPMDS 2019/EMMSAD 2019, LNBIP 352, pp. 103–111, 2019.
https://doi.org/10.1007/978-3-030-20618-5_7

The rest of this paper is written according to the following plan. In Sect. 2, we give a short overview of the FEM to give the reader a possibility to comprehend this paper without studying the papers where the FEM was originally introduced. Section 3 present a case study of building the FEM. Section 3 presents the details of a business case, how the model has been built, for which purpose, and the way it has been used. Section 4 covers the lessons learned, including reflections on the challenges of using the FEM technique in practice.

2   Background – the Fractal Enterprise Model

The Fractal Enterprise Model (FEM) [1] includes three types of elements: business processes (more exactly, business process types), assets, and relationships between them; see Fig. 1, in which a fragment of a model for a management consulting company is presented. Graphically, a process is represented by an oval; an asset is represented by a rectangle (box), while the relationship between a process and an asset is represented by an arrow. We differentiate two types of relationships in the fractal model. One type represents the relationship of a process "using" an asset; in this case, the arrow points from the asset to the process and has a solid line. The other type represents a relationship of a process changing the asset; in this case, the arrow points from the process to the asset and has a dashed line. These two types of relationships allow tying up processes and assets in a directed graph.

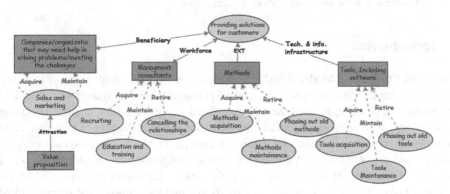

Fig. 1. A fragment of a FEM representing a management consulting company

In the FEM, a label inside an oval names the given process, and a label inside a rectangle names the given asset. Arrows are also labeled to show the type of relationships between the processes and assets. A label on an arrow pointing from an asset to a process identifies the role the given asset plays in the process, for example, *workforce*, *infrastructure*, *Execution Template* (EXT), etc. A label on an arrow pointing from a process to an asset identifies the way in which the process affects (i.e. changes) the asset. In the FEM, an asset is considered as a pool of entities capable of playing a given role in a given process. Labels leading into assets from the supporting processes reflect the way the pool is affected, for example, the label *acquire* identifies that the process can/should increase the pool size.

Note that the same asset can be used in two different processes playing the same or different role in them, which is reflected by labels on the corresponding arrows. It is also possible that the same asset can be used for more than one role in the same process; in this case, there can be more than one arrow between the asset and the process, but with different labels. Similarly, the same process could affect different assets, each in the same or in different ways, which is represented by the corresponding labels on the arrows. Moreover, it is possible that the same process affects the same asset in different ways, which is represented by two or more arrows pointing from the process to the asset, each with its own label.

Labels inside the ovals, which represent processes, and rectangles, which represent assets, are not standardized. They can be set according to the terminology accepted in the given domain, or be specific for a given organization. Labels on arrows which represent the relationships between processes and assets, however, can be standardized. This is done by using a relatively abstract set of relationships, like *workforce*, *acquire*, etc., which are clarified by the domain- and context-specific labels inside the ovals and rectangles. Standardization improves the understandability of the models.

3   Case Study – a Large Manufacturing Company

3.1   The Company and Problem Description

Harju Elekter has been manufacturing electrical equipment since 1968. Harju Elekter Group has seven subsidiaries (fully owned); our case study was conducted at Harju Elekter Elektrotehnika that produces equipment for power distribution networks, and industrial control and automation systems for the energy and industrial sectors as well as for public utilities.

The quality management of the company is based on a process model built a number of years ago. The process model is decomposed into six levels [4]; altogether, there are 260 process models containing 1400 tasks in the repository [5]. Process diagrams follow the BPMN [6] format. The quality of the syntax and completeness [7] of the diagrams are relatively good; validity (i.e. relation to the current state of the business) could be better, which would require a live update of the diagrams.

The area chosen for this case study was the preparation for manufacturing a batch of products. Every batch is unique and it is treated as a project that starts with a client ordering a product (white shape "Ordering" in Fig. 2), which in turn triggers the whole process of batch manufacturing (the final step is "Production", highlighted with the white shape in the right-upper corner in Fig. 2). For the production, it must be ensured that all necessary resources, e.g. material or equipment, are available at the batch start. There are two project phases to ensure the availability of resources: pre-planning, which takes place a couple of weeks before the production, and operative planning to double-check the availability of materials and resources before production, which happens a couple of days before production.

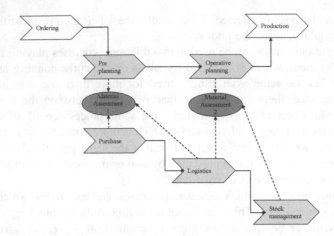

Fig. 2. Process diagrams and focus of the FEM (Color figure online)

From the process view accepted in the company, pre-planning and operative planning phases are not depicted as a sub-process, but are spread between several processes as represented in Fig. 2. In the diagram in Fig. 2, there are 5 (sub-)processes (green shapes) that include the activities related to pre-planning and operative planning phases (at the top of the diagram) and three other processes that indirectly participate in the preparation of the batch: *Purchase, Logistic* and *Stock Management*, as shown at the bottom of the diagram.

To represent the activities that are of interest in the current study, but are spread between the processes identified in the company process documentation, a different process view is needed. For this purpose, we identify two sub-processes, which are not presented as green shapes in the diagram of Fig. 2. We introduce them in the diagram as oval magenta shapes called Material Assessment 1, and Material Assessment 2. Dashed arrows pointing from the green shapes show which of these three original processes contribute to the newly identified sub-processes.

Both planning phases are quite similar but differ by the type of how assessment is done and the roles involved in them: **Pre-planning** is completed on the "virtual" stock by *Production Planner* and *Buyer* (a role responsible for making purchases); **Operative planning** is completed on the real stock by *Production Supervisor* (although *Production Planner* and *Buyer* could be involved).

The focus of the pre-planning is on the forecast. The Production Planner has to match material requirements relating to the product to be produced in the batch and the two-weeks-forecast of the stock position; the Buyer has to match the stock position, material purchase and shipment. Moreover, the Production Planner cannot handle all details (mainly risks) concerning the purchase and delivery; the Buyer is not aware of all details concerning the production and the client behind the batch product.

There is no forecast during the operative planning phase. The *Production Supervisor* completes a similar process to pre-planning on the real stock. Any problem discovered by the Production Supervisor triggers tasks similar to the pre-planning process; the main difference is that instead of a couple of weeks (as it was during pre-planning phase), there are just a few days (sometimes hours) for resolving the material delivery problems.

The first objective of the case study was to improve the data context for material assessment during the pre-planning process in order to provide better information to the *Production Planner* and the *Buyer* when they work on the forecast. As regards this objective, the focus of the modeling was on analyzing and improving the *quality of data and data exchange* (*Material Assessment 1* in Fig. 2). The second objective of the case study was related to the material assessment in operative-planning – how to produce an adequate, i.e. prompt, *response to the problems* discovered by the *Production Supervisor* under *Material Assessment 2* (see Fig. 2).

3.2   Building and Using the FEM

When applying FEM concepts and graphical presentation in this case, the focus of what is the object (or subject) of modeling has been changed in comparison to the original idea behind the FEM [1]. Originally, the FEM presents relationships between the process types (ovals), and "global", i.e. organization-wide, assets that are necessary for the uninterrupted start and finish of process instances. In the current case, the FEM was built to highlight the relationship between the sub-processes related to one production batch and thus can be considered as a part of the whole manufacturing process. The instances of these sub-processes produce and use assets that we can call "local", i.e. assets related to a particular instance of one (sub-)process or connected instances of different (sub-)processes.

The model as-is for this case is presented in Fig. 3. It was built mainly on the basis of the information from the process model repository of the company which has been created and is maintained using a software tool called Conciliate 2c8 [8]. The process diagrams in the repository contain various context elements (called assets in the FEM) related to the tasks of processes [5], in particular: related **actors** (represented by swim-lines in process diagrams); related **data elements** (represented as Documents and Information Systems in process diagram); related **materials** (represented as Materials in a process diagram).

Data was exported from five process models/diagrams (highlighted with green arrow shapes in the previous figure, Fig. 3). Based on the exported data, two contexts related to two material assessments from Fig. 2 were modeled and analyzed in Fig. 3.

- Green rectangles in Fig. 3 identify roles that participate in a process; they have approximately the same meaning as a workforce in the original FEM.
- Blue rectangles in Fig. 3 identify local assets of the type data; they do not have direct analogues in the original FEM.
- Yellow rectangles in Fig. 3 identify the communication assets produced in one sub-process and consumed/used in another sub-process.
- A dashed arrow directed to a local asset in Fig. 3 shows the sub-process that generates this asset. A solid arrow from an asset points to a sub-process that uses this asset. Thus the arrows have the same meaning as in original FEM.

- Red arrows in Fig. 3 identify that local assets connected by them are produced and consumed to handle exceptions/deviations that occur during the preparation of a batch.

The first draft of the FEM that we got with the formal procedure described above contained several redundancies and some incorrectness: several **tasks not relevant** for our consideration were automatically included in the model; some **context elements were missing** (as they were not included in the process diagrams); some **errors in the process diagrams were imported** to our FEM (these errors, mainly, concerned relations between *Tasks* and *Documents*; in addition, a couple of semantic errors).

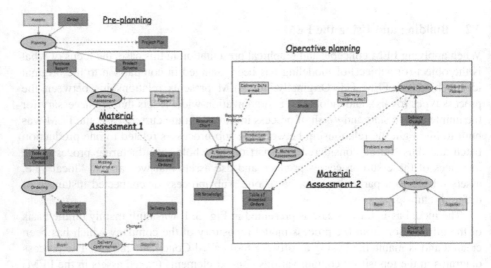

Fig. 3. FEM diagram (As-Is) for the industry case. (Color figure online)

The improvement of the first FEM draft was completed in the following fashion. Firstly, we merged/grouped some tasks to diminish the number of oval nodes in the FEM. In terms of process architecture [4], we moved up about one level, i.e. from level 6 to level 5. In addition, we eliminated tasks not directly related to our consideration (e.g. Stock management and Book-keeping).

Secondly, we improved the context representation related to the sub-processes. Namely, missing context elements were added, and a few errors that had been discovered were eliminated.

Also, the layout of the FEM has been changed so that the horizontal dimension started to highlight time-axes and the vertical dimension started to represent parallel sub-processes. As we can see in Fig. 3, the general strategy of the layout is similar to a typical process diagram. However, arrows have a different meaning: instead of showing the sequence of execution, they connect sub-processes to the related context elements (local assets).

After introducing the improvements, we had a separate discussion with employees participating in the business activities. The primary goal was to improve communication between the parallel sub-processes. We analyzed what information (local assets) is provided to actors and whether this information is sufficient for completing the activities. The analysis showed that the informational assets provided to the parallel sub-processes were not equal. For example, while the *Production planner* participating in *Material Assessment* had knowledge on the product related to the batch under preparation, the *Buyer* participating in *Delivery Confirmation* did not have this information. The difference resulted in misunderstandings that were solved in erratic email communication.

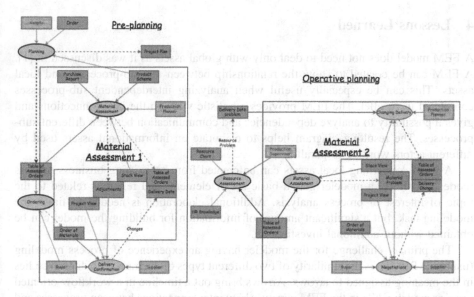

Fig. 4. FEM diagram (to-be) for the industry case.

Based on the analysis, an attempt has been made to redesign the local assets for the sub-processes to make them more unified so that parallel sub-processes would have the same informational assets in their disposition. The redesign resulted in a to-be FEM presented in Fig. 4. The new aggregated local informational assets are encapsulated in red squares in Fig. 4. These were designed according to the following principles:

- *Order of Materials* and *Table of Assessed Orders* were transferred from the as-is model in Fig. 3.
- Essential data concerning purchase and logistics, *Stock View*, were provided for *Production Planner* completing *Material Assessment*.
- Data concerning the product and project (batch), *Project View*, were provided for *Buyer* completing *Delivery confirmation*.
- Missing material e-mails were substituted by common view called *Adjustments* to be made in the project plan.

Providing a richer set of informational assets simplifies communication and makes sub-processes implemented in parallel to run smoother.

Similar changes were proposed for the operative-planning phase (completing a few weeks later) where *Material Assessment* will be implemented by *Production Supervisor*. If problems appear (*Material Problem* - some materials are not delivered in the stock and the production cannot start), then *Product Planner* and *Buyer* will be involved to solve the delivery problem, using the same data context they are familiar with (used already during the pre-planning phase). These changes are expected to produce more effect on the overall effectiveness, as there is much less time to solve the material problems before the batch starts in comparison to pre-planning.

4   Lessons Learned

A FEM model does not need to deal only with global assets as it was discussed in [1]. A FEM can be created to show the relationship between the sub-processes and local assets. This can be especially useful when analyzing interdependent sub-processes completed in parallel. The FEM provides a holistic view on the interconnections and gives a possibility to analyze dependencies and communication between different sub-processes. The resulting diagram helps to elaborate on informational assets used by different actors working in parallel.

A FEM concerning local assets can be created from an existing business process model repository; a modeler gets a basic set of elements and relations related to the topic of interest of process analysis. Additional elaboration is needed to finish the modeling task, but a significant amount of information for building the model can be obtained without additional investigation.

The primary challenge for the modeler having an experience of process modeling (using the BPMN) is the similarity of two different types of diagram. The difference lies in the meaning assigned to arrows. Arrows bring out a timeline in a workflow-oriented process model; while in the FEM, arrows show interconnections between processes and assets. It takes some time to get used to two diagrams where nodes are similar, but arrows emphasize different aspects.

References

1. Bider, I., Perjons, E., Elias, M., Johannesson, P.: A fractal enterprise model and its application for business development. Softw. Syst. Model. **16**(3), 663–689 (2017)
2. Bider, I., Perjons, E.: Defining transformational patterns for business model innovation. In: Zdravkovic, J., Grabis, J., Nurcan, S., Stirna, J. (eds.) BIR 2018. LNBIP, vol. 330, pp. 81–95. Springer, Cham (2018). https://doi.org/10.1007/978-3-319-99951-7_6
3. Josefsson, M., Widman, K., Bider, I.: Using the process-assets framework for creating a holistic view over process documentation. In: Gaaloul, K., Schmidt, R., Nurcan, S., Guerreiro, S., Ma, Q. (eds.) CAISE 2015. LNBIP, vol. 214, pp. 169–183. Springer, Cham (2015). https://doi.org/10.1007/978-3-319-19237-6_11
4. Dumas, M., La Rosa, M., Mendling, J., Reijers, H.A.: Fundamentals of Business Process Management. Springer, Berlin (2013). https://doi.org/10.1007/978-3-642-33143-5

5. Elias, M., Johannesson, P.: A survey of process model reuse repositories. In: Dua, S., Gangopadhyay, A., Thulasiraman, P., Straccia, U., Shepherd, M., Stein, B. (eds.) ICISTM 2012. CCIS, vol. 285, pp. 64–76. Springer, Heidelberg (2012). https://doi.org/10.1007/978-3-642-29166-1_6

6. Chinosi, M., Trombetta, A.: BPMN: an introduction to the standard. Comput. Stand. Interfaces **34**(1), 124–134 (2012)

7. Lindland, O.I., Sindre, G., Solvberg, A.: Understanding quality in conceptual modeling. IEEE Softw. **11**(2), 42–49 (1994)

8. 2Consiliate Business Solutions: 2c8 Modeling Tool. https://www.2c8.com/en/products/2c8-modeling-tool/

Transformative Business Process Modeling, Development, and Support (BPMDS 2019)

Augmented Reality-Based Process Modelling for the Internet of Things with HoloFlows

Ronny Seiger[✉], Maria Gohlke, and Uwe Aßmann

Software Technology Group, Technische Universität Dresden,
01062 Dresden, Germany
{ronny.seiger,maria.gohlke,uwe.assmann}@tu-dresden.de

Abstract. Workflow technologies can be handy to model, execute and analyse simple processes in Internet of Things (IoT) environments. End-users are enabled to compose processes and thereby automate basic repetitive tasks involving one or more IoT devices. However, the modelling of these IoT workflows currently relies on rather bloated and complex desktop applications, deep knowledge of the underlying process notations and a high level of abstraction, which makes workflow modelling too complicated for end-users. In this work we propose to use augmented reality (AR) to simplify the modelling and configuration of IoT workflows. With our *HoloFlows* app for smart glasses end-users are able to explore their surrounding IoT environment and model various types of basic processes involving sensors and actuators by simply connecting two or more physical IoT devices via virtual wires. AR technology hereby facilitates the understanding of the physical contexts and relations among the IoT devices and provides a new and more intuitive way of modelling workflows in the cyber-physical world. We demonstrate the HoloFlows app with the help of various IoT workflows from the smart home domain.

Keywords: Process modelling · Augmented reality ·
Internet of Things

1 Introduction

Business Process Management (BPM) and workflow technologies have increasingly found their way into new emerging research fields such as the Internet of Things (IoT) and Cyber-physical systems (CPS). With the help of concepts and technologies from the BPM domain processes in the physical world among the sensors, actuators, smart objects and humans as well as in the virtual world among the services and apps of an IoT environment can be modelled, executed and analysed. Related research discusses the extension and integration of these new cyber-physical entities into established BPM concepts and modelling tools. Especially the process modelling tools are mostly heavy-weight applications that

© Springer Nature Switzerland AG 2019
I. Reinhartz-Berger et al. (Eds.): BPMDS 2019/EMMSAD 2019, LNBIP 352, pp. 115–129, 2019.
https://doi.org/10.1007/978-3-030-20618-5_8

rely on a deep understanding of the underlying process notations (e.g., BPMN 2.0 [19]) and require domain and expert knowledge as well as a high level of abstraction regarding the business process elements, which hinders the creation of workflows in many IoT domains involving end-users. The smart home is an excellent example of an IoT environment with end-users as main target group. This user group needs simplified tools for workflow modelling and configuration to wire and coordinate existing IoT devices, automate basic repetitive tasks, and customize simple processes and routines.

In this work, we investigate the application of augmented reality (AR) technology to facilitate the modelling and coordination of simple processes among the typical devices of an IoT environments. We present the *HoloFlows* application that uses the physical location of IoT devices and everyday metaphors to provide a simple and intuitive generic tool for modelling and executing IoT processes in smart spaces (e.g., smart homes). With HoloFlows end-users are able to create simple processes among IoT devices by drawing virtual wires between the respective sensors and actuators at their physical locations. With this prototype we investigate the application of new technologies such as IoT and AR in the BPM domain. The paper is structured as follows: Sect. 2 presents basic information on IoT processes and AR. Section 3 discusses related work. Section 4 presents the *HoloFlows* AR app for IoT process modelling with examples from the smart home domain. Section 5 briefly presents a preliminary user study. Section 6 discusses our approach. Section 7 concludes the paper and shows starting points for future work.

2   Background

2.1   Internet of Things Entities

The Internet of Things (IoT) can be regarded as the "world-wide network of interconnected objects uniquely addressable based on standard communication protocols" [10]. Key components of IoT-enabled smart objects and IoT environments are sensors, actuators and microprocessors to consume data from the physical world, act on the physical world, process data and communicate with other smart objects and computers. With our work, we follow the suggestions of the *IoT Reference Model* [3] and view *Sensors* and *Actuators* as main classes of IoT devices. An IoT device may also be composed of one or more of these components. The functionality of these devices can be accessed and controlled via software-based *Services*. *Sensors* are able to measure physical properties and produce continuous or discrete events. We also view more abstract event sources producing data as (virtual) sensors. *Actuators* receive active commands and manipulate the physical world by executing these commands. Actuators also often have physical or virtual states that are again regarded as sensor data. IoT devices are usually compounds of sensors and actuators of varying complexity.

2.2 Augmented Reality with HoloLens

An Augmented Reality (AR) system "supplements the real world with virtual (computer-generated) objects that appear to coexist in the same space as the real world" [2]. We rely on AR technology to project extended information about the IoT devices as overlay information above the physical devices in the smart glasses. The Microsoft® HoloLens^{TM} platform is used for this purpose [1]. These head-mounted smart glasses use various cameras to create a spatial 3D map of their surroundings. With that it is possible to display holographic images in the see-through displays of the glasses and also fix these holograms at specific physical spots in the virtual scene, where they will stay due to the spatial understanding of the room. The user interacts with the holograms by controlling a virtual mouse pointer via his/her head and eye movements and performing air tap gestures (pinching of thumb and index finger) to "click" the mouse pointer. The built-in front cameras of the smart glasses are able to recognise this gesture.

3 Related Work

The application of business process management (BPM) technologies to model and execute processes in IoT environments and Cyber-physical Systems (CPS) has been vibrantly discussed over the recent years. Various works identified new challenges that emerge with the tighter coupling of the physical and virtual worlds in BPM [12,17]. With our work, we address the simplified modelling of processes in IoT for end-users (*end-user development*), which includes the concretion of abstract process models, the breaking down of end-to-end processes, the placement of sensors in a process-aware way and the bridging of the gap between event-based and process-based systems [12]. Lots of related works exist that address the modelling of IoT processes using conventional applications. The application of AR technology to model IoT workflows as a combination of transformative technologies for BPM is a rather new research field.

3.1 Internet of Things Process Modelling

Literature surveys regarding the modelling of IoT-aware business processes can be found in [4,5]. Many approaches propose extensions of existing business process notations with new elements for IoT/CPS-related sensor and actuator tasks and entities. Sensor-related tasks and conditions are introduced to the WS-BPEL language in [6]. The majority of related work discusses extensions of BPMN 2.0 to support new IoT and CPS related features. Business process tasks related to sensor networks are addressed by the *BPMN4WSN* extension [25]. Meyer et al. discuss the integration of IoT devices as business process resources in [18] as dedicated lanes in a business process. Specific new process tasks for sensing and actuating in an IoT/CPS context as well as dedicated pools and lanes for these tasks are discussed in various works [9,15,26]. Complementary work discusses ways of integrating IoT devices as process resources (e.g., by Friedow et al. [7]).

All these approaches propose new formalisms and extensions to integrate IoT-related tasks and devices into business processes. They extend existing process notations and modelling tools accordingly. These tools are often rather complex desktop or web applications that require domain experts and deep knowledge about the underlying formalisms to model the processes. Pools and lanes as well as special tasks are used for representing the activities of IoT devices, which requires a high level of abstraction from modelling the process with a desktop tool and a formal representation of the process to its actual execution in the physical world. We propose to use AR to decrease this complexity and simplify the creation of IoT workflows by taking the physical contexts of the devices into account and directly present offered functionality and states at the IoT devices' physical locations. This will enable end-users to model basic IoT workflows themselves.

3.2   Augmented Reality in Workflow Applications

Interactive business process management in combination with mobile devices, IoT and augmented reality has so far only been discussed by few works. Approaches for mobile business process management and guidance in the context of IoT are proposed in [8,21]. In [30] the authors propose new interaction devices as event sources for business processes and patterns for new interaction techniques (e.g., augmented reality) based on these interaction devices.

AR technology is currently mostly used in workflow contexts for process guidance and advisory purposes, e.g., in manufacturing [13], assembly [28] and maintenance [14]. An approach for the automatic device recognition and process-based configuration in smart environments with the help of AR is proposed in [16]. In [20] the authors present a prototype of an augmented reality collaborative modelling tool for business processes based on the BPMN 2.0 language. The system presented by Pryss et al. in [21] is accompanied by 3D augmented reality application to configure and visualize assistance workflows.

In general, we see approaches applying AR technology to improve understanding and collaboration by visualizing important data in location-related contexts. The physical world contexts play a key role when designing, modelling and operating IoT environments as they enable the end-users to relate virtual data and information about IoT devices to the physical counterparts (*Digital Twins* [27]). The works discussing the application of AR to BPM [20,21] still rely on abstract workflow notations and do not make use of the location contexts of process participants and devices. In contrast to these approaches, we will use AR technology to directly compose workflows among the available IoT device instances at their physical locations without requiring an understanding of abstract BPM concepts. Especially in smart home environments end-users have to be provided with an intuitive and easy way to explore and manage their IoT infrastructure as well as the devices' interactions and processes [29].

4 IoT Process Modelling with HoloFlows

In this section we present an AR application for modelling and executing holographic workflows (*HoloFlows*) in IoT environments. Examples from the smart home domain illustrate the usage of the application. This work is an extended version of a demo presented in [24] featuring a revised user interface, an extended set of modelling elements, operational modes and configuration options.

4.1 Design Principles

The goal of the HoloFlows app is to simplify the modelling of basic IoT workflows by using AR technology to provide a better understanding of the physical contexts, relations and effects of the individual devices and their actions. With our target group being end-users in the respective IoT environments, we rely on the following design principles regarding the implementation of a user interface and interactions for end-user development and control of IoT workflows.

Ubiquitous Exploration. HoloFlows allows the users to explore their surroundings: all instances of IoT devices that can be interacted with are augmented with extra information including the devices' properties, states and functionality. These information are shown at the physical location of the device, which also enables the discovery of hidden physical devices embedded into the smart space (*Ubiquitous Systems* [29]). That way the user is able to get an understanding of the surroundings, available devices, their functionality as well as their physical (spatial) relations to other devices in the room. The smart glasses facilitate this exploration in a mobile and hands free manner with embodied natural interactions (head movement, air tap gestures) to interact with the IoT environment.

Reduced Information. When presenting information regarding sensors, actuators and workflows to the user in AR, we reduce the amount of details to only relevant information necessary to understand the properties and states of the devices and the configurations of the existing workflows. Figure 1 shows an excerpt of the AR scene presenting states and functionality of a barometer and humidity sensor, a door actuator and the parameters of a simple workflow. For workflow modelling, we perform automatic pre-checking of the compatibility of IoT devices based on the device selected as first workflow participant to then only show compatible devices to create the specific workflow (cf. Sect. 4.3) which also reduces the amount of information and possible configurations.

Creation & Correlation. With the design of the user interface in HoloFlows, we put focus on having an easy to learn tool for exploring and controlling the cyber-physical environment. AR hereby helps the user to understand the properties and functionality of the IoT devices as well as the effects of executing their operations by adding relevant information to their physical context.

When controlling the devices and creating processes, the users do not have to rely on complex modelling tools that require an abstract understanding of the physical relations of the devices (e.g., represented as individual swimlanes [18]). In HoloFlows they can simply connect and correlate the desired devices with each other via virtual wires drawn between the physical devices.

Everyday Metaphors. To reach a high level of usability and create a steep learning curve, we apply various metaphors from everyday life in the HoloFlows app. Examples include virtual buttons displayed at the respective IoT devices that can be pushed in the AR scene via an air tap gesture to trigger the execution of the respective functionality; and the drawing of virtual wires between the devices that should be connected as part of a workflow (cf. Fig. 1). Arrows indicate the direction of control or data flow from source to target device. In addition we provide visual feedback by highlighting actively focussed and selected components or operations to facilitate navigation and control in the AR scene.

4.2   HoloFlows Operational Modes

The operation of HoloFlows relies on a state machine consisting of the following operational modes, which depend on the current user tasks and interactions.

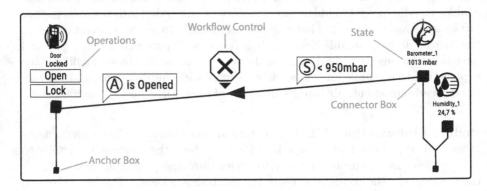

Fig. 1. Simple workflow between sensor and actuator created with HoloFlows.

Exploration Mode. The application's default mode is the *Exploration Mode* where the user is able to explore and control all IoT devices and IoT workflows in the vicinity. Holograms above the respective devices show general information (name and type), their current states and control functionality that can be triggered via an air tap gesture. Figure 1 shows these exemplary holograms for a barometer and humidity sensor (both attached to a single device) and for a door actuator. In this mode the user is always presented with a small unobtrusive menu to switch to the *Manual Placement Mode* or *Workflow Modelling Mode*.

Manual Placement Mode. In the *Manual Placement Mode* the user is able to position holograms for the individual IoT devices at their physical locations in the holographic scene. Upon selecting the hologram's Anchor Box (cf. Fig. 1) the hologram can be moved to the desired location and its position fixed with another air tap on the anchor box. The hologram will then stay at this exact position. We currently rely on a manual placement of these holograms by the user, i. e., the hologram positions have to be adjusted in case the device is moved.

Workflow Modelling Mode. The *Workflow Modelling Mode* allows the user to create different types of workflows as described in Sect. 4.3 in more detail. A menu is displayed once this mode becomes active from which the user is able to select additional workflow elements, safe the current state of the workflow, delete the workflow and leave the workflow modelling mode.

Workflow Mode. The *Workflow Mode* enables the user to control individual workflows, which have been created in the workflow modelling mode. Upon clicking on the respective control panel of a workflow (cf. Fig. 1), an expanded control menu for the workflow is presented to the user. Here the user is able to edit the workflow configuration (enter the workflow modelling mode), delete it, execute it and upload it to an external workflow management system (WfMS).

4.3   AR-based IoT Workflow Modelling

The HoloFlows app shows properties, states and available functionality of IoT devices as holograms directly above the individual sensors and actuators. These information are provided by a central middleware having a semantic model of the devices, their contexts, relations as well as available instances stored in its knowledge base [11]. To create a workflow between two or more devices the user enters the workflow modelling mode and selects the first device's connector box (cf. Fig. 1). Depending on the type of this first device (sensor or actuator) the user then selects a compatible second device or logic element–compatibility is checked automatically–to create a connection between both workflow participants. Afterwards some parameters have to be set for each device being part of the workflow. Currently we support the following basic types of IoT workflows depending on the type of the first and the second IoT device. More complex workflows can be created by chaining of multiple of these basic processes.

Conditional Sensor–Actuator Workflows. Simple workflows between a sensor and an actuator with a condition for activating the actuator–event-condition-action (ECA) rules–can be created using HoloFlows. Upon selecting a sensor first and connecting it to a compatible actuator, the user sets a sensor-related condition for defining the activation. Figure 2 shows a workflow with a condition triggering the activation of the connected actuator when the value of the "Barometer_1" sensor is smaller than 950 mbar. The user then sets the activity to be executed by the actuator upon activation of the workflow connection.

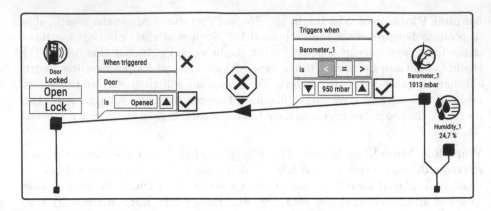

Fig. 2. Creating a conditional sensor–actuator workflow.

Figure 2 shows the "Door" actuator to be opened when the connection to the sensor is triggered. Conditional sensor–actuator workflows are used to define simple automation rules; more complex workflows can be created by chaining conditional sensor–actuator workflows that connect actions with subsequent events from sensors that are influenced by these actions, e.g., switching on the light when it becomes too dark; and start brewing coffee when the light sensor surpasses a certain value. Other sensors integrated into the HoloFlows app comprise an NFC tag reader (e.g., to create an authentication workflow to open the door when a certain NFC tag is present) and a wearable hand movement sensor (e.g., to switch on the light via a simple swipe gesture). Figure 3 shows a live view of the HoloFlows app in modelling mode with two sensor–actuator workflows: one defining that if the light levels are below 150 Lux then the coffee maker should start brewing; and one defining that if the temperature is above 26 °C then the power level of the fan should be switched to 100%.

Direct Sensor–Actuator Workflows. The values of some sensors can serve as direct input to control the states of actuators in a continuous control loop of an IoT workflow. Upon selecting a compatible sensor first, the user has to select if it should be used to create a conditional sensor–actuator workflow (cf. previous section) or a direct sensor–actuator workflow. The sensor is then directly connected to a compatible actuator by the user without the need for additional configuration. The data produced by the sensor has to be compatible with or at least convertible to input data for the respective actuator commands. Figure 4 shows an exemplary direct sensor–actuator workflow between a "ColorSensor" sensor and a "HueLamp" actuator. Once connected and activated, the current color detected by the color sensor is sent as an input value for the lamp to set its current light color to a certain value. Another example included in the HoloFlows application is the direct connection between a potentiometer as sensor (values from 0 to 100%) to the power level of a dimmer switch controlling a lamp (values from 0 to 100%) as shown in Fig. 5 or to the power level of a fan (values from 0

Fig. 3. Live view of two conditional sensor–actuator workflows.

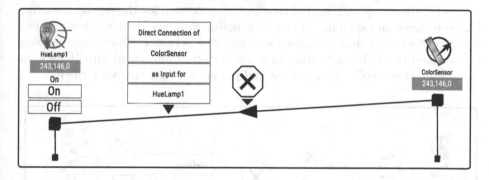

Fig. 4. Creating a direct sensor–actuator workflow.

to 100%). The compatibility checks and conversions of sensor output to actuator input data are currently implemented directly in the HoloFlows app.

Actuator–Actuator Workflows. IoT devices may often serve as sensors and actuators at the same time as their states can also be interpreted as sensor values. To create a sequence of actuator related activities to be executed in a row in a workflow, the user has to select the first IoT device's connector box–and choose between it acting as an actuator or as a sensor in case the device offers both functionalities. Actuators can only be connected to other actuators in a sequence of activities. Following, the user selects the second actuator to connect it with. The activity to be executed by the first actuator is then selected from

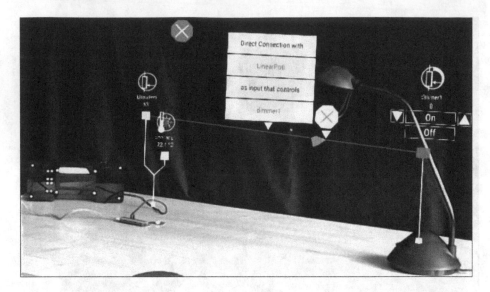

Fig. 5. Live view of a direct sensor–actuator workflow.

a list of available operations, followed by the same step for the second actuator. Figure 6 shows an exemplary actuator–actuator workflow defining that first the actuator "Door" should be opened and then the actuator "HueLamp1" should be switched on. Other actuators that are currently integrated into HoloFlows comprise a smart coffee maker, light and power switches, and a door bell.

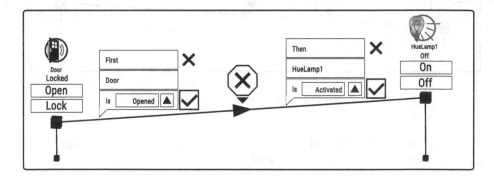

Fig. 6. Creating an actuator–actuator workflow.

IoT Workflows with Split and Join Operations. In the workflow modelling mode the user is presented with a menu to select additional logic elements and place the respective *OR* and *AND* cube holograms freely within the holographic scene. Connections from and to other sensors and actuators can be created by either first selecting the logic element and then the sensor/actuator or by first selecting the sensor/actuator and then the logic element. This way workflows with multiple sensor-related conditions and parallel actuator calls can be defined. Figure 7 shows the live view of a workflow defining that if the light levels are below 100 Lux then the power levels of Lamp 1 should be increased to 50% **AND** of Lamp 2 to 79% in parallel. Figure 8 shows a workflow defining that the door should be opened if the humidity exceeds 65.8% **OR** the temperature is above 28.4 °C.

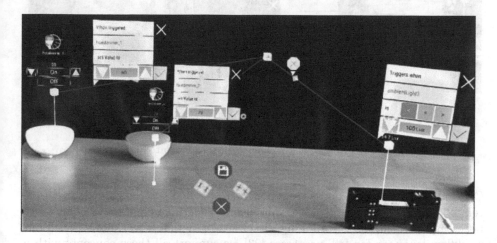

Fig. 7. Live view of a workflow with an actuator-related AND-split.

4.4 Implementation

The HoloFlows[1] app is an AR application implemented for the Microsoft HoloLens. We rely on the *openHAB*[2] middleware to connect and unify the heterogeneous set of sensors and actuators. A semantic model describes the properties, functionalities and relations of the individual IoT devices [11]. The IoT middleware provides service-based interfaces to all devices to retrieve data and send commands from the HoloFlows app. The modelled workflows can be executed directly in HoloFlows or they can be uploaded to the PROtEUS WfMS for IoT [22].

4.5 Mapping to Business Process Elements

To execute the IoT processes on external WfMSes, a mapping to process notations supported by the respective WfMS is required. The individual IoT devices can be viewed as process participants and represented by *pools/lanes*. The activation of actuator functionality relies on simple service calls as *service tasks*.

---

[1] https://github.com/IoTUDresden/HoloFlows.

[2] https://www.openhab.org/.

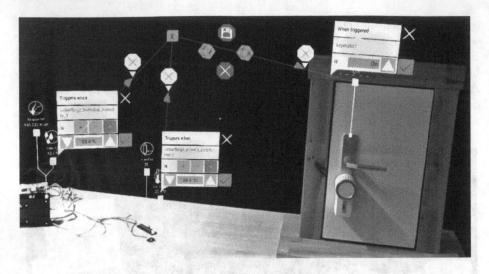

Fig. 8. Live view of a workflow with sensor-related OR-split.

OR and AND elements can be viewed as *inclusive* and *parallel* gateways; sensor-related decisions as *events* with subsequent *conditional* gateways. *Loops* are necessary for continuously running direct sensor–actuator workflows. With our workflow language for IoT processes [23] we support all these concepts with a focus on sensor-related activities based on complex event processing.

5 Preliminary User Study

The goal of HoloFlows is to provide end-users with a simple intuitive tool for modelling processes in IoT environments using AR technology. We claim that AR helps users to better understand the IoT environment, its devices and their relations. Users are able to put devices in their physical context and directly correlate them with others in the form of IoT workflows.

We presented the HoloFlows app to approx. 60 to 70 people in the context of conference demos, (student) project exhibitions, trade fairs, project presentations and visits of guests from academia and industry to our lab. Among the participants were mostly students and experts from IT with little to no knowledge about (business) process modelling, but a general interest and understanding of IoT and AR. We also had guests with no IT or scientific background. The age spectrum ranged from approx. 20 years to 65 years.

Similar to our previous AR demos in IoT contexts [14], users were curious about using the smart glasses and excited to try out the demo after a short introduction and demonstration of the app by a HoloFlows expert. The app was well received by the participants as being very innovative and appealing for various kinds of end-users and application domains. The exploration of IoT devices, their states and direct control were straightforward without the necessity of instructing users. Regarding process modelling, we observed a steep learning curve as the users were able to create and configure the different types of basic processes after a short demo of modelling an exemplary workflow by an expert. Once the basic process creation was mastered, the users quickly moved on to create a larger number and more complex IoT workflows and try out different combinations of sensors and actuators. With HoloFlows we are able to simplify the workflow creation to the act of simply drawing virtual wires between devices and setting some additional parameters–a deep knowledge of BPM concepts or domain-specific processes is not required. However, a basic understanding of the IoT devices (sensors, actuators and their properties) and program logic (ECA rules, AND/OR splits/joins) is necessary to configure the IoT workflows. A more formal user study based on these preliminary observations and lessons learned has to be conducted in future work to verify our claims of HoloFlows being more intuitive and providing a better usability for non-experts.

6 Discussion

HoloFlows supports the types of processes among the sensors and actuators of an IoT environment described in Sect. 4.3 as basic building blocks for composing more complex workflows, which fulfil most of the automation requirements in simple IoT environments such as the smart home. The application of the concepts in other IoT domains (e.g., smart factories or smart hospitals) may also provide an improved experience for end-users and simplify exploration and work-flow modelling to create and optimize processes. However, these domains usually comprise more complex IoT devices and workflows, which is why HoloFlows has to be evaluated and extended according to the requirements of the individual domain. The set of actual business process modelling elements supported by HoloFlows is currently very limited and also has to be extended with new concepts for representing the respective workflow elements in AR [20].

HoloFlows supports the coordination and control of known sensor and actuator instances, whose properties are provided by the IoT middleware. The integration and configuration of IoT devices–known or unknown–is currently rather complex and static requiring manual placement of the holograms. We are currently working on simplifying these steps by automatically identifying the IoT devices and dynamically adding/retrieving necessary information from/to the middleware to also integrate unknown devices as proposed in [16].

7 Conclusion and Future Work

In this work we investigated the application of AR technology to support the modelling of basic processes in IoT domains. The resulting HoloFlows app can be viewed as an intuitive and easy to use process modelling, configuration and execution application that enables non-experts to create individual processes in the respective IoT domain without BPM knowledge. In contrast to related work relying on abstract representations of process elements, HoloFlows exploits

AR technology and the physical contexts of devices to directly connect and coordinate instances of sensors and actuators of the IoT environment to form basic real world processes that can be composed to more complex workflows. With HoloFlows we present a vision of combining new emerging technologies– AR and IoT–with the BPM domain.

Future work includes the extension of supported workflow/business process elements and a revision of the user interface to further simplify the parameter configurations and provide better overviews of IoT environments with many devices and workflows. In this context we will also investigate the application of HoloFlows in smart factories and facilities as IoT domains. A more formal and systematic user study comparing HoloFlows with classical desktop and web-based process modelling tools to evaluate the usability and efficiency of the application and support our claims of HoloFlows being intuitive and easy to use will also be conducted as future work.

Acknowledgements. This research has received funding under the grant number 100268299 by the European Social Fund (ESF) and the German Federal State of Saxony. Kudos to our student Henrik Schole for his support regarding the implementation.

References

1. Avila, L., Bailey, M.: Augment your reality. IEEE Comput. Graph. Appl. **36**(1), 6–7 (2016)
2. Azuma, R., Baillot, Y., Behringer, R., Feiner, S., Julier, S., MacIntyre, B.: Recent advances in augmented reality. Technical reports, Naval Research Lab, Washington, DC (2001)
3. Bauer, M., et al.: IoT reference model. In: Bassi, A., et al. (eds.) Enabling Things to Talk, pp. 113–162. Springer, Heidelberg (2013). https://doi.org/10.1007/978-3-642-40403-0_7
4. Brouns, N., Tata, S., Ludwig, H., Asensio, E.S., Grefen, P.: Modeling iot-aware business processes-a state of the art report. arXiv preprint arXiv:1811.00652 (2018)
5. Chang, C., Srirama, S.N., Buyya, R.: Mobile cloud business process management system for the internet of things: a survey. ACM Comput. Surv. **49**(4), 70 (2016)
6. Domingos, D., Martins, F., Cândido, C., Martinho, R.: Internet of Things aware WS-BPEL business processes - context variables and expected exceptions. J. UCS **20**(8), 1109–1129 (2014)
7. Friedow, C., Völker, M., Hewelt, M.: Integrating IoT devices into business processes. In: Matulevičius, R., Dijkman, R. (eds.) CAiSE 2018. LNBIP, vol. 316, pp. 265–277. Springer, Cham (2018). https://doi.org/10.1007/978-3-319-92898-2_22
8. Giner, P., Cetina, C., Fons, J., Pelechano, V.: Developing mobile workflow support in the Internet of Things. IEEE Pervasive Comput. **9**(2), 18–26 (2010)
9. Graja, I., Kallel, S., Guermouche, N., Kacem, A.H.: BPMN4CPS: a BPMN extension for modeling cyber-physical systems. In: 2016 IEEE 25th International Conference on Enabling Technologies: Infrastructure for Collaborative Enterprises (WET-ICE), pp. 152–157, June 2016
10. Gubbi, J., Buyya, R., Marusic, S., Palaniswami, M.: Internet of Things (IoT): a vision, architectural elements, and future directions. Future Gener. Comput. Syst. **29**(7), 1645–1660 (2013)

11. Huber, S., Seiger, R., Kühnert, A., Theodorou, V., Schlegel, T.: Goal-based semantic queries for dynamic processes in the Internet of Things. Int. J. Semant. Comput.
10(02), 269–293 (2016)
12. Janiesch, C., et al.: The Internet-of-Things meets business process management:
Mutual benefits and challenges. arXiv preprint arXiv:1709.03628 (2017)
13. Kammerer, K., Pryss, R., Sommer, K., Reichert, M.: Towards context-aware process guidance in cyber-physical systems with augmented reality. In: 2018 4th International Workshop on Requirements Engineering for Self-Adaptive, Collaborative,
and Cyber Physical Systems (RESACS), pp. 44–51. IEEE (2018)
14. Korzetz, M., Kühn, R., Gohlke, M., Aßmann, U.: HoloFacility: get in touch with
machines at trade fairs using holograms. In: Proceedings of the 2017 ACM International Conference on Interactive Surfaces and Spaces, pp. 336–341. ACM (2017)
15. Martins, F., Domingos, D.: Modelling IoT behaviour within BPMN business processes. Procedia Comput. Sci. **121**, 1014–1022 (2017)
16. Mayer, S., Inhelder, N., Verborgh, R., Van de Walle, R.: User-friendly configuration of smart environments. In: 12th IEEE International Conference on Pervasive
Computing and Communication (PERCOM), pp. 163–165. IEEE (2014)
17. Mendling, J., Baesens, B., Bernstein, A., Fellmann, M.: Challenges of smart business process management: an introduction to the special issue. Decis. Support Syst.
100, 1–5 (2017)
18. Meyer, S., Ruppen, A., Magerkurth, C.: Internet of Things-aware process modeling:
integrating IoT devices as business process resources. In: Salinesi, C., Norrie, M.C.,
Pastor, Ó. (eds.) CAiSE 2013. LNCS, vol. 7908, pp. 84–98. Springer, Heidelberg
(2013). https://doi.org/10.1007/978-3-642-38709-8_6
19. OMG: Business Process Model and Notation (BPMN), Version 2.0, January 2011
20. Poppe, E., Brown, R.A., Recker, J.C., Johnson, D.M.: A prototype augmented
reality collaborative process modelling tool (2011)
21. Pryss, R., Reichert, M., Bachmeier, A., Albach, J.: BPM to go: supporting business
processes in a mobile and sensing world (2015)
22. Seiger, R., Huber, S., Schlegel, T.: Toward an execution system for self-healing
workflows in cyber-physical systems. Softw. Syst. Model. **17**, 551–572 (2018)
23. Seiger, R., Keller, C., Niebling, F., Schlegel, T.: Modelling complex and flexible processes for smart cyber-physical environments. J. Comput. Sci. **10**, 137–148 (2015)
24. Seiger, R., Korzetz, M., Gohlke, M., Aßmann, U.: Mixed reality cyber-physical systems control and workflow composition. In: Proceedings of the 16th International
Conference on Mobile and Ubiquitous Multimedia, pp. 495–500. ACM (2017)
25. Sungur, C.T., Spiess, P., Oertel, N., Kopp, O.: Extending BPMN for wireless sensor
networks. In: IEEE 15th Conference on Business Informatics, pp. 109–116 (2013)
26. Suri, K., Gaaloul, W., Cuccuru, A., Gerard, S.: Semantic framework for internet of things-aware business process development. In: IEEE 26th International
Conference on Enabling Technologies: Infrastructure for Collaborative Enterprises
(WETICE), pp. 214–219. IEEE (2017)
27. Walch, M., Karagiannis, D.: Service-driven enrichment for KbR in the OMiLAB
environment. Serviceology for Services. LNCS, vol. 10371, pp. 164–177. Springer,
Cham (2017). https://doi.org/10.1007/978-3-319-61240-9_16
28. Wang, X., Ong, S.K., Nee, A.Y.: A comprehensive survey of augmented reality
assembly research. Adv. Manuf. **4**(1), 1–22 (2016)
29. Weiser, M.: The computer for the 21st century. Sci. Am. **265**(3), 94–104 (1991)
30. Yousfi, A., Hewelt, M., Bauer, C., Weske, M.: Towards uBPMN-based patterns
for modeling ubiquitous business processes. IEEE Trans. Ind. Inf. **14**, 3358–3367
(2018)

The Rise of Enforceable Business Processes from the Hashes of Blockchain-Based Smart Contracts

Sara Migliorini[1]($\boxtimes$) (iD), Mauro Gambini[1] (iD), Carlo Combi[1] (iD),
and Marcello La Rosa[2] (iD)

[1] Department of Computer Science, University of Verona, Verona, Italy
{sara.migliorini,mauro.gambini,carlo.combi}@univr.it
[2] School of Computing and Information Systems, The University of Melbourne,
Melbourne, Australia
marcello.larosa@unimelb.edu.au

Abstract. Over the past few decades, the automation of inter-organizational processes has been the focus of several research efforts that have produced a broad spectrum of design methods and technologies. Recently, some experiments have shown how in principle a Decentralized Autonomous Process-Aware Information System (DAIS) can be implemented by means of Blockchain-based Smart Contracts (BSCs). In this paper, we cast a shadow on this novel approach by arguing that such kind of contracts cannot be considered an optimal abstraction to specify inter-organizational process models. We base our analysis on contractual incompleteness, a pivotal concept in widely accepted economic theories. We identify the main weakness in the conflict between the immutability-by-default of the BSCs and the nature of inter-organizational processes. As a result of this analysis, we introduce the concept of *enforceable business process* that is more in line with the original idea of smart contract and extends it to better match the essential requirements of a DAIS.

Keywords: Blockchain · Smart Contracts · Network coalition ·
Process-Aware Information System · Enforceable Business Process

1 Introduction

Modern life is embodied in a striking complex socio-economic infrastructure. In many countries, such infrastructure is effective enough that people can take for granted the availability of a wide range of products and services, safely ignoring the complexity of the underlying processes and means of production. The socio-economic infrastructure is made of people that takes part in several emergent or consolidated forms of organization. We can identify at least three ideal forms that we call here *competitive market*, *hierarchical firm* and *network coalition* [8,9,12].

S. Migliorini and M. Gambini—Member of the IEEE Blockchain Technical Community.

I. Reinhartz-Berger et al. (Eds.): BPMDS 2019/EMMSAD 2019, LNBIP 352, pp. 130–138, 2019.
https://doi.org/10.1007/978-3-030-20618-5_9

In their essence, the competitive market is an emergent form of coordination, the hierarchical firm is a designed form of cooperation and the network coalition is a concerted form of cooperation, where cooperation is intended here as the process of coordinating a group of actors with the explicit purpose of achieving a common goal. Supply chains, strategic business alliances, joint ventures, and also decentralized cryptocurrencies can be good examples of coalitions. Conversely, consortia are rarely considered coalitions, because their inter-organizational processes are related to the optimal allocation of shared resources, not necessarily to the achievement of a common goal.

This paper focuses on the problems that coalitions have to face in automating inter-organizational processes: due to their cooperative and exogenous nature, these processes can be neither delegated to the market nor managed entirely inside the boundary of a single hierarchical firm. To fix these concepts, we define an inter-organizational business process, or more briefly an *Exogenous Business Process (XBP)*, as a cooperative stable process, managed by a coalition of two or more mutually independent organizations, in order to pursue a common goal. By postulating its stability, we are emphasizing that the process is repetitive in nature and its identity is preserved over time, while being mutually independent implies the lack of an established central authority. An XBP often arises from repetitive casual market interactions, a typical example is a firm that acquires from the market a specific component on a regular basis. In order to reduce uncertainty and lower transaction costs, such firm can steadily choose the same supplier, building up a trustworthy relation that can be eventually formalized by a contract. Broadly speaking, any organization is established through a contract expressed in more or less formal terms. Here we consider a contract any agreement on a collection of mutual obligations that after being accepted by the parties, can be enforced in some way, for instance by social pressure or law.

The aim of this paper is to investigate how XBPs can be designed, enacted and monitored by a network coalition. In particular, we examine the limits in automating such processes by means of *Blockchain-based Smart Contracts (BSCs)* provided by the existing blockchain technology [1,3]. In doing this, we will attempt to face the challenges exposed by Mendling et al. in their exploratory work about how blockchain-based systems can support inter-organizational processes [6]. As emphasized by the authors, there is no general acceptance on how these processes can be managed. Several technologies can be deployed to streamline and automate them, but no one seems able to offer a complete solution. They also speculate that smart contracts and the blockchain technology can provide a new way to overcome these obstacles. Unfortunately, this new approach comes with its own challenges: it not clear how XBPs should be modeled as BSCs and then interpreted by an effective trustless Decentralized Autonomous Process-Aware Information System (DAIS).

In this paper, we argue that BSCs are too limited and not very suitable to automate XBPs, because they neglect renegotiation. The Caterpillar project [3] shows how in principle process models can be mapped to one or more BSCs and executed on a blockchain platform, but this mapping does not change the underlying semantics of such contracts. The lack of support for renegotiation in the current BSCs does not dismiss the potentiality of the blockchain technology, but this problem has to be carefully stated before proposing new solutions. We identify in the immutability-by-default of BSCs one of their major drawbacks that does not fit very well with the nature of network coalitions which are rooted on long-term incomplete contracts. Contractual incompleteness is a pivotal concept of several economic theories that can be traced back to the seminal work of Williamson [11], Hart and Holmström [5]. To the best of our knowledge, this is the first time that contractual incompleteness is used for shedding new light on the inter-organizational process automation. We use such concept to characterize XBPs, analyze the limits of BSCs and capture the essential requirements of a DAIS. In order to scale up, network coalitions require not only enforceable and verifiable, but also easily renegotiable contracts that can foster a continuous improvement of their contractual terms. We capture these features with the notion of *Enforceable Business Process* (*EBP*) which is essentially an XBP model archetype representing a renegotiable smart contract. The notion of EBP could be a good starting point to design an effective DAIS.

2   Incomplete Contracts

In an ideal world with a costless and flawless legal system, opportunistic behavior can be prevented by drawing up a complete contract that precisely dictates, for any future eventuality, which actions the parties should take, with the related incentives and penalties and no trust needs to be factored in. Unfortunately, law enforcement can be very expensive and actual contracts are far from being complete. Contracts are often poorly written, ambiguous and even purposely silent in many respects, to the point that virtually any contractual dispute brought before the courts concerns an incompleteness problem [4,5].

In the last few decades, prominent economists have recognized that many relevant economic phenomena can be explained in terms of contractual incompleteness, making the notion of *incomplete contract* a pivotal concept of several theories, such as Transaction Cost Economics and Contract Theory [5,11]. Contractual incompleteness can have manifold origins, for instance (1) the impossibility to predict all the relevant eventualities, (2) the costs to describe all the identified eventualities in advance, (3) the impossibility to observe certain actions of the contracting parties, and (4) the difficulty to make the observable actions verified by a trusted third-party. During the contracting process, the parties evaluate costs and benefits of including additional contractual terms. In light of these costs, even if in principle the parties would be able to draw up a complete formal contract, they can rationally choose to omit several details and leaving out many unlikely eventualities. Given these facts, it is reasonable to assume that any contract, even the most formal one, could be *intentionally* incomplete. Short-term contracts representing occasional relationships in a market setting do not escape this logic: an ideal contract of this kind should include a formal specification of the offered product, but this practice can be unacceptably expensive for any nontrivial product. These problems are exacerbate in case of long-term contracts on which network coalitions are grounded. In long-term interactions, purposely incomplete contracts can mitigate renegotiation costs, but at the expense of a higher dependence on trust.

3   Szabo's Smart Contracts (SSCs)

The original concept of *smart contract* has been introduced by N. Szabo to ease the definition of legal contracts and reduce the related transaction costs [10]. A *Szabo's Smart Contract (SSC)* is a computerized transaction protocol that formalizes and secures a set of relationships over computer networks. It is an agreement between two or more parties that can be automatically enforced without the need for a trusted third-party intermediary. An SSC should communicate the protocol semantics to the parties through good visual representations of the contract elements, so that each party has a clear understanding about the contract content. We generalize this requirement saying that any SSC realization should foster *intelligibility* as a primary concern.

The essential property that makes a contract *smart* w.r.t. a traditional one is its *automatic enforceability*, namely the execution of an SSC can be forced without relying on a trusted intermediary, because replaced by a trustworthy machine or network. Besides intelligibility and automatic enforceability, an SSC should ensure three other important properties: observability, verifiability, and privity. *Observability* is the ability of each party to observe the actions performed by others, or similarly to prove the execution of some actions to other parties. *Verifiability* is the ability of a party to prove to an adjudicator that a contract has been poorly performed or breached. Finally, *privity* states that no third-party has control over the enforcement of a contract, except for the appointed intermediaries or adjudicators but only in case of a dispute. These properties can substantially reduce the transactional costs associated to a contract.

The original work of Szabo [10] is focused on protocol design for algorithmically specifiable relationships and no specific SSC feature seems to directly address contractual incompleteness. In our context, XBPs are grounded on long-term contracts, more or less formalized in legal terms, and in this setting, we consider contractual incompleteness and renegotiation two primary concerns.

4   Blockchain-Based Smart Contracts (BSCs)

A *blockchain* is essentially a temporally ordered list of permanent data blocks. Blocks are considered immutable because the effort needed to revert them could be quite expensive and the probability of observing a replaced block decreases over time as new blocks are added in front of it. The key innovation of the blockchain technology is a decentralized emergent consensus protocol that enables a group of agents to reach an agreement about a global state by accepting data transmitted across an open byzantine Peer-to-Peer (P2P) network. The blockchain technology appeared for the first time in the implementation of the Bitcoin protocol [7] as a innovative solution to the double-spending problem that does not require a trusted central authority. In Bitcoin, each block contains a set of transactions representing a transfer of tokens from a source to a destination account address. BSC platforms extend this basic functionality by supporting the execution of general-purpose on-chain stored procedures.

The core idea behind BSCs can be found in the Bitcoin scripting mechanism, but a fully working BSC implementation has been offered by successive systems, like Ethereum [1]. The Ethereum platform can run general-purpose scripts encoding arbitrary state transition functions that are automatically enforced when a certain event occurs, for instance when a transaction is scheduled. Every smart contract deployed on Ethereum is unique and no modification is allowed.

BSCs are sufficiently expressive to create new cryptocurrencies and to establish novel network coalitions in the form of Decentralized Autonomous Organizations (DAOs). However, immutability-by-default of BSCs can generate subtle problems when used for organizational purposes. A clear evidence is provided by the history of The DAO project that was one of the first attempts to found a large network coalition on the Ethereum platform. The BSCs encoding its governance rules were not able to capture the actual intents of the parties and all the future eventualities, namely they were fatally incomplete. In June 2016, a bug, or a feature for the immutability-by-default proponents, has allowed an attacker to subtract about USD 50M from The DAO project. The ad-hoc updating procedure included by The DAO developers in their BSCs was not sufficient to fix the breach. The problem caused these contracts was partially solved outside The DAO authority by forking the entire Ethereum platform.

5   Enforceable Business Process (EBP)

In the previous sections, we argued that cost-optimized contracts could be intentionally incomplete and network coalitions are generally established by long-term contracts which should be considered inherently renegotiable. We also explained why BSCs are poor abstractions for modeling XBPs. In this section, we outline an alternative notion that would better match the requirements of a DAIS. We define an *XBP specification* as a potentially incomplete, renegotiable, procedural contract. A contract is said to be procedural if all its completely specified parts can be directly interpreted by a DAIS without additional details. Following the SSC intelligibility principle, we also define an *XBP model* as an XBP specification built using graphical constructs with a clearly stated semantics. Visually, an XBP model can be represented as a common business process model enhanced with banking abstractions and temporal constraints [2]. This additional features are required to make the XBP activities effectively enforceable in a decentralized way by means of incentives and deadlines. We can now introduce an evolution of the SSC concept that should better match the discussed XBP traits. An *Enforceable Business Process (EBP)* is an XBP model archetype, characterized by five primary life cycle phases or states (S1–S5), four enforcement modes (E1–E4) and eight fundamental contractual properties (P1–P8). To ease the discussion, phases and enforcement modes are depicted in Fig. 1.

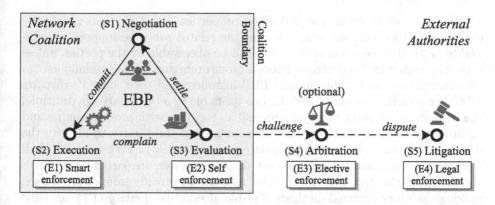

Fig. 1. The life-cycle of the Enforceable Business Process (EBP).

The EBP life cycle is made of three recurring phases (S1–S3) that are managed inside a coalition and two external phases (S4–S5) that could lead to the process disposal or even to the coalition dissolution. In the *negotiation* phase (*S1*) the parties discuss a new EBP or refine an existing one until a good compromise is reached, namely until a specific XBP model is committed. When an EBP is ready, it can be instantiated several times on demand during the *execution* phase (*S2*). The contracting parties will follow the agreed protocol by performing the required tasks. This phase can terminate if a party rises a complain. In the *evaluation* phase (*S3*), the EBP performance is discussed. One or more parties may not be satisfied and may opt for a compensation, opening a dispute. If an agreement is reached, the EBP enters in a new negotiation phase, where it can be improved; otherwise, it can enter into a phase of arbitration or litigation. The *arbitration* phase (*S4*) is useful when the parties are not able to settle a dispute, but they can agree on a trusted third-party arbitrator, see (E3) below. Finally, in the *litigation* phase (*S5*) the EBP and the related tamper-proof logs will be brought before a court for adjudication, see (E4) below.

An EBP can be subject to four different kinds of enforcement, two of them can be implemented by a DAIS, while the other two should be supported as fail-safe methods to settle a dispute. *Smart* (*E1*) is an automatic enforcement mode that can be obtained by running the EBP instances in a trustless system, similarly to what happens for BSCs. *Self* (*E2*) is an autonomous enforcement mode triggered by one or more parties to complain about the overall EBP performance. A voting mechanism may be used to solve the raised conflicts. *Elective* (*E3*) is an external enforcement mode that can be applied when the contracting parties are not able to settle a dispute on their own, but they can reach an agreement about a trusted third-party arbitrator. Finally, *legal* (*E4*) is an external enforcement mode that brings the dispute before the court. The blockchain logs can be in principle used by an adjudicator as evidences to solve a conflict.

An EBP shall fulfill the following properties (P1–P8) that should be expressed by its executable semantics and the related run-time support. *Observability (P1)*: the execution of an EBP shall be observable by the parties, unless otherwise stated in the contract. Process monitoring and mining techniques can be adapted to examine the running EBP instances and their logs. *Verifiability (P2)*: the performance of an EBP shall be verifiable by a third-party. In principle, the blockchain property of being irreversible, together with process mining and auditing techniques, could be used by a designated third-party to identify the divergent behaviors and act appropriately. *Enforceability (P3)*: an EBP shall support the four kinds of enforcement discussed above. In particular, a DAIS shall support the first two enforcement modes and provide tamper-proof logs, making the other external methods a viable alternative. *Privity (P4)*: an EBP shall affect only the contracting parties and only such parties have the rights to interpret it and disclosure its content whenever necessary. A third-party should interfere with the process only when explicitly solicited. *Intelligibility (P5)*: an EBP shall be as clear as possible for the end-users. User-friendly interfaces, graphical notations and simulation techniques could be applied to enhance comprehensibility. *Underspecifiability (P6)*: a DAIS shall support an EBP with a best-effort execution where incomplete parts are manually handled by the contracting parties. For instance, an override mechanism is necessary for any task without an explicitly stated deadline. *Renegotiability (P7)*: an EBP shall always be renegotiable by the contracting parties even when it is explicitly stated otherwise: in line with contractual incompleteness and privity, a non-negotiable statement may not match the actual aims of the parties that can agree on changing it. *Durability (P8)*: an EBP represents a long-term contract and its execution shall persist over time, its logs shall be recoverable in case of a system failure.

Example – The program committee of a conference can be considered a network coalition whose common business goal is selecting the most valuable contributions, improving the quality of the conference at every edition. The actual process is refined during the negotiation phase (S1) through which the parties decided important details such as the prescribed deadline for the revisions, the number of reviewers for each paper, the minimum evaluation for the acceptance, and so on. When an agreement is reached, the process enters into the execution phase (S2) during which the automatic enforcement (E1) of some tasks may happen. For instance, the automatic assignment of some papers to a reviewer that does not promptly communicates any preference. Moreover, during the execution some complains may arise, for instance some reviewers may not be able to meet the deadline or a reviewer may disagree with the evaluation performed by another one. An evaluation phase (S3) can start during which the program committee can decide to modify the original process, for instance by changing the deadline or by requiring an additional revision. This phase may involve a self enforcement (E2) eventually implementing a voting mechanism. In case the parties are not able to reach an agreement, the process can enter into an arbitration phase (S4) during which the conference chairs unilaterally decide the actions to perform (E3). The parties can be subject to some form of incentives and penalties, for example can be encouraged with some discount on the conference price.

6   Conclusion

In principle, a broad uptake of the blockchain technology can induce a paradigm shift in the way network coalitions design and automate their inter-organizational processes. In this paper, we have investigated what are the limits of the BSCs in supporting such kind of processes. We have based our analysis on contractual incompleteness, a key concept of quite a few economic theories. We have seen that XBPs are grounded in potentially incomplete, inherently renegotiable, long-term contracts. In contrast, BSCs are intended to be immutable, relegating renegotiability as a secondary class feature. We found in this mismatch a major concern that hinders the development of an effective DAIS. To characterize this problem, we have proposed the notion of EBP, an evolution of the original SSC concept that better captures the requirements of a DAIS. In a foreseeable future, a new generation of decentralized information systems built around the notion of EBP could substantially lower the contractual costs, opening the path to innovative large-scale network coalitions and changing the actual socio-economic landscape.

Acknowledgment. This work is partially supported by the Italian National Group for Scientific Computation (GNCS-INDAM) and by "Progetto di Eccellenza" of the Computer Science Department, University of Verona, Italy.

References

1. Buterin, V.: A Next-Generation Smart Contract and Decentralized Application Platform (2014). http://github.com/ethereum/wiki/wiki/White-Paper. Accessed 04 2019
2. Combi, C., Gambini, M., Migliorini, S., Posenato, R.: Representing business processes through a temporal data-centric workflow modeling language: an application to the management of clinical pathways. IEEE Trans. Syst. Man Cybern. Syst. **44**(9), 1182–1203 (2014)
3. García-Bañuelos, L., Ponomarev, A., Dumas, M., Weber, I.: Optimized execution of business processes on blockchain. In: Carmona, J., Engels, G., Kumar, A. (eds.) BPM 2017. LNCS, vol. 10445, pp. 130–146. Springer, Cham (2017). https://doi.org/10.1007/978-3-319-65000-5_8
4. Hart, O.: Incomplete contracts and control. Am. Econ. Rev. **107**(7), 1731–1752 (2017)
5. Hart, O., Holmström, B.: The Theory of Contracts. Econometric Society Monographs, pp. 71–156. Cambridge University Press, New York (1987)
6. Mendling, J., et al.: Blockchains for business process management - challenges and opportunities. ACM Trans. Manage. Inf. Syst. **9**(1), 4:1–4:16 (2018)
7. Nakamoto, S.: Bitcoin: a peer-to-peer electronic cash system (2008). http://www.bitcoin.org/bitcoin.pdf. Accessed 04 2019

8. Powell, W.W.: Neither market nor hierarchy: network forms of organization. Res. Organ. Behav. **12**, 295–336 (1990)
9. Simon, H.A.: Organizations and markets. J. Econ. Persp. **5**(2), 25–44 (1991)
10. Szabo, N.: Formalizing and securing relationships on public networks. First Monday **2**(9) (1997). https://doi.org/10.5210/fm.v2i9.548. Accessed Apr 2019
11. Williamson, O.E.: The Economic Institutions of Capitalism: Firms, Markets, Relational Contracting. The Free Press. A division of Macmillan, Inc. New York (1985)
12. Williamson, O.E.: Comparative economic organization: the analysis of discrete structural alternatives. Adm. Sci. Q. **36**(2), 269–296 (1991)

Foundations of Modeling and Method Engineering (EMMSAD 2019)

A Continuous Delivery Pipeline for EA Model Evolution

Simon Hacks[1]($\boxtimes$), Andreas Steffens[1], Peter Hansen[2], and Nikhitha Rajashekar[2]

[1] Research Group Software Construction, RWTH Aachen University,
Aachen, Germany
{hacks,steffens}@swc.rwth-aachen.de
[2] RWTH Aachen University, Aachen, Germany
{peter.hansen,nikhita.rajashekar}@rwth-aachen.de

Abstract. The pace of changing structures and complexity within enterprise architecture (EA) models is expected to increase. This will challenge existing maintenance processes of EA models. To tackle this challenge, we propose to adapt the well-known concept of continuous delivery (CD) from the agile software development domain. We propose to automate the necessary steps to ensure EA model quality by applying multiple validation and analysis steps. Therefore, this results shorter feedback loops and helps to uncover possible conflict as early as possible.

Keywords: EA model evolution · Continuous delivery ·
EA model maintenance

1 Introduction

Since it beginnings in the 1980's [25], Enterprise Architecture (EA) has developed to an established discipline [32,34]. The ISO 42010:2011 defines architecture as the "fundamental concepts or properties of a system in its environment embodied in its elements, relationships, and in the principles of its design and evolution" [20]. As this definition implies, the EA model, comprised by the organization elements and relationships, is a central artifact of EA. Additionally, EA has to provide important and up-to-date information of the organization to its stakeholders.

There are a many different sources for changes of the EA model [9], which contribute to a continuous evolution of the EA model. As our research assumes a project-driven environment, we will refer to projects as example for the main source of changes. However, our approach sticks not solely to projects, which can also be replaced by teams working in a more agile environment.

EA models are currently mostly modeled manually and changes require notable manual efforts. This is especially true when complex organizational structures need to be covered and the organization is constantly changing. The pace of changing structures and complexity is expected to increase and this

I. Reinhartz-Berger et al. (Eds.): BPMDS 2019/EMMSAD 2019, LNBIP 352, pp. 141–155, 2019.
https://doi.org/10.1007/978-3-030-20618-5_10

makes it even more challenging [40]. In recent years, the field of enterprise architecture management already adopted techniques to reduce model maintenance effort. However, there are still challenges in regards to conflicting changes, different semantics and responsibilities [8].

In the field of software engineering, changing requirements are also very common. Software engineering deals with this by becoming as agile as possible and uses various social and technical techniques to improve towards this direction [14].

Examples for social techniques are the ongoing adoption of agile process models like scrum or kanban and even techniques directly related to the development itself like pair programming. Technical examples are the rise of continuous integration and delivery. All of these techniques lead to the same shared goal: Shorten feedback loops [17]. Techniques used for software engineering are also being adopted for other parts of organizations: With the DevOps movement, which emphasizes on the collaboration of development and operations, infrastructure is being covered using techniques typically used in the context of software engineering and processes are also adopted [6].

To overcome the aforementioned problems of EA modeling, we proposed already an architecture roundtrip process [13]. However, this process is still abstract and needs to be instantiated. To do so, we facilitate the well-known technique of continuous delivery (CD) and realize the architecture roundtrip process. Accordingly, we formulate our research question:

Can a continuous delivery help to overcome the challenges of manual EA model's maintenance?

So far, existing research on EA model maintenance automatizing has focused either on collecting information from different external sources (e.g. [4,18]), trying to bring contradictory information together (e.g. [22,38]), or proposing an overall process for maintenance (e.g. [9,13]). To the best of our knowledge, there is no research around trying to adapt the technique of CD to the domain of EA model maintenance. Our results contribute to the existing body of knowledge by enhancing the proposed processes with the benefits of CD and offering new possibilities to connect further sources of information to the central EA model.

In the rest of this paper, we will elaborate on this question. First, we will present work related to automatic maintenance/evolution of EA models. Second, we sketch our research design, before we give insights into the design and implementation of our pipeline. Next, we demonstrate our pipeline by a fictitious example and discuss the findings of the experiment. Last, we conclude our work and give an impression of future research.

2   Related Work

EA is used in large organizations and different departments often own information, which is used within the EA. This makes it hard for a central enterprise architecture team to gather all information and keep them up-to-date. Fischer et al. proposed a semi-automated federated approach for the maintenance of EA models [10]. The main idea is that the data is kept within specialized architectures and linked to a central EA repository.

Other approaches to automatize EA model maintenance are presented e.g. by Buschle et al. [4], who facilitate an ESB (Enterprise Service Bus) to extract EA models automatically. In contrast, Holm et al. [18] concentrate more on technically observable components as they map the output of a network scanner to ArchiMate. An extension of this work is presented by Johnson et al. [22], who incorporate uncertainty into the mapping. The work of Välja et al. [37,38] focuses on uniting different information from contradictory sources. Hence, they try to estimate the trustworthiness of the sources.

EA related research did not only elaborate solely on the technical aspects of EA model maintenance. For example, Kirschner and Roth [24] rely on a human component to solve arising conflicts from different sources. Further, Khosroshahi et al. [23] investigated the social factors influencing the success of federated EA model maintenance. A slightly different point of view is taken by Hauder et al. [15] as they focused on the challenges of a federated EA model maintenance.

Further related research to our work can be identified in the field of continuous delivery. Humble and Farley [19] define continuous delivery as a set of practices, which enables to speed-up, automate and optimize the delivery of software artifacts to the customer with higher quality and lower risks in a continuous manner. Continuous delivery uses an automated development infrastructure, called deployment pipeline, which automates nearly every step of the delivery process. Each commit of a developer enters the deployment pipeline and an automated process is started, which produces a new software increment as a result artifact.

The deployment pipeline incorporates all activities known from continuous integration [7] as automatic build, unit testing, and static code analysis. In addition to these, the pipeline performs testing activities like integration, performance, and security testing. All these tasks are executed in a defined order of stages. After each stage, the test results are evaluated at a quality gate, which stops the processing if the quality conditions are not met. If all quality gates are passed, the software artifact is stored and can be accessed and used from external clients; it is released.

In recent research many challenges of adopting continuous delivery have been found [5,26,28] and coping with software evolution and heterogeneity can be identified as the major technical obstacles for a continuous delivery system. To overcome many of these obstacles, we proposed a generalized model and architecture for a new generation of continuous delivery systems [35].

Lastly, our process relies heavily on the quality of the EA model. Regarding to ISO/IEC 25010 quality "is the degree to which a product or system can be used by specific users to meet their needs to achieve specific goals with effectiveness, efficiency, freedom from risk and satisfaction in specific contexts of use" [21]. In the context of EA research Ylimäki states that "a high-quality EA conforms to the agreed and fully understood business requirements, fits for its purpose [...] and satisfies the key stakeholder groups' [...] expectations" [42, p. 30]. In general, research regarding EA quality agrees that it is defined by the ability to meet the EA users' requirements [27,30]. Most of the related work divides quality aspects of EA into the quality of EA products, its related services, and EA processes [27,30].

In the discipline of enterprise modeling there are approaches that discuss model quality in general, without focusing on a certain modeling structure. Becker et al. [2] define six principles that have to be considered when assessing an enterprise model's quality. Sandkuhl et al. [33] apply these principles to evaluate the quality of their modeling language 4EM and further depict concrete quality attributes.

3   Research Design

Design science research (DSR) is a widely applied and accepted means for developing artifacts in information systems (IS) research. It offers a systematic structure for developing artifacts, such as constructs, models, methods, or instantiations [16]. As our research question indicates the development of means, the application of a DSR is appropriate. We stick to the approach of Peffers et al. [31], since it transpired as effective in former research. It is split up into six single steps and two possible feedback loops:

- **Identify Problem & Motivate:** As previous research has shown, reasons to change the EA model are manifold [9] and raise many different challenges [15]. One of them is to handle different sources and another to design a suitable process for EA model maintenance. We believe that the principle of continuous delivery offer efficient means to support the EA model maintenance process.
- **Define Objectives:** Based on our research problem stated before, we identified mainly three sources for objectives: First, Farwick et al. [8] identified a set of 23 requirements on automated EA model maintenance grouped into categories like architectural, organizational, or data quality. Those requirements should be incorporated into a feasible solution. Second, Fischer et al. [10] describe an EA model maintenance process comprised by activities that mainly are related to data collection, quality checks, and delivery of the new information. Additionally, Fischer et al. define four roles, which are either related to process coordination (EA Coordinator, EA Repository Manager), data delivery (Data Owner), or quality checks (EA Coordinator, EA Stakeholder). Last, we presented a process for a distributed EA model evolution [13] describing different tasks and their sequence focusing on a continuous evolution of the EA model.
- **Design & Development:** To realize an artifact in accordance to the beforehand identified objectives, first, we align the input of the three objectives' sources. Then, we design an abstract process model using Business Process Model and Notation (BPMN) [39] and implement it using JARVIS [35]. Our derived integrated EA maintenance process consists of activities, which will be implemented as microservices following JARVIS's architectural framework. In addition to the activities defined in our objectives, we include additional steps inspired by principles found in the continuous delivery domain.
- **Demonstration:** The demonstration is put into practice by applying the proposed means to a single fictitious case study. Single case studies gain a

first, in-depth reflection on means in real life scenarios [41]. Moreover, single case studies are a feasible instrument to show applicability. Our case study is based on an EA model illustrating an airport. Within this case study, we show that a CD pipeline can reduce the manual effort in EA model maintenance.

- **Evaluation:** We identified 54 equivalence classes of possible actions, which should be considered in our pipeline. Therefore, we created for each class an exemplary test case as a representative for this class [3, p. 623].
- **Communication:** The communication is done with this paper itself and its presentation on a conference.

4 A Pipeline for EA Model Evolution

Following, we will sketch our pipeline for an EA model maintenance. Fischer et al. [10] contribute two main findings to our pipeline. First, they propose an EA model maintenance process, which we unite with our work from [13]. Second, they offer a fine-grained role concept, which we incorporate in the pipeline as well.

To implement our deployment pipeline for EA model maintenance, we opt for our prototype JARVIS [35]. It allows integrating the proposed processes into a deployment pipeline and we create a BPMN version of the process as JARVIS is equipped to use BPMN as a modeling language. From this model, we derive the necessary activities, which needs to be implemented as microservices. During this, we transform the process model to reflect better the principles of JARVIS and continuous delivery in general. Figure 1 shows the resulting model for EA model maintenance.

The first process steps from Fischer et al. and Hacks et al. of initializing and collecting the necessary data of the EA model evolution can be omitted. We assume, that in an environment following the principles of continuous delivery from Humble et al. [19] all artifacts like the global and the special EA models are under version control and stored in an appropriate system like subversion or git. Each change to one of these models by the responsibles within in projects needs to be committed to the repository. A change is resulting in a new version of the model. Whenever a change is committed to the repository for the special architecture our deployment pipeline is triggered automatically.

The technical infrastructure of the SCM and the deployment pipeline ensure the automatic processing of the first process steps of both proposed maintenance processes. Necessary notifications can be sent by the system if we need to be compliant to the overall process, but effectively we want the stakeholders only to be involved if really necessary.

The pipeline starts by first checking out the new models versions from the repository and provide both to the first transformation activity. This activity is called "Compute Change Set" and uses the provided input models to compute the existing deviations between both and provide these as a new artifact called "Change Set".

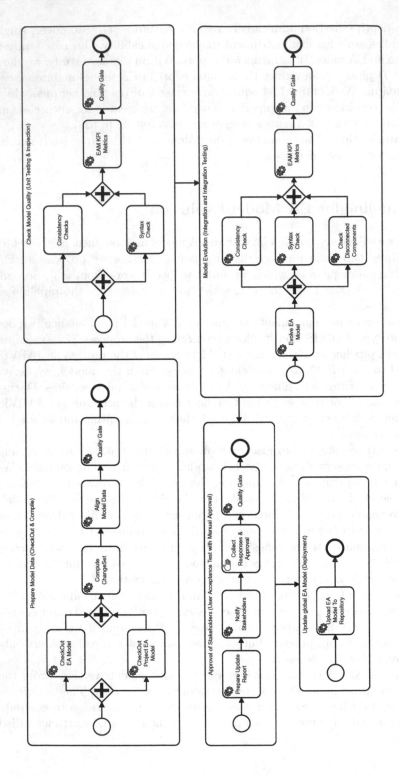

Fig. 1. EA maintenance deployment pipeline as BPMN

All existing artifact are now processed in the next transformation activity "Align Model Data". Hacks and Lichter [13] argue that a specific project may contain more detailed information than the more general global EA model. Therefore, the model provided by the project has to be aligned in order to be effectively compare- and merge-able to the central model. This includes a necessary meta-model transformation as well as an adaption of the provided model to the same level of detail presented in the central model. The following quality gates check the successful execution of the proceeded activities and the existence of the three artifacts. Afterwards, the first stage of our deployment pipeline is finished. This stage corresponds to the checkout and compile stages in classic software delivery pipelines.

Fischer et al. and Hacks and Lichter both incorporate steps to check the model quality like consistency or correctness of syntax. In our pipeline, we model these as assessments, which are performed on the model singular artifacts of the proceeding stage and which produce a report for each assessment. This stage corresponds to static analysis for software source code. Duval et al. [7] incorporate an inspection phase into his continuous integration model in which relevant metrics for software quality are measured and evaluated. We adopt this by applying well-known EAM KPIs [29] to models inside the pipeline.

In the next stage, the artifacts are integrated to produce a new and updated candidate for the EA model by reproducing the changes made by the project on the central EA model. This candidate is then examined by the same assessments as before. The modular architecture allows us to integrate even more sophisticated assessments, which can be performed on EA models. We integrated a check for disconnected components, which checks if parts of the resulting EA model candidate has components, which are not connected to the rest of the model. Based on the assessment reports the quality gate decide if the pipeline should continue to the next stage where the candidate is presented to the stakeholders of the overall process.

Up to this point the pipeline is performing its tasks completely autonomous, so the stakeholder are only involved if the model candidate has reached a certain degree of quality due to the assessments performed before. The manual approval of the stakeholders corresponds to the User Acceptance Test (UAT) stage in classic pipelines. Bass et al. [1] define the UAT stage as the last one before going to production and are meant to ensure these aspects of the delivery process which cannot be automated.

If this stage is successfully executed, the EA model candidate is promoted to the final stage where it is deployed to the EA model repository. The next run of the pipeline will use this new version of the EA model and so the roundtrip is completed.

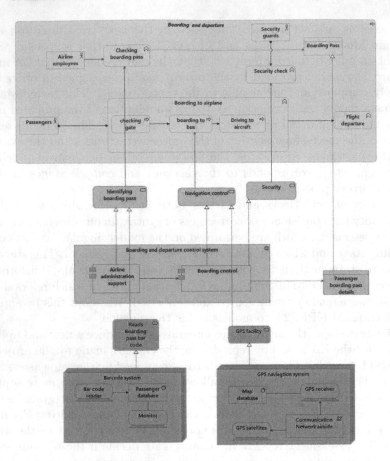

Fig. 2. Excerpt of the boarding and departure process

5 Demonstration

5.1 Exemplary EA Model

To demonstrate and evaluate our artifact, we conduct a fictitious case study. Therefore, we facilitate the example of an airport departure system. This example was originally developed to illustrate the realistic use of ML and graph analytic methods in the context of analyzing EA models. Following, we illustrate a scenario of airport departure system, which depicts the functionality of the passengers before boarding to an aircraft.

This example is modelled as an EA model based on ArchiMate 3.0.1 [36]. The model incorporates all the ArchiMate layers beginning with business, application, and technology architectures. It consists of 171 different elements and 250 relations. We will further discuss in detail the core layers of the system. An excerpt of the model is presented in Fig. 2.

The business layer depicts the business services offered to the customers, which is mainly used to build business architecture [12]. In this example, the active entities of the business layer are airline employees, passengers, and security guards. Four functions are provided by boarding and departure process. The function boarding to airplane is internally divided into three sub-processes.

The application layer includes for example the airline administration support, which is responsible for handling check-in process, and the boarding control, which handles boarding process. Furthermore, two application components collaborate in boarding and departure control system, i.e., the airline administration component and the boarding control to provide application level services like identifying boarding pass, security and navigation control support.

The technology layer offers several components to the application layer. E.g., there is a barcode system offering the needed means to validate the barcodes of the boarding tickets and a GPS navigation system guiding the bus drivers to the right plane on the airfield.

5.2   Facilitated Metrics

To simulate the "Check Model Quality" step of the pipeline, we check the EA model against KPIs from the EAM KPI Catalog [29]. As we do not want to implement all KPIs of the catalog, we randomly chose three of them as representatives for all KPIs. Those KPIs are only exemplary and can be replaced by any other calculable metrics. Nonetheless, we have to keep in mind that it can be quite challenging to assess the necessary input parameters (e.g., if interviews have to be conducted).

PM guideline adherence checks if IT projects adhere to the stated PM guideline [29, p. 28]. As the information model of the KPI catalog is not directly reflected in ArchiMate, we identify work package as an IT project and business object with a property PMguideline as PM guideline. To compute this KPI, the project managers, first, answer the degree the project adheres to every guideline. Second, we compute the average for every project along all guideliness. The catalog defines three categories of adherence. If a project adheres to 100% to the guideline it is full adherence. Between 100% and 75% it is a minor deviation which will cause a warning in our pipeline. With less than 75% it is a major deviation causing a fail of the pipeline.

Application continuity plan availability [29, p. 19] measures the degree how completely IT continuity plans for business critical applications have been drawn and tested for the IT's application portfolio. To reflect the information model in ArchiMate, we map the application to application component and continuity plan to business object with the property ContinuityPlan. The responsible for the operation of the applications answer if there exists a continuity plan for a certain application and if it is tested. The KPI is then computed by the number of critical applications where a tested continuity plan is available divided by the total number of critical applications. The value is good above 80%. Normally, the value will between 60% and 80% resuming in a warning to related stakeholders. If the value drops beyond 60% the value is problematic and the pipeline fails.

IT process standard adherence [29, p. 33] checks if a certain application (application component in ArchiMate) adheres to the IT standard processes (application process in ArchiMate). This is answered by the process responsible and then calculated by the number of applications, which adhere to an IT standard process, divided by the total number of applications. The value is good at 100%. Normally, the value will between 80% and 100% resuming in a warning to related stakeholders. If the value drops beyond 80% the value is bad and the pipeline fails.

Besides the EAM KPI Catalog, we check also the *connectivity* of the graph representing the EA model, where the elements of the EA model represent nodes within the graph and their connections represent edges. A graph is connected if there is a path between every pair of nodes. We assume that the model of an EA should be always connected. If the model contains isolated elements or sub-graphs, there are parts in the organization, which are not related to the other parts. So to say, there are parts in the EA pursuing different goals and, therefore, different organizations within the organization. Nevertheless, for two organizations there would be two EA's. Consequently, we expect the model of the EA to be connected. Otherwise, the pipeline should fail.

5.3   Implementation of the Pipeline

Our designed pipeline for EA model maintenance was implemented for the continuous software delivery system JARVIS [35] and each activity in the pipeline model was implemented as an independent microservice following the architectural framework of JARVIS. From JARVIS, we reused the complete infrastructure and general activities like the git checkout activity and the quality gate activity.

6   Evaluation

To evaluate our pipeline, we conduct an equivalence class test [3, p. 623] where the values of the metrics serve as input parameters (three respectively two classes per KPI) and the behavior of the pipeline (i.e., successful, warning, and fail) represents the output. To test the pipeline, we combine each possible input class and determine the expected output for each combination resulting in 54 test cases. We choose always the worst expected output (fail<warning<successful) if different outputs would be possible. An extract of four exemplary test cases is presented in Table 1.

For the execution, the presented example model from Sect. 5.1 was stored in a git repository and used as the global EA model. A variant of the model was stored in a second repository and was used as the repository for a simulated specific project model. This variant was altered for each test case to represent the different test cases and resulting behavior of the pipeline is checked against its expected behavior.

Table 1. Exemplary test cases

Test case ID	Input				Expected output
	PM guideline adherence	Application continuity plan availability	IT process standard adherence	Connected	
1	100%	100%	100%	TRUE	fail
6	100%	70%	100%	TRUE	warning
7	100%	70%	90%	TRUE	warning
8	100%	50%	100%	TRUE	success

The execution of the test cases by triggering the pipeline with different inputs showed that our approach is feasible. The expected behavior of our pipeline could be observed. In case of a failing pipeline the execution always stopped at the first KPI assessment in the Model Quality stage. The reason for this is, that we already test the KPIs on each model in this stage, so the assessment of the project model results in a fail. By deactivating this assessment, the pipeline performs the Model Execution stage and fails at this point. Both behaviors are correct. Due to this phenomenon we recognize, that our pipeline is already performing a simpler inspection process for the project mode, it is embedded in the global EA model maintenance process.

7   Discussion

Before, we presented our pipeline and its application on a fictitious example. Our results show that the existing approaches are missing certain steps, which we incorporated into our pipeline. For example, our roundtrip process lacks a step for an evaluation of EA KPIs, which are represented in the Model Quality stage and in the Model Evolution stage of our pipeline. As the KPIs can be easily computed and automatically evaluated, we can naturally apply it inside in a continuous delivery pipeline. Besides, it has to be mentioned that the calculation of a KPI is only easy as long as the basic measures are provided, which can be quite challenging.

Furthermore, the pipeline incorporates a simple inspection process of the project model, which is presented by its own independent pipeline and is executed during the project solution development. This leads to a similar result as with Continuous Integration and Continuous Delivery. Continuous Delivery can be seen as an extension of Continuous Integration as Fowler argued [11]. The project pipeline would only consider the single project model as our maintenance process also considers the global EA model and an EA model candidate, which integrates changes from the project model into the EA model.

In addition, the roundtrip approach lacks the incremental and iterative nature of an agile development process. The project solution delivers its model only one time to the maintenance process. With incorporating continuous delivery, the project can deliver the changed model every time to the overall maintenance process. Therefore, the project will get feedback on the compatibility with the global EA model earlier and can adopt to this feedback more easily. The deviations between global and specific model are therefore minimized.

On the other hand, changes to the EA model are much earlier distributed to other projects in the organization, as there maintenance process will use the adapted EA model also for other active projects. So the deviations between the various projects are minimized. In result, the automation of the maintenance process may lead to more relevant EA model, which represents the current state of the organization and its enterprise architecture in a much more accurate way. Furthermore, the whole process is completely transparent and most important traceable, which supports further requirements regarding compliance and security.

The process of Fischer et al. [10] lacks the roundtrip approach. As we count on short feedback cycles as typical for agile development, we overcome this shortcoming. In addition, our proposed means reduces the involvement of stakeholders and the necessary manual work to a minimum. Stakeholders only assess EA model candidates, which has achieved a certain degree of quality.

Lastly, we introduced a new metric to measure the connectivity of the EA model represented by a graph. For our case study, we assume that the complete graph needs to be connected. However, depending on the needs of the organization under observation multiple connected components are desired. Another organization's need could be for a metric to assess the certain degree of connectivity for the whole EA or its sub-graphs. As our case study is only fictitious, it does not offer further insights into these aspects and need to be investigated in future research.

8   Conclusion

EA models are currently mostly modeled manually and changes require huge manual efforts. This is especially true when complex organizational structures need to be covered and the organization is constantly changing. The pace of changing structures and complexity is expected to increase and this makes it even more challenging [40]. In recent years, the field of enterprise architecture management already adopted techniques to reduce model maintenance effort. We contribute to this field of research by adapting the means of continuous delivery to shorten feedback cycles and providing a higher degree of automatizing.

To do so, we facilitated existing EA model maintenance processes and implemented them within our tool JARVIS. Our first evaluation shows that existing maintenance processes benefit from the ideas of the agile domain leading from a model maintenance to a model evolution perspective. Additionally, we could show that the interaction between stakeholder and enterprise architects can be further reduced. Consequently, both can concentrate more on the essential parts of EA than on technically related issues.

However, our research includes still some limitations. First, we were not able to test our approach in a natural environment. Such a field evaluation may raise additional issues, especially related to the influence of our approach on the sociological environment. So far, we focused only on technical aspects, but internal resistance might hinder our approach.

Second, we just took a single project as data provider for our pipeline into account. A plenty of distributed data provider might cause issues, we did not consider thus far. In particular, we encourage short feedback cycles, which might cause problems as well if the mindset of the involved employees is missing.

Third, today most EA models are maintained in a central EA model tool, which apply version control mainly internally. To apply our approach to those environments, the tools need to provide an interface providing model information for interaction with our pipeline. However, this needs a change of thinking at EA tool providers from a single, closed tool to an integrated tool, which is part of a bigger environment.

Fourth, we took a very technical view on the problem. For instance, we assumed for simplicity reasons that the needed input for the KPIs we facilitate for our quality gate can be computed easily. However, the assessing of certain inputs for the KPIs can be quite challenging, which needs to be further evaluated in future research. Additionally, there might be not only one perception of a KPI as multiple stakeholders with a diverse background and possibly different expertise and expectations contribute to its assessment and interpretation, which has to be taken into account.

References

1. Bass, L., Weber, I., Zhu, L.: DevOps: A Software Architect's Perspective, 1st edn. Addison-Wesley Professional, New York (2015)
2. Becker, J., Probandt, W., Vering, O.: Grundsätze ordnungsmäßiger Modellierung: Konzeption und Praxisbeispiel für ein effizientes Prozessmanagement. BPM kompetent. Springer, Heidelberg (2012)
3. Burnstein, I.: Practical Software Testing: A Process-Oriented Approach. Springer, New York (2006). https://doi.org/10.1007/b97392
4. Buschle, M., Ekstedt, M., Grunow, S., Hauder, M., Matthes, F., Roth, S.: Automating enterprise architecture documentation using an enterprise service bus. In: 18th Americas Conference on Information Systems (2012)
5. Chen, L.: Continuous delivery: overcoming adoption challenges. J. Syst. Softw. **128**, 72–86 (2017)
6. Debois, P.: Agile infrastructure and operations: how infra-gile are you? In: Agile 2008 Conference, pp. 202–207 (2008)
7. Duvall, P., Matyas, S.M., Glover, A.: Continuous Integration: Improving Software Quality and Reducing Risk (The Addison-Wesley Signature Series). Addison-Wesley Professional (2007)
8. Farwick, M., Agreiter, B., Breu, R., Ryll, S., Voges, K., Hanschke, I.: Requirements for automated enterprise architecture model maintenance - a requirements analysis based on a literature review and an exploratory survey, In: ICEIS (2011)

9. Farwick, M., Schweda, C.M., Breu, R., Voges, K., Hanschke, I.: On enterprise architecture change events. In: Aier, S., Ekstedt, M., Matthes, F., Proper, E., Sanz, J.L. (eds.) PRET/TEAR -2012. LNBIP, vol. 131, pp. 129–145. Springer, Heidelberg (2012). https://doi.org/10.1007/978-3-642-34163-2_8
10. Fischer, R., Aier, S., Winter, R.: A federated approach to enterprise architecture model maintenance, In: EMISA (2007)
11. Fowler, M.: Continous integration (2006). http://martinfowler.com/articles/continuousIntegration.html
12. Guild, B.A.: A Guide to the Business Architecture Body of Knowledge (BIZBOK Guide), vol. V04 (2014)
13. Hacks, S., Lichter, H.: Towards an enterprise architecture model evolution. In: Czarnecki, C., Sultanow, E., Brockmann, C. (eds.) Workshops der Informatik 2018. Lecture Notes in Informatics, Gesellschaft für Informatik e.V, Bonn (2018)
14. Hanssen, G.K., Smite, D., Moe, N.B.: Signs of agile trends in global software engineering research: a tertiary study. In: 2011 IEEE Sixth International Conference on Global Software Engineering Workshop, pp. 17–23, August 2011
15. Hauder, M., Matthes, F., Roth, S.: Challenges for automated enterprise architecture documentation. In: TEAR/PRET (2012)
16. Hevner, A.R., March, S.T., Park, J., Ram, S.: Design science in information systems research. MIS Q. **28**(1), 75–105 (2004)
17. Highsmith, J., Cockburn, A.: Agile software development: the business of innovation. IEEE Comput. **34**, 120–122 (2001)
18. Holm, H., Buschle, M., Lagerström, R., Ekstedt, M.: Automatic data collection for enterprise architecture models. Softw. Syst. Model. **13**(2), 825–841 (2014)
19. Humble, J., Farley, D.: Continuous Delivery: Reliable Software Releases through Build, Test, and Deployment Automation, 1st edn. Addison-Wesley Professional, Upper Saddle River (2010)
20. ISO, IEC, IEEE: Systems and software engineering - Architecture description (01122011)
21. ISO/IEC 25010: Systems and software engineering - Systems and software Quality Requirements and Evaluation (SQuaRE) - System and software quality models, ISO/IEC, vol. 25010. ISO, Geneva (2011)
22. Johnson, P., Ekstedt, M., Lagerström, R.: Automatic probabilistic enterprise IT architecture modeling: a dynamic bayesian networks approach. In: Franke, U., Lapalme, J., Johnson, P. (eds.) 20th International Enterprise Distributed Object Computing Workshop (EDOCW), pp. 123–129 (2016)
23. Aleatrati Khosroshahi, P., Aier, S., Hauder, M., Roth, S., Matthes, F., Winter, R.: Success factors for federated enterprise architecture model management. In: Persson, A., Stirna, J. (eds.) CAiSE 2015. LNBIP, vol. 215, pp. 413–425. Springer, Cham (2015). https://doi.org/10.1007/978-3-319-19243-7_38
24. Kirschner, B., Roth, S.: Federated enterprise architecture model management: collaborative model merging for repositories with loosely coupled schema and data. In: Multikonferenz Wirtschaftsinformatik 2014 (2014)
25. Kotusev, S.: The history of enterprise architecture: an evidence-based review. J. Enterp. Archit. **12**(1), 31–37 (2016)
26. Laukkanen, E., Itkonen, J., Lassenius, C.: Problems, causes and solutions when adopting continuous delivery-a systematic literature review. Inf. Softw. Technol. **82**, 55–79 (2017)

27. Lim, N., Lee, T.G., Park, S.G.: A comparative analysis of enterprise architecture frameworks based on EA quality attributes. In: 2009 10th ACIS International Conference on Software Engineering, Artificial Intelligences, Networking and Parallel/Distributed Computing, pp. 283–288 (2009)
28. Marín, P.R., et al.: Continuous deployment of software intensive products and services: a systematic mapping study. J. Syst. Softw. **123**, 263–291 (2017)
29. Matthes, F., Monahov, I., Schneider, A.W., Schulz, C.: EAM KPI Catalog v1.0. Garching (2011)
30. Niemi, E., Pekkola, S.: Enterprise architecture quality attributes: a case study. In: 2013 46th Hawaii International Conference on System Sciences, pp. 3878–3887. IEEE (2013)
31. Peffers, K., Tuunanen, T., Rothenberger, M.A., Chatterjee, S.: A design science research methodology for information systems research. J. Manage. Inf. Syst. **24**(3), 45–77 (2007)
32. Saint-Louis, P., Lapalme, J.: Investigation of the lack of common understanding in the discipline of enterprise architecture: a systematic mapping study. In: Franke, U., Lapalme, J., Johnson, P. (eds.) 20th International Enterprise Distributed Object Computing Workshop (EDOCW) (2016)
33. Sandkuhl, K., Stirna, J., Persson, A., Wißotzki, M.: Enterprise Modeling. TEES. Springer, Heidelberg (2014). https://doi.org/10.1007/978-3-662-43725-4
34. Simon, D., Fischbach, K., Schoder, D.: An exploration of enterprise architecture research. Commun. Assoc. Inf. Syst. **32**(1), 1–72 (2013)
35. Steffens, A., Lichter, H., Doring, J.S.: Designing a next-generation continuous software delivery system: concepts and architecture. In: 2018 IEEE/ACM 4th International Workshop on Rapid Continuous Software Engineering (RCoSE), pp. 1–7, May 2018
36. The Open Group: ArchiMate 3.0.1 Specification (2017)
37. Välja, M., Korman, M., Lagerström, R., Franke, U., Ekstedt, M.: Automated architecture modeling for enterprise technology management using principles from data fusion: a security analysis case. In: Portland International Conference on Management of Engineering and Technology (PICMET) (2016)
38. Välja, M., Lagerström, R., Ekstedt, M., Korman, M.: A requirements based approach for automating enterprise IT architecture modeling using multiple data sources. In: 19th International Enterprise Distributed Object Computing Workshop (2015)
39. White, S.A.: BPMN Modeling and Reference Guide: Understanding and Using BPMN. Future Strategies Inc., Lighthouse Point (2008)
40. Winter, K., Buckl, S., Matthes, F., Schweda, C.M.: Investigating the state-of-the-art in enterprise architecture management method in literature and practice. In: 5th Mediterranean Conference on Information Systems, AIS (2010)
41. Yin, R.K.: Case Study Research: Design and Methods, 5th edn. Sage Publications, Thousand Oaks and London and New Delhi (2013)
42. Ylimäki, T.: Potential critical success factors for enterprise architecture. J. Enterp. Architect. **2**(4), 29–40 (2006)

A Situational Approach to Data-Driven Service Innovation

Marlies van Steenbergen[1(✉)], Jeroen van Grondelle[1],
and Lars Rieser[2]

[1] HU University of Applied Sciences, Padualaan 99, 3584 CH Utrecht,
The Netherlands
{marlies.vansteenbergen, jeroen.vangrondelle}@hu.nl
[2] Open University, Valkenburgerweg 177, 6419 AT Heerlen,
The Netherlands
lars.rieser@ou.nl

Abstract. Though organizations are increasingly aware that the huge amounts of digital data that are being generated, both inside and outside the organization, offer many opportunities for service innovation, realizing the promise of big data is often not straightforward. Organizations are faced with many challenges, such as regulatory requirements, data collection issues, data analysis issues, and even ideation. In practice, many approaches can be used to develop new data-driven services. In this paper we present a first step in defining a process for assembling data-driven service development methods and techniques that are tuned to the context in which the service is developed. Our approach is based on the situational method engineering approach, tuning it to the context of data-driven service development.

Keywords: Method engineering · Data-driven services · Service innovation

1 Introduction

In many organizations the availability of data leads to the search for new opportunities to gain competitive advantage or to better service customers or clients. Data-driven services open the possibility of offering services that are more to-the-point, timely and accurate, and thus more appealing to consumers. Realizing the promise of big data is not straightforward, however. Issues that must be addressed concern how to collect data, analyze it and translate it into service, both from a technical point of view and a regulatory as well as ethical point of view. The latter is becoming increasingly important. In programs such as the Dutch National Science Agenda researchers are looking for ways to create value with data in a responsible manner. The question we address in this paper is how to make the results of such, and other, academic research broadly accessible and usable in the market, especially for small and medium-sized organizations. In practice, the implementations of processes such as service innovation,

© Springer Nature Switzerland AG 2019
I. Reinhartz-Berger et al. (Eds.): BPMDS 2019/EMMSAD 2019, LNBIP 352, pp. 156–168, 2019.
https://doi.org/10.1007/978-3-030-20618-5_11

portfolio management and product management vary across organizations. Small and medium-sized organizations may not possess a dedicated data-science unit, whereas large organizations often have such capabilities in house. Large organizations tend to make decisions in a more hierarchical manner than smaller organizations, with more involvement of specialized roles. In addition, organizations in specific sectors such as health and finance may have to meet special requirements and constraints when dealing with data. No single approach therefore is suitable for all organizations. Depending on their situation and context, the right techniques and approaches must be identified and combined into a data-driven service development process. In this paper we focus on how to describe available techniques and approaches to make them findable. Our approach is based on situational method engineering. The purpose of the present study is to design a metamodel for characterizing data-driven service development method fragments that enables the retrieval of suitable method fragments in a specific data-driven service innovation situation. We start with deriving a generic metamodel from the literature on situational method engineering. Next, we tune this metamodel to the domain of data-driven service innovation, based on specificities of this domain found in literature. To demonstrate its usefulness, we apply it to the development of a data-driven service in oral care. The ultimate goal of our research project is to build a method base with method fragments for data-driven service development, derived from either practice or academic research.

In the next section we provide the theoretical background to our research, situational method engineering and data-driven service innovation. In Sect. 3 we combine the insights from situational method engineering and data-driven service innovation into a metamodel for defining method fragments. We illustrate and discuss the use of the metamodel in the context of preventive healthcare in Sect. 4. Section 5 contains conclusions and further research.

2 Theoretical Background

We base our study on situational method engineering. Brinkkemper [1] introduces method engineering as a research framework for information systems development methods and defines method engineering as: "method engineering is the engineering discipline to design, construct and adapt methods, techniques and tools for the development of information systems". A method is defined by Brinkkemper as "an approach to perform a systems development project, based on a specific way of thinking, consisting of directions and rules, structured in a systematic way in development activities with corresponding development products" (p. 275–276).

In our case the information systems concerned are data-driven services. Situational method engineering is motivated by the conviction that the suitability of an IS development method depends on the situation and that there is no one-size-fits-all method that suits all situations. Therefore, the goal of situational method engineering is to enable method engineers to build a method tailored to the situation based on reusable method fragments that are stored in a method base (Fig. 1).

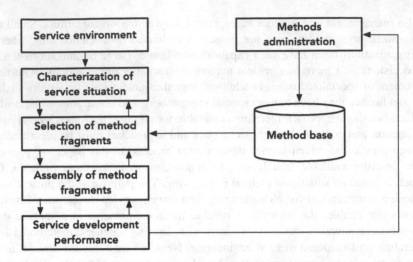

Fig. 1. Method engineering (adapted from [1]).

The method engineering process contains three main steps: (1) characterize service situation, which leads to method requirements [2], (2) select method fragments, (3) assemble method fragments. In this paper we focus on how to describe method fragments in the method base in order to enable effective selection (step 2). We aim to identify the characteristics that can be used to select appropriate method fragments.

In [1] method fragments are defined as coherent pieces of IS development methods. A distinction is made between product fragments and process fragments. Other authors allow fragments that contain both product and process elements in the same fragment [3]. In [4] the concept of a method chunk is used to refer to method fragments consisting of one process fragment and one product fragment. Cossentino et al. [5] compare various method fragment metamodels and arrive at the general metamodel depicted in Fig. 2.

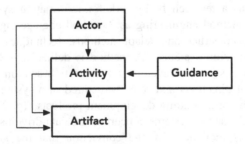

Fig. 2. General metamodel summarizing the fundamental elements of method fragment approaches (adapted from [5])

The metamodel of [5] is comparable to the metamodel for development methodologies defined in ISO/IEC 24744. This standard refers to both methodologies and their instances (in the form of endeavors), as well as to five aspects of the modeled method components [6]: Work Units (cf. Activity), Work Products (cf. Artifact), Producers (cf. Actor), Model Units (cf. Guidance) and Stages. The concept of stages is not present in Cossentino's metamodel. However, stage can be regarded as part of the context in which the fragment can be used, rather than of the fragment itself. Börner [7] refers to 'any reasonable combination of method elements representing a coherent part of a method' as a method fragment, where method elements are techniques, activities, roles and results. In Börner's definition a method fragment can contain any of these elements in any number, including nil. We will use Börner's definition of method fragment in this paper.

In addition to the content of the method fragment, for it to be reusable, information is needed about the context in which the fragment can be used. Mirbel and Ralyté [2] describe a method chunk as consisting of (1) a body, which contains a process part (process fragment) and a product part (product fragment), (2) an interface, containing the situation in which the method chunk can be used (i.e. precondition, usually containing obligatory input products, e.g. "problem statement") and the intention the method chunk can achieve (e.g. "to construct a use case model"), and (3) a descriptor providing the contextual information about the context in which the method chunk is applicable. The interface and body are used for method construction and evaluation. The descriptor is purely used to select method chunks from the method base [8]. It contains a reuse context describing criteria for use of the method chunk and a reuse intention describing the goal that can be achieved by the method chunk. The descriptor is the link to the situational context in which a method chunk can be used.

To achieve method fragment selection, the method fragment characteristics must be matched to the situational factors of the context. This means that the descriptor part of the fragment, consisting of the criteria for use (reuse context) and the goals that can be achieved (reuse intention) must be matched with situational factors. The values describing a method fragment must be chosen in such a way that they can be matched with specific context. Thus, it is useful to know by which situational factors a context can be defined (step 1: characterize service situation).

Mirbel and Ralyté [2] present categories of criteria for selecting method fragments: human, application domain, and organizational, subdividing the latter into system engineering activities, contingency factors and project management. Each of these categories of criteria is represented by a tree of criteria. The reuse context of a method fragment may refer to one or more trees and one or more criteria from the trees. At least some of these criteria seem to be very close to what might be regarded situational factors, e.g. project clarity & stability or high technology innovation level. Mirbel and Ralyté indicate that an organization must build its own reuse frame.

Other authors too, make a selection of criteria suited to their purposes [2, 7, 9–13]. Comparing the situational factors identified by these authors, we find that the diversity is large, as these seven authors together mention a total of 90 situational factors. It seems there is no common agreed upon set of relevant situation factors. Thus, it does not provide us with a solid base for defining the values with which to populate the method fragment metamodel.

3   Data-Driven Service Development Method Fragment Model

To describe method fragments for data-driven service development, we combine the method chunk metamodel of [2] with the definition of method fragments used by [7], by allowing in the body part of the method fragment any combination of activities to be done, results produced, techniques used, and roles involved (Fig. 3).

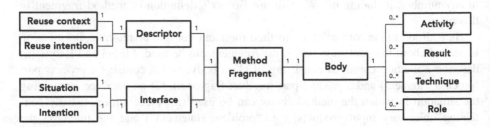

Fig. 3. Method fragment metamodel

Though in more recent studies, the distinction between descriptor and interface as described by [2] is not explicitly made [14, 15], we find the distinction useful to accommodate the difference between the specific goal that can be achieved with a method fragment from a method construction perspective (interface intention) and a more generic purpose a method fragment can contribute to (descriptor reuse intention). The interface intention is expressed from the perspective of the method fragment and what it can do, whereas the descriptor reuse intention is expressed from the perspective of possible contexts and what is needed. A descriptor reuse intention can be contributed to by different interface intentions, dependent on context and situation.

To further tune the metamodel to the domain of data-driven service development, we turned to the literature about data-driven services, using the metamodel as a lens. Based on literature on service innovation and information systems, Troilo et al. [16] provide a framework relating data-rich environments and service innovation. The framework distinguishes three intertwining key dimensions of service innovation: service concept, customer experience, and service process. Innovation can take place along each of these dimensions. Service concept innovation concerns offering a new solution to a need or problem. Customer experience innovation concerns the interaction between service provider and customer. Service process innovation concerns more efficient or effective delivery of services. Specific to data-driven service innovation is the concept of datafication [17, 18]. Datafication means that data are detached from the material world (dematerialization), manipulated, moved around and (un)bundled (liquidity), and again rematerialized by converging data in a particular context, time and place to create value (density). The latter, the data density processes, are the mechanism by which service innovation is realized. It makes the insights generated by data analytics actionable. Troilo et al. [16] further elaborate the data density processes into three types, i.e. pattern spotting, real-time decisioning and synergistic exploration.

Pattern spotting analyzes past data to improve on service delivery. Its objective is explanation and its main aim is service process innovation. Real-time decisioning applies data-analytics to (near) real-time data to identify suitable responses to real-time events. It is primarily aimed at prediction to enable customer experience innovation. Synergistic exploration explores data from a great variety of sources to search for new service concepts. From a method fragment metamodel perspective the types of data density processes can be categorized as activities, their immediate objectives are examples of interface intentions and their ultimate aims can be categorized as descriptor reuse intentions.

Sivarajah et al. [19] perform a structured literature review on big data challenges and analytical methods. They classify big data analytical methods into descriptive analytics, inquisitive analytics, predictive analytics, prescriptive analytics and pre-emptive analytics. Descriptive analytics are aimed at describing a current situation. Inquisitive analytics, such as factor analysis, use data to confirm or reject propositions. Predictive analytics uses data to make predictions about the future. Prescriptive analytics turns data into improvement actions. And pre-emptive analytics use data to mitigate anticipated undesirable future events. In method fragment metamodel terms these types of analytics are techniques with associated interface intentions.

Gandomi and Haider [20] discuss the basic concepts relating to big data. They too mention various techniques available for big data analytics, but from the perspective of type of data being analyzed: text analytics, which can be used for information extraction, text summarization, question answering and sentiment analysis; audio analytics for large-vocabulary continuous speech recognition or a phonetic-based approach; video analytics in which they distinguish server-based architecture and edge-based architecture; social media analytics such as content-based analytics or structure-based analytics; and predictive analytics, for which new statistical techniques are needed because of the big data characteristics of heterogeneity, noise accumulation, spurious correlation and incidental endogeneity.

Maglio and Lim [21] present four archetypes for the design of smart service systems. They define a smart service system as a "configuration of people, information, organizations, and technologies that operate together for mutual benefit and is capable of learning, dynamic adaptation, and decision-making based upon data received, transmitted, and/or processed to improve its response to a future situation" [21, 22]. Maglio and Lim [21] use two dimensions to distinguish four ways of using big data in smart service systems: the source of data (mainly from people or mainly from objects) and the use of data (informing people or managing objects directly). 'Smart operations management' uses data from objects to manage objects. 'Smart customization and prevention' uses data from people to manage objects. 'Smart coaching' uses data from people to inform people. 'Smart adaptation and risk management' uses data from objects to inform people. The dimensions source of data and use of data may be relevant for the descriptor reuse context. For instance, because data sourced from people may have more privacy issues connected to it.

Lim et al. [23] use a framework for discussing cases that contains four generic service design process phases: preliminary investigation and opportunity identification, service idea generation and refinement, service concept and delivery process design, and validation and implementation issue identification. These four phases can be used as descriptor reuse contexts. They also identify 11 managerial issues that should be considered in using data to advance service. When fed with solutions, these issues might be considered examples of interface intentions. In addition, they argue that the application domain, such as the health sector, may pose requirements on data-driven services. This makes application domain a candidate for reuse context.

Table 1 maps the concepts from the literature discussed above to our metamodel of a data-driven service development method fragment. It illustrates the type of values that may be relevant to describe data-driven service development method fragments.

Table 1. Data-driven service metamodel values from literature.

Metamodel concept	Possible values derived from literature
Body – activity	– This may be very diverse, including any activity that may be performed in any of the stages of the method outline depicted in Fig. 4. Examples are pattern spotting, real-time decisioning and synergistic exploration [16]
Body – result	– Interventions [16] – Decisions [21] – Predictions [19]
Body – technique	– Source-dependent Analytic techniques: Text analytics; Audio analytics; Video analytics; Social media analytics [20] – Purpose-dependent Analytic techniques: descriptive analytics, inquisitive analytics, predictive analytics, prescriptive analytics and pre-emptive analytics [19]
Body - role	– Besides the obvious role of data scientist, one can also think about domain experts (for instance medical doctors) supporting the analysis process and evaluating outcomes or legal experts consulting on data use limitation in industries handling sensitive data [23]
Interface – situation	– Actuality of data: past, present [16]
Interface – intention	– Explain, Optimize, Predict, Respond, Explore, Diversify [16] – Collecting data, Protecting Customer values, Integrating data sources [23]
Descriptor – reuse context	– Application domain: health, chemical industry, finance [23] – Type of data: people, objects [21] – Type of use: inform people, manage objects [21] – Dominant V of data: volume, velocity, variety [16] – Service development phase: preliminary investigation and opportunity identification; service idea generation and refinement; service concept and delivery process design; validation and implementation issue identification [23]
Descriptor – reuse intention	– Innovation type: Service process innovation; Customer experience innovation; Service concept innovation [16]

Figure 4 shows a preliminary population of the metamodel for data-driven services.

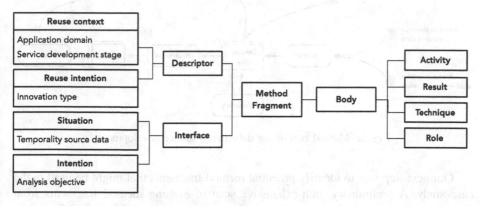

Fig. 4. Data-driven service development method fragment metamodel.

Application domain is the domain in which the method fragment is appropriate, for instance Health, Finance or Industry. Service development stage indicates in which phase of the development process a method fragment can be used: preliminary investigation and opportunity identification; service idea generation and refinement; service concept and delivery process design; validation and implementation issue identification. Innovation type refers to the distinction between service process innovation, customer experience innovation and service concept innovation. Temporality source data indicates whether the method fragment needs past or present data as input. And analysis objective distinguishes between method fragments used for explanation, optimization, prediction, responding, exploring or diversifying. The metamodel is to be further refined in case studies.

4   Demonstration

To conduct a preliminary test of the metamodel we applied it to the first phase of the design of a data-driven service in the context of preventive healthcare. A data-driven service development process was initiated with the oral care unit of a health clinic, with the purpose of validating various research results from our research project. We defined a generic method outline, largely based on [23], to use as an initial framework (Fig. 5): the stages ideation, idea selection, realization and use in the method outline correspond to the four stages distinguished in [23].

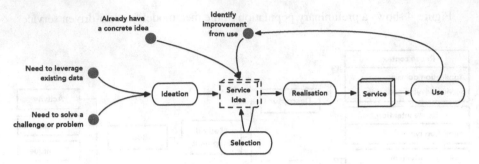

Fig. 5. Method outline for data-driven service development

Our next step was to identify potential method fragments that might be used in the case study. A preliminary, non-exhaustive scan of existing method fragments from literature or practice by the researchers in the project, generated 22 method fragments that might potentially be used in a data-driven service development process, depending on the situation. An example is the real-time decisioning data density process discussed in [16]. Describing this process in terms of the metamodel results in Table 2.

Table 2. Real-time decisioning described as method fragment.

Metamodel concept	Possible values derived from literature
Body – activity	– Real-time decisioning
Body – result	– Intervention
Body – technique	– Prescriptive analytics
Body – role	– Provider
Interface – situation	– Actuality of data: present
Interface – intention	– Predict and Respond
Descriptor – reuse context	– Type of use: inform people – Service development phase: use
Descriptor – reuse intention	– Innovation type: Customer experience innovation

Next, in an interactive session the researchers in the project selected five method fragments to be used in the ideation phase of the oral care service to be developed: (1) long-term goal definition, (2) empathy map, (3) discovery of relevant values, (4) story board, and (5) operationalization of relevant values. Method fragments 1, 2 and 4 are well-known fragments from professional publications, fragments 3 and 5 are the result of research done by the project team. The selected fragments were elaborated with the aid of the metamodel. For illustration purposes we present the method fragments *empathy map* and *discovery of relevant values* in Tables 3 and 4.

Table 3. Example method fragment from practice: empathy map

Name fragment	Empathy map
Body – activity	1. Roughly sketch a persona of the consumer 2. Each team member writes observations in the appropriate quadrant of the map 3. Identify unknowns for later inquiry or validation 4. Discuss observations and fill in gaps collaboratively
Body – result	A visualization of what is known about a consumer
Body – technique	An empathy map is divided into 4 quadrants (Says, Thinks, Does, and Feels), with the consumer, user or persona in the middle The **Says** quadrant contains quotes and defining words of the consumer The **Thinks** quadrant captures what the consumer is thinking throughout the experience The **Feels** quadrant is the consumer's emotional state The **Does** quadrant contains the actions of the consumer
Body – role	Marketeers, service designers and software developers
Interface – situation	Optional: qualitative or quantitative inputs like interviews, field studies, consumer data, or qualitative surveys Optional: the empathy map is ideally being used in conjunction with data discovery. There is a continuous interaction between requirement articulation and exploration of data
Interface – intention	Explore: creating user/customer/consumer insight by visualizing and categorizing the user's needs
Descriptor – reuse context	Ideation stage
Descriptor – reuse intention	Service concept innovation: externalizing knowledge and experience about consumers in order to create a shared understanding of consumer needs

Table 4. Example method fragment from research: discovery of relevant values

Name fragment	The discovery of relevant values
Body – activity	Answering 28 questions about how values may be impacted by the new service
Body – result	List of relevant values that must be addressed in the design of the new service
Body – technique	Moral dialogue
Body – role	Designers and potential users
Interface – situation	A concrete idea for a data-driven service
Interface – intention	Explore: find the values that are relevant to, inspire, or inform the design project
Descriptor – reuse context	Health domain Ideation or Selection stage
Descriptor – reuse intention	Service concept innovation: Value Sensitive Design of a data-driven service

The empathy map is an instrument for understanding audiences, including users, customers, and other players in any business ecosystem, originating from practice and developed by XPLANE [24]. It is a qualitative instrument aimed at understanding and categorizing the needs of a prospective service user. We used the empathy map to generate ideas for a data-driven service, but the fragment can also be used for services that are not data-driven, as can be deduced from the interface intention.

The method fragment *discovery of relevant values* aims to identify the values of direct and indirect stakeholders that may be impacted by a data-driven service in the health domain. This method fragment is aimed specifically at data-driven services, as can be deduced from the interface situation and the descriptor reuse intention.

Both fragments depicted in Tables 3 and 4 can be used in the ideation stage. Comparing the body result and the interface situation of both fragments, however, indicates that the method fragment *empathy map* should be applied before the method fragment *discovery of relevant values*: the result of *empathy map*, a visualization of what is known about the customer, is part of gaining a concrete idea of a service, which is a prerequisite for *discovery of relevant values*.

The two fragments are a preliminary result and discussed here primarily for illustrative purposes. More fragments will be collected, both from academics and from practice, in the context of the preventive health service, and used to test the metamodel and further populate it with optional or obligatory value ranges for the interface and descriptor parts of the model.

5   Conclusion

In this paper we present a metamodel to describe data-driven service development method fragments with the purpose of making method fragments from both academics and practice accessible to the market. Based on literature on situational method engineering and data-driven service innovation we defined a metamodel and made a first inventory of relevant values to populate the metamodel. We applied the metamodel to defining a development method for the ideation phase of a data-driven service development process in preventive healthcare.

The main contribution of this paper is the metamodel to describe data-driven service development method fragments. The metamodel is an essential part of a situational method engineering approach to data-driven service development. It is part of the method base architecture. Besides validating the metamodel in more depth, further research will focus on the situational method engineering phases of characterization of the situation and selection of method fragments, i.e. matching situational characteristics with method fragment characteristics.

Acknowledgements. This work is part of the VWDATA research program with project number 400.17.605, which is financed by the Netherlands Organization for Scientific Research (NWO).

References

1. Brinkkemper, S.: Method Engineering: Engineering of Information Systems Development Methods and Tools. Inf. Softw. Technol. **38**(7), 275–280 (1996)
2. Mirbel, I., Ralyté, J.: Situational method engineering: combining assembly-based and roadmap-driven approaches. Requirements Eng. **11**(1), 58–78 (2006)
3. Deneckère, R., Iacovelli, A., Kornyshova, E., Souveyet, C.: From method fragments to method services. In: Halpin, T., Proper, E., Krogstie, J., Franch, X., Hunt, E., Coletta, R. (eds.) Proceedings of the 13th International Workshop on Exploring Modeling Methods for Systems Analysis and Design (EMMSAD 2008), CEUR Workshop Proceedings, Montpellier, France, vol. 337, pp. 80–96 (2008)
4. Henderson-Sellers, B., Ralyté, J.: Situational method engineering: state-of-the-art review. J. Univ. Comput. Sci. **16**(3), 424–478 (2010)
5. Cossentino, M., Gaglio, S., Henderson-Sellers, B., Seidita, V.: A metamodelling-based approach for method fragment comparison. In: Krogstie, J., Halpin, T., Proper, E. (eds.) Exploring Modeling Methods for Systems Analysis and Design, CEUR Workshop Proceedings, EMMSAD 2006, vol. 364, pp. 57–70 (2006)
6. Gonzalez-Perez, C.: Supporting Situational Method Engineering with ISO/IEC 24744 and the Work Product Pool Approach. In: Ralyté, J., Brinkkemper, S., Henderson-Sellers, B. (eds.) Situational method engineering: fundamentals and experiences. ITIFIP, vol. 244, pp. 7–18. Springer, Boston, MA (2007). https://doi.org/10.1007/978-0-387-73947-2_3
7. Börner, R.: Applying situational method engineering to the development of service identification methods. In: Proceedings of the Sixteenth Americas Conference on Information Systems, Lima, Peru, August 12–15 (2010)
8. Henderson-Sellers, B., Gonzalez-Perez, C., Ralyté, J.: Comparison of method chunks and method fragments for situational method engineering. In: Proceedings 19th Australian Software Engineering Conference. ASWEC2008, IEEE Computer Society, pp. 479–488, Los Alamitos, CA, USA (2008)
9. Ralyté, J.: Situational method engineering in practice: a case study in a small enterprise. In: CAiSE 2013 Forum at the 25th CAiSE, CEUR-WS.org, Valencia, Spain, pp. 17–24 (2013)
10. Kalus, G., Kuhrmann, M.: Criteria for software process tailoring: a systematic review. In: Proceedings of the 2013 International Conference on Software and System Process, ICSSP 2013, pp. 171–180. ACM, New York (2013)
11. van Slooten, K., Hodes, B.: Characterizing is development projects. In: Brinkkemper, S., Lyytinen, K., Welke, R. (eds.) Proceedings of IFIP TC8 Working Conference on Method Engineering: Principles of Method Construction and Tool Support, pp. 29–44. Chapman & Hall, Great Britain (1996)
12. Nguyen, V.P., Henderson-Sellers, B.: Towards automated support for method engineering with the OPEN approach. In: Proceedings of the 7th IASTED Sea Conference, pp. 691–696. Acta Press, Anaheim (2003)
13. Bekkers, W., van de Weerd, I., Brinkkemper, S., Mahieu, A.: The influence of situational factors in software product management: an empirical study. In: Proceedings of the 21th International Workshop on Software Product Management (IWSPM 2008), Barcelona, Spain, pp. 41–48 (2008)
14. Henderson-Sellers, B., Ralyté, J., Ågerfalk, Pär J., Rossi, M.: Situational Method Engineering. Springer, Heidelberg (2014). https://doi.org/10.1007/978-3-642-41467-1
15. Franch, X., et al.: A situational approach for the definition and tailoring of a data-driven software evolution method. In: Krogstie, J., Reijers, Hajo A. (eds.) CAiSE 2018. LNCS, vol. 10816, pp. 603–618. Springer, Cham (2018). https://doi.org/10.1007/978-3-319-91563-0_37

16. Troilo, G., de Luca, L.M., Guenzi, P.: Linking data-rich environments with service innovation in incumbent firms: a conceptual framework and research propositions. J. Prod. Innov. Manage **34**(5), 617–639 (2017)
17. Lycett, M.: Datafication: making sense of (big) data in a complex world. Eur. J. Inf. Syst. **22** (4), 381–386 (2013)
18. Normann, R.: Reframing Business: When the Map Changes the Landscape. Wiley, West Sussex (2001)
19. Sivarajah, U., Kamal, M.M., Irani, Z., Weerakkody, V.: Critical analysis of big data challenges and analytical methods. J. Bus. Res. **70**, 263–286 (2017)
20. Gandomi, A., Haider, M.: Beyond the hype: big data concepts, methods, and analytics. Int. J. Inf. Manage. **35**(2), 137–144 (2015)
21. Maglio, P.P., Lim, C.H.: Innovation and big data in smart service systems. J. Innov. Manage. **4**(1), 11–21 (2016)
22. Medina-Borja, A.: Smart things as service providers: a call for convergence of disciplines to build a research agenda for the service systems of the future (Editorial). Serv. Sci. **7**(1), ii–v (2015)
23. Lim, C., Kim, M., Kim, K., Kim, K.: Using data to advance service: managerial issues and theoretical implications from action research. J. Serv. Theo. Pract. **28**(1), 99–128 (2018)
24. XPLANE site. https://gamestorming.com/empathy-mapping/. Accessed 06 Mar 2019

On the Need for Intellectual Property Protection in Model-Driven Co-Engineering Processes

Salvador Martínez[1]($\boxtimes$), Sebastien Gerard[1], and Jordi Cabot[2]

[1] CEA-LIST, Paris, France
{salvador.martinez,sebastien.gerard}@cea.fr
[2] ICREA-UOC, Barcelona, Spain
jordi.cabot@icrea.cat

Abstract. We live in an increasingly complex world where all systems tend to include heterogeneous and interconnected components. To cope with these systems, industry is shifting towards co-engineering development processes where partners with very different roles and access needs must collaborate together. Therefore, protecting the intellectual property (IP) of the shared assets is a must. Model-Driven Engineering (MDE) may play a key role in the successful enactment of industrial co-engineering processes but only if it succeeds at integrating at its core the concern for IP protection, that has been up to the date largely ignored. In order to advance in this direction, we provide in this paper an initial roadmap towards the holistic protection of IP in collaborative modeling scenarios and we discuss how existing technologies such as Cryptography, Access-control (AC) or Digital Rights Management (DRM) are adapted and integrated in a framework for IP protection in the MDE.

1 Introduction

Systems are becoming more and more complex every day and often integrate IoT components, AI, Big data, and other heterogeneous subsystems. As a result, outsourcing parts of the system design process becomes a necessity. In a classical supply chain, an original equipment manufacturer (OEM) shares parts of its design artefacts with its direct suppliers (tier 1) so that they can perform their tasks. In turn, tier 1 suppliers may also share their artefacts with their own suppliers (tier 2) and so on. This is also becoming true for *digital* assets in what constitutes a paradigm shift towards the co-engineering of systems design.

Model-Driven Engineering (MDE), due to its capacity to specify and reason on digital assets at a high abstraction level, can become a key enabler of this industrial co-engineering shift by helping all participants to contribute to a common project using different (modeling) languages and tools depending on their technical profile and level of expertise. However, for this to happen, MDE should integrate at its core the concerns for Intellectual Property (IP) protection that so far have been largely ignored.

© Springer Nature Switzerland AG 2019
I. Reinhartz-Berger et al. (Eds.): BPMDS 2019/EMMSAD 2019, LNBIP 352, pp. 169–177, 2019.
https://doi.org/10.1007/978-3-030-20618-5_12

A modeling project is typically composed of models and metamodels[1] but also of transformations, queries and constraints on those (meta)models. All of them must be protected in such a way that only what is strictly necessary for a given task is shared with the relevant partners.

Nevertheless, and no matter the strength of the security mechanisms in place, the event of an IP leakage from authorized parties may not be discarded. Thus, an effective IP protection system for a collaborative modelling framework must also deal with such events by providing mechanisms to deal with stolen IP.

These aspects are a major hurdle for any collaborative modeling project. The French Alternative Energies and Atomic Energy Commission (CEA) has struggled with this challenge when trying to set up collaborations with partners in projects involving MDE and where, due to industrial confidentiality agreements, it has to ensure the disclosure of the full details of the models or had to ensure the IP preservation. This was the initial motivation of this work.

To advance in this direction, we provide in this paper an initial roadmap towards the holistic protection of IP in collaborative modelling scenarios. Partial approaches based on access-control [13, 21], cryptography [5] and/or encapsulation (such as Functional Mock-up Units (FMUs)) [7] have been explored in the past. We go beyond these approaches by pushing for the first unified solution including advanced access-control, cryptography and digital rights management (DRM) techniques for collaborative modeling.

The rest of the paper is organized as follows. Section 2 describes existing mechanism successfully used in other domains for the protection of digital assets. Then, Sect. 3 details how we propose to adapt them to the modeling technical space and enable their integration in an IP protection framework for model-based collaborative development. Finally, Sect. 4 outlines a working plan to achieve this goal and Sect. 5 presents our conclusions and further work.

2   IP Protection Mechanisms

A number of different mechanisms have been successfully employed to protect digital assets. They are clear candidates to be part of an IP protection framework for MDE. Here we summarize the main "families" of (complementary) approaches we will reuse and discuss the, very few, previous attempts on porting them to the MDE realm.

- Authorization policies are a mechanism to assign permissions, e.g. the capability of performing actions on resources within a system, to users depending on certain conditions like role and time. Many different access-control paradigms exist such as Role-Based Access-Control (RBAC) [8] or Attribute-Based Access-Control (ABAC) [22]. Privacy policies are conceptually similar but add conditions on the intent and purpose for the data to be shared to protect the user privacy.

---

[1] Metamodels define the abstract syntax of a modeling language, i.e. they specify the elements that can appear in a model and how they can be related to each other. Metamodels are usually represented as models themselves.

- Cryptography is a mechanism to assure the secrecy of information by converting ordinary information into unintelligible information. Typically, cryptography relies on the use of keys and on two encryption and decryption functions. Obfuscation is a similar concept.
- Digital Rights Management (DRM) refers to the mechanisms used to restrict the usage of proprietary resources with the purpose of preventing IP to be shared freely. It involves access-control mechanisms such as *pay-per-view* or *membership-based* content access **but also mechanisms intended to provide prosecution evidence for legal purposes.** The former can be regarded as part of the "Authorization policies" family mentioned above. The latter are typically implemented via digital watermarking and fingerprinting technologies. *Watermarking* consists in embedding in an object imperceptible marks that can be subsequently used to determine IP ownership. *Fingerprinting*, unlike watermarking, does not involve the modification of a resource. It relies on the identification of *unique* features of a resource so that its *fingerprint* can be stored by a trusted arbiter to resolve potential IP conflicts.

MDE has been largely employed to model (and generate) security aspects of the software artefacts to be developed [17] but very few works focus on protecting MDE artefacts themselves and no other approach tries to combine several in one MDE IP framework as we propose. First steps towards providing access-control for model artefacts are proposed by Debreceni et al. [6], whereas obfuscation has been explored by Fill [9]. Industry-wise, popular tools such as such as CDO [19] and Viatra [20] provide, respectively, model access-control and obfuscation. Some of our own works will also be adapted in the building of this framework as we will see next.

3   IP Protection Framework for MDE

Our framework requires two main components (Fig. 1): (1) a *design time* component to enable the specification of the **IP protection policy** of the collaborative project and (2) a *runtime* component in charge of **evaluating and enforcing that policy** upon model access and manipulation requests from users during the collaborative modeling process.

We use the term *megamodel* [2] to refer to the whole set of interrelated modeling artefacts involved in the project. This includes all kinds of model manipulation operations (like model transformations) that from a MDE perspective can also be regarded as models themselves. This allows for a uniform treatment of all artefacts.

3.1   IP Protection Policy Setup

The IP protection policy is expressed via an IP policy language that integrates the definition of **classical authorization** constraints plus advanced **conditions** to refine those authorizations and additional **obligations** the IP protection mechanism must satisfy before delivering the requested modeling artefact.

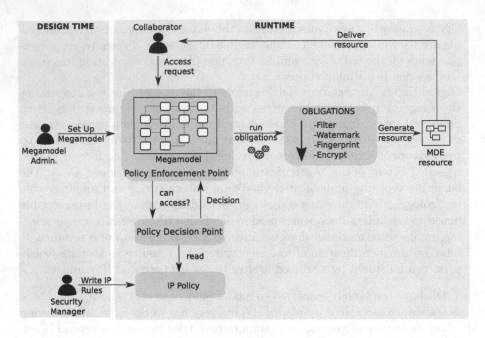

Fig. 1. IP protection approach

The same language can be used to define policies to restrict both internal and external access to the model elements, depending on the required security level.

Authorization. The IP policy language must support the definition of authorization rules where each *rule* specifies whether a *Subject* can perform a given *Action* (typically *read* or *write*) on a given *Object* by attaching to this triple a *decision* element (e.g. *allow* or *deny*)[2]. Effectively, this corresponds to a classical discretionary access-control policy as discussed in [18].

These concepts are generic enough to cover authorization needs on all kinds of modeling artefacts but we also foresee their refinement when more domain-specific actions are required (e.g. the need to indicate whether a transformation can be executed and not only read or written).

For this global policy, the granularity is set at the model level (i.e. users can request access to complete modeling artefacts). More specific permissions, for instance to grant access on specific parts of a model, are managed with the *Filter* obligation described below.

Conditions. To increase the expressiveness (w.r.t. protection needs) of the IP protection rules, the language must include context conditions such as time

---

[2] You can also add a *default* authorization policy to indicate whether allow or deny access to elements when an explicit permission is not provided.

(i.e. the model can only be accessed within a given time interval) and geographical location as well as privacy concepts, such as the purpose of the request.

Obligations. Even when all conditions are met we may still want to process the model before we deliver it to the user. As such, obligations are tasks to be conducted by the security engine before, after or together with the enforcement of the authorization decisions.

The IP policy language must support, at least, the following *Obligations*: *Watermark, Fingerprint, Encrypt* and *Filter*. The *Filter* obligation is linked to a function that calculates a view on the model based on the user requesting the access. This view is "the" model from the perspective of that user. If existing, this is the first obligation to be executed. Then we can proceed to watermark/fingerprint the model (for IP protection) or encrypt it (e.g. for a secure transmission).

Listing 1.1 shows an example of an IP policy where companies try to access an important resource, the *ArchitectureModel*. As we trust those partners holding the *TrustedPartner* role, we state in the first rule that they have the right to read it but only between 9:00 and 17:00. Even when access is granted, the model resource is sent encrypted and watermarked in order to protect our IP. Instead, partners holding the *Contractor* role are in charge of developing specific parts of the system and do not need access to the *ArchitectureModel*. Thus, in the second rule we forbid them to *read* the model.

Listing 1.1. Policy Example

```
Rule r1 (
    Subject S1 {attributes <'role' = 'TrustedPartner'>},
    Object ArchitectureModel,
    Action Read,
    Time 9:00-17:00
) -> Accept [encrypt, watermark]

Rule r2 (
    Subject S2 {attributes <'role' = 'Contractor'>},
    Object ArchitectureModel,
    Action Read
) -> Deny
```

3.2   Enforcement at Runtime

Given an IP policy, our framework needs to combine a number of runtime components to enforce it. We first discuss the mechanism for evaluating the rules and then those in charge of fulfilling the obligations.

Authorization Evaluation and Enforcement. The recommendation in the implementation of modern policy frameworks is separating the infrastructure logic from the application logic by using a *reference monitor* architecture [1].

This architecture consists in two basic components: a Policy Enforcement Point (PEP) and a Policy Decision Point (PDP). Every model access action requested by a subject is intercepted by the PEP that, in turn, forwards it to the PDP to yield an access decision. Note that values for attributes such as location or time (or any other contextual attribute referenced in the access conditions) must be attached to the access-request (or directly taken from the runtime environment) in order for the PDP to evaluate the match.

We follow this architecture. Concretely, we intercept access requests to any of the artefacts in the megamodel by hooking our framework to the API of the modeling technology stack. The request data is then forwarded to our PDP to resolve the request. The PDP is implemented as a model transformation itself [15] to facilitate its execution within the context of modeling tools.

The access decision yielded by the PDP includes the obligations to be fulfilled which are passed on to the next components in the framework.

Filtering Mechanisms for MDE. The filtering obligation aims to provide a finer degree of access-control (at the model element level) for the users. Its implementation requires an efficient fragmentation mechanism for models.

Given the nature of collaborative projects, where many distributed and remote users may require quick access to the models elements, we settled down for a *materialized view* mechanism as the most adequate solution. That is, once a user requests access to a model, she will get back a view of the model containing all the elements she has read access to. This view will be materialized (instead of calculated on the fly every time the user needs to access a different element within the model) and, from a user point of view, it will be indistinguishable from a "normal" model while protecting the parts of the original model users should not even know they exist.

These kind of *materialized views* may be derived by using techniques such as bidirectional transformations [11] or virtual models [4], being the latter our choice. In this sense, the filter obligation must be accompanied by a view definition. This view definition can be automatically inferred from the model-element level access-control policy as we show in [14]. Note that, to ensure that the generated view is always consistent, the view inference process follows a number of permission propagation and consistency rules. In short, these rules propagate permissions across the containment and hierarchy relationships to assign permissions to any element not directly mentioned in the access-control policy. This propagation takes into account that no elements whose access depends on a forbidden element can be part of the view, no matter their individual permission.

If the user is allowed to perform modifications, she can send back the updated view and the changes will be propagated to the original model under some strict and well-known (especially in the database community) limitations.

Cryptography for MDE. The adaptation of encryption techniques for models depend on the storage format used to exchange them. In the simplest scenario (models exchanged as XMI files), encryption can be directly performed with off-the-shelf crypto tools for XML. Similarly, for models stored in a relational or NoSQL databases, available encryption mechanisms in those platforms could be directly used with some adaptations.

Watermarking and Fingerprinting for MDE. Contrary to the previous obligation, standard watermarking techniques cannot be applied to protect the IP of modeling artefacts. To begin with, watermarking for non-media data is challenging as the toleration level to modifications is much lower than for media data. And the few approaches for non-media data (e.g. for XML or graphs) rely on a number of assumptions (basically related to the existence of non mutable identifiers and abundant numerical data) that are not true for models. Therefore, we have developed a new robust (i.e. resistant to data modification to a certain degree) labelling mechanism that uniquely identifies model elements considering both their contents and position (i.e. relationships with other elements) in the model [16].

This labelling mechanism enables us to then reuse in MDE state-of-the-art watermarking algorithms for non-media data. The process of watermarking uses our labelling mechanism to select a small percentage of the total number of elements to be part of the watermark. Then, we could either include the water-mark directly in the model (by making some minor, and mostly imperceptible changes, on the element data like modifying the less relevant digits in numbers or other types of data) or calculate and store the watermark corresponding to the selected elements outside the model (e.g. encrypted on a trusted third party). By using our method with different degrees of robustness in the tolerance to modifications, it can be used to both, identify ownership and tampering, this is, watermarking and fingerprinting.

4   Roadmap

We believe the framework we have proposed provides the basis for the holistic IP protection of MDE artifacts in collaborative modeling scenarios. It reuses, integrates and adapts a number of model-driven technologies and security mechanisms to protect IP by concealing access and tracking leaks. A preliminary implementation of the main components of this framework has been conducted as a proof-of-concept.

Nevertheless, plenty of interesting challenges to consolidate and expand the framework must be addressed before it can actually represent a valid solution for IP protection in industrial projects. In what follows we discuss some of these challenges. Challenges are divided in conceptual, technical and domain specific challenges.

On a conceptual level, we consider interesting to explore the integration of: (1) Peer-to-peer collaboration scenarios where there is no central partner that defines the global protection policy, (2) Multi-level security policies, and (3) functional encryption [3] results, where a decryption key enables a user to learn a specific function of the encrypted data (this could be assimilated to the concept of model query) but nothing else about the data itself.

On a technical level, the framework may be enhanced to support: (1) content-based requests where users define the type of data they need without even knowing in what model/s that data is located, (2) advanced integration of user updates on model fragments to deal with the "view updating" problem.

On a domain-specific level, when collaboration occurs in the development of critical systems such as those integrated in the automobile and avionics domains, traceability and accountability become essential security properties. The history of a model must be thus immutable and verifiable. In that sense our framework may be enhanced by the use of blockchain technologies. Initial steps towards the use of blockchain for model-based knowledge management provided in [10] and [12] may be integrated in our approach so that access and manipulation requests may be stored in a blockchain together with the model modification for further use in verification and certification processes.

5   Conclusions and Future Work

We have presented an approach aimed at providing the basis for the holistic protection of MDE artefacts in collaborative model-based co-engineering scenarios. Our approach is based on the coordination and adaptation to the modeling technical space of several different IP protection mechanisms such as Cryptography, Access-control and Digital Rights Management. This is achieved through a framework composed of two main components: (1) a policy language, that enables the specification of the IP protection policy of the collaborative project; and (2) a megamodel-based runtime infrastructure, in charge of evaluating and enforcing that policy upon model access and manipulation requests from users during the collaborative modeling process.

As future work, we envisage several extensions to our approach. From the challenges outlined in Sect. 4, we intend to preferentially focus on the domain-specific challenges. Concretely, we intend to study the adaptation of our framework to critical domains such as the aerospace and automotive domains. We are specially interested in dealing with traceability and accountability issues together with an on-the-fly validation & verification of security properties. This requires the adaptation and integration of additional mechanisms, such as blockchain and solvers, into our framework.

Acknowledgement. This work is partially funded by the H2020 ECSEL Joint Undertaking Project "MegaM@Rt2: MegaModelling at Runtime" (737494) and the Spanish Ministry of Economy and Competitivity through the project "Open Data for All: an API-based infrastructure for exploiting online data sources" (TIN2016-75944-R).

References

1. Information technology - Open Systems Interconnection - Security frameworks for open systems: Access control framework (International Standard ISO-10181-3/X.812) (1996)

2. Bézivin, J., Jouault, F., Valduriez, P.: On the need for megamodels. In: OOP-SLA/GPCE Workshops (2004)
3. Boneh, D., Sahai, A., Waters, B.: Functional encryption: a new vision for public-key cryptography. Commun. ACM **55**(11), 56–64 (2012)
4. Bruneliere, H., Perez, J.G., Wimmer, M., Cabot, J.: EMF views: a view mechanism for integrating heterogeneous models. In: Johannesson, P., Lee, M.L., Liddle, S.W., Opdahl, A.L., López, Ó.P. (eds.) ER 2015. LNCS, vol. 9381, pp. 317–325. Springer, Cham (2015). https://doi.org/10.1007/978-3-319-25264-3_23
5. Cai, X., He, F., Li, W., Li, X., Wu, Y.: Encryption based partial sharing of CAD models. ICAE **22**(3), 243–260 (2015)
6. Debreceni, C., Bergmann, G., Ráth, I., Varró, D.: Enforcing fine-grained access control for secure collaborative modelling using bidirectional transformations. In: SOSYM, pp. 1–33 (2017)
7. Durling, E., Palmkvist, E., Henningsson, M.: FMI and IP protection of models: a survey of use cases and support in the standard. In: Modelica Conference, Prague, Czech Republic, 15–17 May 2017, no. 132, pp. 329–335 (2017)
8. Ferraiolo, D., Cugini, J., Kuhn, D.R.: Role-based access control (RBAC): features and motivations. In: ACSAC, pp. 241–248 (1995)
9. Fill, H.-G.: Using obfuscating transformations for supporting the sharing and analysis of conceptual models. In: Multikonferenz Wirtschaftsinformatik 2012 - Teilkonferenz Modellierung betrieblicher Informations systeme, Braunschweig (2012)
10. Fill, H.-G., Härer, F.: Knowledge blockchains: applying blockchain technologies to enterprise modeling. In: HICSS (2018)
11. Foster, J.N., Greenwald, M.B., Moore, J.T., Pierce, B.C., Schmitt, A.: Combinators for bidirectional tree transformations: a linguistic approach to the view-update problem. TOPLAS **29**(3), 17 (2007)
12. Härer, F.: Decentralized business process modeling and instance tracking secured by a blockchain. In: ECIS (2018)
13. Kim, T., Cera, C.D., Regli, W.C., Choo, H., Han, J.: Multi-level modeling and access control for data sharing in collaborative design. AEI **20**(1), 47–57 (2006)
14. Martínez, S., Fouche, A., Gérard, S., Cabot, J.: Automatic generation of security compliant (virtual) model views. In: Trujillo, J.C., et al. (eds.) ER 2018. LNCS, vol. 11157, pp. 109–117. Springer, Cham (2018). https://doi.org/10.1007/978-3-030-00847-5_10
15. Martínez, S., García, J., Cabot, J.: Runtime support for rule-based access-control evaluation through model-transformation. In: SLE, pp. 57–69 (2016)
16. Martínez, S., Gérard, S., Cabot, J.: On watermarking for collaborative model-driven engineering. IEEE Access **6**, 1 (2018)
17. Nguyen, P.H., Kramer, M., Klein, J., Le Traon, Y.: An extensive systematic review on the model-driven development of secure systems. IST **68**, 62–81 (2015)
18. Sandhu, R.S., Samarati, P.: Access control: principle and practice. IEEE Commun. Mag. **32**(9), 40–48 (1994)
19. Stepper, E.: CDO model repository (2010)
20. Varró, D., Balogh, A.: The model transformation language of the VIATRA2 framework. Sci. Comput. Program. **68**(3), 214–234 (2007)
21. Wang, Y., Ajoku, P.N., Brustoloni, J.C., Nnaji, B.O.: Intellectual property protection in collaborative design through lean information modeling and sharing. JCISE **6**(2), 149–159 (2006)
22. Yuan, E., Tong, J.: Attributed based access control (ABAC) for web services. In: ICWS (2005)

Enterprise, Business Process and Capability Modeling (EMMSAD 2019)

Dynamic Adaptation of Capabilities: Exploring Meta-model Diversity

Georgios Koutsopoulos$^{(\boxtimes)}$, Martin Henkel, and Janis Stirna

Department of Computer and Systems Sciences, Stockholm University,
Stockholm, Sweden
{georgios,martinh,js}@dsv.su.se

Abstract. Environmental dynamism is constantly gaining ground as a driving force for enterprise transformation. The enterprise capabilities need to adapt as well and capability modeling can facilitate the process of transformation. A plethora of approaches for capability modeling exist. This study aims to explore how adaptability has been addressed in the meta-models of these approaches, visualize relationships among adaptability concepts, and identify ways to improve capability modeling in terms of adaptability. The concepts are visualized in a map and a framework is developed to assist the identification of concepts relevant for adaptation. Similarities and differences among the existing models are discussed, leading to suggestions towards improvements of capability modeling for capability adaptation.

Keywords: Capability · Enterprise modeling · Adaptability

1 Introduction

Environmental dynamism is a factor of major significance concerning changes occurring in every modern organization. The challenging part of changes in the environment is that they are often unpredictable and sudden, yet, they require an immediate response [1]. In addition, organizations become increasingly dependent on information systems (IS), which can no longer be considered a separate feature of an organization; they are an innate part of the business. Therefore, any discussion about organizations that need to be highly adaptive, also refers to highly adaptive IS, which need to be constantly available and adapting to changing environmental conditions and requirements [2].

As a response to this situation, dynamically adaptive IS emerged exhibiting degrees of variability depending on user requirements and contextual run-time fluctuations. These systems are built with several predefined variation points, and depending on the state of the context, a suitable variant is selected to realize a variation point [2].

It is required for any modern IS to be able to deliver business value in accordance with contextual variations, for example user preferences, business models of suppliers, local legislations, resource pricing or location [1]. Furthermore, even if adapting single aspects of an organization is important, the endgame of an adaptive organization is to adapt what it is capable of. The concept of capability encompasses a wide spectrum of concepts and associations among different aspects of an organization. Therefore, an

© Springer Nature Switzerland AG 2019
I. Reinhartz-Berger et al. (Eds.): BPMDS 2019/EMMSAD 2019, LNBIP 352, pp. 181–195, 2019.
https://doi.org/10.1007/978-3-030-20618-5_13

organization that desires to be flexible, requires capability modeling approaches that address the adaptive and dynamic nature of its capabilities.

A plethora of capability modeling techniques and methods exist that employ different sets of concepts in their meta-models in order to reflect the nature of the capabilities of an organization. However, despite the fact that the concept of capability is used with relative conceptual consistency, different purposes for developing a meta-model result in different sets of concepts [3], and hence, significantly different meta-models.

The objective of this paper is to explore how the meta-models depict capability adaptability and present findings along with suggestions for improving dynamic adaptations through capability modeling. As a part of this work, a framework is developed to facilitate the identification of the adaptability elements before exploring their associations and modeling decisions in depth.

The rest of the paper is structured as follows. Section 2 presents a brief overview of the concepts of interest for this study and related literature. Section 3 provides an overview of the methods employed. Section 4 presents the results. Section 5 discusses the findings of Sect. 4 and suggests possible improvements. Section 6 presents concluding remarks.

2   Background and Related Research

The notion of capability has been defined in various ways in the literature. For example [4] defines that capability "is the ability and capacity that enables an enterprise to achieve a business goal in a certain context". It assumes that capability is always defined by certain intention (goal), a defined operational context, and means of achieving the goal. According to the literature search, no studies similar to this one have been conducted before, specifically focusing on capability meta-models and their adaptability concepts. However, there have been studies that can be considered related, having as main topic capability modeling, capability as used in enterprise architecture, the dimensions of adaptability.

Modeling of capabilities is an ongoing research field. Koç [5] has conducted a systematic mapping of methods of modeling, designing and developing capabilities, identifying that having a Resource Based View and changing environments were the main motivations for using the concept of capability. Developments approaches and frameworks were the main solution artifacts from the research. It was also found that methodological support for capability management was scarce and finally, the finding that was considered most important, was that enterprise models were only exploited to some extent. In another study, Koç et al. [6], performed a systematic literature review on context modeling, being an essential element of capability management, and identified the lack of methodology or language to model context.

To some degree, the concept of capability has found its way into *enterprise architecture*. Zdravkovic et al. [3, 7] analyzed how the concept of capability is employed in various Business Architecture, Enterprise Architecture, Enterprise Modeling, and business analysis frameworks. The results state that the concept is used in a similar way, i.e. to represent the ability to achieve a certain result, in all the studied frameworks.

There are however significant differences in the point of focus around capabilities which is a result of the different purposes of the frameworks, e.g. in [8], the focus is on the strategic viewpoint of capabilities which results in including the concept of goal.

Capability adaptations have been addressed in terms such as business services, business process variants, and delivery adjustments. The purpose of capability delivery adjustments is to change capability delivery as response to the changing context and delivery performance without the need to redesign the capability and underlying IS [9].

A common approach to describe adaptability is by identifying the dimensions and functionalities of adaptive systems. In [10], the concept of adaptability of capabilities is tackled by introducing a framework that includes the main dimensions and interrelated aspects for analyzing and evaluating enterprise adaptability. Their framework consists of three dimensions, namely (i) complexity of the environment, (ii) managerial profiling, and (iii) artifact-integrated components. Similarly, [11, 12] are two studies that include such dimensions. They are described in detail in Sect. 3.3. The distinction between functionalities and knowledge in these two studies was the inspiration for the framework presented in the following section.

3 Methodology

This section presents the three activities for the exploration process. The collection of the set of capability meta-models, the visualization of the meta-model concepts and the development of an adaptability framework.

3.1 Capability Meta-model Collection

The process of identifying capability meta-models in the literature was initiated by keyword searches in dblp.org using the terms «capabilit* AND model» and Google Scholar using the terms «"capability OR capabilities AND model" AND "enterprise modelling OR modeling"». The reason behind the difference in the search terms lies in the fact that dblp.org is a database specialized in computer science literature, therefore, the search in Google Scholar had to be narrowed down with extra search terms. This resulted in a set of 672 papers in dblp.org and 169 papers in Scholar.

The inclusion criterion for a study was to contain a conceptual meta-model that contains at least one capability concept. After removing duplicates, a starter set of papers was formed and a snowballing technique was applied using the references in the papers to identify more sources of meta-models until a point of saturation had been reached. Several included meta-models are different versions belonging to the same project, however, they reflect different elaboration levels and include variations in their concept sets, therefore, they were deemed worth exploring. Finally, several documentations and specifications of well-known enterprise architecture frameworks [13–17] and modelling languages [1, 18] that include capability viewpoints were included in order to complete the final set of meta-models to be explored. The number of the included meta-models is 64. It is worth mentioning that approaches based on capability mapping, for example [19], despite being valid approaches, have not been included in the study unless a meta-model existed as well.

3.2   Visualization of Capability Meta-model Concept Map

The purpose of this part is to provide an overview of the capability meta-model concepts. After collecting the meta-models, every single term in the meta-models was manually extracted, put in a database and imported into the VOSviewer tool [20]. The tool is useful in showing occurrences and co-occurrences of terms in the meta-models, along with grouping of concepts based on common co-occurrences. It is commonly used for the automatic visualization of bibliographic networks but can be valuable for visualizing any type of network. However, in this case, the task was performed manually. The items in the map have been imported using a .ris file which was developed after extracting the concepts from the selected meta-models. The clustering is performed automatically by the tool.

All terms with at least two occurrences are included to avoid domain-specific terms that have only been used once. This does not exclude domain-specific terms that have been used in different versions of domain-specific meta-models. Certain terms have been converted from plural to singular number, e.g. "resources" to "resource" and British to American English.

3.3   Adaptability Framework

In this work we employ a framework in order to compare existing models used for representing capability adaptation. The framework is based on work done in the area of adaptive IS and contains the basic elements that are needed to express adaptability. In order to present the framework, we first introduce the work of Weyns et al. [11] and Morandini et al. [12] that the framework is inspired from.

Weyns et al. [11] have conducted a study concerning software development, however, their contribution can be generalized to adaptive and self-adaptive systems in general, since software, nowadays, is naturally associated to business, being a part of the business or supporting it. Weyns et al. suggest that a model should be capable of describing and reasoning about (i) how the system monitors the environment, referring to context-awareness, (ii) how the system monitors itself, referring to self-awareness, (iii) how the system adapts itself, and (iv) how the system coordinates monitoring and adaptation. In addition, the work suggests that besides addressing a wide spectrum of perspectives, a model should also be extensible for future refinements.

In a similar way, Morandini et al. [12] identify the three core functionalities of adaptive and, in particular, self-adaptive systems being (a) sensing the environment in order to recognize "problems", (b) taking decisions in which behavior to exhibit, and (c) realizing the behavior change by adaptation. They state that, as a result to the abovementioned functionalities, a system needs information about (α) what to monitor and for which symptoms, (β) which alternative behaviors are available, and (γ) the decision criteria for a specific behavior. Thus, they differentiate between needed functions (a–c) and information (α–γ).

As shown in Fig. 1, the two studies are consistent with each other and enable a conceptual composition that, in return, provides a basis for a capability adaptability framework. For instance, how the system monitors the environment and itself is associated to the monitoring function and to what to monitor and for which symptom

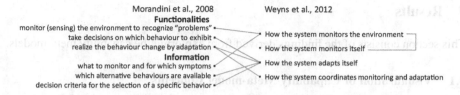

Fig. 1. The association between the two studies.

types of information. How the system adapts itself is associated to taking a decision on behavior and realization of the behavior functions and to the available alternative behaviors and decision criteria types of information. The coordination between monitoring and adaptation is associated to the realization of the selected behavior function.

Identifying the concepts that exist in a capability model can also be assisted by predefined sets of adaptability concepts. Grabis and Kampars [21] have suggested a set of concepts dedicated to adaptive capability run-time adjustments consisting of:

- Capability
- KPI
- Goal
- Process
- Adjustment
- Context element

Abstraction has been applied on this set of concepts. For example, "intention" is derived from abstracting "goal". Combining the result with the abovementioned findings from literature, results in a framework for evaluating the adaptability attributes of capabilities in existing meta-models. The framework, which is a combination of a top-down approach using the adaptability requirements and a bottom-up approach using the predefined set of concepts, is shown in Table 1 below.

Table 1. Capability adaptability framework.

Function elements	Information elements	Example terms
Observation	Measurement	KPI, metric
	Context	Context element, environment
	System itself	Capability
Orientation & decision	Intention	Goal, objective
	Alternatives	Variation
	Criteria	Policy
Coordination & delivery	Delivery	Process, service
	Capability architecture	Dependency, specialization

The framework function elements bear similarities to Boyd's OODA loop [22], from which the functionality names "observation", "orientation" and "decision" have been inspired. More details on the framework components exist in the results section.

4   Results

This section consists of the findings derived from exploring the capability meta-models.

4.1   Visualization of Capability Meta-model Concepts

The interconnections among the concepts have been visualized using VOSviewer [20]. 707 unique concepts were identified in the 64 sources. All 153 concepts with at least two occurrences have been included. Figure 2 depicts the visualized result. The size of the circular elements and their labels reflect their number of occurrences across all models, the distance among the elements reflects their relatedness and the thickness of the connecting lines reflects the strength of the link between the two elements, in other words, the frequency of co-occurrence in the meta-models [20].

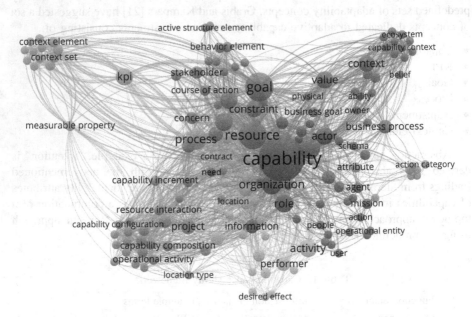

Fig. 2. A visualized network of the identified capability meta-model elements.

Filtering out the majority of the included concepts by setting the occurrence limit to seven occurrences, results in an abstracted version of the visual network that facilitates identifying the most common concepts encountered in capability meta-models. The abstract version is shown in Fig. 3. The most common concepts encountered in capability meta-models, based on the number of occurrences that is shown in the parentheses, are:

- Goal (23)
- Resource (21)
- Process (12)

- Service (12)
- Organization (11)
- Role (9)
- Driver (9)
- Activity (9)
- Value (8)
- Actor (8)
- Requirement (8)
- KPI (8)
- Constraint (7)
- Context (7)

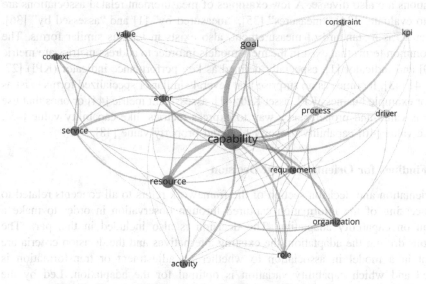

Fig. 3. The visualized network of elements (minimum 7 occurrences)

It is notable that the majority of the commonly encountered concepts are also associated to the adaptability of capabilities matching the examples in the framework or being associated to the explored information elements. For example, activity is a delivery element and requirement is a criterion element.

4.2   Findings for Observation

The term observation refers to monitoring a capability by capturing external and internal data associated to it. As suggested in the framework, important elements associated to observation are the measurement of a capability's attributes along with the sources of data, both contextual and internal. On a generic level, observation elements in a model act as a means to depict the sources of data that can be used in order to evaluate a capability's performance. The majority of the meta-models, in particular, 54 out of 64, included at least one concept associated to observation.

There have been several similarities and differences identified among the models during the analysis. Context seems to be one of the more common concepts included in a capability meta-model. However, various terms have been used to describe it, sometimes using similar terms, for example, context, environment or ecosystem, or by specializing the included model concepts like environmental factor [23], situation [24], location [25], service context [26] or context set [27]. The same trend has been observed concerning measurement and metrics. Measurement [28], calculation [29], computation action [30] and assessment [31] are examples of similar concepts that refer to the activity of measuring a capability. There are also specializations of the concept, e.g., capability calculation [32] and scorecard [33]. An interesting fact concerning measurement is that many of the meta-models have selected to include the concept not as a class item, but as an association between classes. The textual descriptions of the associations are also diverse. A few examples of measurement related associations are "used to evaluate" [34], "measures" [35], "measured by" [1] and "assessed by" [36]. The metric, as a standard of measurement, also exists in various similar forms. The most common terms that exist in the meta-models in order to address metrics are metric [37–40] and indicator [1], especially defined as key performance indicator (KPI) [27, 34, 36, 41–43]. It comes as no surprise that several similar or specialized forms exist as well, for example business KPI, asset KPI [41], assessment metric [44] or ones that use the terms value and property as a way to express metrics, like capability value [45], attribute value [46] capability property [47] and property value [48].

4.3   Findings for Orientation and Decision

The orientation and decision section of the framework refers to all concepts related to the processing of the information captured through observation in order to make a decision on capability adaptation. The decision is also included in this part. The intentions driving the adaptation, the existing alternatives and the decision criteria are relevant in a model in association to whether an adjustment or transformation is required and which capability variation is optimal for the adaptation. Led by the popularity of the concepts depicting intention, this set of concepts concerning orientation and decision has been the most popular one. Only seven out of the 64 meta-models have not included any orientation and decision concepts.

A capability is meant to fulfill a purpose. Hence, the intention concepts are the most popular theme among the ones explored in this study. There have been several similar concepts to depict intention with the most popular being goal as, for example in [51, 54, 56], followed by driver, as in [28, 34, 52, 58] and objective, as in [59], and requirement [40]. Other variations that have been used to depict intention are business goal [60], capability goals [61], task and mission goal [62], mission [63], desired effect [64], need [65] and enterprise vision as in [16]. There also exist specific intention concepts like competitive advantage and superior profit [66]. Finally, there are associations that imply intentionality, e.g. the association "accomplishes" [67].

Capability alternatives have been modeled by various means. The most self-explanatory terms used are current and planned capability [61], current and desired capability [41] and emerging capability [53]. Less obvious concepts that, however, imply the existence of capability alternatives are process variant [1], alternative relation

[8], capability enabling bundle [68], the attribute "potential" in a capability class [69], along with the concepts configuration [37] and capability configuration [23], which imply the existence of multiple configurations for a capability.

The criteria for decisions on capability adaptations or adjustments have been modeled with a diversity of terms as well. Any concept that guides or affects a decision can belong to this set. A few examples that exist in the meta-models are condition and rule [64], plan [70], capability planning [71], policy [49], course of action [14], guidance [25], capability roadmap [44], capability offer [18] or even more specialized like contextual constrains [72].

4.4 Findings for Coordination and Delivery

Coordination and delivery of capabilities refers to how the decision on adaptation is applied affecting the way a capability is delivered and how capabilities' interrelationships are affected by run-time adaptations. As a result, important elements are the delivery of the capability and the capability architecture existing within an organization. This set of concepts has also been widely observed due to the inclusion of delivery concepts. Only ten among the 64 selected meta-models did not contain any delivery or capability architecture concepts.

In the vast majority of capability definitions, the concept is considered associated to the delivery of value. Therefore, a capability that changes is most likely to affect its delivery as well. Examples of the most common concepts that exist in meta-models and reflect capability delivery are the concepts of process, as in [73], business process [52], service [50, 74], business service [15], behavior element [68], capability realization [75], task [76], action [57], and activity [17]. There have also been associations depicting delivery for example "delivers" [36] and "realizes" [55]. Activity modifier [77] and adjustment [14] are interesting concepts, since they refer specifically to the modification of the capability.

Several approaches have been selected as well to address capability architecture in the meta-models. The concept refers to capability interrelationships and interactions. First of all, distinguished classes have been used, for example, capability composition [59], capability dependency [13] or capability relation [8]. In addition, several associations have been used to depict capability relationships, recursive associations of capabilities being the most common case observed. In particular, "has" [52], "realizes" [68], "interacts with" [69], "specifies" and "extends" [78], aggregation [57], "can be combined with", "is decomposed into" and "used by" [38], "contains" [16] and "is part of" [60] are only a few examples of recursive associations. Finally, specializations and generalizations have been used to depict capability interrelations. In particular, examples of specializations of capability are external and internal capability [8], simple and complex capability [62], business capability and technological capability [38]. Meta-capability connected to capability with an association "alters/designs" [26] is another way selected to depict capability interrelationships.

5 Discussion

As far as adaptability of capabilities depicted through Enterprise Modeling is concerned, there are areas for improvement. Despite the differences concerning the scope of the explored meta-models, being business, IT or both, or their domain, being general purpose or domain-specific, e.g., military or transportation, important similarities have been identified in the form of commonly used concepts. Even in domain-specific models, there are major similarities despite the non-overlapping domains. This fact indicates that the utility of capabilities is not bound to specific domains, and optimizing its adaptability may have major impact in several domains.

A fact that needs to be taken into consideration is that not all capability meta-models address adaptability in detail but this cannot be considered a deficiency. Domain-specific approaches serve their purpose by including the specifics of the given domain. Every model or meta-model is an artifact developed in order to address these specific needs. However, adaptability is becoming the new constant in enterprise transformation, and Enterprise Modeling, which is used to support organizations, should aim to support the transformation. This support can be assisted by this study's findings. In particular, what can be suggested is:

– Aligning modeling approaches. The fact that the meta-model concepts that were identified as the most common are significantly overlapping with the ones that address the adaptive nature of capabilities, means that the task of improving capability modeling for adaptations is an achievable task since a solid basis already exists. What may be useful is performing an alignment of meta-models, merging all the relevant concepts.
– Reducing the level of abstraction of adaptability elements. Abstract concepts exist in several models that are a possible source of confusion, since the associations between the concepts related to them are associated to capability, however, the way they are associated is not entirely clear. For example, the concept Gap in [15, 58] could be an efficient way to identify the need for change adaptation, however, it needs to be decomposed before being valuable for capability adaptation. So, reducing the level of abstraction is one way towards optimization.
– Adding the concepts which are implied, yet, missing. A phenomenon whose occurrence in the meta-models is quite common is that there are concepts that are not included as classes or even associations, however, their existence and relation is implied. For example, "capability meets goal" implies measurement concepts. In another example, the association "accomplishes" implies the existence of a goal and associated measurements. Including any implied concepts is another way to optimize the models of adaptive or self-adaptive capabilities.
– Identifying other missing useful concepts. Finally, there are probably concepts that can provide valuable assistance in modeling adaptive capabilities that are still missing from the existing meta-models, however, they should be included in an optimal method. Identifying these concepts is the next future step of this research project as a means to achieve optimization of capability modeling.

6 Conclusion

This study addressed the problem of having a plethora of capability modeling approaches that depict adaptability elements in different ways. A framework has been developed in order to facilitate the identification of adaptability elements in capability meta-models. The framework contains the main functionalities of an adaptive or self-adaptive capability-oriented system. Observation, orientation and decision, coordination and delivery are the main function elements. Each of them is associated to a set of concepts that have been modeled with more similarities than differences in the 64 analyzed capability meta-models. In addition, an overview of the concepts in the meta-models and their association to function elements has been investigated. This exploration contributes towards the identification of the techniques and concepts required for an improved modeling method that focuses on dynamic adaptation of capabilities.

References

1. Sandkuhl, K., Stirna, J. (eds.): Capability Management in Digital Enterprises. Springer, Cham (2018). https://doi.org/10.1007/978-3-319-90424-5
2. Morin, B., Barais, O., Jezequel, J.-M., Fleurey, F., Solberg, A.: Models@ Run.time to support dynamic adaptation. Computer **42**, 44–51 (2009)
3. Zdravkovic, J., Stirna, J., Grabis, J.: A comparative analysis of using the capability notion for congruent business and information systems engineering. Complex Syst. Inform. Model. Q., 1–20 (2017)
4. Grabis, J., Zdravkovic, J., Stirna, J.: Overview of capability-driven development methodology. In: Sandkuhl, K., Stirna, J. (eds.) Capability Management in Digital Enterprises, pp. 59–84. Springer International Publishing, Cham (2018). https://doi.org/10.1007/978-3-319-90424-5_4
5. Koç, H.: Methods in designing and developing capabilities: a systematic mapping study. In: Ralyté, J., España, S., Pastor, Ó. (eds.) PoEM 2015. LNBIP, vol. 235, pp. 209–222. Springer, Cham (2015). https://doi.org/10.1007/978-3-319-25897-3_14
6. Koç, H., Hennig, E., Jastram, S., Starke, C.: State of the art in context modelling – a systematic literature review. In: Iliadis, L., Papazoglou, M., Pohl, K. (eds.) CAiSE 2014. LNBIP, vol. 178, pp. 53–64. Springer, Cham (2014). https://doi.org/10.1007/978-3-319-07869-4_5
7. Zdravkovic, J., Stirna, J., Grabis, J.: Capability consideration in business and enterprise architecture frameworks. In: Sandkuhl, K., Stirna, J. (eds.) Capability Management in Digital Enterprises, pp. 41–56. Springer International Publishing, Cham (2018). https://doi.org/10.1007/978-3-319-90424-5_3
8. Loucopoulos, P., Kavakli, E.: Capability modeling with application on large-scale sports events. In: AMCIS 2016 Proceedings, pp. 1–10. Association for Information Systems, San Diego (2016)
9. Grabis, J., Kampars, J.: Design of capability delivery adjustments. In: Krogstie, J., Mouratidis, H., Su, J. (eds.) CAiSE 2016. LNBIP, vol. 249, pp. 52–62. Springer, Cham (2016). https://doi.org/10.1007/978-3-319-39564-7_5

10. Petrevska Nechkoska, R., Poels, G., Zdravkovic, J.: Enterprise adaptability using a capability-oriented methodology and tool support. In: Proceedings of the 2nd International Workshop on Practicing Open Enterprise Modelling within OMiLAB (PrOse) Co-located with 11th IFIP WG 8.1 Working Conference on the Practice of Enterprise Modelling (PoEM 2018), Vienna, Austria, 31 October 2018, pp. 61–72 (2018)
11. Weyns, D., Malek, S., Andersson, J.: FORMS: unifying reference model for formal specification of distributed self-adaptive systems. ACM Trans. Auton. Adapt. Syst. **7**, 1–61 (2012)
12. Morandini, M., Penserini, L., Perini, A.: Towards goal-oriented development of self-adaptive systems. In: Proceedings of the 2008 International Workshop on Software Engineering for Adaptive and Self-managing Systems - SEAMS 2008, p. 9. ACM Press, Leipzig (2008)
13. NATO: NATO Architecture Framework v.4 (2018). https://www.nato.int/nato_static_fl2014/assets/pdf/pdf_2018_08/20180801_180801-ac322-d_2018_0002_naf_final.pdf
14. The Open Group: Archimate 3.0.1. Specification (2017). https://publications.opengroup.org/i162
15. The Open Group: The TOGAF® Standard, Version 9.2 (2018). https://publications.opengroup.org/standards/togaf/specifications/c182
16. UK Ministry of Defence: Ministry of Defense Architecture Framework V1.2.004 (2010). https://www.gov.uk/guidance/mod-architecture-framework
17. USA Department of Defense: Department of Defense Architecture Framework 2.02 (2009). https://dodcio.defense.gov/Library/DoD-Architecture-Framework/
18. Object Management Group (OMG): Value Delivery Modeling Laguage (2015). https://www.omg.org/spec/VDML/1.0
19. Beimborn, D., Martin, S.F., Homann, U.: Capability-oriented modeling of the firm. Presented at the IPSI Conference, Amalfi, Italy, January (2005)
20. van Eck, N.J., Waltman, L.: Software survey: VOSviewer, a computer program for bibliometric mapping. Scientometrics **84**, 523–538 (2010)
21. Grabis, J., Kampars, J.: Adjustment of capabilities: how to add dynamics. In: Sandkuhl, K., Stirna, J. (eds.) Capability Management in Digital Enterprises, pp. 139–158. Springer International Publishing, Cham (2018). https://doi.org/10.1007/978-3-319-90424-5_8
22. Boyd, J.R.: The essence of winning and losing. Unpubl. Lect. Notes **12**, 123–125 (1996)
23. MODAF ontological data exchange mechanism (MODEM). https://www.gov.uk/government/uploads/system/uploads/attachment_data/file/63980/20130117_MODAF_MODEM.pdf
24. Rauffet, P., Da Cunha, C., Bernard, A.: Conceptual model and IT system for organizational capability management. Comput. Ind. **63**, 706–722 (2012)
25. Antunes, G., Borbinha, J.: Capabilities in systems engineering: an overview. In: Falcão e Cunha, J., Snene, M., Nóvoa, H. (eds.) IESS 2013. LNBIP, vol. 143, pp. 29–42. Springer, Heidelberg (2013). https://doi.org/10.1007/978-3-642-36356-6_3
26. Danesh, M.H., Loucopoulos, P., Yu, E.: Dynamic capabilities for sustainable enterprise IT – a modeling framework. In: Johannesson, P., Lee, M.L., Liddle, Stephen W., Opdahl, Andreas L., López, Ó.P. (eds.) ER 2015. LNCS, vol. 9381, pp. 358–366. Springer, Cham (2015). https://doi.org/10.1007/978-3-319-25264-3_26
27. Stirna, J., Zdravkovic, J.: Development of a modeling language for capability driven development: experiences from meta-modeling. In: Comyn-Wattiau, I., Tanaka, K., Song, I.-Y., Yamamoto, S., Saeki, M. (eds.) ER 2016. LNCS, vol. 9974, pp. 396–403. Springer, Cham (2016). https://doi.org/10.1007/978-3-319-46397-1_30

28. du Toit, F.A., Tanner, M.: A business architecture capability meta model and tool-set for providing function point estimation for enterprise architecture management. In: Proceedings of the International MultiConference of Engineers and Computer Scientists, Hong Kong, pp. 482–494 (2015)
29. Pastor, O., Ruiz, M., Koç, H., Valverde, F.: Capability-based communication analysis for enterprise modelling. Enterp. Model. Inf. Syst. Architectures **13**, 1–24 (2018)
30. Wang, Z., Zhang, W., Dong, Q., He, H., Zhao, W.: A light way of enterprise modeling and simulation for C4ISR system based on xUML. J. Command Inf. Syst. **8**, 2829–2838 (2012)
31. Iacob, M.-E., Quartel, D., Jonkers, H.: Capturing business strategy and value in enterprise architecture to support portfolio valuation. In: 2012 IEEE 16th International Enterprise Distributed Object Computing Conference, pp. 11–20. IEEE, Beijing (2012)
32. Loucopoulos, P., Kavakli, E.: Capability oriented enterprise knowledge modeling: the CODEK approach. In: Karagiannis, D., Mayr, H.C., Mylopoulos, J. (eds.) Domain-Specific Conceptual Modeling, pp. 197–215. Springer, Cham (2016). https://doi.org/10.1007/978-3-319-39417-6_9
33. Rauffet, P., Cunha, C.D., Bernard, A.: Managing resource learning in distributed organisations with the organisational capability approach. Int. J. Technol. Manag. **70**, 300–322 (2016)
34. Becker, C., Antunes, G., Barateiro, J., Vieira, R., Borbinha, J.: Modeling digital preservation capabilities in enterprise architecture. In: Proceedings of the 12th Annual International Digital Government Research Conference on Digital Government Innovation in Challenging Times - Dg.O 2011, p. 84. ACM Press, College Park (2011)
35. Kudryavtsev, D., Grigoriev, L., Bobrikov, S.: Strategy-focused and value-oriented capabilities: Methodology for linking capabilities with goals and measures. In: Molnar, W.A., Proper, H.A., Zdravkovic, J., Loucopoulos, P., Pastor, O., de Kinderen, S. (eds.) Complementary proceedings of the 8th Workshop on Transformation & Engineering of Enterprises (TEE 2014), and the 1st International Workshop on Capability-oriented Business Informatics (CoBI 2014), pp. 15–26. CEUR-WS.org, Geneva (2014)
36. Becker, C., Antunes, G., Barateiro, J., Vieira, R.: A capability model for digital preservation: analysing concerns, drivers, constraints, capabilities and maturities. Presented at the International Conference on Preservation of Digital Objects (iPRES 2011), Singapore, 1 November (2011)
37. Rafati, L., Roelens, B., Poels, G.: A domain-specific modeling technique for value-driven strategic sourcing. Enterp. Model. Inf. Syst. Architectures **13**, 1–29 (2018)
38. Papazoglou, A.: Capability-based planning with TOGAF® and ArchiMate® (2014)
39. Iacobucci, J.V.: Rapid Architecture Alternative Modeling (RAAM): a framework for capability-based analysis of system of systems architectures (2012). https://smartech.gatech.edu/handle/1853/43697
40. TRAK Enterprise Architecture Metamodel (2018). https://sourceforge.net/projects/trakmetamodel/
41. Loucopoulos, P., Kavakli, E., Anagnostopoulos, D., Dimitrakopoulos, G.: Capability-oriented analysis and design for collaborative systems: an example from the Doha 2022 World cup games. In: Proceedings of the 2018 10th International Conference on Computer and Automation Engineering - ICCAE 2018, pp. 185–189. ACM Press, Brisbane (2018)
42. Antunes, G., Barateiro, J., Becker, C., Borbinha, J., Vieira, R.: Modeling contextual concerns in enterprise architecture. In: 2011 IEEE 15th International Enterprise Distributed Object Computing Conference Workshops, pp. 3–10. IEEE, Helsinki (2011)
43. Bergström, S.: Modelling Business Capabilities with Enterprise Architecture: A Case Study at a Swedish Pension Managing Company (2015). http://www.diva-portal.org.ezp.sub.su.se/smash/get/diva2:860618/FULLTEXT01.pdf

44. Malik, N.: Enterprise business motivation model: full model documentation v.4.2 (2013)
45. Straube, C., Kranzlmüller, D.: Model-driven resilience assessment of modifications to hpc infrastructures. In: an Mey, D., et al. (eds.) Euro-Par 2013. LNCS, vol. 8374, pp. 707–716. Springer, Heidelberg (2014). https://doi.org/10.1007/978-3-642-54420-0_69
46. Bhiri, S., Derguech, W., Zaremba, M.: Modelling capabilities as attribute-featured entities. In: Cordeiro, J., Krempels, K.-H. (eds.) WEBIST 2012. LNBIP, vol. 140, pp. 70–85. Springer, Heidelberg (2013). https://doi.org/10.1007/978-3-642-36608-6_5
47. Homann, U., et al.: Efficient and flexible business modeling based upon structured business capabilities (2006). http://patents.google.com/patent/US20060116922A1/en
48. Derguech, W., Bhiri, S., Curry, E.: Designing business capability-aware configurable process models. Inf. Syst. **72**, 77–94 (2017)
49. DeLoach, S.A., Oyenan, W.H., Matson, E.T.: A capabilities-based model for adaptive organizations. Auton. Agents Multi-agent Syst. **16**, 13–56 (2008)
50. Danesh, M.H.: A socio-technical modeling framework for designing enterprise capabilities. In: Proceedings of the Doctoral Consortium Papers presented at the 11th IFIP WG 8.1 Working Conference on the Practice of Enterprise Modelling (PoEM 2018), pp. 31–46. CEUR-WS.org, Vienna (2018)
51. Roubtsova, E., Michell, V.: Behaviour models clarify definitions of affordance and capability. In: Proceedings of the 2014 Workshop on Behaviour Modelling-Foundations and Applications - BM-FA 2014, pp. 1–10. ACM Press, York (2014)
52. Barroero, T., Motta, G., Pignatelli, G.: Business capabilities centric enterprise architecture. In: Bernus, P., Doumeingts, G., Fox, M. (eds.) EAI2 N 2010. IAICT, vol. 326, pp. 32–43. Springer, Heidelberg (2010). https://doi.org/10.1007/978-3-642-15509-3_4
53. Antunes, G., Vieira, R., Borbinha, J.: Capabilities and requirements engineering: research challenges. In: INCOSE International Symposium, vol. 23, pp. 590–605 (2013)
54. Aldea, A., Iacob, M.-E., Hillegersberg, V.J., Quartel, D., Franken, H.: Serious gaming for the strategic planning process. In: Proper, H.A., Lin, K.-J., Marchand-Maillet, S., Ralyte, J. (eds.) Proceedings - 16th IEEE Conference on Business Informatics, CBI 2014, pp. 183–190. Institute of Electrical and Electronics Engineers Inc. (2014)
55. Gongolidis, E., Evangelia, K., Loucopoulos, P., Christos, K.: Migrating eGovernment services in the cloud: a capability modelling approach. In: Proceedings of the 20th Pan-Hellenic Conference on Informatics - PCI 2016, pp. 1–6. ACM Press, Patras (2016)
56. Nunes, I., Faccin, J.G.: Modelling and implementing modularised BDI agents with capability relationships. Int. J. Agent-Oriented Softw. Eng. **5**, 203 (2016)
57. DeLoach, S.A., Garcia-Ojeda, J.C.: O-MaSE: a customisable approach to designing and building complex, adaptive multi-agent systems. Int. J. Agent-Oriented Softw. Eng. **4**, 244–280 (2010)
58. Mikloš, J.: A meta-model for the spatial capability architecture. J. Theor. Appl. Inf. Technol. **43**, 301–305 (2012)
59. Li, W., Badr, Y., Biennier, F.: Improving web service composition with user requirement transformation and capability model. In: Meersman, R., et al. (eds.) OTM 2013. LNCS, vol. 8185, pp. 300–307. Springer, Heidelberg (2013). https://doi.org/10.1007/978-3-642-41030-7_21
60. Bravos, G., Loucopoulos, P., Dimitrakopoulos, G., Anagnostopoulos, D., Kiousi, V.A.: A capability – driven modelling approach applied in smart transportation & management systems for large scale events. EAI Endorsed Trans. Internet Things **3**, 153051 (2017)
61. Walker, S.K.: Capabilities-based planning-how it is intended to work and challenges to its successful implementation. ARMY WAR COLL CARLISLE BARRACKS PA (2005)
62. Qi, Y., Wang, Z., Dong, Q., He, H.: Modeling and verifying SoS performance requirements of C4ISR systems. J. Syst. Eng. Electron. **26**, 754–763 (2015)

63. Zhang, W., Wang, Z., Zhao, W., Yang, Y., Xin, X.: Generating executable capability models for requirements validation. J. Softw. **7**, 2046–2052 (2012)
64. Tingting, Z., Xiaoming, L., Zhixue, W., Qingchao, D.: Capability-oriented architectural analysis method based on fuzzy description logic. Comput. Sci. Inf. Syst. **13**, 287–308 (2016)
65. OASIS Committee: Reference Architecture Foundation for Service Oriented Architecture Version 1.0 (2012). http://docs.oasis-open.org/soa-rm/soa-ra/v1.0/cs01/soa-ra-v1.0-cs01.html
66. Rafati, L., Poels, G.: Capability sourcing modeling. In: Iliadis, L., Papazoglou, M., Pohl, K. (eds.) CAiSE 2014. LNBIP, vol. 178, pp. 77–87. Springer, Cham (2014). https://doi.org/10.1007/978-3-319-07869-4_7
67. Ge, B., Hipel, K.W., Yang, K., Chen, Y.: A data-centric capability-focused approach for system-of-systems architecture modeling and analysis. Syst. Eng. **16**, 363–377 (2013)
68. Azevedo, C.L.B., Iacob, M.-E., Almeida, J.P.A., van Sinderen, M., Pires, L.F., Guizzardi, G.: Modeling resources and capabilities in enterprise architecture: a well-founded ontology-based proposal for ArchiMate. Inf. Syst. **54**, 235–262 (2015)
69. Klinkmüller, C., Ludwig, A., Franczyk, B., Kluge, R.: Visualising business capabilities in the context of business analysis. In: Abramowicz, W., Tolksdorf, R. (eds.) BIS 2010. LNBIP, vol. 47, pp. 242–253. Springer, Heidelberg (2010). https://doi.org/10.1007/978-3-642-12814-1_21
70. Kolini, F., Janczewski, L.J.: Cyber defense capability model: a foundation taxonomy. In: CONF-IRM (2015)
71. Anteroinen, J.: The holistic military capability life cycle model. In: 2012 7th International Conference on System of Systems Engineering (SoSE), pp. 167–172. IEEE, Genova (2012)
72. Malamateniou, F., Themistocleous, M., Prentza, A., Papakonstantinou, D., Vassilacopoulos, G.: A context-aware, capability-based, role-centric access control model for IoMT. In: Perego, P., Andreoni, G., Rizzo, G. (eds.) MobiHealth 2016. LNICST, vol. 192, pp. 125–131. Springer, Cham (2017). https://doi.org/10.1007/978-3-319-58877-3_16
73. Liu, L., Russell, D., Xu, J., Webster, D., Luo, Z., Venters, C., Davies, J.K.: Modelling and simulation of network enabled capability on service-oriented architecture. Simul. Model. Pract. Theory **17**, 1430–1442 (2009)
74. Baccar, S., Rouached, M., Abid, M.: A capabilities driven model for web services description and composition. Int. J. Bus. Inf. Syst. **22**, 26 (2016)
75. Object Management Group (OMG): Service oriented architecture Modeling Language (SoaML) Specification Version 1.0.1 (2012). https://www.omg.org/spec/SoaML/1.0.1/PDF
76. Feltus, C., Petit, M.: Building a responsibility model including accountability, capability and commitment. In: 2009 International Conference on Availability, Reliability and Security, pp. 412–419. IEEE, Fukuoka (2009)
77. Radeck, C., Blichmann, G., Meißner, K.: Modeling and calculating capabilities of composite web applications for assisted end user development. In: Monfort, V., Krempels, K.-H., Majchrzak, Tim A., Traverso, P. (eds.) WEBIST 2016. LNBIP, vol. 292, pp. 58–82. Springer, Cham (2017). https://doi.org/10.1007/978-3-319-66468-2_4
78. Derguech, W., Bhiri, S., Curry, E.: Using ontologies for business capability modelling: describing what services and processes achieve. Comput. J. **61**, 1075–1098 (2018)

A Process for Tailoring Domain-Specific Enterprise Architecture Maturity Models

Mart van Zwienen[1], Marcela Ruiz[1(✉)], Marlies van Steenbergen[2], and Verónica Burriel[1]

[1] Utrecht University, Princetonplein 5, 3584 CC Utrecht, The Netherlands
{m.a.vanzwienen, m.ruiz, v.burriel}@uu.nl
[2] HU University of Applied Sciences,
Padualaan 99, 3584 CH Utrecht, The Netherlands
marlies.vansteenbergen@hu.nl

Abstract. Reference architectures provide strong foundations for the implementation and development of enterprise architecture. It is common for enterprise architects to encounter the challenge of managing an increasingly complex architecture. This management can be enhanced by the application of domain-independent maturity models. Nevertheless, existing maturity models do not provide enterprise architects with metrics and domain-specific solutions to ensure a successful evolution path. This research in progress presents a process for tailoring domain-specific enterprise architecture maturity models. As a proof of concept, we chose the domain of hospitals because of the following reasons: wide variety of interdependencies and many medical disciplines with their own processes, technology, and data requirements; there is no specific maturity model for the enterprise architecture of hospitals; and there are many restrictions (e.g. governmental laws) for the medical domain which are expressed in a reference enterprise architecture. We follow a design science approach from the problem investigation to the treatment design. We conclude this paper with the results of the initial validation that has been conducted with architects from the healthcare domain.

Keywords: Enterprise architecture · Maturity models ·
Reference architecture · Metamodeling · Tailoring process

1 Introduction

Enterprise architecture (EA) is a coherent whole of principles, methods, and models that are used in the design and realization of an enterprise's organizational structure, business processes, information systems, and infrastructures [1]. EA ensures agility, consistency, compliance and efficiency for increasingly complex organizations [2]. Several maturity models and frameworks have been proposed to guide organizations to a more mature EA function [3]. In this context, more mature means better equipped to fulfill its purpose, possibly and hopefully leading to more effectivity [4].

The healthcare domain is characterized by a high level of complexity that stems from a variety of interdependencies and the presence of many medical disciplines with their own processes, technology, and data requirements [5]. It is difficult to cope with

© Springer Nature Switzerland AG 2019
I. Reinhartz-Berger et al. (Eds.): BPMDS 2019/EMMSAD 2019, LNBIP 352, pp. 196–211, 2019.
https://doi.org/10.1007/978-3-030-20618-5_14

this complexity, which is illustrated by the fact that healthcare organizations lag behind other organizations in utilizing IT [6].

Several IT maturity models are tailored to healthcare, showing that the complexity of this highly specialized domain calls for tailored maturity models [7]. However, there is not yet an enterprise architecture maturity model tailored to healthcare.

Another relevant instrument, next to maturity models, to improve the quality of the EA is a reference EA. "A reference EA is a generic EA for a class of enterprises, that is a coherent whole of EA design principles, methods and models which are used as foundation in the design and realization of the concrete EA that consists of three coherent partial architectures: the business architecture, the application architecture and the technology architecture" [8]. Ten Harmsen van der Beek, Trienekes, & Grefen [8] conclude that reference architectures can give support in coping with complexity and are the next step in maturing EA.

The aim of this research is to provide a process to tailor an EA maturity model towards a specific domain with the help of a reference EA. As proof of concept we take the healthcare domain. The scientific contribution herein is two-fold. Firstly, the main artefact of this paper is a process for tailoring an EA maturity model to a specific domain, which can be applied to other domains than healthcare as well. Secondly, the initially validated EA maturity model tailored towards hospitals itself is a contribution to healthcare maturity models.

The paper proceeds in the next section with the research design. Section 3 describes the literature review serving as background for the remainder of the paper. In Sects. 4 and 5 the tailoring process, model, and validation are presented. Finally, conclusions are presented in Sect. 6.

2 Research Design

For the development of the tailoring process, we conducted a design science project according to protocols prescribed by Wieringa [9]. Within design science, the design cycle provides a logical structure of tasks to design an artefact. These tasks are: (1) Problem investigation, (2) Treatment design and (3) Treatment validation. Figure 1 shows the implementation of the design cycle for this research in progress.

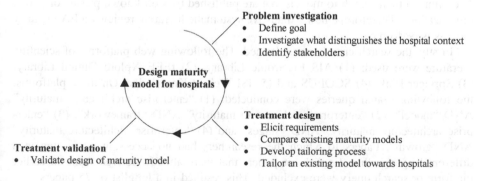

Fig. 1. Design cycle for this research in progress

Part of the goal of this research is to develop the tailoring process for the design of a maturity model for hospitals. The stakeholders are identified during the problem investigation. These stakeholders are also the experts in the semi-structured interviews for eliciting requirements during the treatment design. To tailor an existing EA maturity model towards a specific domain, first, a systematic literature review is performed to find the best fitting existing EA maturity model. The tailoring process is then developed and applied to make the model specific for the healthcare domain.

For the systematic literature review, a method is constructed by adapting the best practices from [10–12]. This resulted in the following steps: (1) define search criteria, (2) identify relevant literature, (3) backward snowballing, (4) forward snowballing and (5) synthesize data. The systematic literature review itself is presented in Sect. 3.

The treatment design step consisted of tailoring an existing maturity model. We constructed a process for integrating a reference EA in an EA maturity model and applied it. This is elaborated in Sect. 4.

To initially validate the tailoring of the EA maturity model, a focus group session is conducted. The session follows the protocol defined in [13]. The key design concepts and the execution of the focus group session are presented in Sect. 5.

3   Theoretical Background

The founder of the maturity approach in the information systems field is considered to be Richard Nolan, who was the first to propose a maturity model in 1973 [14]. In 2002, the Capability Maturity Model was published, which is recognized as a standard maturity model and provides a foundation on which a majority of the maturity models are based [3, 15]. Ross [16] introduced an architecture maturity model in 2003. Her four-stage model became a well-known EA maturity model.

To find a suitable EA maturity model as input for the tailoring, a systematic literature review is performed. Some literature reviews on EA maturity models already exist. In [3] and [17] relevant analyses of EA maturity models are shown, but do not provide a systematic approach. A more recent review from [18] is systematic but not exhaustive on maturity models, since their scope is 'post-implementation evaluation models of enterprise architecture artefacts'. In [19] the authors performed the most recent systematic review on EA maturity models but did not perform it exhaustively. They limited their search to models that are published by well-known private or public organizations. Therefore, a new exhaustive systematic literature review on EA maturity models is performed.

Firstly, the search criteria were defined. The following web platforms of scientific literature were used: (1) AIS Electronic Library, (2) IEEE Xplore Digital Library, (3) Springer Link, (4) SCOPUS and (5) ISI Web of Knowledge. On these platforms, the following search queries were conducted: (1) "enterprise architecture maturity" AND "model", (2) "enterprise architecture maturity" AND "framework", (3) "enterprise architecture maturity" AND "stages" and (4) "enterprise architecture maturity" AND "growth". Papers to which the researchers had no access, were written in a different language than English, or papers that were already derived from an earlier platform or search query were excluded. This resulted in a longlist of 75 papers.

Secondly, relevant literature was identified. For this step we used the following inclusion criteria on the 75 papers: (1) the paper introduces a new EA maturity model, (2) the paper applies an EA maturity model or (3) the paper reviews one or more EA maturity model(s). This resulted in a shortlist of 22 papers.

Thirdly, backward snowballing was performed on the shortlist. By scanning the references of the papers on the shortlist, 11 new relevant papers were identified. The inclusion criterium was that the paper should introduce an EA maturity model. 7 of the 11 papers were white-papers and were therefore not found on the scientific platforms. The other 4 did not surface because they have no mention of EA maturity in their papers. But since at least one of the 22 papers claim that these are EA maturity models, and for the sake of completeness, we included them as well.

Fourthly, forward snowballing was performed. This was only performed on papers that introduce a new EA maturity model, since we want to know whether other new EA maturity models are based on these. We used Google Scholar for the forward snow-balling. Whenever a model was cited more than 100 times, the search string "enterprise architecture maturity" was initiated within these results. From the 279 papers identified through the forward snowballing, none was relevant in the context of EA maturity models that was not already identified earlier in the review, making the review exhaustive.

Finally, the data was synthesized. For this, we adapted the criteria from [3]. The key characteristics and relevant attributes for analyzing the EA maturity models are: (1) the assessment target, (2) number of maturity levels, (3) type of model and (4) type of assessment method. The assessment target can be product-oriented or process-oriented, where product-oriented models focus on products of the enterprise architecture, and process-oriented models focus on processes involved in and around enterprise architecture [3, 20]. Models are of different types: a model can be staged, continuous, or focus area oriented [20]. A staged model has a fixed number, usually 5, of maturity levels with focus areas assigned to each maturity level. Whereas within a continuous model, the same, usually 5, maturity levels are distinguished within each focus area. The focus area oriented model usually has more overall maturity levels and each focus area has its own number of specific maturity levels. Table 1 presents a comparison of the 17 identified EA maturity models.

Earlier reviews have claimed that certain models are suitable for certain purposes. In [3] was discovered that the IT Capability Maturity Framework is capable of serving as an overarching IT maturity model. The review in [17] concluded that the Dynamic Architecture Maturity Matrix (DyAMM) is the most suitable for evaluating EA.

In literature, there are also arguments on why fixed-level maturity models like the staged and continuous models have their limitations. They are not geared to show interdependence between the processes that make up the maturity levels, leading to little guidance in increasing the maturity level [4]. On the other hand, focus area oriented models allow for a finer granularity, also in the improvement measures. These models provide better step by step guidance for improvement [20]. Also, departing from 5 fixed maturity levels makes the model more flexible in defining both focus areas and interdependencies.

Table 1. Comparison between EA maturity models

Model	Assessment target	Nr. of levels	Type of model	Type of method
Maturity Model for Effective Enterprise Architecture [21]	Product-oriented	4	Staged	None explicitly mentioned
Maturity Model based on TOGAF ADM [22]	Process-oriented	5	Staged	None explicitly mentioned
Dynamic Architecture Maturity Matrix [23]	Process- & Product-oriented	12	Focus area oriented	Scoring 136 checkpoints
TOPAZ [24]	Process-oriented	None	Continuous	250 control questions
Normalized Architecture Organization Maturity Index [25]	Process-oriented	None	Unknown	SCAMPI
Extended Enterprise Coherence-Governance Assessment [26]	Product-oriented	5	Continuous	50 gradation questions and 20 open questions
Ross' Four Stages [16]	Product-oriented	4	Staged	None explicitly mentioned
Enterprise Architecture Management Maturity Framework [27]	Product-oriented	6	Staged	None explicitly mentioned
Enterprise Architecture Maturity Model [28]	Product-oriented	5	Staged	A toolkit
IT Architecture Capability Maturity Model [29]	Product-oriented	5	Staged	A scorecard
Extended Enterprise Architecture Maturity Model [30]	Process-oriented	5	Staged	None explicitly mentioned
Enterprise Architecture Assessment Framework [31]	Product-oriented	5	Continuous	KPI's with measurable artefacts
IT Capability Maturity Framework [32]	Process- & Product-oriented	5	Staged	Questionnaire
Strategic Alignment Maturity Assessment Description [33]	Product-oriented	5	Staged	High-level process descriptions
Capability Maturity Model Integration [15]	Process-oriented	5	Staged	SCAMPI
COBIT [34]	Process-oriented	5	Staged	None explicitly mentioned
Enterprise Architecture Value Framework [35]	Product-oriented	4	Continuous	Questionnaire

The finer granularity and flexibility of the focus area oriented models provide a good basis for tailoring. Furthermore, this same granularity provides a better step by step improvement schema [20]. Therefore, we chose to use the DyAMM as existing model to serve as a basis for the tailoring.

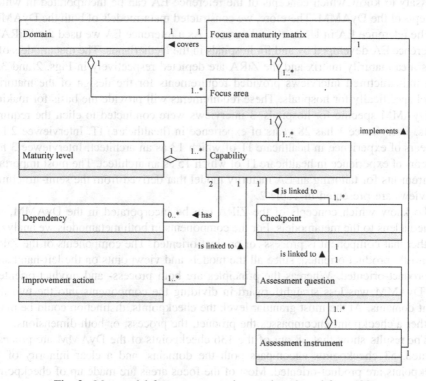

Fig. 2. Metamodel focus area maturity matrix, adapted from [20]

The metamodel of the DyAMM is presented in Fig. 2. The DyAMM is focus area oriented. It has 17 focus areas which represent the performance of the EA function in an organization. Each focus area consists of several capabilities, which represent maturity levels within the focus area. To determine whether an organization fulfills a certain capability within a focus area, checkpoints are introduced. Using the checkpoints, an architecture profile of the organization can be drawn, showing the maturity level of the organization for each focus area. Suggestions for improvement are drawn up for every capability to help organizations improve their maturity. For more detail, we refer to [36, 37].

4 The Tailoring Process

To tailor the matrix towards hospitals, we use a reference EA. This since this is the next step in maturing EA and holds valuable information about a specific domain [8]. It is necessary to know which concepts of the reference EA can be incorporated in which concepts of the DyAMM. Therefore, we constructed meta-models of both the DyAMM and the reference EA in UML class diagrams. As a reference EA we used the 'ZiRA'[1], a reference EA developed by and for hospitals in the Netherlands. The metamodels of a focus area maturity matrix and the ZiRA are depicted respectively in Figs. 2 and 3.

Semi-structured interviews provided requirements for the design of the maturity model specifically for hospitals. These requirements will provide the basis for making the DyAMM specific for hospitals. 3 interviews were conducted to elicit the requirements. Interviewee 1 has 28 years of experience in (healthcare) IT. Interviewee 2 has 18 years of experience in healthcare IT of which 13 as an architect. Interviewee 3 has 37 years of experience in healthcare IT of which 15 as an architect. The most important requirements for tailoring an EA maturity model that derived from the semi-structured interviews are presented in Table 2.

To know which concepts of the ZiRA can be incorporated in the DyAMM, we applied a lens to the metamodels. For the components in both metamodels we analyzed whether that component is process- or product-oriented. The components of the ZiRA are mostly product-oriented, since all the models and viewpoints on the left-hand side are product-oriented. Whereas the principles are both process- and product-oriented. The DyAMM was less straightforward in dividing the components into the two different domains. At the most granular level, the checkpoints, distinction could be made whether a checkpoint encompasses the product, the process, or both dimensions.

The results show that 68 out of the 136 checkpoints of the DyAMM are process-oriented. 53 checkpoints encompass both the domains, and a clear minority of 14 checkpoints are product-oriented. Most of the focus areas are made up of checkpoints that are process-oriented. Only one focus area is mostly made up of checkpoints that are product-oriented.

Table 2. Requirements for an EA maturity model specific for hospitals

Requirement	Source
The model should incorporate parts of the ZiRA	Interviews 2 & 3
The model should evaluate whether the EA is based on standard information concepts	Interview 1
The model should evaluate whether the EA is modular	Interview 1
The model should evaluate the processes involved around the enterprise architecture	Interview 3
The model should evaluate whether the hospital is interoperable in the ecosystem	Interviews 1 & 3

---

[1] https://sites.google.com/site/zirawiki/.

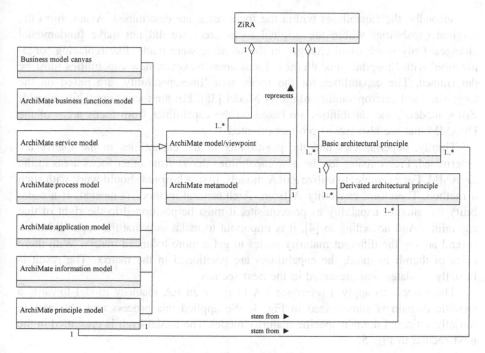

Fig. 3. Metamodel ZiRA

For the tailoring itself, the method described in [4] is used. The steps of designing a focus area maturity model are: (1) identify & scope domain, (2) determine focus areas, (3) determine capabilities, (4) determine dependencies, (5) position capabilities in matrix, (6) develop assessment instrument, (7) define improvement actions, (8) implement maturity model, (9) improve matrix iteratively and (10) communicate results. The first 5 steps are completed in this research, since these make up the scope and design of the initial model. The scope of the model is the EA of hospitals.

Firstly, the focus areas are determined. Interoperability is a main theme in the principles of the ZiRA. It also derived from the semi-structured expert interviews. The DyAMM does not contain a focus area that addresses interoperability. Interoperability was deemed too important and different to incorporate the subject in one of the existing focus areas. Therefore, the focus area 'Interoperability' is added to the model. Also, one of the requirements states that parts of the ZiRA should be incorporated. Most of the knowledge of the ZiRA is incorporated in the ArchiMate models/viewpoints. These are clearly product-oriented concepts, and only one focus area in the DyAMM is mainly oriented on EA products. This focus area however describes the management of the organization's internal architectural product, not whether an external product with its knowledge is involved. Therefore, to fulfill this requirement and to embody the knowledge from these models, we added the focus area 'Utilization of ZiRA models'. From the original focus areas of the DyAMM, none are changed. This since validation through previous research has proved the value of these focus areas [36].

Secondly, the capabilities within the focus areas are determined. Again, from the original capabilities within the original focus areas we did not make fundamental changes. Only some small changes in the wording were made, like replacing 'organization' with 'hospital'. For the new focus areas however, new capabilities must be determined. The capabilities for the focus area 'Interoperability' are based on the Organizational Interoperability Maturity Model [38]. For the focus area 'Utilization of ZiRA models', the capabilities are based on the capabilities from focus areas of the DyAMM that are also (semi) product-oriented.

Thirdly, dependencies and the positioning of the capabilities in the matrix are determined. Prerequisites for the new capabilities derive from other focus areas in the DyAMM. For example, to utilize ZiRA models, first, a hospital should work with such a method. Therefore, capability A from 'Architectural method' is needed. If a capability has another capability as prerequisite, it must be positioned to the right of that capability. And according to [4], it is important to make sure that the capabilities are spread among the different maturity scales to get a more balanced matrix. With these rules of thumb in mind, the capabilities are positioned in the matrix. The result is initially validated and presented in the next section.

The process to apply a reference EA to tailor an EA maturity model towards a specific domain is summarized in Fig. 4. We applied this process and obtained an initially validated domain-specific maturity model. The model itself is presented in the next section in Fig. 5.

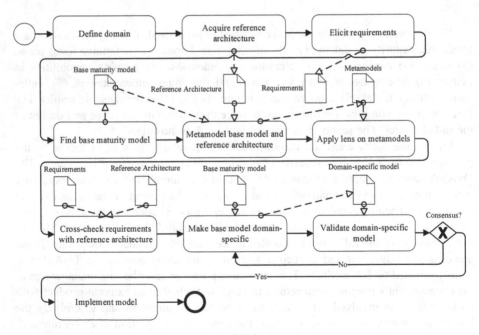

Fig. 4. The tailoring process

5 Initial Validation: A Focus Group Session

We conducted a focus group to initially validate the maturity model as a result from the tailoring process. This initial validation was conducted with the intention to refine the tailoring process and collect evidence on the potential acceptance of the resulting maturity model by architects in the healthcare domain. For the focus group, we follow the protocol prescribed by [13]. The following key design concepts must be defined: (1) the goal of the focus group, (2) the selection of participants, (3) the number of participants, (4) the selection of the facilitator, (5) the information recording facilities and (6) the protocol of the focus group. The goal of this focus group is to gain consensus about whether the execution of the tailoring process, which resulted in additions to the DyAMM, are relevant for assessing the EA maturity of a hospital. The selection of participants was completed from a community of architects in the healthcare domain. An open invite was sent to the community with the following criteria to join: the participant must be a professional who has been working with architecture with at least 3 years of experience in healthcare. From the open invite, 7 participants emerged. Two of them did not meet the criteria to join. However, we did let them participate in the focus group session, since including non-typical participants reduces researcher bias, i.e. the effects of the participants on the researcher [39]. Table 3 shows demographic information about the participants.

Table 3. Participants of the focus group session

Participant	Function	Years of experience in healthcare IT
1	Information architect	10
2	Information architect	25
3	Solution architect	5
4	Enterprise architect	8
5	Data architect	20
6	Freelancer	0
7	Business analyst	2

The main researcher acted as facilitator, since he was most involved in creating the model. The audio was recorded, transcribed and coded in NVivo as means of the information recording facility. Lastly, the protocol of the session was based on the additions made to the DyAMM. For both the new focus areas and all its capabilities, it was asked whether the participants think that that focus area or capability was relevant for assessing the EA maturity of a hospital. They were asked to write on a post-it whether they were positive, negative, or had no opinion about the addition. Whenever there was no unanimous result, a discussion was held to gain consensus about that focus area or capability. After this post-it session, the participants were asked whether they agreed with the checkpoints within each capability.

The results show that the participants unanimously agreed with the focus area 'Interoperability', but that there was some disagreement about the capabilities. It became clear during the discussion that these disagreements mostly involved the phrasing rather than the content. Consensus was reached with choosing the proper phrasing for every capability and its description.

There was no unanimous agreement for the focus area 'Utilization of ZiRA models'. This because some of the participants desired a more generic focus area. One that is not specifically about ZiRA models but also about other domain specific aiding tools. Consensus was reached to change the focus area to a more generic focus area. The first two capabilities within the focus area, were unanimously agreed upon. On the last capability, C, there was another discussion and eventually consensus on the phrasing. Finally, the participants provided some checkpoints from the new focus areas which they also wanted to discuss. There was consensus to remove two checkpoints. Consensus was also reached to change the content of two checkpoints to make them more generic.

Table 4 shows the new focus areas and their capabilities, as initially validated through the focus group session.

Table 4. Capabilities for the new focus areas

Capability	Description
Focus area 'Interoperability'	
A	Ad hoc, limited frameworks are in place which allow for ad hoc interoperability arrangements
B	Collaborative, recognized frameworks are in place to support collaborative interoperability
C	Integrated, shared information services and shared goals on all layers provide integrated interoperability
D	Integral, interoperating by design on a continuing basis makes integral interoperability
Focus area 'Utilization of best-practices'	
A	Ad hoc, when making new architectural products, best-practices are occasionally utilized
B	Structural, best-practices are structurally utilized when making and managing architectural products
C	Embedded, best-practices are embedded in managing the architectural products

The checkpoints of the new focus areas, as formed after validation in the focus group session, are presented in Table 5.

Figure 5 shows the initially validated EA maturity matrix for hospitals. For the descriptions of the capabilities and checkpoints of the original focus areas of the DyAMM, we refer to [37]. The purpose of this figure is to give an indication on how the model looks. The model is not fully elaborated in this paper since the main artefact of this paper is the tailoring process.

Table 5. Checkpoints for the new focus areas

Capability	Checkpoint
Focus area 'Interoperability'	
A	Agreements on interoperability have been made with stakeholders in the ecosystem
A	The architects from involved healthcare organizations do not hesitate to get in touch with one another
B	Message exchange with some stakeholders in the ecosystem is based on standards (e.g. HL7 CDA, HL7 FHIR)
B	Clear agreements are made on which kind of data is exchanged with stakeholders in the ecosystem
C	Exchange of information with stakeholders within the ecosystem is based on established standards
C	The architects from involved healthcare organizations effectively communicate with each other regarding relevant developments in the architectural area
D	Systems store and share information only based on established standards
D	Systems are integrated cross-sector throughout the ecosystem
Focus area 'Utilization of best-practices'	
A	The architects are familiar with the relevant best-practices (e.g. the ZiRA)
A	Best-practices are used as inspiration for the hospital's architectural products
B	The architectural products of the hospital can be linked to best-practices
B	When developing architectural products, best-practices are used as a basis and deviations are substantiated
C	All relevant best-practices are embedded in the architectural products of the hospital

#	Focus Area	0	1	2	3	4	5	6	7	8	9	10	11	12
1	Development of architecture		A			B			C					
2	Use of architecture			A			B				C			
3	Alignment with business strategy		A			B					C			
4	Alignment with realisation			A				B			C			
5	Relationship to the As-Is state					A				B				
6	Responsibilities and authorities				A		B					C		
7	Alignment with change portfolio				A				B		C			
8	Monitoring				A		B		C					
9	Quality assurance								A		B		C	
10	Management of the architectural process							A		B		C		
11	Management of the architectural products					A			B					C
12	Commitment and motivation		A					B		C				
13	Implementation of the architectural role				A		B		C				D	
14	Architectural method				A					B			C	
15	Interaction and collaboration			A		B				C				
16	Architectural tools							A				B		C
17	Budget and planning						A					B		C
18	Interoperability			A			B			C			D	
19	Utilizing domain-specific best-practices						A				B			C

Fig. 5. The EA maturity model for hospitals

5.1 Validity

To increase the validity of the focus group session, some of the methods described in [39] were applied. The participants of the focus group session all worked at different healthcare organizations. This is a form of data source triangulation which increases the legitimation of the evidence. There is an audit trail in place to increase validity as well. Firstly, the raw audio records are available. Secondly, coding the transcription in NVivo provided unitized information.

An inherent validity threat is the researcher bias, since the facilitator was also the main researcher. This bias can and has been reduced by making the researcher's intentions clear at the start of the focus group session and by including non-typical participants [39]. Another validity threat can occur amongst the participants, where they peer pressure each other into a certain decision. This threat was avoided by selecting a heterogeneous sample where none of participants know one another. Also, by letting the participants first write their opinion on a post-it before starting the discussion this threat was reduced.

6 Conclusions

In this paper, we present a process to apply a reference EA for tailoring a domain-specific EA maturity model. This process is executed on the healthcare domain. Therefore, the contribution of this paper is two-fold. The main contribution is this process with the intention to facilitate the tailoring of EA maturity models towards a specific domain with the help of a reference EA. The second contribution is the initially validated maturity model for hospitals, which is a contribution in the field of maturity models for healthcare.

Applying a lens to the metamodels of the reference EA and the base EA maturity model was beneficial. It showed which concepts of the metamodels have similarities and are therefore fit for integration. Especially architectural principles showed to be fit for integration. By using requirements from semi-structured expert interviews, it was ensured that the right alterations were made to the DyAMM, the base model. A more rigorous model was then derived by validating the design through a focus group session with experts.

There are some limitations to this research. Although the model has been initially validated in a focus group, it has not yet been implemented within a hospital. This is a venue for further research, to see whether the model is able to assist in maturing the EA of a hospital. Another limitation is the fact that the alterations to the model are not validated by maturity model experts. A validation with experts in using the DyAMM for example would result in an even more rigorous model. We consider all these aspects as part of our future research endeavors.

Another suggestion for further research is to apply the process to a different domain than healthcare. This will show whether the process is indeed applicable to other domains as well.

References

1. Lankhorst, M.: Enterprise Architecture at Work. Springer, Berlin (2017). https://doi.org/10.1007/978-3-642-29651-2
2. Winter, R., Fischer, R.: Essential layers, artifacts, and dependencies of enterprise architecture. In: 2006 10th IEEE International Enterprise Distributed Object Computing Conference Workshops (EDOCW 2006). IEEE (2006)
3. Meyer, M., Helfert, M., O'Brien, C.: An analysis of enterprise architecture maturity frameworks. In: Grabis, J., Kirikova, M. (eds.) BIR 2011. LNBIP, vol. 90, pp. 167–177. Springer, Heidelberg (2011). https://doi.org/10.1007/978-3-642-24511-4_13
4. van Steenbergen, M., Bos, R., Brinkkemper, S., van de Weerd, I., Bekkers, W.: The design of focus area maturity models. In: Winter, R., Zhao, J.L., Aier, S. (eds.) DESRIST 2010. LNCS, vol. 6105, pp. 317–332. Springer, Heidelberg (2010). https://doi.org/10.1007/978-3-642-13335-0_22
5. Gebre-Mariam, M., Bygstad, B.: The organizational ripple effect of IT architecture in healthcare. In: Proceedings of Twenty-Fourth European Conference on Information System (2016)
6. Romanow, D., Cho, S., Straub, D.: Riding the wave: past trends and future directions for health IT research. MIS Q. **36**, iii–x (2012)
7. Carvalho, J.V., Rocha, Á., Abreu, A.: Maturity models of healthcare information systems and technologies: a literature review. J. Med. Syst. **40**, 1–10 (2016)
8. ten Harmsen van der Beek, W., Trienekens, J., Grefen, P.: The application of enterprise reference architecture in the financial industry. In: Aier, S., Ekstedt, M., Matthes, F., Proper, E., Sanz, J.L. (eds.) PRET/TEAR -2012. LNBIP, vol. 131, pp. 93–110. Springer, Heidelberg (2012). https://doi.org/10.1007/978-3-642-34163-2_6
9. Wieringa, R.J.: Design Science Methodology. Springer, Heidelberg (2014). https://doi.org/10.1007/978-3-662-43839-8
10. Webster, J., Watson, R.T.: Analyzing the past to prepare for the future: writing a literature review. MIS Q. **26**, xiii–xxiii (2002)
11. Wohlin, C.: Guidelines for snowballing in systematic literature studies and a replication in software engineering. In: Proceedings of the 18th International Conference on Evaluation and Assessment in Software Engineering - EASE 2014, pp. 1–10. ACM Press, New York (2014)
12. Tranfield, D., Denyer, D., Smart, P.: Towards a methodology for developing evidence-informed management knowledge by means of systematic review. Br. J. Manag. **14**, 207–222 (2003)
13. Morgan, D.L.: Focus Groups as Qualitative Research. Sage Publications, Thousand Oaks (1996)
14. Nolan, R.L.: Managing the computer resource: a stage hypothesis. Commun. ACM **16**, 399–405 (1973)
15. Chrissis, M.B., Konrad, M., Shrum, S.: CMMI Guidelines for Process Integration and Product Improvement. Addison-Wesley, Boston (2003)
16. Ross, J.W.: Creating a Strategic IT Architecture Competency: Learning in Stages. MIT Sloan Working Paper No. 4314-03; Cent. Inf. Syst. Res. Working Paper No. 335 (2003)
17. Lakhrouit, J., Baïna, K.: State of the art of the maturity models to an evaluation of the enterprise architecture. In: 3rd International Symposium on ISKO-Maghreb, pp. 1–8 (2013)
18. Nikpay, F., Ahmad, R., Rouhani, B.D., Shamshirband, S.: A systematic review on post-implementation evaluation models of enterprise architecture artefacts. Inf. Syst. Front. 1–20 (2016)

19. Vallerand, J., Lapalme, J., Moïse, A.: Analysing enterprise architecture maturity models: a learning perspective. Enterp. Inf. Syst. **11**, 859–883 (2017)
20. van Steenbergen, M., Bos, R., Brinkkemper, S., van de Weerd, I., Bekkers, W.: Improving IS functions step by step: the use of focus area maturity models. Scand. J. Inf. Syst. **25**, 35–56 (2013)
21. Robertson, E., Peko, G., Sundaram, D.: Enterprise architecture maturity: a crucial link in business and IT alignment. In: PACIS 2018 Proceedings (2018)
22. Proenca, D., Borbinha, J.: Enterprise architecture: a maturity model based on TOGAF ADM. In: Proceedings - 2017 IEEE 19th Conference on Business Informatics, vol. 1, pp. 257–266 (2017)
23. van Steenbergen, M., van den Berg, M., Brinkkemper, S.: A balanced approach to developing the enterprise architecture practice. In: Filipe, J., Cordeiro, J., Cardoso, J. (eds.) ICEIS 2007. LNBIP, vol. 12, pp. 240–253. Springer, Heidelberg (2008). https://doi.org/10.1007/978-3-540-88710-2_19
24. Sobczak, A.: Methods of the assessment of enterprise architecture practice maturity in an organization. In: Kobyliński, A., Sobczak, A. (eds.) BIR 2013. LNBIP, vol. 158, pp. 104–111. Springer, Heidelberg (2013). https://doi.org/10.1007/978-3-642-40823-6_9
25. van der Raadt, B., van Vliet, H.: Assessing the efficiency of the enterprise architecture function. In: Proper, E., Harmsen, F., Dietz, J.L.G. (eds.) PRET 2009. LNBIP, vol. 28, pp. 63–83. Springer, Heidelberg (2009). https://doi.org/10.1007/978-3-642-01859-6_5
26. Wagter, R., Proper, H.A., Witte, D.: The extended enterprise coherence-governance assessment. In: Aier, S., Ekstedt, M., Matthes, F., Proper, E., Sanz, J.L. (eds.) PRET/TEAR - 2012. LNBIP, vol. 131, pp. 218–235. Springer, Heidelberg (2012). https://doi.org/10.1007/978-3-642-34163-2_13
27. United States Government Accountability Office: Organizational Transformation: A Framework for Assessing and Improving Enterprise Architecture Management (Version 2.0) (2010)
28. National Association of State Chief Information Officers: NASCIO Enterprise Architecture Maturity Model, Version 1.3 (2003)
29. United States Department of Commerce: Enterprise Architecture Capability Maturity Model, Version 2.0 (2007)
30. Schekkerman, J.: Extended Enterprise Architecture Maturity Model: Support Guide (Version 2.0) (2006)
31. Executive Office of the President of the US - Office of Management and Budget: Improving Agency Performance Using Information and Information Technology (Enterprise Architecture Assessment Framework v3.1) (2009)
32. Curley, M.: Introducing an IT capability maturity framework. In: Filipe, J., Cordeiro, J., Cardoso, J. (eds.) ICEIS 2007. LNBIP, vol. 12, pp. 63–78. Springer, Heidelberg (2008). https://doi.org/10.1007/978-3-540-88710-2_6
33. Luftman, J.: Assessing business-IT alignment maturity. Commun. Assoc. Inf. Syst. **4**, 1–51 (2000)
34. ISACA: COBIT 2019 Framework: Introduction and Methodology (2018)
35. Plessius, H., Slot, R., Pruijt, L.: On the categorization and measurability of enterprise architecture benefits with the enterprise architecture value framework. In: Aier, S., Ekstedt, M., Matthes, F., Proper, E., Sanz, J.L. (eds.) PRET/TEAR -2012. LNBIP, vol. 131, pp. 79–92. Springer, Heidelberg (2012). https://doi.org/10.1007/978-3-642-34163-2_5

36. van Steenbergen, M., Schipper, J., Bos, R., Brinkkemper, S.: The dynamic architecture maturity matrix: instrument analysis and refinement. In: Dan, A., Gittler, F., Toumani, F. (eds.) ICSOC/ServiceWave -2009. LNCS, vol. 6275, pp. 48–61. Springer, Heidelberg (2010). https://doi.org/10.1007/978-3-642-16132-2_5
37. van den Berg, M., van Steenbergen, M.: Building an Enterprise Architecture Practice. Springer, Dordrecht (2006). https://doi.org/10.1007/978-1-4020-5606-2
38. Clark, T., Jones, R.: Organisational interoperability maturity model for C2. In: Proceedings of 1999 Command Control Research and Technology Symposium (1999)
39. Onwuegbuzie, A.J., Leech, N.L.: Validity and qualitative research: an oxymoron? Qual. Quant. **41**, 233–249 (2007)

Ontology-Driven Enterprise Modeling: A Plugin for the Protégé Platform

Benedikt Reitemeyer[1P](✉) and Hans-Georg Fill[2]

[1] Nuremberg, Germany
[2] Department of Informatics - Digitalization and Information Systems Group,
University of Fribourg, Fribourg, Switzerland
hans-georg.fill@unifr.ch

Abstract. The use of ontologies for enterprise modeling has been discussed from different perspectives in the past. In the paper at hand we describe design options for creating enterprise models by using an ontology as a shared domain conceptualization connected through ontology-driven conceptual modeling. The enterprise models thus act as representations of ontology instances. As a major benefit, a coupling between the visual representations of enterprise models and the reasoning capabilities that are typically available for ontologies can be achieved. In addition, we describe options for the realization of such an approach, which ideally builds upon existing platforms for enabling re-use and interoperability. Finally, we present an open-source implementation as a Protégé plugin to show the technical feasibility and its application to a use case in the area of enterprise modeling.

Keywords: Enterprise modeling · Ontologies · System design

1 Introduction

Today, enterprises are confronted with large amounts of data, information, and knowledge that they need to process and manage [31,37]. This concerns for example the analysis of data generated by sensors and engines in production environments, the interpretation of information from various enterprise resource planning systems or the representation of knowledge about business processes and organizational structures [28]. In order to support human actors confronted with these challenges, it is aimed for IT-based solutions that permit the representation, analysis and interpretation of these entities by machines. In this context, techniques developed in conceptual enterprise modeling, Enterprise Ontologies (EO) as well as in information visualization have been found to be beneficial [8,15,35]. Whereas conceptual models (CM) have traditionally focused on improving human understanding and communication by providing semi-formal, visual modeling languages, ontologies in the sense of formal knowledge representation are directed towards machine processing and automated reasoning [34,40].

© Springer Nature Switzerland AG 2019
I. Reinhartz-Berger et al. (Eds.): BPMDS 2019/EMMSAD 2019, LNBIP 352, pp. 212–226, 2019.
https://doi.org/10.1007/978-3-030-20618-5_15

In addition, techniques in information visualization are used to amplify the cognition of information and knowledge [8].

As interface between conceptual modeling and ontologies, the concept of ontology-driven conceptual modeling (ODCM) has evolved aiming on the use of ontological theories for the improvement of conceptual modeling [20].

Although CMs and visualizations share the aspect of graphical representations, they fundamentally differ on the level of semantics. Due to the underlying schema in the form of a modeling language, CMs may be interpreted by machines, at least to a certain extent [4]. In contrast, information visualizations are directed towards human interpretation only and their elements typically have no formal meaning assigned. An exception are visualizations of ontologies, e.g. as available via plugins for ontology editors such as Protégé. Furthermore, information visualizations are generated through algorithms with no or limited editing capabilities for the underlying information structures, whereas CMs may either be created and edited by humans or generated automatically [34,37]. In summary, CMs have the advantage of a visual representation and analysis of knowledge and information structures, ontologies enable machine processing and reasoning based on formal axioms and information visualization targets the analysis of data by amplifying cognition. It thus seems beneficial to investigate ways of how the benefits of these three directions can be joined. This applies both to the design of according solutions as well as their technical realization. In the following we will thus propose design options for what we will call *ontology-based enterprise modeling* and outline how these options can be implemented.

The remainder of the paper is structured as follows. In Sect. 2, some fundamental terms will be defined to achieve a common understanding. Section 3 shows possible technical realization options. Subsequently, an example implementation of a realization option is shown in Sect. 4. In Sect. 5, a practical use case of the approach is discussed. Benefits and drawbacks of our approach are evaluated in Sect. 6. The paper ends with a brief outlook and conclusion in Sect. 7.

2 Foundations

In this section we will briefly explain some fundamental terms regarding conceptual models, visualizations, and ontologies in order to achieve a common foundation for the following elaborations.

2.1 Conceptual Models and Visualizations

CMs and visualizations differ in several aspects, which shall be outlined according to the dimensions *syntax, identity, semantics*, and *machine interpretability* - see also Table 1. First, CMs - in the way we regard them here - are language-based. They depend on a system of symbols and rules for the combination of those symbols, i.e. a grammar or syntax [23,39]. For CMs, the syntax is typically defined in a formal language to ensure its exact interpretation [4]. In contrast, the syntax of visualizations depends on their implementation. If a visualization is constructed using vector graphics, at least the graphical representation and the rules for its composition are based on a formal specification, which can be viewed as a kind of syntax. Otherwise, when pixel graphics are used for their representation, there exists no formal structure at all [10].

Furthermore, elements and relations in CMs have an identity. They can always be distinguished from other elements based on unique identifiers, which permits to modify them individually. Elements in information visualizations do not need to be uniquely identified. Although they may be associated to certain data values that may or may not be unique, they typically need not be individually accessible and modifiable.

While the syntax defines fundamental structures and the way these may be created, its major purpose is to assign semantics, i.e. meaning, to these structures. Here, a large difference between CMs and visualizations exists. Whereas CMs are based on schemata that carry meaning a-priori - either formally defined or given in natural language - information visualizations are directed towards human interpretation, where meaning is assigned to graphical elements as needed, i.e. ex-post. This leads to implications for machine processing. When constructing algorithms for interpreting content, it is considerably easier to do so for CMs due to their grammar and fixed meaning than for information visualizations [4].

Table 1. Differences between conceptual models and visualizations.

	Conceptual models	Visualizations
Syntax	Formal	Formal in case of vector graphics; None in case of pixel graphics
Formal Semantics	Optional	None
Identity of elements and relations	Yes	No
Machine interpretability	Yes, depending on the level of formality	Typically not, only directed towards humans

2.2 Ontology-Driven Conceptual Modeling

Ontology-driven conceptual modeling can be explained as a conceptual connection between conceptual modeling languages (CML) and ontologies. Whereas different kinds of CMLs and ontologies are combined, ODCM approaches can be characterized by different kinds of phenomena: *static phenomena, dynamic phenomena,* and *behavioral and functional phenomena* [44].

In a common definition, ODCM is described as the application of ontological theories, based on broader ontological areas as formal ontology, cognitive science or philosophical logics. Those theories are practically applied in areas such as the development of engineering artifacts, improving the theory, or conceptual modeling [20].

More concretely, various ontology-driven CMs based on different ontology types have been developed, e.g. in the area of foundational ontologies, business and EOs, database design and architecture, or software systems development and architecture [44]. One of the most used foundational ontologies is the Bunge-Wand-Weber (BWW) ontology which was developed to illustrate an information system and provides definitions of important concepts like system, subsystem, and coupling [45]. While the BWW ontology is very high-level, there are more concrete ODCM approaches like the Unified Foundational Ontology (UFO) which has been constructed, aiming on both, improvement of conceptual modeling as theoretically discipline and improvement of practical implications and is used as basis for e.g. OntoUML [3,22] or the UEML approach that puts the BWW into practical use [35]. UFO itself instead aims on improving the semantics of CMLs and not on improving the semantics of specific models.

In a meta study, Verdonck and Gailly [44] count the frequency of scientific appearances of different ontologies and CMLs in ODCM and classify them in terms of their perspective. They distinguish between a *static*, *dynamic*, and *behavioral and functional* perspective. Phenomena in the static perspective describe the structure of a system, such as entity, thing or objects. In contrast, phenomena in the dynamic perspective represent change and time. Lastly, phenomena in the behavioral and functional perspective are social phenomena and states with transitions between them.

2.3   Conceptual Enterprise Models and Enterprise Ontologies

Conceptual models and information visualization can represent enterprise knowledge and information mainly directed to human processing. In contrast, ontologies, as formal representations of knowledge, offer machine processability. Therefore, the differences between CMs and ontologies especially in the enterprise knowledge context must be considered. For our distinction of enterprise models and enterprise ontologies, the dimensions *purpose and goals*, *formal foundation*, *adequacy for automated reasoning*, *inherent visual representation*, and *human-adequate structuring* are considered (see Table 2).

Conceptual enterprise modeling concerns the creation of integrated enterprise models and sub-models which aim at capturing enterprise aspects required for the modeling purpose. Aspects captured by CMs are for instance processes, business rules, or concepts (e.g. information, vision, goals, and actors). Based on those aspects, current and future states of the enterprise are described. Additionally, the conceptual enterprise models contain the enterprise knowledge of the stakeholders which are involved in the modeling process [6]. Conceptual enterprise modeling methods in our understanding are for example the Business Modeling and Notation (BPMN), ArchiMate, or Multi Perspective Enterprise Modelling (MEMO) [16,27].

Ontologies are characterized as "a shared and common understanding of some domain that can be communicated across people and computers" [40, p. 186]. They are represented formally and require capabilities of underlying formal axioms for reasoning and inferences to detect new knowledge [19]. To measure the quality of an ontology various criteria are suggested, e.g. clarity, consistency, accuracy or applicability [7,18,42]. The ontology quality can impact what can be achieved within the reasoning. In an enterprise context, ontologies have the purpose to acquire, represent, and manipulate knowledge based on a formal description of the deep structure behind the surface of an enterprise [9,43]. Examples for enterprise ontologies are TOVE (TOronto Virtual Enterprise) ontology [14] and the Unified Foundational Ontology (UFO) [21].

As we have already shown in Sect. 2, CMs are formally language-based. Conceptual enterprise models, as a specialization of CMs, are therefore language-based as well. Beneath the language-base, the meta meta models and metamodels are used for structuring conceptual enterprises hierarchically. Metamodels and meta meta models are created with own modeling languages, which describe the components of the underlying level. In this way, different abstraction levels of models are formalized.

The formal foundation of ontologies is based on formal languages as well. Various languages like the Resource Description Framework (RDF), DAML+OIL or the Web Ontology Language (OWL) are used for defining ontologies [1,29,32]. In this paper we will limit our focus to OWL, because of its widespread use in ontology engineering and design, and its standardization. OWLClasses are groups of individuals that belong together, because they share properties. Therefore, OWLProperties are needed to state the relationship between individuals or from individuals to data values. Individuals are instances of classes.

Our third dimension for the differentiation of conceptual enterprise models and EOs is the adequacy for automated reasoning. Wang et al. [46] differ between ontological reasoning, which is based on a set of first-order formulas specified through description logic, and user-defined reasoning, which allows users to define their own reasoning rules, e.g. the Semantic Web Rule Language (SWRL) [26]. Therefore, EOs, due to their use of description logics, are adequate for automated reasoning, while conceptual enterprise models are typically not.

For conceptual enterprise models an inherent visual representation is defined by the graphical notation, as well as the ordering rules in terms of the syntax. In contrast, for EOs those inherent visual representations don't exist, despite various approaches in terms of information visualization for ontologies. As EOs are directed towards machine processing, they don't need an inherent visual representation or human-adequate structure. Conceptual enterprise models are directed to human understanding and therefore are human-adequate structured, based on an inherent visual representation.

In enterprise context exist various approaches either for conceptual enterprise models, as well as for EOs. As the analysis of this section showed, both, conceptual enterprise models and EOs, aim for representing enterprise context. Conceptual enterprise models aim for the human-adequate construction of integrated

Table 2. Differences between conceptual enterprise models and EOs.

	Conceptual enterprise models	Enterprise ontologies
Purpose and goals	Integrated enterprise models and submodels for human understanding	Acquire, represent and manipulate machine processable knowledge
Formal foundations	Semi-formal	Formal
Adequacy for automated reasoning	Typically not	Yes
Inherent visual representation	Yes	No
Human-adequate structuring	Model/diagram types	No

enterprise models, based on an inherent visual representation. In contrast, EOs target the acquisition, representation and manipulation of enterprise knowledge, based on a formal foundation, which is machine-processable and appropriate for automated reasoning. Further, the occurring enterprise phenomena can be described from different perspectives, helping to close the knowledge gap between users and modelers. Trying to use the benefits of both concepts, in Sect. 3 different realization options for ontology-based enterprise modeling are developed.

3   Possible Realization Options for a Technical Realization

Based on the presented considerations, several options for an enterprise ODCM software application are possible. In this section those options are discussed, based on *ontology editors*, *enterprise modeling editors* and *hybrid editors*, which combine conceptual modeling and additional semantic information. Subsequently, the options are discussed, and a new approach is introduced. The research method used for this section is argumentative-deductive reasoning [48].

3.1   Ontology Editors

For classifying different ontology editors' various characteristics, such as editing, and browsing are used [47]. As the focus of our work is on *conceptual modeling* and *visualization*, the characterization of the ontology editors focus on those two dimensions and further on the ability of generating knowledge through *reasoning*, and the structure of the foundational *domain knowledge* and *modeling knowledge* - see also Table 3. The characterization includes the editors themselves and additionally possible extensions (e.g. plugins).

Several open-source and commercial ontology editors exist in science and practice. Well-known and widespread editors are for example *Protégé*[1], *TopBraid*

---

[1] https://protege.stanford.edu/.

Composer[2], and *OntoStudio*[3]. The probably most known and used ontology editor is Protégé. Protégé is an open-source platform, offering various plugins [33]. It offers extensive functionality, including visual representation of the developed ontologies, but currently lacks the ability of visually modeling ontologies. The commercial ontology editor TopBraid Composer is based on the Eclipse platform and therefore offers many features and plugins as well [41]. It offers ontology visualization functionalities and the capability of modeling ontologies in an UML-like style. The third example for an ontology editor is OntoStudio which is as well based on the Eclipse platform [47]. OntoStudio and its plugins offer visualization functionality but miss the ability of modeling ontologies.

3.2   Enterprise Modeling Editors

Beneath investigating ontology editors in terms of their modeling functionality, enterprise modeling editors can be investigated in terms of their ontology use. Many different enterprise modeling editors such as the MID Innovator, ADOit, or Sparx Systems Enterprise Architect are used. As far as we investigated, there are currently no full enterprise modeling tools which are based on the ODCM approach. For individual CMLs, approaches and implementations for ODCM-related editors can be found. For example, Benevides and Guizzardi [3] developed an editor for conceptual modeling and ontology engineering. While there are few ODCM editors, still several approaches for connecting CMs and ontologies in a hybrid way are developed.

3.3   Hybrid Editors

Hybrid editors are based on *semantic lifting*, which is defined as "the process of associating content items with suitable semantic objects as metadata to turn unstructured content items into semantic knowledge resources" [2]. Hinkelmann et al. [24] explain various ways for the application of semantic lifting on meta-models referencing different research projects. A practical implementation of the semantic lifting approach is realized in the SeMFIS tool based on the ADOxx platform [11,12]. SeMFIS is an editor for semantic annotations of CMs. It is based on various sets of meta models which enable the visual representation of ontologies and semantic annotations as models [13].

3.4   Comparison

In summary, Ontology editors offer the ability to visual represent knowledge, but have limited ability for the creation of models. They enable reasoning on formal domain knowledge. In contrast, modeling editors offer the ability of creating models and visual representations but have typically no capability for reasoning

---

[2] https://www.topquadrant.com/tools/modeling-topbraid-composer-standard-edition/.

[3] http://www.semafora-systems.com/en/products/ontostudio/.

on the resulting models. Lastly, hybrid editors, enable the visual representation of knowledge, modeling, and reasoning over the results. The domain knowledge is added with semantic lifting in a formal way - see Table 3 for summarizing these results.

Table 3. Comparison of characteristics of ontology, modeling and hybrid editors.

	Ontology editors	Modeling editors	Hybrid editors
Visualization	Yes	Yes	Yes
Modeling	Partly	Yes	Yes
Reasoning	Yes	No	Yes
Domain knowledge	Formal	Informal	Formal
Modeling knowledge	None	Informal	Informal

Relating to the targets described in Sect. 2, creating knowledge that is human and machine-processable and closing the knowledge gap between users and modelers and between modelers we propose a new realization option combining the best of both, ontology editors and modeling editors. For the new approach, the domain knowledge and modeling knowledge are represented as ontologies and combined through mapping, thereby enabling the machine-processing with reasoning functions of ontology editors and creating a common knowledge base for users and modelers. This idea extends the approach of Hinkelmann et al. [25] of ontology-based metamodeling in which ontological metamodels are extended with graphical notations. In addition, a modeling function should be added for the creation of CMs, making modeling and the processing of knowledge by human stakeholders possible. The approach is the realization of the ODCM idea of combining ontologies and CMs.

After the theoretical description of the possible existing realization options and a new realization approach, Sect. 4 introduces the technical realization of the approach, describing our approach as a Protégé-Plugin.

4 Realization as a Plugin of the Protégé Ontology Platform

In this section we describe the implementation of the previously introduced approach in terms of the *Ontological Foundation*, *Technical Foundation*, and *Modeling Mechanism* as a plugin for Protégé platform. The research method used for the development and evaluation of the plugin was prototyping [48].

The approach is based on an ontological foundation consisting of a domain ontology illustrating the technical domain of an enterprise, department, or market sector and a modeling ontology containing the entities and relations of a CML and their necessary attributes like the graphical representation. Both ontologies are implemented in OWL due to its widespread use. The idea is to offer an approach which is as generic as possible to be able to implement various CMLs. While similar approaches like the Meta Object Facility (MOF) [5] and ECore [38] exists, we develop our approach based on the ADOxx meta meta model [12]. Therefore, the modeling ontology is designed based on the meta constructs *model type*, *class*, *relation class* and *attribute* which are stored as OWL classes. Model types like BPMN or UML diagrams contain classes and relation classes. Classes have types like events, activities or gateways depending on the modeling language. Relation classes connect classes. Classes and relation classes can have attributes related through OWL object properties. Attributes for the graphical representation are used for creating the toolbar of the plugin. For relation classes, the OWL object properties *hasStartClass* and *hasEndClass* can be defined and related to class elements with object property assertions. Based on this generic template, the properties of different CMLs can be defined and are created while initializing the toolbar view.

Several options for the technical implementation were considered. Three general implementation options seemed reasonable: a. extend an ontology editor, b. extend a modeling editor or c. create a proprietary software combining the ontology and the modeling concepts. As implementing a new proprietary software is a complex task demanding deep knowledge on either ontology development and modeling, the problem was limited to the decision on extending either an ontology editor or a modeling editor. Based on the idea of using two ontologies, one for the domain knowledge and one for the modeling knowledge, it has been chosen to follow option a. by extending an ontology editor.

The decision for a plugin based on Protégé platform was made, because of its wide use and its openness for external plugins. The plugin is implemented with JAVA, the Graphical User Interfaces (GUI) are designed and realized with JavaFX[4]. They were designed sparsely first, but in a way, they can be extended easily. The plugin is embedded in Protégé as separate Protégé Tab containing a *toolbar view* and a *canvas view* (Fig. 1). The toolbar view contains the modeling language classes and relations as specified in the modeling ontology, which can be added to the canvas view in terms of the modeling process.

The two ontologies approach demands a way of mapping the domain ontology and the modeling ontology for connecting the domain knowledge and the modeling representation. Hinkelmann et al. [24] distinguishes between automated and human-interpreted semantically enrichment of meta models. Our approach uses the human-interpreted approach for adding semantical information in the modeling process. While creating a new modeling entity, a name entered, and a class of the domain ontology must be selected. In the process of adding the graphical element to the canvas, additionally an OWL Individual is created, added to the domain ontology and classified regarding the class that was selected during the modeling procedure. As well, it is annotated with the suiting graphical representation. When a relation between two model elements is created, a name must be entered, and an object property of the domain ontology must be selected. While being added to the canvas an object property assertion to the start element of the relation is made which enables reasoning on the model elements.

---

[4] The plugin is available at https://github.com/benediktreitemeyer/onbacomo.

In this way, the reasoning capabilities for OWL that are provided through Protégé and its external reasoners can be directly applied, e.g. to additionally classify elements of models based on their properties or to apply rules, e.g. using the Semantic Web Rule Language, which could also be specified visually, cf. [36].

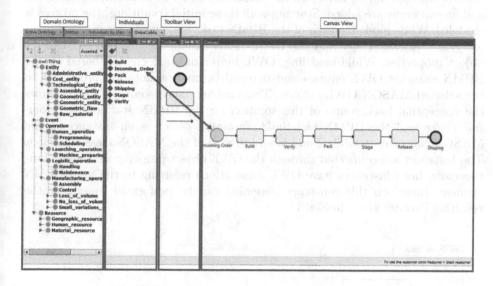

Fig. 1. Layout and GUI of the plugin.

5   Use Case

In this section the application of the plugin is shown with a use case. Therefore, a modeling ontology, which is constructed with *BPMN*, and a domain ontology *Manufacturing's Semantics Ontology (MASON)* [30] are used to show the modeling of a business process. For the practical use case BPMN is used as modeling language and implemented based on the generic modeling ontology template. BPMN is chosen for this case, because it has emerged as a standard notation in process modeling, e.g. for work flows as manufacturing processes, and high-level system design. Beneath its practical use, the comprehensive amount of scientific research on BPMN, e.g. on its formal semantics [49], is an additional reason for its use in the use case. Even though various ontologies representing BPMN exist, the template is used because of its ability to be used with different modeling languages and a simplification of more extensive approaches as e.g. discussed in [17].

In terms of the categorization of ODCM seen in Sect. 2, the implementation could be categorized in the dynamic perspective. Currently, the classes start event, end event and task are implemented with their attributes. They can be connected with the relation class subsequent. Using these elements simple BPMN models can be created. Domain ontology in the use case is the MASON ontology. It is an OWL ontology created with the target to gain a common semantic net for the manufacturing domain. Its practical use is for example automatic cost estimation [30]. An assembly process was modeled, based on the Value-Chain Group's VRM (Value Reference Model) framework. The tasks build, verify, package, stage, and release are modeled as BPMN tasks and connected with the subsequent relation class (see the model in Fig. 1). In addition, a start event and an end event are added. Starting with these initial conditions, the process is modeled. While modeling each of the BPMN tasks and events are mapped manually to MASON classes and the BPMN subsequents are mapped to MASON object properties. While modeling, OWL individuals are created based on the BPMN elements OWL entities and mapped through annotation properties to the selected MASON OWL entities. This enables the reasoning. Figure 2 shows the conceptual background of this solution for the BPMN start event *Incoming Order* and the BPMN task *Build*. *Incoming Order* is an instance of the MASON class *Event*, while *Build* is an instance of the MASON class *Assembly*. The instances are connected through the OWL object property *assembles*. Furthermore, both instances have OWL annotations referring to the used BPMN element. Based on this construct reasoning can be performed leading to the resulting Protégé views in Fig. 3.

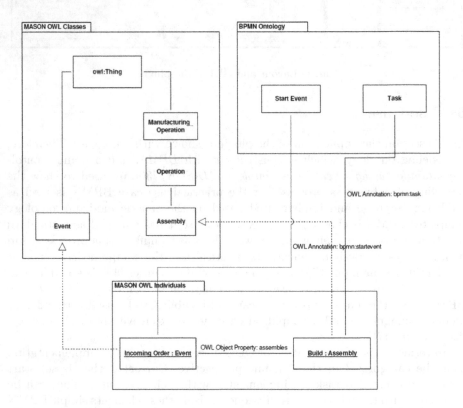

Fig. 2. MASON OWL classes and individuals mapped to BPMN ontology classes.

Fig. 3. Created individuals, annotations and reasoning in the use case

With the implementation and the use case we showed that an approach based on domain and modeling ontologies is feasible. In the next section we will additionally discuss the benefits and drawbacks of the solution.

6   Discussion

In this section the *benefits* and *drawbacks* are discussed. One of the key benefits is that the knowledge gap on domain knowledge and modeling knowledge are closed through commonly used ontologies. Furthermore, the domain and modeling knowledge is not only human-processable but becomes machine-processable. Especially in terms of the machine-interpretation of models this is important and leads to a third important benefit, the ability to apply reasoning on the models and gain new knowledge. We expect finding additional benefits while extending the approach in terms of reasoning.

As the work is still in progress, there are some drawbacks. Currently, the implementation has only been tested with BPMN as modeling language. Implementing other modeling languages can verify the generic approach of the work. Additionally, the current implementations lack BPMN elements like gateways. Regarding the two different reasoning types of Wang et al. [46], we only proved the ability of ontology reasoning, but not the ability of user-defined reasoning.

7   Conclusion and Further Research

In this paper we introduced an ODCM approach based on an ontological foundation of the domain knowledge and the modeling knowledge. For this purpose, we initially differentiated the concepts of visualization and modeling in general and enterprise contexts. The technical feasibility of the approach has been shown by implementing it as a Protégé plugin and applying it to a use case.

The focus of our future research is on completing the BPMN implementation. Further research will include, implementing and testing the plugin with another modeling language for evaluating the generality of the approach. Implementing and evaluating of reasoning e.g. syntax-checking should be investigated. Conceptually, evaluating the quality of the developed ontologies should be performed.

Lastly, a more complex case study which is performed with different editors is necessary to evaluate the advantages of the plugin regarding other modeling editors.

References

1. Antoniou, G., Van Harmelen, F.: Web ontology language: OWL. In: Staab, S., Studer, R. (eds.) Handbook on Ontologies. INFOSYS. Springer, Heidelberg (2004). https://doi.org/10.1007/978-3-540-24750-0_4
2. Azzini, A., Braghin, C., Damiani, E., Zavatarelli, F.: Using semantic lifting for improving process mining: a data loss prevention system case study. In: Accorsi, R., Ceravolo, P., Cudré-Mauroux, P. (ed.) 3rd International Symposium on Data-Driven Process Discovery and Analysis, pp. 62–73. CEUR-WS (2013)
3. Benevides, A.B., Guizzardi, G.: A model-based tool for conceptual modeling and domain ontology engineering in OntoUML. In: Filipe, J., Cordeiro, J. (eds.) ICEIS 2009. LNBIP, vol. 24, pp. 528–538. Springer, Heidelberg (2009). https://doi.org/10.1007/978-3-642-01347-8_44
4. Bork, D., Fill, H.G.: Formal aspects of enterprise modeling methods: a comparison framework. In: 2014 47th Hawaii International Conference on System Science (HICSS), pp. 3400–3409. IEEE (2014)
5. Brockmans, S., Volz, R., Eberhart, A., Löffler, P.: Visual modeling of OWL DL ontologies using UML. In: McIlraith, S.A., Plexousakis, D., van Harmelen, F. (eds.) ISWC 2004. LNCS, vol. 3298, pp. 198–213. Springer, Heidelberg (2004). https://doi.org/10.1007/978-3-540-30475-3_15
6. Bubenko, J., Persson, A., Stirn, J.: User guide of the knowledge management approach using enterprise knowledge patterns, deliverable D3, IST programme project hypermedia and pattern based knowledge management for smart organisations. Technical report, IST-2000-28401, Royal Institute of Technology, Sweden (2001)
7. Burton-Jones, A., Storey, V.C., Sugumaran, V., Ahluwalia, P.: A semiotic metrics suite for assessing the quality of ontologies. Data Knowl. Eng. **55**(1), 84–102 (2005)
8. Card, S.K., Shneiderman, B., MacKinlay, J.D.: Readings in Information Visualization: Using Vision to Think. Morgan Kaufmann, San Francisco (1999)
9. Dietz, J.: Enterprise Ontology - Theory and Methodology. Springer, Heidelberg (2006). https://doi.org/10.1007/3-540-33149-2
10. Fill, H.G.: Visualisation for Semantic Information Systems. Springer/Gabler, Wiesbaden (2009). https://doi.org/10.1007/978-3-8349-9514-8
11. Fill, H.G.: SeMFIS: a flexible engineering platform for semantic annotations of conceptual models. Semant. Web (SWJ) **8**(5), 747–763 (2017). https://doi.org/10.3233/SW-160235
12. Fill, H.G., Karagiannis, D.: On the conceptualisation of modelling methods using the ADOxx meta modelling platform. Enterp. Model. Inf. Syst. Arch. **8**(1), 4–25 (2013)
13. Fill, H.-G.: On the conceptualization of a modeling language for semantic model annotations. In: Salinesi, C., Pastor, O. (eds.) CAiSE 2011. LNBIP, vol. 83, pp. 134–148. Springer, Heidelberg (2011). https://doi.org/10.1007/978-3-642-22056-2_14
14. Fox, M.S., Barbuceanu, M., Gruninger, M.: An organisation ontology for enterprise modelling: preliminary concepts for linking structure and behaviour. In: 4th Workshop on Enabling Technologies: Infrastructure for Collaborative Enterprises, pp. 71–81. IEEE (1995)

15. Fox, M.S., Gruninger, M.: Ontologies for enterprise modelling. In: Kosanke, K., Nell, J.G. (eds.) Enterprise Engineering and Integration. ESPRIT, pp. 190–200. Springer, Heidelberg (1997). https://doi.org/10.1007/978-3-642-60889-6_22

16. Frank, U.: Visual languages for enterprise modelling. In: Arbeitsberichte des Institut für Wirtschaftsinformatik der Universität Koblenz-Landau, no. 18 (1999)

17. Gailly, F., Alkhaldi, N., Casteleyn, S., Verbeke, W.: Recommendation-based conceptual modeling and ontology evolution framework (CMOE+). Bus. Inf. Syst. Eng. **59**(4), 235–250 (2017). https://doi.org/10.1007/s12599-017-0488-y

18. Gruber, T.R.: Toward principles for the design of ontologies used for knowledge sharing? Int. J. Hum.-Comput. Stud. **43**(5–6), 907–928 (1995)

19. Guarino, N.: Formal ontology and information systems. In: Guarino, N. (ed.) Proceedings of FOIS 1998, pp. 81–97. IOS Press (1998)

20. Guizzardi, G.: Ontological foundations for conceptual modeling with applications. In: Ralyté, J., Franch, X., Brinkkemper, S., Wrycza, S. (eds.) CAiSE 2012. LNCS, vol. 7328, pp. 695–696. Springer, Heidelberg (2012). https://doi.org/10.1007/978-3-642-31095-9_45

21. Guizzardi, G., Wagner, G.: Using the unified foundational ontology (UFO) as a foundation for general conceptual modeling languages. In: Poli, R., Healy, M., Kameas, A. (eds.) Theory and Applications of Ontology: Computer Applications, pp. 175–196. Springer, Dordrecht (2010). https://doi.org/10.1007/978-90-481-8847-5_8

22. Guizzardi, G., Wagner, G., Almeida, J.P.A., Guizzardi, R.S.: Towards ontological foundations for conceptual modeling: the unified foundational ontology (UFO) story. Appl. Ontol. **10**(3–4), 259–271 (2015)

23. Harel, D., Rumpe, B.: Meaningful modeling: what's the semantics of "semantics"? Computer **37**, 64–72 (2004)

24. Hinkelmann, K., Albayrak, M., Kritikos, K., Kurjakovic, S., Lammel, B., Woitsch, R.: Modelling framework for BPaaS. CloudSocket (2015). https://site.cloudsocket.eu/documents/251273/350509/CloudSocket-D3.1-BPaaS+Design+Environment+Research.pdf/2ce822b9-3b0f-4602-99dc-c5c32780f511

25. Hinkelmann, K., Laurenzi, E., Martin, A., Thönssen, B.: Ontology-based metamodeling. In: Dornberger, R. (ed.) Business Information Systems and Technology 4.0. SSDC, vol. 141, pp. 177–194. Springer, Cham (2018). https://doi.org/10.1007/978-3-319-74322-6_12

26. Horrocks, I., Patel-Schneider, P., Boley, H., Tabet, S., Grosof, B., Dean, M.: SWRL: a semantic web rule language combining OWL and RuleML. W3C Member Submission 21, 79 (2004)

27. Iacob, M., Jonkers, H., Lankhorst, M., Proper, H.: ArchiMate 1.0 Specification. Van Haren Publishing, Zaltbommel (2009)

28. Karagiannis, D., Mayr, H.C., Mylopoulos, J.: Domain-Specific Conceptual Modeling - Concepts, Methods and Tools. Springer, Cham (2016). https://doi.org/10.1007/978-3-319-39417-6

29. Kifer, M., Lausen, G.: F-logic: a higher-order language for reasoning about objects, inheritance, and scheme. ACM SIGMOD Rec. **18**(2), 134–146 (1989)

30. Lemaignan, S., Siadat, A., Dantan, J.Y., Semenenko, A.: MASON: a proposal for an ontology of manufacturing domain. In: Workshop on Distributed Intelligent Systems, pp. 195–200. IEEE (2006)

31. Maier, R.: Knowledge Management Systems: Information and Communication Technologies for Knowledge Management. Springer, Heidelberg (2004)

32. McBride, B.: The resource description framework (RDF) and its vocabulary description language RDFS. In: Staab, S., Studer, R. (eds.) The Handbook on Ontolgies in Information Systems. INFOSYS, pp. 51–65. Springer, Heidelberg (2003). https://doi.org/10.1007/978-3-540-24750-0_3

33. Musen, M.A.: The protégé project: a look back and a look forward. AI Matters 1(4), 4–12 (2015)

34. Mylopoulos, J.: Conceptual modeling and Telos. In: Conceptual Modelling, Databases and CASE: An Integrated View of Information Systems Development, pp. 49–68. Wiley (1992)

35. Opdahl, A.L., Berio, G., Harzallah, M., Matulevičius, R.: An ontology for enterprise and information systems modelling. Appl. Ontol. 7(1), 49–92 (2012)

36. Pittl, B., Fill, H.G.: A visual modeling approach for the semantic web rule language. Semant. Web J. Pre-Press (2019). https://doi.org/10.3233/SW-180340

37. Sandkuhl, K., et al.: From expert discipline to common practice: a vision and research agenda for extending the reach of enterprise modeling. Bus. Inf. Syst. Eng. 60(1), 69–80 (2018)

38. Staab, S., Walter, T., Gröner, G., Parreiras, F.S.: Model driven engineering with ontology technologies. In: Aßmann, U., Bartho, A., Wende, C. (eds.) Reasoning Web 2010. LNCS, vol. 6325, pp. 62–98. Springer, Heidelberg (2010). https://doi.org/10.1007/978-3-642-15543-7_3

39. Strahringer, S.: Ein sprachbasierter Metamodellbegriff und seine Verallgemeinerung durch das Konzept des Metaisierungsprinzips. Modellierung 98, 15–20 (1998)

40. Studer, R., Benjamins, R., Fensel, D.: Knowledge engineering: principles and methods. Data Knowl. Eng. 25, 161–197 (1998)

41. TopQuadrant: TopBraid Composer 2007 features and getting started guide version 1.0, created by TopQuadrant. TopQuadrant Website (2007)

42. Uschold, M.: Building ontologies: towards a unified methodology. In: Proceedings of 16th Annual Conference of the British Computer Society Specialists Group on Expert Systems. Citeseer (1996)

43. Uschold, M., King, M., Moralee, S., Zorgios, Y.: The enterprise ontology. Knowl. Eng. Rev. 13(1), 31–89 (1998)

44. Verdonck, M., Gailly, F.: Insights on the use and application of ontology and conceptual modeling languages in ontology-driven conceptual modeling. In: Comyn-Wattiau, I., Tanaka, K., Song, I.-Y., Yamamoto, S., Saeki, M. (eds.) ER 2016. LNCS, vol. 9974, pp. 83–97. Springer, Cham (2016). https://doi.org/10.1007/978-3-319-46397-1_7

45. Wand, Y., Weber, R.: An ontological model of an information system. IEEE Trans. Softw. Eng. 16(11), 1282–1292 (1990)

46. Wang, X., Zhang, D.Q., Gu, T., Pung, H.K.: Ontology based context modeling and reasoning using OWL. In: Proceedings of the Second IEEE Annual Conference on Pervasive Computing and Communications Workshops. IEEE (2004)

47. Weiten, M.: Ontostudio® as a ontology engineering environment. In: Davies, J.F., Grobelnik, M., Mladenic, D. (eds.) Semantic Knowledge Management, pp. 51–60. Springer, Heidelberg (2009). https://doi.org/10.1007/978-3-540-88845-1_5

48. Wilde, T., Hess, T.: Forschungsmethoden der Wirtschaftsinformatik. Wirtschaftsinformatik 49(4), 280–287 (2007)

49. Ye, J., Sun, S., Song, W., Wen, L.: Formal semantics of BPMN process models using YAWL. In: 2008 Second International Symposium on Intelligent Information Technology Application, vol. 2, pp. 70–74. IEEE (2008)

Information Systems and Requirements Modeling (EMMSAD 2019)

Review-Based User Profiling: A Systematic Mapping Study

Xin Dong, Tong Li(✉), Xiangyang Li, Rui Song, and Zhiming Ding

Beijing University of Technology, Beijing, People's Republic of China
litong@bjut.edu.cn

Abstract. User profiling is essential for understanding the characteristics of various users, contributing to understanding their requirements better. User reviews by nature are invaluable sources for acquiring user requirements and have drawn increasing attention from both academia and industry, which have not been well explored by traditional user profiling techniques. This paper carries out a systematic mapping study on review-based user profiling. Specifically, 21 out of 1372 papers were carefully selected for investigation under a standardized and systematic procedure. By carrying out in-depth analysis over such papers, we have identified a general process that should be followed to perform review-based user profiling. In addition, we perform multidimensional analysis on each step of the process to review current research progress, identify challenges, and propose potential research directions. The results show that although traditional methods have been continuously improved, they are not effective enough to unleash the full potential of large-scale user reviews, especially the use of heterogeneous data for multi-dimensional user profiling.

Keywords: Review · User profiling · Systematic mapping study · Software requirements

1 Introduction

Software requirements analysis is an important stage of the software life cycle. Precisely understanding user requirements are essential for project success. User profiling is one of the efficient ways to categorize users, which is supposed to profile users through multiple meaningful aspects. Also, it can discover the user's attention and preferences, thus achieving accurate marketing. Although user profiling has been investigated for years, there is a strong need to evolve relevant approaches. User profiling use machine learning techniques to extend the depth of research and mine effective content in user behavior information. As such user profiling techniques can significantly contribute to the understanding of user requirements, and further enable reasonable product recommendations for various groups of people [1].

In recent years, with the rapid development of big data, explosive reviews have attracted the attention of researchers, which are an ideal data source for

© Springer Nature Switzerland AG 2019
I. Reinhartz-Berger et al. (Eds.): BPMDS 2019/EMMSAD 2019, LNBIP 352, pp. 229–244, 2019.
https://doi.org/10.1007/978-3-030-20618-5_16

building accurate models of user preferences and interests. User present their opinions on the web, which include the user's experience and sentiment towards certain products and services. User profiling combined with reviews compensate for the incompleteness of the user's profile information. Although reviews are increasingly used to profile users, there is a lack of systematic research into existing methods. As a critical data source of user profiling, reviews can directly reflect user needs, which are highly valuable for requirements analysis. In particular, with the advent of opinion mining and text analysis techniques, unstructured text reviews can be converted into structured forms. Computer systems can more precisely understand the meaning of reviews and capture the multifaceted nature of user opinions [2]. Many requirements identification approaches have been recently proposed by analyzing user reviews [3–5].

The current general trend towards the current existing literatures on the application of user profiling has led to a new, empirical and systematic research methodology. However, only limited research and findings investigate the implication of using reviews in user profiling from the perspectives of systematic mapping study (SMS). Systematic mapping study is a methodology of defining answerable research questions, searching the literature for the best available evidence, appraising the quality of the evidence, collecting available data for answering the identified questions [6]. Therefore, this paper explores the current research progress of review-based user profiling by conducting a SMS. In particular, we strictly follow the methodology of the SMS to search and filter papers, eventually resulting in 21 papers. This paper focuses on existing methods about review-based user profiling which can provide strong support for the requirements analysis phase. The contributions of this paper are:

- Understand the current state of the user profiling based on the review in selected studies.
- Summarize the general process of user profiling and form a framework for process module analysis.
- Discuss the challenges and potential research directions of user profiling based on reviews.

The rest of the paper is structured as follows. Section 2 describes the research methodology and systematic mapping process, supported by the analysis results in Sect. 3. Section 4 discusses the threats to validity, followed by the related work and conclusions in Sects. 5 and 6.

2   Research Methodology

This study followed the guidelines for SMS developed by Kitchenham et al. [6,7]. In particular, we get three main stages: planning, conducting, and reporting. The process of SMS is completely expressed in Fig. 1. First, we identified meaningful research questions based on the research topic. Second, in the conducting phase, the research literature is searched and screened according to two strategies. Then, we summarize the basic information of the paper and answer the corresponding research questions. Finally, a report of the system research is generated.

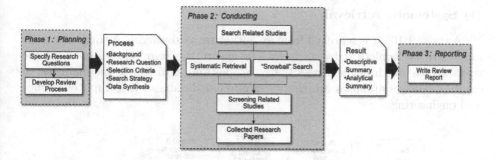

Fig. 1. Systematic mapping process

2.1   Research Questions

The main purpose of this paper is to provide an overview of the research field. Specifically, our work is to determine the number and type of relevant literature, investigate research trends of user profiling, and understand what has been done in this area. These goals are reflected in the following questions.

– **RQ-1 What is the overview of selected studies?**
  The aim is to fully understand the user profiling field from time evolution, domain maturity and scope of application, and to determine what is being studied in this context.
– **RQ-2 What is the generic process for review-based user profiling analysis?**
  The purpose is to understand the advanced frameworks and techniques in the field of user profiling, to master the generic process of research and analysis in this field, and to provide valuable ideas for future research.

– **RQ-3 What are the opportunities and challenges in this field?**
  The aim is to observe future research trends and explore the development of meaningful research directions in this field.

2.2   Search Process

The systematic literature search process for SMS is as follows. Since the electronic-library contains a large number of conference, journal, patent and workshop publications, we first automatically retrieve a large number of related collections from the database through keywords. Second, in order to expand the potential related research, we use the "snowball" technology to search for relevant literature manually [8]. The references in the relevant literature also correspond to the subject of the paper [8]. We used two search strategies to collect existing literature. Figure 2 shows the two parts of the process.

(1) **Systematic retrieval**

As in [6,9,10], it is searched from an authoritative database. A single database may have incomplete data statistics. To ensure the comprehensiveness of the research, we use three databases IEEE, Scopus and, Springer as the main search engines. These databases are the most popular databases in computer science and engineering.

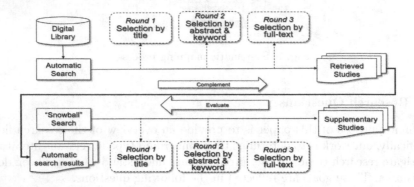

Fig. 2. Screening process

Define a Search Key String. In our experiments, the pilot study method was used [11]. The research uses the research question as a driving factor and judges whether the set string is feasible. Therefore, we identified three keywords of "user profile", "review", "data-driven" initially. We did a variety of string combinations to control the number of the initially searched papers. Finally, we use word variants (singular/plural) and Boolean operators for optimization. Based on these considerations, an optimized search string was obtained:

("user profile" OR "user profiling") AND ("review" OR "reviews") AND ("big data" OR "data-driven")

To ensure that multiple databases are consistent, we make the following settings: (a) The time is setting 1998–2018. (b) Language is only English. (c) Search only in meta-data.

(2) **"Snowball" search**

In order to supplement the research literature, we also carried out a "snowball" search, tracking the links of paper in the systematically retrieve phase and selecting the most relevant reference [12]. In this article, only one layer is expanded because the number of papers retained after screening has been small. The specific screening rules are described in Sect. 2.3.

2.3   Screening Process

According to the proposed research questions, the inclusion and exclusion criteria in the search process are defined in Table 1.

Our research focuses on publications that appear in international journals or conferences. We ignore publications in the form of the book, editorial, poster because their quality is uneven and affects the quality of research (EC1). At the same time, we ignore papers that are less than four pages because their content is relatively simple and the research value is weak (EC2). For the content, papers that are not related to the process and technology about the user's profile should be deleted (EC3). More importantly, if the paper only processes the text of the review without the analysis of the user tag, we should also delete it (EC4).

We include papers using reviews to analyze user behavior (IC1), which means that their main goals and contributions are model building, method research, and user's profile evaluation (IC2). Since user's profiles are a classification of user preferences, we have retained papers that reflect user preferences based on reviews (IC3).

Table 1. The inclusion and exclusion criteria

Inclusion criteria
IC1: Focus on analyzing users through reviews
IC2: Involving specific user profiling modeling methods and evaluation
IC3: Involving the mining of reviews to classify users' preferences
Exclusion criteria
EC1: In the form of a book, editorial, abstract or poster
EC2: In the form of a short paper(less than 4 papers)
EC3: It has little to do with review-based user preference processing
EC4: Only the reviews were analyzed, but the user was not tagged

Using the criteria for inclusion and exclusion presented above, we conducted three rounds of paper screening (Round1, Round2, and Round3). Based on the principle of objectivity and impartiality, three researchers were assigned to conduct three rounds of paper screening. Each paper has two researchers reviewed in each round. In case two researchers come out with adverse decisions, an additional researcher will be involved to resolve the conflict through a joint meeting. The process of the specific literature screening stage is shown in Fig. 2.

- **Round1**: First browse the paper title to eliminate irrelevant papers. If the title of the paper is not relevant to the topic of our research, we will remove it directly according to EC3. Any paper that any researcher believes should be included or uncertain will be passed to the Round2.
- **Round2**: Read the abstract and keywords of the paper by Round1. Through the abstract and the title, we can roughly grasp the basic idea of the paper and filter it according to the criteria. In this phase, we also search keywords across the paper to assist the selection. By searching for "review" and "profile" in the full text, we can efficiently evaluate whether the topic of this paper is related.

– **Round3**: Remaining papers in this stage will be carefully read and evaluated. In particular, we focus on whether the study includes profiling modeling methods and evaluation algorithms, or mines reviews to classify users' preferences.

3   Results and Analysis

In this section, we summarize the results of the SMS considering the research questions (Sect. 3.1). We begin with an overview of the selected studies and then analyze the answers to each of the research questions (Sects. 3.2 and 3.3). Finally, we present constructive reviews on potential opportunities and challenges in this area (Sect. 3.4).

3.1   Search and Selection Results

The detailed screening process and results can be seen in Fig. 3. Initially, we screened 949 papers in the systematic search phase and retained 12 papers. Then, manually screened references to 12 papers and retained 9 papers. Finally, 21 SMS research publications (S1 to S21) were obtained. The list of 21 papers is shown in *Dropbox link*.[1]

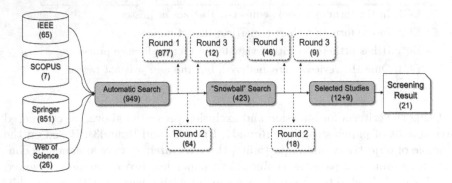

Fig. 3. Paper screening results

3.2   Overview of Selected Primary Studies RQ-1

In this section, the overall status of the selected studies is reported. We focus on the time distribution of the selected papers, as well as the variation of the paper type, the evolution of the publishing venue, and the distribution of the application domain. These all indicate the maturity of the field from different aspects, reflecting the overall situation of research in this field.

---

[1] https://www.dropbox.com/s/rch5ifmzsreltkn/Reference.pdf?dl=0.

The Evolution Trend Over Time. Because user profiling is a relatively new study in big data filed, it is interesting to observe the convergence of these papers. In particular, this is useful to identify when such areas have begun to converge. The time distribution of 21 papers is shown in Fig. 4. Since 2010, it has gradually attracted the attention of researchers, especially in the past five years. A plausible reason for this phenomenon is that the emergence of text analysis technology, unstructured text reviews can be automatically extracted into structured forms [2]. The reduction in the number of papers in 2018 may be because our search time expired in April 2018.

Paper Types. We have labeled the type of selected studies. According to the paper type definition in [12], there are 7 types: proposal, implementation, formalization, meta-study, benchmark, case study, questionnaire and, controlled experiment. The two researchers marked the types of paper separately. If there is an inconsistency, refer to the third researcher's opinion. When labeling types, each paper may belong to many types. Figure 5 shows the distribution of paper types. The proposal is the largest number of paper types, indicating that the field is in the development stage, and new methods are continually being proposed.

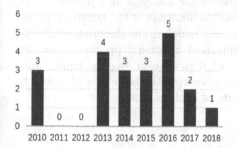

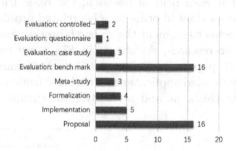

Fig. 4. Time distribution   **Fig. 5.** Paper type distribution

Paper Venues. We believe that in the early stage of research in one field, the number of conference papers was large. As the development of the field expands, the journal paper will gradually increase. As shown in Fig. 6, there are 8 studies published in the conference, and the rest are published in the journal. This shows that the topic has gradually changed from early development to stable development, and has been fully verified and formed a relatively mature research system.

Application Domain. The distribution of the applied topics in the selected papers is displayed in Fig. 7. These specific application areas represent typical scenarios for user profiling. In different scenarios, we can abstract the multimodal user tag model based on the user's social attributes, living habits, and consumer behavior. Product recommendations (14%) and restaurant recommendations (19%) are the two most popular directions. In addition, authorship attribution can provide valuable information in the direction of security and privacy.

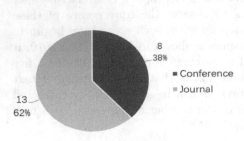

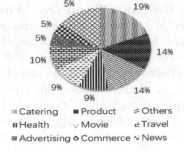

Fig. 6. Paper venues distribution   **Fig. 7.** Application topic distribution

Furthermore, we can identify individuals from a linguistic profiling and identify people of different styles.

3.3 Generic Process of a User Profiling Based on Reviews RQ-2

For each field of research, the basic framework for analysis and processing is important in order to solve related problems. The analysis of the generic process helps to segment the research process, more clearly define the direction available for research. As shown in Fig. 8, we summarized a generic process based on 21 papers, including data sources, mining of review, user tag modeling, and extended applications. This basic framework represents the basic flow of research in this area, and we analyze the current state of each module.

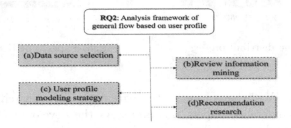

Fig. 8. Analysis framework of general flow

(a) Data sources of user profiling based on reviews

User profiling is often used in areas such as content push, application recommendation, and mobile personalization services. Its data source contains a variety of attributes: static attributes and dynamic attributes. The static attribute of the user refers to the relatively stable data of the user, such as age, gender, and region. The user's dynamic properties vary with the user's behavior, and the data in different domains are different.

The collection and accumulation of user data is the basis of the user profiling. Therefore, we analyze the three aspects of the topic, category, and data acquisition method. The result is shown in Fig. 9. As user behavior changes over time, we need to extend new user data to update user characteristics continually. The standard data sets do not meet the flexibility and versatility of the field. The advantage of using crawlers is that they can be changed according to the requirement of researchers and projects. From the type of data element, the ratings, logs or attribute can provide rich description information.

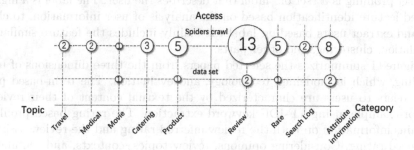

Fig. 9. Data source regarding user profiling

(b) Review information mining

After obtaining the user data, the quality of the data determines the effect of the experiment, and it is necessary to process the text. However, there is a lack of hierarchy and integrity in existing review mining studies, and they do not reflect user evaluation of the product. Therefore, this phase focuses on how to extract opinions about users' preferences from reviews.

As can be seen from Fig. 10, the development of natural language processing (NLP) has promoted the development of user profiling. The reviews reflect the user's emotions and perceptions. From the reviews, we can get a variety of hidden

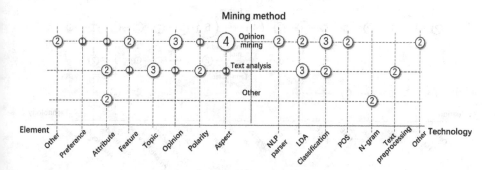

Fig. 10. Mining methods regarding user reviews

information, such as polarity, topic, and opinions [13]. We sorted out the review elements used in these papers and found that many papers used aspect-level information of reviews, which means that review mining can effectively help to describe user characteristics. At the technical level, techniques such as topic models and keyword extraction methods provide tools for accurately extracting valid information from reviews.

(c) Strategy for the construction of user profiling models

User profiling is a "set of" label that describes the user. The label is a highly refined feature identification based on the analysis of user information, to classify and extract users based on labels. It mainly includes the feature similarity calculation, clustering, and other parts.

Figure 11 summarizes the selected papers from the three dimensions of user profiling, which is modeling, technology, and evaluation. The term-based profiling refers to users are characterized by the textual content of their reviews [2], for example, using TF-IDF keyword extraction. The rating based profiling contains information on both the review inferred rating and the review assisted enhanced rating. Considering opinions, review topics, contexts, and sentiment, these multiple features or advanced aspects can explicitly describe her/his preferences. As shown in Fig. 11, the technique of the user profiling is mostly based on similarity calculation and clustering methods, and the use of other ways can assist in the generation of user's profiles. The experimental evaluation method includes accuracy, recall and F value.

(d) Recommendation research based on user profiling

User profiling technologies classify users based on features, with powerful dynamics and spatiotemporal locality. The recommendation system can recommend relevant content according to the user's preferences and characteristics, that is, the user's profile. Therefore, it is reasonable to use the classified user history tags to predict which items the user may be interested in the future.

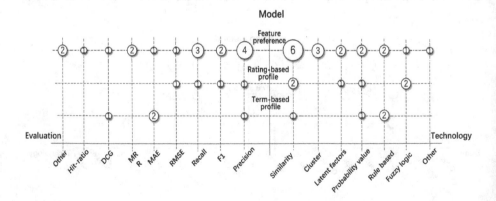

Fig. 11. User profiling modeling method regrading reviews

In the recommendation, we integrated three aspects of type, technology, and model, as shown in Fig. 12. Recommendation methods include content-based (CB), collaborative filtering based (CF) and hybrid recommendations. Collaborative filtering is still the most popular method of recommendation, and recommendations based on similarity and preference are proposed as improved methods. The hybrid approach combines the advantages of CF and CB to promote recommendation effects.

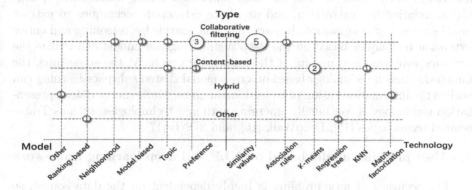

Fig. 12. Recommended types regrading user reviews

3.4   Challenge and Promising Research Directions RQ-3

User profiling use data mining techniques to learn user preferences and build models. With the construction of NLP technology and big data platforms, user reviews in social networks are an important element in the field of user profiling. However, based on the above analysis, we can see that the filed is still in its development stage and we have summarized possible opportunities and challenges in this area.

(1) Multi-source information cross-domain fusion user profiling

User profiling as a human-centered perception can be called group perception. Users generate a large amount of data from both passive sensing and active sensing. As social data acquisition capabilities continue to increase, users' historical records or items in different fields can be captured. For example, a user registers an account on multiple social media. Integrating users' opinions of different social platforms into converged cross-domain information can overcome the incompleteness of information in a single field. At the same time, data modal diversity brings more possibilities for user profiling to extract more certain user preferences. The difference in application context also deepens the complexity of data analysis. For example, in the field of transportation, multi-source data is used to depict profiles of pedestrians and traffic behaviors. Analysis of the similarities and differences of traveler's traffic choice behavior under different traffic conditions can provide quantitative support for traffic planning decisions. In addition, the integration of multi-source information also includes geographic location information, time information, and image information [14].

However, how to build multidimensional behavioral data about user social attributes, living habits, and consumer behavior is a huge challenge. The recent knowledge graph has proposed a new direction for solving this problem. For the massive user data under big data conditions, the effective structuring of explicit knowledge is the goal. We can use deep semantic learning based entity recognition, relationship extraction, and attribute extraction techniques to extract multi-source user information. In particular, the knowledge reasoning and entity extension techniques based on the deep neural language model can realize the dynamic evolution and update of the knowledge graph. At the same time, the knowledge fusion technology based on cross-modal shared subspace learning can realize the information fusion of cross-domain users. Multi-source data representation technology is continually emerging with new technologies, such as Trans-related technologies [15], DeepWalk [16], and SDNE [17].

(2) User profiling model based on NLP and deep learning framework

The accuracy of user profiling is highly dependent on the data source, so improving the usefulness of the review can improve the quality of the user's profile. With the development of NLP technology, the review can be combined with graph algorithms to provide a deep thought for the characterization of user behavior. It is also an optional solution to transfer the application scenarios of the traditional NLP domain topic model to the field of user profiling analysis. In addition, based on the word vector technologies, the similarity of the text can be evaluated, and the reviews with the same semantics can be clustered together. In particular, from the level of the syntax tree, the structural information in the review statement can be mined. For text classification and clustering algorithms, specific algorithmic improvements such as Support Vector Machine (SVM), K-nearest neighbor algorithm (KNN), and Naive Bayes are also valuable aspects of research.

The traditional user analysis method uses a non-end-to-end approach in feature extraction and clustering, which is performed sequentially by multiple independent steps, and the quality of each task affects the results of the entire training. However, deep learning uses an end-to-end approach to avoid a lot of manual annotation problems. For example, various types of data uniformly input through embedding, and a deep prediction model is constructed to solve the representation of heterogeneous data. The social role of the user changes with time, and the concept of timeline adding to the user behavior provides more stereoscopic feature data. The RNN model that senses temporal data can perceive changes in user preferences. The deep neural network model framework and knowledge graph [18] are in the early stage of user profiling technology. The current user profiling technology is not sufficiently scalable in behavior analysis and multi-source information fusion. User profiling techniques for massive user behavior data require more sophisticated algorithmic research to drive.

(3) **Integration with search and recommendation systems**

User profiling has important implications for search and recommendation. As a prerequisite for accurately understanding the user's needs and recommending suitable products for the user, it fully exploits the user's preferences. The traditional recommendation method brings about a cold start problem. In knowledge-based recommendations, ontology [19] and knowledge graphs [18] solve these problems with auxiliary information. Relational extension and reasoning techniques in knowledge graphs can improve the ability of user behavior representation learning in big data environments. The combination of the recommendation algorithm and the time series model can add timing information according to the user's travel process or registration order, especially in the recommended POI field. The traditional recommendation system lacks interpretability, and the knowledge graph algorithm based on reinforcement learning can understand the reason and serve the user better.

In the current recommendation system, when the number of users and the number of products reach a certain number, the recommendation algorithm faces serious scalability problems, and the recommended effectiveness becomes poor. Improving the recommendation speed in algorithms and architecture is difficult. At present, the recommendation speed is improved mainly by introducing clustering technology and improving real-time collaborative filtering algorithm. In terms of architecture, current real-time recommendations mainly include streaming computing based on Spark, Kiji framework and Storm.

4 Threats to Validity

According to the validity classification and definition of [20], the validity of this paper is summarized as follows:

Conclusion validity. Ignore workshop papers, which leads us to miss out on influential work in the field. In our work, the recent papers were not searched enough. The subsequent supplementary research will include manual search, reducing omissions of important papers.

Construct validity. From the results of the search, many documents contain descriptions of user profiling. Although we implemented the search string that we thought was valid, there were fewer types involved in the keyword selection of the search string, which might have caused us to miss some useful information.

Internal validity. When we are reviewing, the professionalism of different researchers may affect the results of the analysis. However, we try to make researchers have relevant background knowledge in the field of user profiling. In the process of marking and analysis, the inconsistencies will be discussed together.

External validity. For external validity, it is crucial to demonstrate sufficient repeatability. If another group of people re-investigate the publication, according to our proposed standards, inconsistent results may result from differences in attitudes and abilities.

5   Related Work

A systematic survey of the literature is a secondary study method that has been proposed and widely used over the last two decades, and that can be seen as an evolution of research based on primary studies of empirical evidence [21]. One of the first systematic surveys was in medicine, a discipline that is particularly invested in evidence-based research. A mapping study is performed at a higher granularity level to identify research gaps and clusters of evidence in order to direct future research. This approach more recently inspired a demand for systematic investigations in the field of information systems, and this concept transferred to, in parallel, software engineering [22].

Over the past decade, some SMSs and literature surveys have summarized these achievements and provided insights in this area [23]. Chen [2] summarized the user profiling based on reviews from standard recommending, review-based user profiling and review-based product profiling. Possible research directions include combining different types of review elements and producing review-based explanations. Suganeshwari and Syed Ibrahim [9] give a detailed explanation of the techniques used in content-based and collaborative filtering in the recommendation system. In [1], the techniques of various user profiling are combined and classified to form a classification tree. The article emphasizes that for new customers who have already registered and have not purchased, as well as old customers who have a purchase record, the same recommendation method cannot be used to personalize. However, these studies only describe some related technologies and do not make a comprehensive and systematic analysis of user's profile.

At the same time, we also refer to system mapping research in different fields. For example, we draw on the systematic mapping process used by Petersen in the precise explanation of software engineering [10]. Specifically, we focus on a map of available work, rather than a detailed survey evaluating publication quality, clearly define our process of finding and including papers, making our research questions clear [9]. Kitchenham et al. provide guidelines for SLRs in software engineering. When applicable, we apply many of these guidelines to our SMS, including clearly specifying a hypothesis, defining populations, defining a process, providing raw data, and making extensive use of graphics [6, 24]. Not only in the process of processing but also much inspiration in the research perspective, such as [12] in the goal-oriented requirements engineering explored venue, citations, co-authors, and other research issues, this is also a problem we need to improve.

6   Conclusion

This paper reports a systematic mapping study of review-based user profiling. In particular, we focus on the latest research trends in user profiling modeling and analysis. We summarize the user profiling process based on the general flow in order to discuss the existing techniques and algorithms in each phase.

Our research shows that traditional methods have been continuously improved to explore user reviews. We discuss future research directions, such as the use of heterogeneous data for multidimensional user analysis. The application of knowledge maps and neural networks should attract more attention from the corresponding research communities.

Acknowledgment. This work is supported by National Key R&D Program of China (No. 2018YFB0804703, 2017YFC0803307, 2017YFC0803300, 2016YFB0901200), the National Natural Science of Foundation of China (No. 91546111, 91646201), International Research Cooperation Seed Fund of Beijing University of Technology (No. 2018B2), and Basic Research Funding of Beijing University of Technology (No. 040000546318516), the Key Project of Beijing Municipal Education Commission (No. SZ201510005002), the State Grid Science and Technology Project (NO. 52272216002B, NO. JS71-16-005).

References

1. Luo, Y.: The comparison of personalization recommendation for e-commerce. Phys. Procedia **25**, 475–478 (2012)
2. Li, C., Chen, G., Wang, F.: Recommender systems based on user reviews: the state of the art. User Model. User-Adap. Inter. **25**(2), 99–154 (2015)
3. T. Dhinakaran, V., Pulle, R., Ajmeri, N., Murukannaiah, P.: App review analysis via active learning: reducing supervision effort without compromising classification accuracy, pp. 170–181, 08 2018
4. Johann, T., Stanik, C., MollaAlizadeh Bahnemiri, A., Maalej, W.: Safe: a simple approach for feature extraction from app descriptions and app reviews, pp. 21–30, 09 2017
5. Williams, G., Mahmoud, A.: Modeling user concerns in the app store: a case study on the rise and fall of yik yak. In: 2018 IEEE 26th International Requirements Engineering Conference (RE), pp. 64–75, August 2018
6. Kitchenham, B.A., Budgen, D., Brereton, O.P.: Using mapping studies as the basis for further research–a participant-observer case study. Inf. Software Technol. **53**(6), 638–651 (2011)
7. Yang, Z., Zhi, L., Zhi, J., Chen, Y.: A systematic literature review of requirements modeling and analysis for self-adaptive systems. In: International Working Conference on Requirements Engineering: Foundation for Software Quality (2014)
8. Wohlin, C.: Guidelines for snowballing in systematic literature studies and a replication in software engineering. In: International Conference on Evaluation & Assessment in Software Engineering (2014)
9. Suganeshwari, G., Syed Ibrahim, S.P.: A survey on collaborative filtering based recommendation system. In: Vijayakumar, V., Neelanarayanan, V. (eds.) Proceedings of the 3rd International Symposium on Big Data and Cloud Computing Challenges (ISBCC – 16). SIST, vol. 49, pp. 503–518. Springer, Cham (2016). https://doi.org/10.1007/978-3-319-30348-2_42
10. Kai, P., Feldt, R., Mujtaba, S., Mattsson, M.: Systematic mapping studies in software engineering. In: International Conference on Evaluation & Assessment in Software Engineering (2008)
11. Lancaster, G.A., Susanna, D., Williamson, P.R.: Design and analysis of pilot studies: recommendations for good practice. J. Eval. Clin. Pract. **10**(2), 307–312 (2010)

12. Horkoff, J., et al.: Goal-oriented requirements engineering: an extended systematic mapping study. Requirements Eng. (5), 1–28 (2017)
13. Sun, Y., Han, J.: Mining heterogeneous information networks: a structural analysis approach. SIGKDD Explor. Newsl. **14**(2), 20–28 (2013)
14. Sarwat, M., Levandoski, J.J., Eldawy, A., Mokbel, M.F.: Lars*: an efficient and scalable location-aware recommender system. IEEE Trans. Knowl. Data Eng. **26**(6), 1384–1399 (2014)
15. Moon, C., Jones, P., Samatova, N.F.: Learning entity type embeddings for knowledge graph completion. In: Proceedings of the 2017 ACM on Conference on Information and Knowledge Management, pp. 2215–2218. CIKM 2017. ACM, New York (2017)
16. Perozzi, B., Al-Rfou, R., Skiena, S.: Deepwalk: online learning of social representations. In: ACM SIGKDD International Conference on Knowledge Discovery & Data Mining (2014)
17. Wang, D., Peng, C., Zhu, W.: Structural deep network embedding. In: ACM SIGKDD International Conference on Knowledge Discovery & Data Mining (2016)
18. Catherine, R., Cohen, W.: Personalized recommendations using knowledge graphs: a probabilistic logic programming approach. In: ACM Conference on Recommender Systems (2016)
19. Ananthapadmanaban, K.R., Srivatsa, S.K.: Personalization of user profile: creating user profile ontology for Tamilnadu tourism. Int. J. Comput. Appl. **23**(8), 42–47 (2011)
20. Opdahl, A.L., Sindre, G.: Experimental comparison of attack trees and misuse cases for security threat identification. Inf. Software Technol. **51**(5), 916–932 (2009)
21. Hayes, W.: Research synthesis in software engineering: a case for meta. In: International Software Metrics Symposium (1999)
22. Sjoberg, D.I.K., Dyba, T., Jorgensen, M.: The future of empirical methods in software engineering research. In: Future of Software Engineering (FOSE 2007), pp. 358–378, May 2007
23. Park, D.H., Kim, H.K., Choi, I.Y., Kim, J.K.: A literature review and classification of recommender systems research. Int. Proc. Econ. Dev. Res. **39**(11), 10059–10072 (2012)
24. Kitchenham, B.A., et al.: Preliminary guidelines for empirical research in software engineering. IEEE Trans. Softw. Eng. **28**(8), 721–734 (2002)

Matching Technology with Enterprise Architecture and Enterprise Architecture Management Tasks Using Task Technology Fit

Sunet Eybers[1]([⊠]) [iD], Aurona Gerber[1,3] [iD], Dominik Bork[2] [iD],
and Dimitris Karagiannis[2]

[1] Department of Informatics, University of Pretoria,
Hatfield 0083, Pretoria, South Africa
{sunet.eybers,aurona.gerber}@up.ac.za
[2] Faculty of Computer Science, University of Vienna,
Waehringer Street 29, 1090 Vienna, Austria
dominik.bork@univie.ac.at, dk@dke.univie.ac.at
[3] Center for AI Research, Pretoria, South Africa

Abstract. Advanced modeling is a challenging endeavor and good tool support is of paramount importance to ensure that the modeling objectives are met through the efficient execution of tasks. Tools for advanced modeling should not just support basic task modeling functionality such as easy-to-use interfaces for model creation, but also advanced task functionality such as consistency checks and analysis queries. Enterprise Architecture (EA) is concerned with the alignment of all aspects of an organization. Modeling plays a crucial role in EA and the matching of the correct tool to enable task execution is vital for enterprises engaged with EA. Enterprise Architecture Management (EAM) reflects recent trends that elevate EA toward a strategic management function within organizations. Tool support for EAM would necessarily include the execution of additional and often implicit advanced modeling tasks that support EAM capabilities. In this paper we report on a study that used the Task-Technology Fit (TTF) theory to investigate the extent to which basic and advanced task execution for EAM is supported by technology. We found that four of the six TTF factors fully supported and one partially supported EAM task execution. One factor was inconclusive. This study provided a insight into investigating tool support for EAM related task execution to achieve strategic EAM goals.

Keywords: Enterprise architecture task execution · Modeling tools ·
Enterprise Architecture Management · Task-Technology Fit

1 Introduction

The development of tool support for advanced modeling remains a challenging and arduous task. Modeling tool developers are confronted with voluminous sets of requirements of which some are straightforward such as user-friendly interfaces and the syntactic and semantic support for a specific modeling language such as UML or ArchiMate. However, some of the modeling requirements that would in the end

© Springer Nature Switzerland AG 2019
I. Reinhartz-Berger et al. (Eds.): BPMDS 2019/EMMSAD 2019, LNBIP 352, pp. 245–260, 2019.
https://doi.org/10.1007/978-3-030-20618-5_17

determine whether a tool is successful and realizes sufficient adoption are implicit or vague because it supports model *use* for, for instance, management tasks that could include using models for communication across business functions, or doing business alignment analysis and managing business transformation using models.

Enterprise Architecture (EA) models are constructed to depict components of an enterprise from different perspectives in order to, for instance, align all aspects of an organization and support business transformation from an As-Is to a To-Be state [1, 2]. EA was traditionally positioned as an IT capability. Recent trends elevate EA as a strategic management function within organizations called *Enterprise Architecture Management* (EAM) [3, 4]. EAM necessarily include the construction of EA models [5]. In modeling tasks for EAM, implicit and advanced modeling functionality form a substantial part of the tool requirements due to the complexity of EA models as well as the complexity of the EAM scenarios that the models should support. In order to support EAM, a tool (the TEAM tool) was developed using the ADOxx platform [6–8].

In this paper we report on a study that was part of a collaboration project on tool support for EAM. A deliverable of the project was the development of the TEAM tool that was evaluated against initial modeling requirements [7]. During the first stage a need for evaluating advanced modeling functionality was identified, which lead to this study that used the Task-Technology-Fit (TTF) theory as proposed by Goodhue [9] to investigate the extent to which TEAM as technology 'fit' the execution and subsequent completion of tasks associated with basic as well as advanced modelling tasks required by EAM. Basic tasks would include the construction of EA models, CRUD and search functionality. Advanced EAM tasks would include the *use* of EA models inlcuding analysis across layers, governance and management tasks. The main focus of this study was the evaluation of six out of the eight factors of the Task-Technology Fit theory, namely *quality, locatability, compatibility, production timelines, systems reliability*, and *ease-of-use*. TTF is a widely adopted theory that specifically focuses on a particular technology that supports the execution of a user task, which in this case refer to EAM tasks. If the task is executed and completed successfully, a higher level of benefits (or increase performance) will be reached. The primary research question under investigation is *"Using the task-technology fit theory, to what extent did the technology (TEAM tool) support the execution of EAM tasks?"*.

We found that four of the evaluated factors (locatability, production timelines, systems reliability and ease-of-use) supported the execution and completion of EAM tasks. Through the use of the existing TEAM modeling tool, one factor (quality) partially supported EAM, whilst the findings pertaining to the compatability factor was inconclusive. The objective of the study was not to replace proper end-user testing of a modelling tool such as TEAM, but specifically focused on the extent to which the technology enhanced the execution and completion of tasks. It should also be noted that that six of the eight measures were considered, omitting both the *authorization* and *relationship with users* measures due to the evaluation scenario for reasons explained later in the paper. The remainder of this paper starts with background on the TTF theory, EAM and TEAM followed by a section on the research method, and sections that present the results and findings, and conclude.

2 Background

2.1 Task-Technology Fit

The Task-Technology-Fit theory as introduced by Goodhue [9] focus on the "degree to which a technology *assists* an individual in performing his or her tasks". In instances where technology provide a higher degree of assistance to perform a task, performance is increased. The theory, in its original form, used elements from the 'Utilization focus' school of thought which focused on 'user attitudes and beliefs' to predict information system utilisation [10]. It subsequently included theory that focused on the extent to which the task requirements 'fit' or meet the needs of the individual to successfully complete a task. The TTF model (Fig. 1) represents the two dimensions or main areas that influence the extent to which information technology can be used to increase performance (the so-called task-technology fit), namely *task characteristics* and *technology characteristics*.

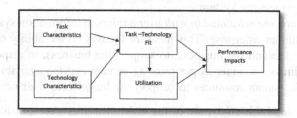

Fig. 1. The TFF model (reproduced from [10]).

Task characteristics refer to the tasks or actions completed by a user in direct response to a particular need or input. For example, in this study, (given a particular case study), part of the business requirements might be to create an architecture vision, in particular a stakeholder viewpoint modelling the stakeholders, their concerns, and the assessment of the concerns. *Task/job characteristics measures* focus on "task equivocality" and "task interdependence". Task equivocality refers to unstructured, infrequent business problems whereas Task interdependence refers to interdepartmental business questions posed across business functions.

The *Technology characteristics* could refer to information systems in general, or to a particular tool or technology. In this study technology refers to the TEAM tool, i.e. the tool used to create an architecture vision.

The *utilisation component* refers to the extent to which the technology is used in completing the task(s). In this study, the user might decide to use the technology, i.e. TEAM tool, only once or repetitively.

The *Task-Technology Fit* dimension focuses on eight factors that could possibly have a performance impact or an impact on the utilization of technology [10]:

- *Quality* refers to data quality characteristics such as the currency of the data available, the maintenance of data and the availability of an adequate level of detail of data;
- *Locatability* focuses on the identification of the location of data, i.e. what the source of data is as well as the metadata, i.e. the meaning of data elements on both a technical and business level;
- *Authorization* refers to the permission required to access certain data elements in order to complete a task or overall job;
- *Compatibility* refers to the ability to combine data from disparate sources;
- *Production timelines* refer to the success of information systems to meet operational timelines;
- *System reliability* (also referred to as 'uptime') evaluates the dependency and consistency of systems by considering the availability of the system.
- The system under evaluation should be *easy to use* and it should be *easy to train* or educate users to use the system;
- The last measure, *the relationship with users*, refers to information systems business functions within an enterprise. This measure focuses on the ability of the business function to understand the business, to support the business, to respond to service request in a timeous manner as per prior agreement and the availability of skilled, knowledgeable human resources to support the business in their needs.

For the purpose of this study, six of the eight measures were considered, omitting both the *authorization* and *relationship with users* measures due to the evaluation scenario. The target population/respondents to the study did not experience any challenges with regards to accessing certain data elements in the TEAM tool (*authorization*) and the *relationship with users* was not applicable as the study was conducted outside a formal information systems enterprise and subsequent business unit.

Lastly, the *performance impact* measures focus on the influence of information systems on individual job productivity as well as the service and support provided by IS systems on job effectiveness. For the purpose of this study this dimension evaluated the performance impact of the TEAM tool on the overall effectiveness and efficiency of the tasks completed by users.

2.2 Enterprise Architecture and Enterprise Architecture Management

One of the goals of EAM is to provide a high level overview of all aspects and components of an enterprise including the relationships between them [1, 11, 12]. The rationale include that organizations having a holistic view can manage and anticipate the impact of future changes in their business [13]. Such organizations use EA models to understand the various facets or perspectives of their enterprise (such as the business architecture, information architecture, data architecture, applications and technology architecture), supported by capabilities such as people, content, processes and tools, organizations [14]. Several EA frameworks are available, which mostly consist of a common vocabulary, models and taxonomy to establish the EA [15–18]. Most EA frameworks are supported by a variety of modelling tools and environments supporting specific EA languages and tasks such as ArchiMate [19, 20].

EAM is a relatively new development to the EA discipline. In contrast to EA initiatives that were managed from IT departments, EAM proposes that EA is a strategic management practice that establishes, maintains and uses a coherent set of guidelines, architecture principles and governance regimes that provide direction and practical help in the design and development of an enterprise's EA to achieve its vision and mission [3, 21–23]. In order to support EAM and the efficient and effective management of the enterprise, the actual EA *modeling* process is of strategic importance. EA models represent knowledge and support communication and consensus. EAM tasks would necessarily include tool support to manage EA models including comparison of models across various layers or viewpoints (such as the application and business layers). In this paper we focus on the execution of both basic and advanced EAM modeling tasks in the TEAM tool.

2.3   The TEAM Tool

In order to support EAM modeling, the Open Models Laboratory (OMiLAB, www.omilab.org) developed the TEAM tool. OMiLAB provides an open platform for conceptual modeling and almost 50 different modeling methods have already been successfully conceptualized within OMiLAB [8, 24, 25]. The TEAM tool that supports EAM was implemented as a project within OMiLAB in multiple design science research cycles in which different prototypes of TEAM were released [7]. The initial cycles focused on the development of basic EA and ArchiMate modeling capability. The study reported on in this paper considers the execution of basic as well as advanced modeling tasks, which is only possible once a basic stable version of the TEAM tool is available for modeling. In the next section a short overview of ArchiMate for EAM modeling is provided.

2.4   ArchiMate

ArchiMate is a common EA modeling language that was formalized as an open and independent standard by the Open Group [19, 26].

The purpose of ArchiMate is to support enterprise architecture modeling given a layered view of an enterprise (the ArchiMate Framework) depicted in Fig. 2 [27, 28]. Each layer within the ArchiMate framework provides services to the layers above it. The core layers are the *business*, *application* and *technology* layers, which can be subdivided into further layers as indicated by the colours in Fig. 2 [4]. ArchiMate uses a service model and a service is constructed using three aspects as indicated by the columns in Fig. 2 namely *Passive Structure*, *Behavior* and *Active Structure* [19]. The latest version of ArchiMate include Views and Viewpoints to support the specific modeling requirements of different stakeholders.

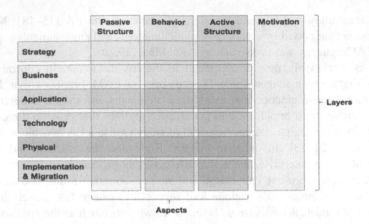

Fig. 2. The ArchiMate framework [19].

3 Methodology

As mentioned, this study form part of a larger research collaboration project on advanced modelling tool support for enterprise architecture management. The project consistent of two phases: Phase 1 developed and evaluated the TEAM tool [7, 25]. Phase 2 of which this study forms part, investigated advanced modelling support using TEAM. The research steps for the execution of this study were: (1) identifying a suitable theory for evaluation of advanced nodeling; (2) developing a data collection instrument based on the theory; (3) data collection and (4) data analysis.

We identified the Task-Technology fit theory as a theory that could be used to investigate the capability of TEAM for advanced modelling, and we developed an online questionnaire instrument based on the TTF theory. An interpretive, qualitative approach was followed to gather data from EAM students and scholars who used the TEAM tool during two main engagement sessions (one in Austria and another in South Africa). During the first part of both sessions a speaker on the topic of EAM explained basic terminology and the context of EAM to the audience using the TEAM tool where applicable for demonstration. The latter part of the session offered students the opportunity to perform EAM tasks using TEAM and the ArchiSurance[1] Case study [29]. Due to time constraints, participants were instructed to create the architecture vision based on the case study. Figure 3 depicts the high level architecture vision.

On completion, participants created a high level model to display one of the business goals as identified in the high level architecture vision, namely profitability (see Fig. 4a). One of the many actions to increase profitability was to reduce costs depicted in the business models in Fig. 4 (a and b). Hands-on support was available to participants during the execution of tasks to create the models in the TEAM tool. On completion, participants had the opportunity to complete the online questionnaire based

---

[1] ArchiSurance is a fictitious case study developed by the OpenGroup to illustrate the ArchiMate modelling language using the TOGAF framework.

on the TFF theory. The tasks in the case study included model analysis using meta-specification of model functionality provided by TEAM.

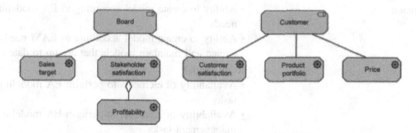

Fig. 3. ArchiSurance – high level architecture vision model

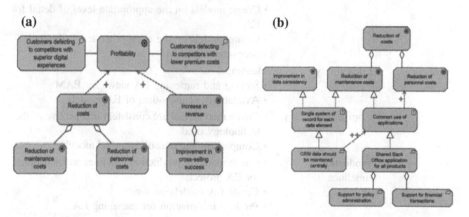

Fig. 4. a. ArchiSurance – high level profitability business goal model. b. ArchiSurance – EA model displaying the reduction of costs goal

3.1   Online Questionnaire Based on TTF

The Task-Technology-Fit (TTF) theory [9] has proven to be an extensively used theory for investigating the extent to which technology support the execution of tasks. For using TTF we made a distinction between basic modeling tasks (create, read, update, delete (CRUD) and search) for EA models. EAM use EA models to do strategic management and advanced tasks mostly entail *using* EA models (analysis, governance, management) e.g. doing a cross-comparison of models across different architectural layers to detect inconsistencies or incompleteness. Participants were made aware of the difference between basic and advanced modeling tasks i.e. basics that involved model CRUD and search, and *using* models for EA *management*. Each of the TTF constructs was used to assess the ability to execute basic and advanced modelling tasks according to end-users. The EAM modeling tasks were mapped to the TTF constructs as indicated in Table 1 below.

Table 1. Mapping of tasks to TTF constructs

Dimensions	Factor name	Sub item
Technology dimension	Quality	Currency • Ability to create model according to EA modeling needs • Ability to create model according to EAM needs • Create and maintain models that are up to date
		Right model • Availability of elements to perform EA modeling tasks • Availability of elements to perform EA modeling management tasks
		Right level of detail • Performing EA modeling maintenance • Create models on the appropriate level of detail for EA • Create models on the appropriate level of detail necessary for EAM
	Locatability	Meaning • Storing and retrieving EA views for EAM • Availability of meta-data of EA models
	Compatibility	• Create models that are consistent irrespective of the technology used • Comparison and consolidation of models
	Production timelines	• Create/maintain production timelines and schedules for EA projects • Create EA models on time • Produce information for managing EA
	Systems reliability	• Platform available during task execution
	Easy of use/training	• TEAM is easy to learn • TEAM is easy to use for EAM • Training is available
Task/job characteristics	Task equivocality	• Ability to create models for ill-defined modeling tasks • Complete ad-hoc, non-routine modeling tasks • Create models responding to new questions
	Task interdependence	• View/create models for more than 1 business function
Performance impact measures	Performance impact of EAM tools	• The TEAM tool supports me in the execution of my tasks to increase job performance

Although questions pertaining to the task characteristic and performance impact measures were included in the questionnaire, the main focus remained on the six factors of the task/technology dimension as it could be directly linked to the EAM task requirements. A Likert scale was used as measurement scale. Available options ranged from strongly agree over undecided to strongly disagree. The questionnaire was deployed online via the online questionnaire software QuestionPro [30].

3.2   Data Collection

Using the developed instrument, we collected data during two different contact sessions. The online questionnaire consisted of three parts focusing on evaluating the basic and advanced modeling tasks using the TEAM modeling tool: *Part 1* explained the objective of the questionnaire, namely "to investigate the extent to which the TEAM modeling platform assist or support enterprise architecture modeling and management tasks using the task-technology fit theory". Even though the audience were mostly familiar with EA and EAM, the key technological terminology such as enterprise architecture, enterprise architecture models and enterprise architecture management were clarified. *Part 2* collected biographical information from participants such as country, current job title, and designation. *Part 3* contained questions focusing on each of the two dimensions as specified in the TFF model namely task and technology as well as the subsequent six factors namely *Quality, Locatability, Compatibility, Ease of use/training, Production timelines* and *Systems reliability*.

Data from the two contact sessions were analyzed using the online analytical capability of the questionnaire tool QuestionPro [30].

4   Results and Discussion

The first contact session was conducted during the Next-generation Enterprise modeling (NEMO) summer school in 2018 (Session A). The session was attended by a diverse audience from all over the world including senior level students from more than ten countries. The positions held included Masters and Doctoral students, Software Developers, Researcher, Enterprise Architect, Software developer, Entrepreneur, General Manager and Electrical Engineer. 81.25% of the respondents had less than 2 years' experience in the area of EA including any EA tool; 12,5% had between 2 to 5 years' experience, whilst only 6.25% had more than 10 years' experience. All the respondents had less than 2 years' experience with the TEAM tool. A total of 18 respondents completing the questionnaire after a short tutorial and practical hands-on session where they had opportunity to use the tool.

The second contact session was conducted in South Africa. All the participants were residing in South Africa. Two participants were students and two EA consultants/ solution architects, the remainder were associated with an academic environment. 37.5% of respondents have between 5 and 10 years' experience in the area of EA and EAM, whilst 62,5% have experience in using a particular EA *platform*. None of the participants used the TEAM modeling tool before. A total of 8 participants completed the online questionnaire (referred to as Session B).

4.1   Task-Technology Fit Characteristics

Quality (Currency):

Session A: Respondents had diverse opinions when asked if there were EA modeling platforms available that meet their modeling needs. 26% of respondents agreed, 32% were undecided whilst 37% disagreed. A small minority indicated that the question was not applicable (5%). When asked if the TEAM tool offered the necessary functionality to fulfil their EA modeling needs, all respondents agreed. In terms of the EA *management* capability respondents felt that there is no EAM tool available to utilise (31%), whilst 32% were undecided 32% disagreed and 5% felt that the question was not applicable. However, all the respondents agreed that the TEAM modeling tool could assist them in future in achieving EAM task requirements.

Session B: Almost half of the respondents indicated that there are currently EA modeling platforms available to meet their modeling as well as EAM needs. 33% of respondents felt that the TEAM tool can also be used and is up to date and offers all the functionality required to perform EAM tasks.

Quality (right model):

Session A: The majority of the respondents (47%) indicated that the TEAM modeling tool has the capability to carry out their EA modeling tasks. A total of 10.5% of respondents indicated that the question was not applicable whilst another 10.5% were 'undecided'. 31,7% of respondents indicated that the TEAM tool did not provide all the capability required. The majority of participants (52.5%) furthermore indicated that current modeling platforms are missing critical EA modeling functionality that would be useful in completing their tasks. 32% of respondents were undecided, while 5% disagreed that the EA modeling tools will be useful. 10.5% felt that the question was not applicable.

From an EA *management* perspective, 37% respondents indicated that the TEAM modeling tool provides capability when engaging in EAM tasks, 31.5% of respondents were undecided whilst 10.5% felt that the question was not applicable. 21% indicated that the TEAM modeling tool did not provide them with useful and applicable capability to complete EAM tasks. 53% of respondents indicated that current modeling platforms available to them are missing critical EAM functionality that would be useful in completing their jobs; 26% were undecided; 11% indicated that the question was not applicable whilst 10% disagreed.

Session B: 25% of respondents indicated that the TEAM modeling tool offers the necessary capability to carry out EA modeling tasks and fulfil their functional needs to perform EA management. Despite the (negative) responses, 50% of respondents felt that they could not decide if the current modeling platforms are missing critical capability (including EA management) for them to complete their EA related tasks.

Quality (right level of detail):

Session A: The maintenance of EA models are an advanced EA management task requirement. The majority of respondents agreed that the TEAM modeling tool allowed them to maintain their EA models (52.5%) whilst 37% of respondents were indecisive. Only 5% disagreed whilst another 5% felt that the question was not applicable. Respondents further indicated (49%) that the TEAM modeling tool allowed for the maintenance of respondent's enterprise models on the correct level of detail – another important advanced EAM requirement. The number of indecisive respondents were

32% whilst a bigger number of participants felt that the question was not applicable (10.5%) or was in disagreement (5%). Focusing on the ability of the TEAM modeling tool to support detailed management tasks, the majority of respondents agreed that the platform support the capability (42%) whilst 10.5% disagreed; 37% disagreed and another 10.5% felt that the question was not applicable to the tool.

Session B: Between 37.5% of respondents felt that the TEAM modeling tool allows them to maintain their EA models on an appropriate level to support their EA tasks including their EA management tasks.

Locatability:

Session A: 77% of respondents indicated that they could easily find and view models that are maintained in the TEAM modeling tool whilst 67% indicated that it was easy to locate the appropriate layer inside the tool without any prior experience with the tool.

Session B: 25% of respondents felt that it was easy for them to find and maintain their EA models even if they have not used the TEAM modeling tool before.

Locatability (meaning):

Session A: When using EA modeling tools, the majority of respondents (72%) could easily store and obtain the exact definition, properties or attributes of their current EA models. This was also the case when using the TEAM modeling tool (77% of respondents agreed).

Session B: Metadata, such as the definition of properties or attributes of enterprise architecture models related to respondents EA modeling tasks were easy to store and maintain whilst keeping all the elements in a place that is easy to find.

Compatibility:

Session A: Almost an equal number of respondents agreed (42%) or were indecisive (44%) when asked to compare models or detect inconsistencies between two different EA layers or views using TEAM. 31% of respondents indicated that they find it difficult to compare or consolidate two models from two different EA layers or views and (55.5%) were indecisive.

Session B: 37% of respondents indicated that they could not decide if models from different EA layers inside the TEAM modelling tool are inconsistent and 37% of respondents indiacted that it was difficult to compare models from different layers.

Production timelines:

Session A: An equal number of respondents (41%) agreed and were indecisive when asked if the TEAM modeling tool could assist in completing tasks to meet EA production schedules whilst advanced requirement support to complete EA managerial activities (such as decision making support and project migration schedules) scored slightly higher (47%). The remainder of the respondents were indecisive.

Session B: The respondents "more or less agree" that the TEAM modeling tool assist with the EA production schedules such as information delivery and decision support to relevant stakeholders.

Systems reliability:

Session A: Although the majority of the respondents were undecided when asked if the TEAM modeling tool is susceptible to crashes (65%) the respondents indicated that they could count on the tool being available when needed (59%).

Session B: The majority of respondents felt that TEAM tool is reliable and did not experience software "crashes" or problems. 37% of respondents indicated that they could not decide if they agree with the statement that the TEAM tool is available when needed.

Ease of use (of software)

Session A: The majority of respondents (69%) indicated that TEAM is easy to learn and use. When asked if the tool was convenient and easy to use 57% of respondents felt that they agree with that statement whilst 31% were indecisive, 6% disagreed and 6% felt that the questions was not applicable.

Session B: 25% of respondents felt that TEAM was easy to learn and convenient.

Ease of use (training)

Session A: 31.25% of respondents indicated not enough training to support them in using TEAM, 37.5% were indecisive whilst 31.25% indicated that sufficient training opportunities exist.

Session B: 50% of the respondents could not decide if there were enough training offered in order to understand and access the TEAM modeling tool.

4.2 Task/Job Characteristic Measures

Task equivocality

Session A: Half of the respondents indicated that they currently work on ill-defined, ad-hoc and non-routine business and/or modeling tasks whilst 37% were indecisive. 12.5% of respondents indicated that the question was not applicable.

Session B: Very few respondents indicated that they are working on ill-defined, ad-hoc, non-routine business and/or modeling tasks.

Task interdependence

Session A: 43.75% of respondents indicated that they frequently deal with more than one business function whilst 37.5% is indecisive and 18.75% indicated that the question was not applicable. 43,75% indicated that they were indecisive when asked if they work with more than one EA layer or view at a time whilst 37.5% indicated that they indeed work with multiple layers.

Session B: Very few respondents work on modeling tasks that involve more than one business function or more than one EA layer or view.

4.3 Performance Impact Measures

Performance impact of enterprise architecture tools

Session A: 43,75% of respondents indicated that the current EA environment has a big, positive impact on their effectiveness and productivity in their jobs, whilst 3.75% were indecisive and 18.75% indicated that the question was not applicable. 43.75% of respondents indicated that they were indecisive when asked if they felt that EA modeling platforms are an important and valuable aid to them in performing their jobs; 37,5% felt that EA modeling platforms are important whilst 18.75% indicated that the question in not applicable.

Session B: 25% of respondents indicated that EA modeling platforms play an important part and act as valuable aid to them in performing tasks, whilst three respondents indicated that the EA environment has a positive impact on their effectiveness and job productivity.

5 Findings

From a *quality (currency)* perspective respondents were divided when asked if appropriate EAM tools exist. Respondents from the session in Austria (involving a more diverse group of participants) were more prone to consider using TEAM to perform EAM tasks, whilst the South African group was more skeptical.

Focusing on the *quality (right model)* respondents indicated that TEAM did provide them with all the modeling task capability, however a substantial percentage of respondents disagreed (31%) but could not indicate the reason for their statement due to the nature of the questionnaire. Respondents further indicated that EA modeling tools would be useful in completing their jobs. The majority of respondents indicated that TEAM provides the capability to carry out advanced EAM tasks. However, the majority of the Austria respondents felt that current modeling platforms are missing critical EAM functionality that would be useful in their jobs whilst South African participants were indecisive. From an advanced EAM requirement the majority of the participants agreed that TEAM allows them to not only maintain their EA models but also at the appropriate level of detail to support their enterprise (quality - right level of detail dimension). The platform furthermore allows them to maintain their EA models at an appropriate level of detail to support their enterprise architecture *management* tasks.

Focusing on the *Locatablity* perspective, respondents from Austria agreed that the TEAM modeling tool allows them to easily view and maintain their EA models even if they have not used the platform before. This was also the case when respondents were asked to what extend TEAM provided for the definition of metadata about their existing EA models such as properties and attributes (locatability – meaning dimension).

Focusing on the *Compatibility* perspective there was no clear, undisputed feedback from respondents when asked if two different EA layers or views were inconsistent when compared or consolidated due to the inherent underlying definitions of the models or architecture layers. ArchiMate enforces these EA model definitions and the need for tool support to assist with the advanced task of model consolidation was thus emphasized.

Focusing on *production timelines* there was a strong indication from respondents that the TEAM modeling tool supports the advanced requirements. These include the capability to meet the needs of stakeholders in terms of decision-making, information delivery schedules as well as project migration schedules.

Focusing on the systems *reliability* factor, TEAM was perceived as being stable with high availability even though it was not used extensively used for long periods.

The ease of use dimension focused on how easy it was to use TEAM as well as the availability of training material to support the acquisition of knowledge to use the tool. The majority of respondents indicated that it was easy and convenient to use TEAM. Respondents furthermore felt that although not enough training was conducted when using TEAM, more training opportunities were made available. Unfortunately, respondents from South Africa disagreed that the system was easy to use possibly due to the limited level of exposure of participants to TEAM. Participants from Austria attended an extensive summer school focusing on the topic of EAM whilst participants from South Africa only attended a half-day seminar.

With regards to *task/job measures*, the majority of respondents indicated that they currently work on ill defined, ad-hoc and non-routine business and/or modeling tasks (task equivocality). They furthermore work frequently with more than one business function although fewer respondents worked with multiple enterprise architecture layers at a time (task interdependence).

With regards to *performance impact meas*ures, the majority of respondents indicated that the current enterprise architecture environment and subsequent tools available to them has a big, positive impact on their task execution effectiveness and productivity in their jobs. This is not surprising if considered their specialised work area. However, this offers new research opportunities to identify the true impact of technology on the effectiveness and subsequent performance impact of successfully executed EA and EAM tasks.

6 Conclusion

In this paper we report on a study that used the Task-Technology Fit (TTF) theory as proposed by Goodhue [9] to investigate the extent to which the TEAM tool assisted in the execution of EAM tasks. TTF was suitable for the study as it assists with understanding how technology supports the execution of a user task, which in this case included advanced tasks such as required by EAM. The main focus was the eight TTF characteristics, of which six factors were evaluated (quality, locatability, compatibility, production timelines, systems reliability, ease of use). The research question under investigation was *"Using the task-technology fit theory, to what extent did the technology (TEAM tool) support the execution of EAM tasks?"*.

The results indicate that, through the use of the TEAM tool, the quality factor partially supported EAM whilst the findings pertaining to the compatibility factor was inconclusive. The remainder of the factors (locatability, production timelines, systems reliability and ease of use) evaluated by the participants when executing EAM tasks using TEAM indicates that TEAM readily supports these tasks.

This study provides a starting point for evaluating the task execution support of the TEAM modeling tool to perform EAM tasks. Further research will focus on extending the research to investigate in-depth analysis of the impact of successful EAM task execution on both individual and organizational performance.

Acknowledgment. Part of this research has been funded through the South Africa/Austria Joint Scientific and Technological Cooperation program with the project number ZA 11/2017.

References

1. Lapalme, J.: Three schools of thought on enterprise architecture. IT Prof. **14**, 37–43 (2012). https://doi.org/10.1109/MITP.2011.109
2. Hinkelmann, K., Gerber, A., Karagiannis, D., Thoenssen, B., van der Merwe, A., Woitsch, R.: A new paradigm for the continuous alignment of business and IT: combining enterprise architecture modelling and enterprise ontology. Comput. Ind. **79**, 77–86 (2016). https://doi.org/10.1016/j.compind.2015.07.009
3. Ahlemann, F., Stettiner, E., Messerschmidt, M., Legner, C. (eds.): Strategic Enterprise Architecture Management. Springer, Heidelberg (2012). https://doi.org/10.1007/978-3-642-24223-6
4. Weiss, S., Aier, S., Winter, R.: Institutionalization and the Effectiveness of Enterprise Architecture Management, 19
5. Winter, K., Buckl, S., Matthes, F., Schweda, C.M.: Investigating the state-of-the-art in enterprise architecture management methods in literature and practice. MCIS **90** (2010)
6. Fill, H.-G., Karagiannis, D.: On the conceptualisation of modelling methods using the ADOxx meta modelling platform. Enterp. Model. Inf. Syst. Architectures **8**, 4–25 (2013). https://doi.org/10.1007/BF03345926
7. Bork, D., et al.: Requirements engineering for model-based enterprise architecture management with ArchiMate. In: Pergl, R., Babkin, E., Lock, R., Malyzhenkov, P., Merunka, V. (eds.) EOMAS 2018. LNBIP, vol. 332, pp. 16–30. Springer, Cham (2018). https://doi.org/10.1007/978-3-030-00787-4_2
8. Bork, D., Miron, E.T.: OMiLAB - an open innovation community for modeling method engineering. In: ICMIE 2017, pp. 64–77 (2017)
9. Goodhue, D.L.: Understanding user evaluations of information systems. Manage. Sci. **41**, 1827–1844 (1995). https://doi.org/10.1287/mnsc.41.12.1827
10. Goodhue, D.L., Thompson, R.L.: Task-technology fit and individual performance. MIS Q. **19**, 213 (1995). https://doi.org/10.2307/249689
11. Zachman, J.: A framework for information systems architecture. IBM Syst. J. **26**(3), 276–292 (1987)

12. Lapalme, J., Gerber, A., van der Merwe, A., de Vries, M., Hinkelmann, K.: Exploring the future of enterprise architecture: a Zachman perspective. Comput. Ind. **79**, 103–113 (2016)
13. Rogers, C.: Proposed Enterprise Architecture solutions for Industry 4.0 Manufacturing simulation information assets based on TOGAF. University of Denver University College (2016)
14. Lankhorst, M.M.: Enterprise architecture modelling—the issue of integration. Adv. Eng. Inform. **18**, 205–216 (2004). https://doi.org/10.1016/j.aei.2005.01.005
15. de Vries, M., van der Merwe, A., Gerber, A.: Towards an enterprise evolution contextualisation model. Presented at the first international conference on enterprise systems (ES 2013), Cape Town (2013)
16. de Vries, M., Gerber, A., van der Merwe, A.: The nature of the enterprise engineering discipline. In: Aveiro, D., Tribolet, J., Gouveia, D. (eds.) EEWC 2014. LNBIP, vol. 174, pp. 1–15. Springer, Cham (2014). https://doi.org/10.1007/978-3-319-06505-2_1
17. The Open Group: TOGAF®, an Open Group standard. http://www.opengroup.org/subjectareas/enterprise/togaf
18. Zachman, J.A.: The Zachman Framework for Enterprise Architecture. Zachman International (2011). http://www.zachman.com/
19. OMG: ArchiMate® 3.0.1 Specification. The Open Group (2016). http://pubs.opengroup.org/architecture/archimate3-doc/
20. Lankhorst, M.M., Proper, H.A., Jonkers, H.: The anatomy of the archimate language. Int. J. Inf. Syst. Model. Des. **1**, 1–32 (2010). https://doi.org/10.4018/jismd.2010092301
21. Jonkers, H., Lankhorst, M.M., ter Doest, H.W.L., Arbab, F., Bosma, H., Wieringa, R.J.: Enterprise architecture: management tool and blueprint for the organisation. Inf. Syst. Front. **8**, 63–66 (2006). https://doi.org/10.1007/s10796-006-7970-2
22. Matthes, F., Buckl, S., Leitel, J., Schweda, C.M.: Enterprise architecture management tool survey 2008. Techn. Univ. München (2008)
23. Ross, J.W., Weill, P., Robertson, D.: Enterprise Architecture as Strategy: Creating a Foundation for Business Execution. Harvard Business Press, Boston (2006)
24. Karagiannis, D., Mayr, H.C., Mylopoulos, J. (eds.): Domain-Specific Conceptual Modeling. Springer, Cham (2016). https://doi.org/10.1007/978-3-319-39417-6
25. Bork, D., Buchmann, R., Karagiannis, D., Lee, M., Miron, E.T.: An open platform for modeling method conceptualization: the OMiLAB digital ecosystem. Communications of the Association of Information Systems (2019)
26. Josey, A., Lankhorst, M., Band, I., Jonker, H., Quartel, D.: An Introduction to the ArchiMate® 3.0.1 Specification. The Open Group (2016)
27. Lankhorst, M. (ed.): Enterprise architecture at work: modelling, communication, and analysis. Springer, Berlin, New York (2005)
28. Lankhorst, M., The ArchiMate team: The ArchiMate Language Primer (2004). https://web.archive.org/web/20110724162610/https://doc.novay.nl/dsweb/Get/Document-43839/
29. ArchiSurance Case Study, Version 2. https://publications.opengroup.org/y163
30. FREE Survey Software: Online Survey Software | QuestionPro®. https://www.questionpro.com/

A Method for Database Model Selection

Noa Roy-Hubara[1]([⊠]), Peretz Shoval[1,2], and Arnon Sturm[1]

[1] Ben-Gurion University of the Negev, Be'er Sheva, Israel
nro@post.bgu.ac.il
[2] Netanya College, Netanya, Israel

Abstract. In the last decade, new types of database models emerged, most notably the NoSQL database models. Within this family of databases there are specific models, such as Document-based, Graph-based and more, each of which, in additional to the Relational model, may fit to specific types of applications. Hence, the issue of which database model to select for a given application becomes important. Nowadays, to the best of our knowledge, the selection of a database model is not based on systematic methods that consider the specific requirements and characteristics of the sought application. In this paper we propose a structured method for database model selection. The method considers a variety of factors, including data-related requirements, functional requirements and non-functional requirements. Based on these factors the method proposes the most appropriate database models for that application. We demonstrate the method through a running example.

Keywords: Database selection · Database models · NoSQL · NewSQL

1 Introduction

Databases are a fundamental part of every information system. They are created and manipulated by special types of software termed database management systems (DBMS). These are usually classified according to data models, meaning the way/structure the data are stored in the database. Relational databases, which were developed in the 1970s, dominate the market for a long time; in fact, they are still one of the top solutions to date[1]. Over the years many other database models have emerged, including object-oriented (OO), and more recently NoSQL (Not Only SQL) and NewSQL databases. A major advantage of OO databases is that they are integrated with OO programming languages and thus overcome the mismatch impedance between the Relational database and the programming languages. NoSQL databases are flexible, horizontally scalable that aim at overcoming the Relational databases rigidity. Lastly, NewSQL databases are a combination of the Relational and NoSQL databases, aimed to converge the advantages of both technologies.

Since many database models are available nowadays, there is a need for a method to select the most suitable database models for a specific application. Related studies mostly compare different DBMSs based on technical aspects such as replication type,

---

[1] https://db-engines.com/en/ranking.

© Springer Nature Switzerland AG 2019
I. Reinhartz-Berger et al. (Eds.): BPMDS 2019/EMMSAD 2019, LNBIP 352, pp. 261–275, 2019.
https://doi.org/10.1007/978-3-030-20618-5_18

atomicity type, data model, etc. These studies are useful for understanding different technical aspects of the databases. However, they hardly deal with how well the various databases fit with the specific requirements of an application. Practitioners who deal with the selection problem use three major strategies: (1) Agenda-based strategy, meaning that the selection is based on trends and on strong desire to learn something new. Since many new technologies emerge daily, some of them tend to gain a lot of attention. When being exposed to a new technology, practitioners tend to adapt it mainly because of the attention it is getting; (2) Knowledge-based strategy, meaning that the selection is based on personal or organizational knowledge or experience with previously used databases; and (3) Exploration-based strategy, meaning that the selection is based on analysis of the problem (data analysis, goal analysis) and finding the best DBMSs that fit the problem. Obviously, the third option is appealing; unfortunately, it is less used and is not structured or well-established.

In this study we propose a method for a database model selection that emphasizes the users' requirements, including data-related requirements, functional requirements and non-functional requirements. The proposed method will assist practitioners to choose the best database model. The sought method will "replace" the much needed analysis that practitioners require but lack to perform, and will help to save time and money, that might be wasted while selecting unfitting database model.

The rest of the paper is structured as follows. In Sect. 2 we review existing studies and best practices. In Sect. 3 we set the ground and formalize the proposed method. In Sect. 4 we provide an example that demonstrates the method. Finally, in Sect. 5 we summarize this study and elaborate on our plans for future research.

2   Related Work

Many technologies emerged in the database field. Various surveys, such as [3, 4, 6, 8, 9, 12, 14], discuss characteristics, capabilities and benefits of various database technologies. These characteristics include technical aspects such as supported query languages, index implementation, availability, consistency, etc. Yet, they usually do not deal with the issue of how to select a database model based on the users' needs and the requirements of the application.

Nevertheless, we found some studies that refer to the issue of database selection to some extent. For example, [1] compared different graph databases and their features, including storing features, querying features and data structures. [5] and [7] conducted empirical comparisons of different types of workloads, such as data insertion time and traversal time for different databases. [13] compared the performance of five NoSQL databases. The authors exclude graph database providers from their study since they claim that its use cases are different from the other three NoSQL database models. They defined three types of workloads and tested execution time and throughput for the five databases. While the study involved DBMSs of specific providers, the authors claim that "Document databases, followed by Column-family databases, have a good average performance since they own both efficiency and scalability". In [2] six database systems were compared based on different aspects. These were divided into functional, non-functional requirements and techniques. With respect to functional requirements, the authors compared supported types of queries, such as sorting, joins, transactions, etc. With respect to non-functional requirements, they compared latency and availability. With respect to techniques, they looked at technical aspects such as replication, logging and analytic framework. The authors provided a decision tree, consists of three levels, that maps some of the aspects to the different database providers.

In summary, the above studies did not deal specifically with how to select the appropriate database models based on the users' needs and requirements. In the next section, we propose a method that aims at bridging that gap.

3 The Proposed Selection Method

The proposed method for selecting database models considers various types of users' requirements. It is meant to be used in early stages of the application development process so the database model will fit the users' requirements. The method consists of the following steps:

1. Gather and specify the **data-related** requirements and express them using a conceptual data model. In this work we use the UML class diagram.
2. Gather and specify the **functional** requirements that are related to database operations, i.e., data retrievals and updates operations. Hereafter, we call them queries.
3. Gather and specify the **non-functional** requirements that are related to the data requirements and the queries.
4. Based on the above, consider to divide the conceptual data model into fragments, each of which has different characterizations (different performance requirements and different consistency requirements). The result of this step may be a selection of more than one database model.
5. Select the most suitable database model for each fragment. This will be based on a general-purpose pre-defined profile of each database model. A pre-defined profile consists of a set of non-functional properties associate with each database model.

Before proceeding into the details of each step, we provide a few basic definitions.

Definition 1. A *Database Specifcation* (DBS) is a pair of <SV, BV>. SV refers to the Structural View and BV refers to the Behavioural View.

Definition 2. A *Structural View* consists of classes, the relationships among them, and non-functional requirements (NFR): SV = <C, R, NFR>.

- C represents classes, each of which has attributes along with variability indicator.

$$c \in C, c = (name, ATTR), attr \in ATTR, attr = (name, type, var).$$

The variability indictor (*var*) indicates whether the attribute is common to all instances (marked M for mandatory) or only to some of them (marked O for optional). This indicator may affect the selection process. That is, many optional attributes would probably mean high flexibility.

– R represents binary relationships between related classes, their multiplicity, and variability.

$$r \in R, r = (source, target, scard, tcard, var), source, target \in C$$

scard and tcard indicate the multiplicity constraints, and var is the variability indicator.

– NFR represents the non-functional requirements related to the various classes and relationships. $nfr \in NFR, nfr = (e \in C \cup R$, requirement-type, requirement-value). At this stage we refer to the following requirement-types: {Consistency, Integrity, Flexibility, Volume, Velocity, Veracity}. Yet these can be change later on.

Definition 3. A *Behavioral View* consists of query quartettes = <type, query, C, NFRs>.

– type: insert, update, delete, select.
– query: refers to the actual query specification.
– C: refers to the classes involved within the specific query.
– NFRs is a list of (requirement-type, requirement-value). At this stage frequency is the only requirement-type that is addressed.

Definition 4. A Fragment (F) is a sub-set of the DBS specification, **F** ⊂ *DBS*.

In the following we elaborate on the various steps of the method.

Step 1: Gather and specify the data-related requirements

This step is not different from what is "traditionally" done in databases design: creating a conceptual database schema based on the users' requirements, using an existing conceptual modeling method. In this study we use the UML class diagram, consisting of data classes along with their attributes, the relationships between the classes, and various constraints.

Step 2: Gather and specify the functional/query requirements

Functional requirements are usually not considered in existing practices of database design. We claim that it is important to consider such requirements for the purpose of selecting the proper database model. Actually, we consider here only data-related functional requirements, i.e., requirements dealing with update and retrieval operations. Obviously, other functional requirements are also gathered and specified as part of the development process of the sought application, but these are not considered here with respect to database model selection.

It is assumed that relevant functional requirements (queries) are gathered from the users who express their needs in natural language. We plan to convert each such "natural language" query into a SQL-like query using syntax adopted from [10]. SQL-like syntax is relatively easy to learn and can be used later on to analyze the query. Here are some examples of this language:

• **Return** – returns listed items to the user.
• **All** – returns all relevant items.

- **From** – where is the data taken from. Data can be taken from one or several classes.
- **Where** – filtering conditions. This will probably be accompanied by '?' to state the parameter of the filter.
- **Query type** – one of **Update/ Insert/ Delete** – the needed changes. **Set** – the actual insert or update; **Connect** – create relationship among classes.
- **Rel** – represents the relationship type in the Where and Set clauses; used when several relationships exist between the same two classes in order to distinguish between them.
- **As** – used in the From clause where there is a cyclic query and the same class is used multiple times.

From the given queries, we determine their complexity using a scale of 1–5. The complexity value of a query depends on the complexity of its functions. For example, a simple Get or Set query gets a complexity value 1. A path finding query gets a complexity value 5. Complexity values 2–4 are assigned to queries involving filtering, joins and advanced search, respectively, representing the complexity of these operations. We assign these values of complexity based on different surveys [2, 4, 6], yet, it is might be that another analysis would results in different values.

Step 3: Gather and specify the non-functional requirements (NFR)
NFRs play a major role in software system design. In this study we focus on specific NFRs that affect the database selection. For example, when referring to data consistency, relational DBMSs support ACID and thus provide high consistency compare to most NoSQL systems that support eventual consistency.

Based on the literature on database technology [2, 6], in the following we present a list of possible NFRs. Each NFR is associated with a weight that determines its **importance**. High weight for an NFR means that it might have higher impact on the classes' similarity. We chose the weights based on Analytical Hierarchy Process (AHP) [11]. The pairwise comparisons, which compose the input for the AHP, were chosen based on previous knowledge and surveys on the different databases such as [3, 4, 6]. We determine that *consistency* is the most important NFR since it has the biggest impact on the chosen model. For example, if two data classes require strong consistency they are similar and more likely to be in the same fragment. *Integrity* and *flexibility* are of second and third importance, respectively, with relatively high importance. The other three NFRs (*velocity*, *volume* and *veracity*) are of less importance, while *Veracity* is the least important. These weights of importance may be changed as we gain further understanding.

The following demonstrate the chosen NFRs, their possible values, and weights. At this stages, the values are categorical. In the next steps they are transformed into numerical values. In the future, we might include more fined-grained numerical values.

- Consistency – Eventual Consistency, Strong Consistency. (Note that there are different levels to consistency in different DBMSs.). **AHP Weight: 0.46.**
- Integrity – Low (system may contain incorrect data, e.g., DOB > today), High (data must be correct at all times). **AHP Weight: 0.25.**

- Flexibility – Very low (changes are needed once a month or slower), low (once a week), medium (several times a week), high (less than twice a day), very high (several changes per day). **AHP Weight: 0.12.**
- Velocity – Data arrives very slow (once a month or slower), slow (once a week), medium (several times a week), fast (less than twice a day), very fast (e.g. several times per day). **AHP Weight: 0.08.**
- Volume – Based on the estimated size of the entities, between 0 and 1. **AHP Weight: 0.05.**
- Veracity – High (data is very noisy/sparse/abnormal), medium (data might be noisy/sparse/abnormal), low (data is not noisy/sparse/abnormal). **AHP Weight: 0.04.**

In addition to the general NFRs, we also take into consideration a specific NFR that relates to queries, the frequency of each query, how many times the query is expected to run per a time unit (e.g., second, day). In this step the frequency of each query is defined.

Step 4: Consider to divide the conceptual data model into fragments
Relatively large applications with many users and diverse needs may have to be implemented with more than one database model; a method for database selection should also deal with such possibility. This means that we need to examine the different requirements and check if and how to divide the conceptual schema into fragments. Each of the fragments may be implemented with a different database model.

When implementing the application with several database models, we need to take into account that joining data from different sources in code could decrease performances. However in the era of data variety, different data might require different treatment and storage. Therefore, fragmentation may improve performance for each fragment individually.

For this step, we need to analyze the proximity among the data classes and cluster closely related classes. For that purpose, we define the notion of proximity matrix.

Definition 5. A *class proximity matrix* determines the closeness among pairs of classes in the conceptual data model. The values of this matrix are normalized to 0-1.

Definition 6. A *relationship proximity matrix* determines the structural closeness among all pairs of classes. This is determined by the number of relationships among all pairs of classes.

Definition 7. A *functional proximity matrix* determines the functional closeness among all pairs of classes. This is determined by the number of classes' pairs within the queries.

Definition 8. A *non-functional proximity matrix* determines the closeness among all pairs of classes based on similarity of their non-functional requirements. The similarity is a weighted non-functional similarity function that is defined as follows: $nfs(c_1, c_2) = \sum \alpha_i * (1 - (\beta_i(c_1) - \beta_i(c_2)))$, where α_i is the weight of the i-nfr (introduced in step 3) and β_i is the value of the i-nfr. $\sum \alpha_i = 1$.

Having defined the three proximity matrices, the next step is to merge them into a single matrix reflecting the unified proximity of classes. This is done by weighting the normalized values within the three matrices, based on weights determined by AHP. The unified proximity matrix is used as an input for a clustering algorithm that gathers closely related classes into fragments.

For clustering the classes we adopt the DBSCAN algorithm[2]. DBSCAN receives as input a distance matrix (inverse of the proximity matrix in Definition 5), and finds the best number of clusters and the clustering partition. We chose this algorithm due to the fact that it receives a distance matrix and determines the best number of clusters, while other algorithms, such as K-Means, require to define beforehand the number of needed (K) clusters.

Step 5: Select the most suitable database model for each fragment

To select the most suitable database model for each fragment, we define profiles.

Definition 9. A profile is a vector of non-functional requirements pairs: P = {(nfr-name, nfr-value)}. We define profiles of database models and profiles of fragments.

For a profile we consider only non-functional requirements and query complexity, since these factors determine the differences between database models. Based on the literature we define profiles for the different database models, as follows.

Most of the NFRs differentiate between NoSQL and Relational databases. NoSQL databases support eventual consistency and low integrity. In addition, since they lack schemas, they are more flexible and by definition they support many type of data (i.e., variety) [2, 3, 6]. Within the family of NoSQL databases different systems handle size, data model, and query complexity differently. There is a tradeoff between size and complexity, as can be seen in Fig. 1, adapted from [6]: the bigger the database, the smaller its complexity. Therefore, we decide to define the size of data as a function of the data (and therefore) query complexity, as shown in Tables 1 and 2.

Table 1. NFRs values for the different DBMSs

	Consistency	Integrity	Flexibility	Volume	Velocity	Veracity	Query complexity
RDBMS	Strong	High	Low	Low	Low	Low	Low
Key-value	Eventual	Low	High	High	High	High	Very low
Column based	Eventual	Low	High	High	High	High	Medium
Graph	Eventual	Low	High	High	High	High	Very high
Document	Eventual	Low	High	High	High	High	High
NewSQL	Strong	High	Low	High	Low	Low	Low

---

[2] https://scikit-learn.org/stable/modules/generated/sklearn.cluster.DBSCAN.html.

Table 2. NFRs numerical values (the databases' profiles)

	Consistency	Integrity	Flexibility	Volume	Velocity	Veracity	Query complexity
RDBMS	2	2	1	0.05	1	1	3
Key-value	1	1	5	1	5	3	1
Column based	1	1	5	0.5	5	3	2
Graph	1	1	5	0.2	5	3	5
Document	1	1	5	0.25	5	3	4
NewSQL	2	2	1	1	1	1	3

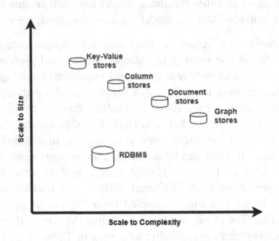

Fig. 1. NoSQL solutions: complexity vs. size - adopted from [6].

Table 1 shows NFR values for the different databases, whereas Table 2 further drills down into the differences between the database models and assigns numerical values. Each database model receives a query complexity value between 1 and 5. We decided to locate RDBMS query complexity between the Column and Document databases, and assign it a complexity value 3, since RDBMS supports more complex capabilities such as joins, but it does not support traversal or full text search. For NoSQL databases we use the said complexity to calculate the data volume (size) using the function: size = 1/complexity. Since RDBMS (within a single server), relatively to NoSQL databases, is used for low data volume, we set a lower value of 0.05 and NewSQL was assigned with the value 1.

Finally, a fragment's profile is calculated as an average of each of the non-functional requirements of the participating classes. The selection of the appropriate database model will be based on the weighted distance between each fragments' profile and the profiles of the database models.

Definition 10. *Profile similarity* is defined as inverse of weighted Manhattan distance[3] between the database model profile and the fragment profile. The chosen database model is the one with the minimal distance, i.e., with the most similar profile.

4 Example

In this section we demonstrate the proposed method using an IMDB[4]-like system (i.e., "Movies" database). This system stores data about watch items (movies, series and episodes) and their ratings by users who watched them. For each watch item the system stores data about its directors, producers and actors. For each actor the system stores various properties such as name and role in each watch item. A user of this system may login in order to rate a watched item. For each item the system also stores special information such as goofs, trivia information (as 'did you know?') and funny/sentimental quotes.

According to the first step, Fig. 2 presents the structural view, i.e. a conceptual database model in the form of a UML class diagram.

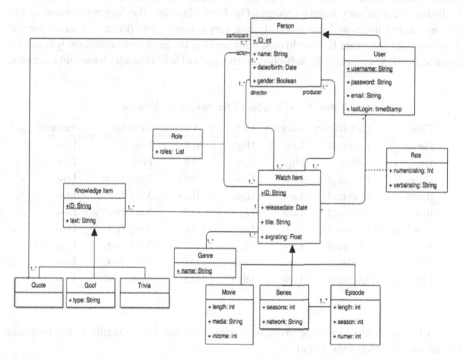

Fig. 2. Class diagram representing the conceptual database model for the "Movies" database

---

[3] https://xlinux.nist.gov/dads/HTML/manhattanDistance.html.
[4] https://www.imdb.com/.

In the second step, we gather and specify the functional view in the form of 5 queries:

- **Query 1.** Login (RETURN password FROM User where username = ?)
- **Query 2.** Simple search (RETURN ALL FROM Watch Item where title = ?)
- **Query 3.** Addition of all entities and relationships (two examples: Insert Person SET name = ?, CONNECT Person, Watch Item WHERE name = ? and title = ? SET REL = ?)
- **Query 4.** Recommendation query (RETURN rec.title FROM watch item as rec, watch item AS org WHERE org.Genre = rec.Genre and type(org) = type(rec) and rec.releasedate BETWEEN org.releasedate += 10)
- **Query 5.** ALL persons (of type) for a watch item (RETURN Person.All FROM Watch Item, Person where title = ? and rel = Actor)

In the third step, the NFRs are gathered. Table 3 presents a possible way to specify the NFRs and their values for the constructs of the conceptual database model. The example includes only classes; yet these might apply to other components of the conceptual model (relationships, attributes and constraints), as defined in the previous sections under the structural view. In Table 3, both *User* and *Genre* classes have low flexibility because they hardly change. The *User* class has the highest volume in this system – many users will use it. *Genre* is a very limited class (there is a small number of genres) and therefore has the lowest volume. Due to space limitations we ignored the Knowledge Item class and its sub-classes; the method will take all classes into account.

Table 3. NFR table of the "Movies" database

Class	Consistency	Integrity	Flexibility	Volume	Velocity	Veracity
Person	Eventual	Low	High	0.8	Fast	Low
User	Strong	High	Low	0.9	Fast	Low
Genre	Eventual	Low	Low	0.01	Very slow	Low
Role	Eventual	Low	High	0.55	Very fast	Low
Rate	Eventual	Low	High	0.7	Very fast/Fast	Low
Watch item	Eventual	Low	High	0.6	Very fast	Low
Series	Eventual	Low	High	0.1	Very fast	Low
Movie	Eventual	Low	High	0.2	Very fast	Low
Episode	Eventual	Low	High	0.3	Very fast	Low

To further demonstrate the process, we translate the requirements to the proposed formalism in Definitions 1 and 2.

- The application database specification, DBS:
  - The structural view SV, in which we will focus on C and NFR. We follow the form of (ClassName, {ATTR}, {NFRs Values: Consistency, Integrity, Flexibility, Volume, Velocity, Veracity}). Following a partial example of the SV:

- **(Person**, {(ID, int, M), (name, string, M), (dateofbirth, Date, O), (gender, Boolean, O)}, {Eventual, Low, High, 2 (0.01 Users), Fast, Low})
- **(User**, {(ID, int, M), (name, string, M), (dateofbirth, Date, O), (gender, Boolean, O), (username, string, M), (password, string, M), (email, string, M), (lastlogin, DateTime, M)}, {Strong, High, Low, 1, Fast, Low})
- **(Genre**, {(name, String, M)}, {Eventual, Low, Low, 6 ($\sim$50), Very Slow, Low})

- The behavioral view BV, in which we define the frequency in time per minute (tpm)
    - **Query 1**. (SELECT, return password FROM user WHERE username = ?, {User}. {60 tpm}) **Complexity level: 2**
    - **Query 2**. (SELECT, return All FROM Watch Item WHERE title = ?, {Watch Item}, {3 tpm}) **Complexity level: 2**
    - **Query 3a**. (INSERT, Insert Person SET name = ?, {Person}, {1 tpm}) **Complexity level: 1**
    - **Query 3b**. (INSERT, Insert rel = ? Of Person, Watch Item WHERE name = ? and title = ?{Person, Watch Item}, {4 tpm}) **Complexity level: 3**
    - **Query 4**. (SELECT, Return rec.title FROM Watch Item as rec, Genre, Watch Item as org WHERE org.Genre = rec.Genre and type(org) = type(rec) and rec.releasedate between org.releasedate += 10, {Watch Item, Watch Item, Genre}, {6 tpm}) **Complexity level: 3**
    - **Query 5**. (SELECT, return Person.All FROM Watch Item, Person WHERE title = ? and rel = Actor, {Watch Item, Person}, {1 tpm}) **Complexity level: 3**

Based on these definitions the related proximity matrices can be derived.

Table 4. Relationship proximity matrix for the IMDB-like case

Class	Person	User	Genre	Role	Rate	Watch item	Series	Movie	Episode
Person	0								
User	1	0							
Genre	0	0	0						
Role	1	0	0	0					
Rate	0	1	0	0	0				
Watch item	3	1	1	1	1	0			
Series	0	0	0	0	0	1	0		
Movie	0	0	0	0	0	1	0	0	
Episode	0	0	0	0	0	1	1	0	0

Table 4 presents the relationship proximity matrix in which we count the relationships that exist between the classes in the structural view. Since the *Person* class has three different relationships with the *Watch Item* class, the relationship value for the two classes is 3.

Table 5 presents the functional proximity matrix in which we count the number of queries in which a pair of classes appear together. Table 6 is calculated based on the formula in Definition 8.

Table 5. Functional proximity matrix for the IMDB-like case

Class	Person	User	Genre	Role	Rate	Watch item	Series	Movie	Episode
Person	0								
User	0	0							
Genre	0	0	0						
Role	0	0	0	0					
Rate	0	0	0	0	0				
Watch item	2	0	1	0	0	1			
Series	0	0	0	0	0	0	0		
Movie	0	0	0	0	0	0	0	0	
Episode	0	0	0	0	0	0	0	0	0

Table 6. Non-functional proximity matrix for the IMDB-like case

Class	Person	User	Genre	Role	Rate	Watch item	Series	Movie	Episode
Person	1.00								
User	0.22	1.00							
Genre	0.84	0.18	1.00						
Role	0.97	0.19	0.85	1.00					
Rate	0.99	0.21	0.85	0.99	1.00				
Watch item	0.97	0.19	0.84	0.99	0.98	1.00			
Series	0.93	0.15	0.88	0.95	0.94	0.96	1.00		
Movie	0.94	0.16	0.87	0.96	0.95	0.97	0.99	1.00	
Episode	0.95	0.17	0.87	0.97	0.96	0.98	0.98	0.99	1.00

Table 7. Final proximity matrix

Class	Person	User	Genre	Role	Rate	Watch item	Series	Movie	Episode
Person	0.54								
User	0.17	0.54							
Genre	0.45	0.10	0.54						
Role	0.58	0.10	0.46	0.54					
Rate	0.54	0.17	0.46	0.53	0.54				
Watch item	0.98	0.16	0.66	0.59	0.58	0.69			
Series	0.50	0.08	0.48	0.51	0.51	0.57	0.54		
Movie	0.51	0.09	0.47	0.52	0.51	0.58	0.54	0.54	
Episode	0.51	0.09	0.47	0.52	0.52	0.58	0.58	0.54	0.54

Table 7 is the final proximity matrix. In this table we present the weighted average of the three proximity matrices (Tables 4, 5 and 6), based on the weights chosen by AHP. The matrix in Table 4 received the weight of 0.16; the matrix in Table 5 received the weight of 0.3; and the matrix in Table 6 received the weight of 0.54. These weights indicate that relationship proximity is the least important: the fact that two classes are linked in the conceptual model, should have less impact on them being clustered together. However, if two classes are queried together or more importantly, share the same non-functional characteristics; the need to be clustered these together is much more important. As in the case of the weights for the different NFRs, these weights might be changed as we gain further understanding.

Applying the DBSCAN algorithm on the proximity matrix (Table 7) resulted with the suggestion of two clusters: one for the *User* class, and another for the rest of the classes.

Observing Table 3, we note the difference between the *User* class and the other classes. The *User* class requires strong consistency and integrity since it contains information regarding user password, which has to be correct at all times and changed immediately throughout the entire system. In addition, the user data in itself is not flexible (username will probably not change and password will be always in the same format) and queries that refer to the *User* class do not refer to other classes. Therefore, it is likely to define a separate fragment for the *User* class. This can be clearly seen in the matrix on Table 7 in which the *User* class has low proximity with the other classes based on the NFRs.

Another observation is that the Genre class is a bit different from other classes with respect to flexibility and velocity: Genres are pretty static since new genres are hardly like to occur; therefore the velocity is slow, and their properties are also static and therefore have low flexibility. However, since this class is used as part of a query with other classes (such as recommendation queries, as can be seen in Table 5) and not on its own, it is not justified to create a separate fragment for it.

After partitioning the conceptual database model into two fragments, we attach the respective queries along with their functional and non-functional requirements to each fragment. In the next step we select the proper database model for each fragment, based on these elements.

For each fragment we calculated its profile. For the fragments' profile, we calculate for each NFR the average of the values associated with the fragment elements (i.e., classes and queries). The results of this calculation is presented in Table 8. In the next step, we calculate the distance between the fragments' profile and the different databases' profiles shown in Table 2. The distance is calculated based on weighted normalized (i.e., a number between 0 and 1) Manhattan distance. Table 9 shows the normalized distances for each fragment.

Based on the above process, we recommend that the IMDB-like system should use two database models: a NewSQL system for the *User* data and a Column-based system for the rest of the data. Another option for the rest of the data is a Document model, which received a similar low score to column based.

Table 8. Profiles of the fragments

User

	Consistency	Integrity	Flexibility	Volume	Velocity	Veracity	Query complexity
avg =	2	2	5	0.9	1	3	2

Rest

	Consistency	Integrity	Flexibility	Volume	Velocity	Veracity	Query complexity
avg =	1	1	2.25	0.407	1.75	3	2.875

Table 9. Distance for the fragments

User

	Consistency	Integrity	Flexibility	Volume	Velocity	Veracity	Query complexity	Distance
RDBMS	0	0	1	0.85	0	1	0.25	0.443
Key-value	1	1	0	0.1	1	0	0.25	0.479
Column based	1	1	0	0.4	1	0	0	0.486
Graph	1	1	0	0.7	1	0	0.75	0.636
Document	1	1	0	0.65	1	0	0.5	0.593
NewSQL	**0**	**0**	**1**	**0.1**	**0**	**1**	**0.25**	**0.336**

Rest

	Consistency	Integrity	Flexibility	Volume	Velocity	Veracity	Query complexity	Distance
RDBMS	1	1	0.31	0.36	0.19	1	0.03	0.556
Key-value	0	0	0.69	0.59	0.81	0	0.47	0.366
Column based	**0**	**0**	**0.69**	**0.09**	**0.81**	**0**	**0.22**	**0.259**
Graph	0	0	0.69	0.21	0.81	0	0.531	0.320
Document	0	0	0.69	0.16	0.81	0	0.28	0.277
NewSQL	1	0	0.31	0.59	0.19	1	0.03	0.589

5 Summary and Future Work

In this paper we propose a method for selecting the most fitting database model(s) for a set of requirements. The method contains five steps beginning with the creation of a conceptual database model (i.e., a UML class diagram), and terminating with the selection of the most fitting database models for the sought application. We demonstrated the method on a small example. We plan to test the method in real applications to further determine the required weights and to test its usefulness. We also plan to develop software tools to support utilization of the method.

We also plan to add a sixth step that will deal with designing the database schemas for the selected database models. Methods for designing Relational and some NoSQL database schemas already exist; we plan to develop methods for designing database schemas for other types on NoSQL database models.

References

1. Angles, R.: A comparison of current graph database models. In: 2012 IEEE 28th International Conference on Data Engineering Workshops, pp. 171–177. IEEE, April 2012
2. Gessert, F., Wingerath, W., Friedrich, S., Ritter, N.: NoSQL database systems: a survey and decision guidance. Comput. Sci. Res. Dev. **32**(3–4), 353–365 (2017)
3. Han, J., Haihong, E., Le, G., Du, J.: Survey on NoSQL database. In: 2011 6th International Conference on Pervasive Computing and Applications, pp. 363–366. IEEE, October 2011
4. Haseeb, A., Pattun, G.: A review on NoSQL: applications and challenges. Int. J. Adv. Res. Comput. Sci. **8**(1), 203–207 (2017)
5. Jouili, S., Vansteenberghe, V.: An empirical comparison of graph databases. In: 2013 International Conference on Social Computing, pp. 708–715. IEEE, September 2013
6. Khazaei, H., et al.: How do I choose the right NoSQL solution? A comprehensive theoretical and experimental survey. Big Data Inf. Anal. (BDIA) **2**, 1 (2016)
7. Kolomičenko, V., Svoboda, M., Mlýnková, I.H.: Experimental comparison of graph databases. In: Proceedings of International Conference on Information Integration and Web-based Applications & Services, p. 115. ACM, December 2013
8. Kumar, R., Parashar, B.B., Gupta, S., Sharma, Y., Gupta, N.: Apache Hadoop, NoSQL and NewSQL solutions of big data. Int. J. Adv. Found. Res. Sci. Eng. (IJAFRSE) **1**(6), 28–36 (2014)
9. Lourenço, J.R., Cabral, B., Carreiro, P., Vieira, M., Bernardino, J.: Choosing the right NoSQL database for the job: a quality attribute evaluation. J. Big Data **2**(1), 18 (2015)
10. Mior, M.J., Salem, K., Aboulnaga, A., Liu, R.: NoSE: schema design for NoSQL applications. IEEE Trans. Knowl. Data Eng. **29**(10), 2275–2289 (2017)
11. Saaty, T.L.: Decision making with the analytic hierarchy process. Int. J. Serv. Sci. **1**(1), 83–98 (2008)
12. Storey, V.C., Song, I.Y.: Big data technologies and management: what conceptual modeling can do. Data Knowl. Eng. **108**, 50–67 (2017)
13. Tang, E., Fan, Y.: Performance comparison between five NoSQL databases. In: 2016 7th International Conference on Cloud Computing and Big Data, pp. 105–109. IEEE, November 2016
14. Tudorica, B.G., Bucur, C.: A comparison between several NoSQL databases with comments and notes. In: 2011 RoEduNet International Conference 10th Edition: Networking in Education and Research, pp. 1–5. IEEE, June 2011

Domain-Specific and Ontology Modeling (EMMSAD 2019)

Towards Ontological Support
for Journalistic Angles

Andreas L. Opdahl$^{(\boxtimes)}$ and Bjørnar Tessem

Department of Information Science and Media Studies,
University of Bergen, 5020 Bergen, Norway
{Andreas.Opdahl,Bjornar.Tessem}@uib.no
http://www.uib.no/en/rg/ssis

Abstract. Journalism relies more and more on information and communication technology (ICT). New journalistic ICT platforms continuously harvest potentially news-related information from the internet and try to make it useful for journalists. Because the information sources and formats vary widely, *knowledge graphs* are emerging as a preferred technology for integrating, enriching, and preparing journalistic information. The paper explores how journalistic knowledge graphs can be augmented with support for *news angles*, in order to help journalists detect newsworthy events and present them in ways that will interest the intended audience. We argue that finding newsworthy angles on news-related information is important as an example of a more general problem in information science: that of finding the most interesting events and situations in big data sets and presenting those events and situations in the most interesting ways.

Keywords: Computational journalism · ICT tool for journalists ·
News platforms · Newsroom systems · Knowledge graphs · Ontology

1 Introduction

Journalism relies more and more on computers and the internet [17]. News platforms such as Event Registry [14], Reuters Tracer [15], and Bloomberg's knowledge graph [29] continuously harvest potentially news-related information from the internet and try to make it useful for journalists. Because the information sources and formats vary widely, *knowledge graphs* and related semantic technologies [1] are emerging as preferred solutions for integrating, enriching, and preparing journalistic information. Semantic technologies support information *integration* because they offer a standard Resource Description Format (RDF) for representing and exchanging facts [1]. They support information *enrichment* because they represent resources—such as concepts and concrete objects (people, organisations, locations, works...)—using standard IRIs that provide access to further information about the resources. And they support reasoning techniques,

© Springer Nature Switzerland AG 2019
I. Reinhartz-Berger et al. (Eds.): BPMDS 2019/EMMSAD 2019, LNBIP 352, pp. 279–294, 2019.
https://doi.org/10.1007/978-3-030-20618-5_19

for example using OWL DL or rule languages, that can be used for *preparing* information for journalists.

The paper explores how journalistic knowledge graphs—represented in RDF, a type of property graph—can be augmented with support for *news angles* that can be used to detect newsworthy events and present those events in interesting ways. Finding or inventing good news angles on unfolding events is a central journalistic skill, which we seek to formalise in order to help journalists with: responding quickly to newsworthy events; identifying appropriate angles on those events; and backing those angles up with relevant information. Examples of angles are *conflict, local person*, and *fall from grace*. Some angles are more detailed versions of others, such as *David-versus-Goliath*, a subtype of *conflict*. The paper proposes OWL ontologies that can be used to organise knowledge graphs that support news angles. We ask: *how can ontologies be used to organise journalistic knowledge graphs and augment them to support news angles.* To answer this question, the rest of the paper is organised as follows: Sect. 2 reviews existing work. Section 3 proposes suitable ontologies. Section 4 discusses our approach, before Sect. 5 concludes the paper and offers paths for further work.

2   Existing Work

2.1   Computational and Data Journalism

There are different ways to use computational resources in journalism [3,25]: precision journalism, computer-assisted journalism, data journalism, database journalism, data-driven journalism, and finally computational journalism. The latter is characterised by its focus on computation and software as driving tools for creating journalistic content, whereas data journalism places the journalist in the driver's seat in the creation and presentation of content [25]. Following this typology, our paper presents a *computational journalism* approach, albeit one that aims at supporting journalists rather than automating journalism.

2.2   AI-support for Journalism

Artificial intelligence (AI) in journalism can be divided into four areas: data mining, topic selection, commentary moderation, and news writing [19]. Commercial companies such as Narrative Science and Automated Insights have already developed journalistic robots that automatically generate news reports in areas such as finance and sports [13]. In 2016 alone, Automated Insight's Wordsmith tool wrote and published 1.5 billion news reports, possibly more than all the human journalists in the world [19].

2.3   News Platforms

Recent developments in AI have been driven in part by the availability of *big and open data sources* that are relevant for journalism. For example, researchers have investigated how news events can be extracted from big-data sources such as Tweets [12] and other texts [10].

We define a *news platform* [3] as an integrated system that continually *harvests* potentially news-related information from a variety of sources, *integrates* the information, *prepares* it for journalistic use, and *provides* potentially relevant information to journalists or the general audience, whether passively on demand or proactively through event detection. Reuters Tracer [15] is a news platform with similar goals to ours. It targets journalists, but does not use knowledge graphs and ontologies and does not support angles.

2.4 Knowledge Graphs for Journalists

Event Registry [14] is a news platform that collects news messages and lifts them into a semantic *knowledge graph* (in RDF) in order to detect and describe news events in real time. Bloomberg's knowledge graph [29] is a similar platform. They are both based on semantic technologies, but Event Registry targets a wider audience, and neither platform supports news angles.

Beyond news platforms, researchers have used semantic technologies in other ways to make big and open data sources more readily available for journalists [27] and journalistic AI tools [7]. Fernandez et al. [4] propose an ontology for streamlining news production and distribution. Heravi et al. [9] advocate *social semantic journalism*, which uses natural-language processing (NLP) and semantic metadata together to: detect news events from socially-generated big data; verify information and its sources: identify eyewitnesses; and contextualise news events and their coverage.

2.5 News Hunter

In collaboration with Wolftech, a developer of news-production software for the international market, our research group is developing News Hunter, a knowledge-graph based news platform for journalists [2, 20]. News Hunter is a proof-of-concept prototype that has been designed to continually harvest news items and social media messages from the web; analyse and represent them semantically in a knowledge graph; classify, cluster, and label them; enrich them with additional information from encyclopedic and other reference sources; and present them in real time to journalists as suggestions for new or updated reports.

This paper builds on previous papers that: give an overview of the previous News Hunter prototype (which did not support angles) [2]; discuss the concept of news angles and outline a suitable big-data architecture [5]; and investigate reasoning approaches for detecting news angles along with suitable ontologies [26]. Compared to a previous short paper [26], the present one: develops the ontologies further; discusses them in more detail; places them in an architectural context; and illustrates them using a real news event as a running example.

3 Ontologies

To prepare for a knowledge-graph based ICT platform for journalists, this section will present core ontologies for representing: potentially news-relevant information in semantic form; potentially newsworthy events detected and aggregated from that information; and possible news angles on those events. Building on our experiences from earlier News Hunter prototypes, this section will present the three corresponding ontologies and outline the roles they will play in the augmented News Hunter platform. For each ontology, we will first explain the *role* it plays in the News Hunter architecture; then the *ontology* itself and its central terms; the *processing* techniques that can be used to populate and analyse it; and finally an *example* graph in RDF, serialised using Turtle notation.

3.1 News Items

News Hunter will continuously harvest potentially news-relevant information *items* from a variety of sources in different formats. So far, we have explored harvesting of: messages from social media like Facebook and Twitter; articles from newspapers on the web; and items from RSS. But relevant information items are available from a much wider range of sources that include: commercial news services like AP and Reuters; the home pages of commercial companies and public authorities; and the Internet of Things (IoT). We have so far focussed on textual items, but strive to develop a platform that is open to also include images, audio, and video in the future.

Architectural Role: Harvested items are first filtered. The ones that are deemed potentially news-related are *lifted* into semantic form and represented as *item (sub-)graphs* of the central knowledge graph. A driving idea behind News Hunter is that the graph may facilitate reasoning that goes beyond standard text-based similarity searches: detecting and populating news angles is one example. Nevertheless, we also store each filtered item closer to its original form as a JSON object in a database, indexed from the knowledge graph.

Ontology: Figure 1 shows how a potentially news-relevant **Item** is represented semantically as an item graph.[1] Each item has an **originalTitle**, an **originalText**, and a **sourceIRL** among its attributes. It has a **Person** as its **contributor**, perhaps contributing through or on behalf of a **source Agent**. The agent can be, e.g., an organisation or web site, whereas the contributor can be a natural person or a social-media handle.

The item's semantics is represented by **Annotations**, each of which contains a single piece of semantic information about the item. In Fig. 1, the **Annotation**

---

[1] This and later OWL ontologies have been created using Protege-OWL and rendered using WebVOWL [16].

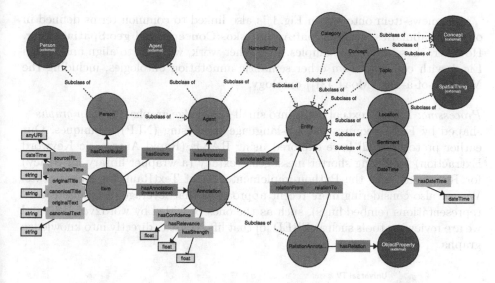

Fig. 1. Ontology for representing news items semantically as knowledge graphs.

class is therefore in turn related to an **Entity** in the knowledge graph, of which there are several subtypes:

- A **NamedEntity** mentioned in the text, possibly a named geolocation.
- A **Concept**, **Topic**, or **Category** reflected in the text, all of them subtypes of **skos:Concept**. The difference is that a concept must be a word or phrase used in the text, whereas topics and categories can be latent. Categories must also be taken from a restricted vocabulary, such as the IPTC media topics [11].
- A **Location** (**geo:SpatialThing**) or a **DateTime** (**xsd:dateTime**) associated with the text.
- A **Sentiment** reflected in the text.

Each instance of these classes (**NamedEntity, Concept, Topic, Category, Location, DateTime**, and **Sentiment**) has an IRI and can be extended with triples from the Linked Open Data (LOD) cloud and from proprietary resources. A **RelationAnnotation** can even represent a semantic relation between a pair of entities annotating the same item, using the **hasRelation** property to indicate the semantic relationship intended.

Each annotation has a **confidence** that expresses trust in its sources and a **relevance** that expresses how semantically central it is to the item. A relation annotation can also have a **strength** that expresses how forcefully the relation holds, if it is of a graded type. An annotation can also have a **foaf:Agent** as its **annotator**, which will usually be a piece of software or a service, such as a named entity linker or sentiment analyser. We expect that linking annotations to their annotators in this way will be useful whenever the semantic-lifting software is later improved or turns out to have been imprecise or faulty.

The news-item ontology in Fig. 1 is also linked to common terms defined in other vocabularies, such as **foaf:Agent**, **skos:Concept**, and **geo:SpatialThing**. However, these are just examples. In further work, we want to align and enrich Fig. 1 with concepts from other semantic annotation ontologies, including the Meaning-of-a-Tag (MoaT [21]) ontology.

Processing: Lifting textual items into small knowledge graphs—or *item graphs*—shaped by Fig. 1 requires natural-language processing (NLP) techniques. Our earlier prototypes [2] have explored using RAKE (Rapid Automatic Keyword Extraction) for lifting shorter messages, Textacy (a wrapper library for Spacy) for RSS feeds, and the Python-implementation of TextRank for longer texts. We are also considering more recent approaches that leverage distributed word representations (embeddings), such as the ones provided by word2vec [18], and we are reviewing tools such as FRED [6] that lift NL texts directly into knowledge graphs.

Fig. 2. An example tweet written in Somali, announcing that President Farmajo has appointed Hassan Sheikh Ali as the new prime minister of Somalia.

Example: Figure 2 shows a tweet posted by Universal Somali TV early in the morning on February 23rd 2017. Listing 1 shows an item graph that could result from lifting the text in this tweet, supported by the context provided by the news article it links to.[2] The tweet proclaims that President Mohamed Abdullahi Farmajo appoints Hassan Ali Khayre as the new Prime Minister of Somalia. Importantly, the lifting process has resolved the Somalian name Xasan Khayre Cali to its international counterpart: Hassan Ali Khayre. President Farmajo has been successfully resolved to a DBpedia IRI, whereas the new prime minister Khayre is not yet defined in DBpedia or Wikidata and is therefore given an internal News Hunter IRI that begins with `:unres/...` for *unresolved*.

Outside north-eastern Africa, the Somalian prime-minister appointment might not warrant prominent mention in the news. But a Norwegian newsroom could detect it as potentially newsworthy, because the newsroom's knowledge graph might already contain triples about the similar unresolved IRI `:unres/Hassan_Khaire`, shown in Listing 2, that was harvested and lifted from a YouTube video caption uploaded by The Royal House of Norway in 2010.

---

[2] For the purpose of the example, we have used Google Translate and adapted the outputs of IBM Watson's Natural Language Understanding service. We have enriched the resulting item graph with additional triples from DBpedia and Wikidata.

Listing 1. The tweet in Figure 2 represented semantically as an item graph.

```
:twitter834619575509594114 a :Item;
    :source dbp:dbpedia.org/resource/Universal_Television_(Somalia);
    :sourceIRL "https://twitter.com/ ... /834619575509594114";
    :originalText "WAR DEG DEG: Madaxweyne Farmaajo oo ..."@so;
    :canonicalText "PRESS RELEASE: President Farmajo appointed
                    Hassan Sheikh Ali as new prime minister";
    :hasAnnotation [    a :Annotation;
                        :hasEntity dbp:Mohamed_Abdullahi_Farmajo;
                        :hasConfidence 0.9;
                        :hasRelevance 0.33;
                        :hasStrength 1.0                            ];
    :hasAnnotation [    a :Annotation;
                        :hasEntity :unres/Hassan_Ali_Khayre        ];
    :hasAnnotation [    a :RelationAnnotation;
                        :hasRelation wn:appoint;
                        :relationFrom dbp:Mohamed_Abdullahi_Farmajo;
                        :relationTo :unres/Hassan_Ali_Khayre       ];
    :hasAnnotation [    a :RelationAnnotation;
                        :hasRelation wde:Q14212;
                        :relationFrom :unres/Hassan_Ali_Khayre;
                        :relationTo dbp:Prime_minister             ]
```

3.2   News Events

To represent potentially newsworthy *events*, the individual item graphs must be clustered, merged, and enriched to form *event (sub-)graphs* of the central knowledge graph. Because they are aggregated, event graphs provide more complete and precise information than individual item graphs, many of which may only describe a small part or aspect of an event. Event graphs are also corroborated by more sources, which is particularly important for social-media messages that originate from less known contributors and whose annotations may have low confidence.

Architectural Role: Items are clustered into event graphs according to their annotations, such as their named entities, concepts/topics/categories, locations and date-times, most of which will be shared by many item sub-graphs. Clustering can take into account item annotations that are identical as well as related: either semantically, for example through taxonomical or mereological relations, or lexically, for example using Levenshtein distance or similar measures to detect different spellings of the same name. To the extent possible, cluster detection should also identify how larger events are composed of sub-events with temporal, causal, and other relations between them. Annotation entities and relations from item graphs in the same cluster are then merged to form the event graph, whose entities can be enriched with further triples taken from the Linked Open Data

Listing 2. An existing item graph with facts about Hassan Khaire harvested from YouTube's video descriptions dated 2010.

```
:youtubetMkyoqpM4Pc a :Item;
    :source dbp:Norwegian_royal_family;
    :sourceIRL "https://www.youtube.com/watch?v=tMkyoqpM4Pc";
    :originalText "Intervju med Hassan Khaire ..."@no;
    :canonicalText "Interview with Hassan Khaire ...";
    :hasAnnotation [    a :Annotation;
                        :hasEntity :unres/Hassan_Khaire              ];
    :hasAnnotation [    a :Annotation;
                        :hasEntity dbp:Norwegian_Refugee_Council    ];
    :hasAnnotation [    a :RelationAnnotation;
                        :hasRelation wdp:P39;
                        :relationFrom :unres/Hassan_Khaire;
                        :relationTo dbp:Norwegian_Refugee_Council   ];
    :hasAnnotation [    a :RelationAnnotation;
                        :hasRelation dbo:location;
                        :relationFrom dbp:Norwegian_Refugee_Council;
                        :relationTo dbr:Norway                      ]
```

(LOD) cloud and other sources, either by linking to external knowledge graphs or by downloading and inserting RDF triples into the event graph.

Ontology: Figure 3 shows how a potentially newsworthy **Event** is represented semantically as an event graph. Each **Event** is **describedBy** one or more **Items** that it has been derived from. It can come *before* or *after* and it can *cause* other events, and it can have *subevents*. The semantics of an **Event** is represented in further detail by **Descriptors**, each of which contains a single piece of semantic information about the event. Analogously to item annotations, each **Descriptor** is further related to an **Entity** with subtypes as in Fig. 1. There are also **RelationDescriptors** that represent semantic relationships between pairs of entities in the same event graph.

Figure 3 also shows how event **Descriptors** have *confidence*, *strength*, and *relevance* values in the same way as item annotations. In addition, **Descriptors** can hold *before*, *during*, and/or *after* the **Event**.

Pointing forward to the next section, an event can *match* one or more **NewsAngles**, of which two subtypes are shown: **LocalPerson** and **Nepotism**. They will be explained in Sect. 3.3. In further work, we want to align and enrich Fig. 3 with concepts from other event ontologies and frameworks, such as the Event Ontology[3], the ACE framework[4], and the Simple Event Model (SEM [28]), and Eso [23].

---

[3] http://motools.sourceforge.net/event/event.html.
[4] https://www.ldc.upenn.edu/collaborations/past-projects/ace.

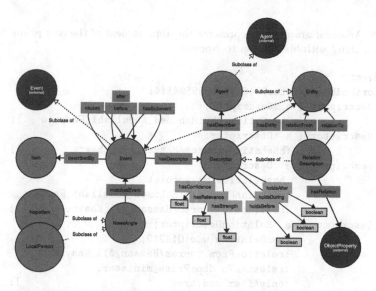

Fig. 3. Ontology for representing news events semantically as knowledge graphs.

Processing: Simple clustering of item graphs by annotation similarity is straight-forward. An earlier prototype used Scikit-learn's DBSCAN algorithm, which offers scalability and focus on neighbourhood size at the expense of uneven cluster sizes [2]. Other researchers have investigated detection of events in knowledge graphs [22], as well as relations between events. Merging entities and relations from item graphs belonging to the same event is also straightforward. An earlier prototype enriched the knowledge graph with DBpedia triples [2]. Wikidata, the triple-oriented fact database behind Wikipedia and its sister projects, is a more recent alternative. Compared to DBpedia, it offers a more uniform ontology and property-level provenance.

Example: In the example from Listing 1, Universal Somali TV could be a trusted source whose news item might suggest a new event without further corroboration. But confidence in the new event would increase as news items from other sources independently reported the same information. Listing 3 shows an event graph that might result from enriching the facts in Listing 1 with facts from external sources like DBpedia and Wikidata and from the related item graph shown in Listing 2, assuming that the similar-looking IRIs for Hassan Ali Khayre have been resolved to the same individual.

3.3 News Angles

Some exceptional events are newsworthy in themselves. But most events have to be made newsworthy by presenting them according to a *news angle*. Matching event graphs with news angles is a bi-directional process, in which the core facts of the event suggest candidate news angles and the candidate news angles in

Listing 3. An event graph that represents the appointment of the new prime minister of Somalia, along with his relation to Norway.

```
[   a :Event;
    :describedBy :twitter834619575509594114;
    :hasDescriptor [ a :Descriptor;
                     :hasEntity dbp:Mohamed_Abdullahi_Farmajo   ];
    :hasDescriptor [ a :Descriptor;
                     :hasEntity :unres/Hassan_Ali_Khayre        ];
    :hasDescriptor [ a :Descriptor;
                     :hasRelation wn:appoint;
                     :relationFrom dbp:Mohamed_Abdullahi_Farmajo;
                     :relationTo :unres/Hassan_Ali_Khayre       ];
    :hasDescriptor [ a :RelationDescriptor;
                     :hasRelation wde:Q14212;
                     :relationFrom :unres/Hassan_Ali_Khayre;
                     :relationTo dbp:Prime_minister;
                     :onlyAfter xsd:true                        ];
    :hasDescriptor [ a :Descriptor;
                     :hasEntity dbp:Norwegian_Refugee_Council   ];
    :hasDescriptor [ a :RelationDescriptor;
                     :hasRelation wdp:P39;
                     :relationFrom :unres/Hassan_Ali_Khayre;
                     :relationTo dbp:Norwegian_Refugee_Council  ];
    :hasDescriptor [ a :RelationDescriptor;
                     :hasRelation dbo:location;
                     :relationFrom dbp:Norwegian_Refugee_Council;
                     :relationTo dbr:Norway                     ];
    :hasDescriptor [ a :RelationDescriptor;
                     :hasRelation :basedNear;
                     :relationFrom :unres/Hassan_Ali_Khayre;
                     :relationTo dbr:Norway                     ]
]
```

turn encourage additional facts to be sought, whether manually or by automated means.

Although news angles and values are common journalistic ideas mentioned in many text books, e.g., [24, p. 115], they have not yet, to our knowledge, been analysed in depth from a knowledge representation and reasoning perspective. As a starting point, we have compiled a list of angles from academic textbooks [24] and web sites[5]. Table 1 lists examples of potential angles on the tweet from Fig. 2.

---

[5] Brad Phillips, December 10th 2014: https://www.prdaily.com/Main/Articles/16_story_angles_that_reporters_relish_17748.aspx; Wesley Upchurch, September 1st 2018: http://www.streetdirectory.com/etoday/ten-common-news-angles-for-media-releases-uuofou.html.

Table 1. Alternative news angles on the tweet from Fig. 2.

Event:	*President Farmajo has appointed Hassan Ali Khaire as the new prime minister of Somalia*
Human interest:	"Sheikh Ali was forced to leave his home country as a young man."
Proximity:	"Hassan Ali Khaire has lived as a refugee here in Vestre Slidre."
Actionability:	"Join our congratulations of the new Somalian prime minister!"
Influence:	"Khaire inherits a decade-long destabilising conflict with Ethiopia."
Milestone:	"Next year marks the 30th anniversary of the first peace treaty between Somalia and Ethiopia."
Conflict:	"Farmajo and Khaire's clans clashed during the southern unrest."
Recency:	"Khaire was not thought to be a contender for this position."

Architectural Role: News angles are important both for detecting newsworthy events and for presenting them in ways that may interest the intended audience. A news angle can be understood as a pattern with which an event graph can potentially be matched and which offers one or more extended patterns according to which the event graph can be enriched in interesting ways. The part of an event graph that matches a news angle becomes a *fabula (sub-)graph*. The term *fabula* adopted from literary theory [8] to denote *the facts that a story is about* in contrast to the *narrative*, which denotes the presentation of those facts as a *story*. Although our representations of news angles and fabulas might support automatic narration as well, our work in News Hunter is currently limited to proposing angled events as fabulas to journalists as an aid.

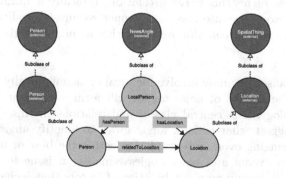

Fig. 4. Ontological representation of the local-person news angle.

Ontology: Figure 4 shows how the **LocalPerson** news angle can represented in OWL. It is a particularly simple angle, matched whenever a central **Person** in an event graph is **relatedToLocation** to a particular **Location** that is of importance to the journalist's intended audience. Figure 3 already showed how such an **Event** can be **matched** by a **NewsAngle** to form a fabula. It is possible that Fig. 4 and our other news-angle ontologies will need to be supplemented with additional rules and constraints in further work, perhaps using domain-specific modelling notations on top of our ontological approach.

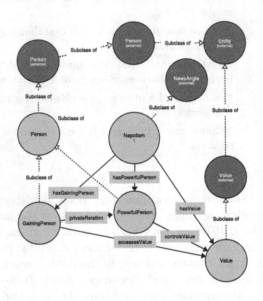

Fig. 5. Ontological representation of the nepotism news angle.

Figure 5 illustrates a more complex news angle, that of **Nepotism** [26], in which a **PowerfulPerson controls** a **Value** which a **GainingPerson** achieves **access** to because of her/his **privateRelation**, typically a **familyRelation**, to the **PowerfulPerson**. Because neoptism proper requires causality, the angle in Fig. 5 represents a weaker *potential nepotism* that mandates further investigation by journalists.

Processing: Because they may involve identical or taxonomically related classes and relations, the library of news angles will form a more or less connected news-angle ontology. The central classes and relations in this slowly evolving ontology will suggest what to look for in order to identify angles in the much more rapidly changing event sub-graphs. Selecting the best or most promising matches between events and news angles remains an issue for further work. Most likely, it will depend on a combination of factors that include recency and reliability of the event and originality and fit of the angle.

We envisage a News Hunter architecture in which many collaborating agents specialise in maintaining and leveraging specific classes and relations in the connected news-angle ontology, continuously looking for changes that contribute towards enabling or disabling particular angles in response to unfolding events. For example, a *local-person* agent would specialise in deriving **Person-relatedToLocation-Location** triples from semantically related facts in the knowledge graph, including **basedNear** and **location** facts.

Example: Listing 4 shows the *fabula graph* that results from matching the facts in Listing 3 with the news angle in Fig. 4. This graph comprises only a single triple, possibly derived by a *local-person agent* from triples stating that Khayre has worked for the Refugee Council located in Norway. Although the graph is simple, its triple is important as it forms the core fabula of the angled news report, to which interesting related facts from the LOD cloud could be added.

Listing 4. The small fabula graph that results from matching the facts from the Somalian prime minister tweet with the local-person news angle.

```
[   a :LocalPerson;
    :hasPerson unres/Hassan_Ali_Khayre;
    :hasLocation dbr:Norway;
] .
:unres/Hassan_Ali_Khayre :relationToLocation dbp:Norway
```

4   Discussion

We have proposed OWL ontologies that can be used to organise journalistic knowledge graphs and augment them with support for news angles. To the best of our knowledge, this is the first attempt to analyse and represent news angles as OWL ontologies. We also think that developing a news platform that supports news angles is new, and we suggest for the first time how ontologies for annotations, events and news angles can be combined in a journalistic platform.

We expect the proposed ontologies to evolve as we develop the News Hunter proof-of-concept architecture and prototype. Additional ontologies will also be needed, for example to: organise different types of input items; represent available analysis techniques and tools; propagate information about provenance/confidence and terms-of-use; reason about privacy; describe editorial and journalistic preferences; etc. Although we have presented them separately in this paper, we see the ontologies merely as alternative thematic windows into a single logically contiguous, but perhaps physically distributed, knowledge graph.

Our paper has focussed on ontology—and thus knowledge-graph—structure, leaving architectural and algorithmic issues to parallel [5,26] and future work. Our ontology structure can potentially also shape News Hunter's processing structure, so that different sub-systems, perhaps implemented as collaborating agents, can take responsibility for different ontologies. For example, one group of agents would lift data into item graphs, another would collate item graphs into events, a third would match event graphs with news angles, etc. In such an architecture, the knowledge graph would be split by ontology into contiguous and sometimes overlapping *smart graphs* that comprise both ontology definitions (TBox) and corresponding RDF triples (ABox), and associated software agents with responsibility for maintaining and leveraging the triples.

5 Conclusion

In a world of ever-increasing information, journalists are not the only ones facing the challenge of: finding the most interesting events and situations in big data sets and presenting those events and situations in the most interesting ways. We therefore hope our results will be useful for and inspire practice and research in other information systems areas beyond journalism and the news.

Our work on News Hunter and its parent project News Angler is just starting, and interesting paths for further work include: developing the architecture further and populating it with live and test data; collecting libraries of news angles, both manually and automatically; adapting and extending suitable analysis techniques for analysing news items, detecting and aggregating events, finding suitable news angles, and identifying causal and other relations between events; and selecting the most suitable and appropriate empirical research goals and evaluation approaches for the different parts of our project.

Acknowledgement. The News Angler project is funded by the Norwegian Research Council's IKTPLUSS programme as project 275872.

References

1. Allemang, D., Hendler, J.: Semantic Web for the Working Ontologist: Effective Modeling in RDFS and OWL. Elsevier, Waltham (2011)
2. Berven, A., Christensen, O.A., Moldeklev, S., Opdahl, A.L., Villanger, K.J.: News Hunter: building and mining knowledge graphs for newsroom systems. In: NOKO-BIT, vol. 26 (2018)
3. Diakopoulos, N.: Computational journalism and the emergence of news platforms. In: The Routledge Companion to Digital Journalism Studies. Routledge, Taylor and Francis Group, London (2016)
4. Fernández, N., Fuentes, D., Sánchez, L., Fisteus, J.A.: The NEWS ontology: design and applications. Expert. Syst. Appl. **37**(12), 8694–8704 (2010)
5. Gallofré, M., Nyre, L., Opdahl, A.L., Tessem, B., Trattner, C., Veres, C.: Towards a big data platform for news angles. In: 4th Norwegian Big Data Symposium – NOBIDS 2018, November 2018
6. Gangemi, A., Presutti, V., Recupero, D.R., Nuzzolese, A.G., Draicchio, F., Mongiovì, M.: Semantic web machine reading with FRED. Semant. Web **8**(6), 873–893 (2017)
7. García, R., Perdrix, F., Gil, R., Oliva, M.: The semantic web as a newspaper media convergence facilitator. Web Semant. Sci. Serv. Agents World Wide Web **6**(2), 151–161 (2008)

8. Gervas, P.: Computational approaches to storytelling and creativity. AI Mag. **30**(3), 49–62 (2009)
9. Heravi, B.R., McGinnis, J.: Introducing social semantic journalism. J. Media Innov. **2**(1), 131–140 (2015)
10. Hogenboom, F., Frasincar, F., Kaymak, U., De Jong, F.: An overview of event extraction from text. In: Workshop on Detection, Representation, and Exploitation of Events in the Semantic Web (DeRiVE 2011) at 10th ISWC 2011, vol. 779, pp. 48–57. Citeseer (2011)
11. International Press Telecommunications Council. Media Topics: Subject taxonomy for the media – the successor of the Subject Codes
12. Jackoway, A., Samet, H., Sankaranarayanan, J.: Identification of live news events using Twitter. In: Proceedings of 3rd ACM SIGSPATIAL International Workshop on Location-Based Social Networks, pp. 25–32. ACM (2011)
13. Latar, N.L.: The robot journalist in the age of social physics: the end of human journalism? In: Einav, G. (ed.) The New World of Transitioned Media. TEICE, pp. 65–80. Springer, Cham (2015). https://doi.org/10.1007/978-3-319-09009-2_6
14. Leban, G., Fortuna, B., Brank, J., Grobelnik, M.: Event Registry: learning about world events from news. In: Proceedings of the 23rd International Conference on World Wide Web, pp. 107–110. ACM (2014)
15. Liu, X., et al.: Reuters Tracer: a large scale system of detecting & verifying real-time news events from Twitter. In: Proceedings of the 25th ACM International on Conference on Information and Knowledge Management, pp. 207–216. ACM (2016)
16. Lohmann, S., Link, V., Marbach, E., Negru, S.: WebVOWL: web-based visualization of ontologies. In: Lambrix, P., et al. (eds.) EKAW 2014. LNCS (LNAI), vol. 8982, pp. 154–158. Springer, Cham (2015). https://doi.org/10.1007/978-3-319-17966-7_21
17. Machill, M., Beiler, M.: The importance of the internet for journalistic research: a multi-method study.... J. Stud. **10**(2), 178–203 (2009)
18. Mikolov, T., Sutskever, I., Chen, K., Corrado, G.S., Dean, J.: Distributed representations of words and phrases and their compositionality. In: Advances in Neural Information Processing Systems, pp. 3111–3119 (2013)
19. Miroshnichenko, A.: AI to bypass creativity. Will robots replace journalists? (The answer is "yes"). Information **9**(7), 183 (2018)
20. Opdahl, A.L., Berven, A., Alipour, K., Christensen, O.A., Villanger, K.J.: Knowledge graphs for newsroom systems. In: NOKOBIT, vol. 24 (2016)
21. Passant, A., Laublet, P.: Meaning of a Tag: a collaborative approach to bridge the gap between tagging and linked data. In: LDOW, vol. 369 (2008)
22. Rospocher, M., et al.: Building event-centric knowledge graphs from news. J. Web Semant. **37**, 132–151 (2016)
23. Segers, R., Vossen, P., Rospocher, M., Serafini, L., Laparra, E., Rigau, G.: ESO: a frame based ontology for events and implied situations. In: Proceedings of MAPLEX 2015 (2015)
24. Shoemaker, P.J., Reese, S.D.: Mediating the Message: Theories of Influences on Mass Media Content. Longman, White Plains (1995)
25. Stavelin, E.: Computational Journalism. When journalism meets programming. Ph.D. thesis, University of Bergen (2013)
26. Tessem, B., Opdahl, A.L.: Supporting journalistic news angles with models and analogies. In: Proceedings IEEE RCIS 2019, Brussels (2019)

27. Troncy, R.: Bringing the IPTC news architecture into the semantic web. In: Sheth, A., et al. (eds.) ISWC 2008. LNCS, vol. 5318, pp. 483–498. Springer, Heidelberg (2008). https://doi.org/10.1007/978-3-540-88564-1_31
28. Van Hage, W.R., Malaisé, V., Segers, R., Hollink, L., Schreiber, G.: Design and use of the simple event model (SEM). Web Semant. Sci. Serv. Agents World Wide Web 9(2), 128–136 (2011)
29. Voskarides, N., et al.: Weakly-supervised contextualization of knowledge graph facts. In: The 41st International ACM SIGIR Conference on Research & Development in Information Retrieval, pp. 765–774. ACM (2018)

A System for Semi-automatic Construction of Image Processing Pipeline for Complex Problems

Asha Rajbhoj[1]([✉]), Shailesh Deshpande[1], Jayavardhana Gubbi[2],
Vinay Kulkarni[1], and P. Balamuralidhar[2]

[1] TCS Research, Pune, India
{asha.rajbhoj, shailesh.deshpande,
vinay.vkulkarni}@tcs.com
[2] TCS Research, Bangalore, India
{j.gubbi, balamurali.p}@tcs.com

Abstract. Creation of an image processing pipeline for solving complex problems is a tedious task. Current industry practices largely rely on the image processing domain experts for this. Given the image processing problem have multiple viable solutions. Thus, the search space of creating suitable solution using available algorithms for a given goal in a given constrained infrastructure is generally large. The exploratory work to choose an optimal image processing solution is an effort-, time- and intellect-intensive endeavor. To address these issues we propose a system for automatic construction of the pipeline that can improve domain expert's productivity by creating a solution quickly. The proposed system externalizes image processing domain knowledge in the form of object model and a set of rules defined over it. Recommendations are given to choose suitable algorithm/s for carrying out the image processing tasks. On successful creation of the pipeline, the system generates deployable code. It also generates trace data that can help for cognitive knowledge upgrade. We showcase ongoing work on this system and its early results using the simple working example.

Keywords: Image processing · Recommender system · Meta model · Model based system · Model engineering

1 Introduction

Creating an image processing pipeline, that is, a sequence of atomic image processing functions, for a given scene understanding (including quantification) is a challenging task. First, many parts of the human vision are not very well understood yet [1–3]. Hence, mundane tasks for human vision may remain complex for computational methods. Developing the image processing algorithm that generalizes well and work in different situations similarly to human vision is a dream goal [4]. For example, attention model, foreground-background recognition. Second, combining different image processing services of atomic nature to achieve a desired end goal requires a sound understanding of the domain, the data, and the goal. Naturally, the creation of

© Springer Nature Switzerland AG 2019
I. Reinhartz-Berger et al. (Eds.): BPMDS 2019/EMMSAD 2019, LNBIP 352, pp. 295–310, 2019.
https://doi.org/10.1007/978-3-030-20618-5_20

optimal image processing pipeline for a given end goal is handled by experts. However, the manual approach is effort intensive requiring exploratory empirical work, and the approach may lead to a biased, subjective solution for a specific goal [5–7].

Because of exponential increases in industrial and consumer grade imaging devices, the number of situations requiring image processing solutions are increasing at a rapid rate [7]. Each of these solutions may use different image acquisition platform, and may be applied to many different situations, for example, the satellite imagery for monitoring crop-produce, the image by a cell phone for detecting damages in household equipment. A specific image processing task can be achieved by many different algorithms with different qualities. The current practices rely on experts to choose the most appropriate algorithm/s based on the end goal and sub-goals. There is a prior art related to automating specific image processing tasks [5, 8]. However, to the best of our knowledge, there is no work reported on automation support for the image processing pipeline to satisfy a complex goal structure.

We present, in this paper, a solution precisely to this problem. In the present research, we examine the modeling approach for designing the system, which can create an image processing pipeline automatically. The main research questions that we investigate are: (1) What is the efficacy of modelling techniques for image processing knowledge representation? (2) What all challenges of image processing pipeline creation can be addressed through automation. We propose the system for automatic construction of a pipeline that can improve domain expert's productivity by creating a solution quickly. The proposed system models the image processing goals in abstract task categories and externalize image processing domain knowledge as an object model and a set of rules defined over it. Rules codifies task template selection criteria and algorithm selection criteria for implementing a task. Recommendations are provided to choose the suitable algorithm/s for carrying out image processing tasks. Effects of algorithm execution are recorded in the context and considered for subsequent tasks recommendations. Most importantly, state of execution is stored, which enables rerouting the execution to initial stages if required. The system generates deployable code after successful creation of a pipeline. Furthermore, the system generates the useful trace information, which can be used further for knowledge upgrade to improve results over a period. We present the ongoing work on this system and its early results using the simple working example.

The rest of the paper is organized as: Sect. 2 briefs about related work, Sect. 3 outlines the approach, Sect. 4 describes system meta models, Sect. 5 shows instantiation of these meta models for image processing domain, Sect. 6 describes overall process used in pipeline generation, Sect. 7 demonstrate use of the system with example. Finally, we share lesson learnt and planned future work in Sect. 8.

2   Related Work

The earlier efforts in automated image processing systems model the knowledge for a very specific image processing tasks. These systems separate image processing logic for object identification and the control logic [5, 8, 9]. However, these systems don't generalize well and work in constrained conditions [5]. Moreover, they do not address the question, "how to create an image processing pipeline quickly for a given problem, in case the system does not produce the desired results?"

Although these early systems do not automate the task of building the processing pipeline, some of the work provide insights into the problems and attempt semi-automated systems. Rost and Munkel (1998) developed a knowledge-based system to make an image processing algorithm adaptable in changing condition. The rule base captures the expert knowledge for configuration of steps and for changing the algorithm parameter values based on the feedback [6]. The work by Renouf *et al.* (2007) developed ontology for describing the image processing objectives and image class model. The system constructs the image processing formulation by using 300 concepts, 23 roles and 183 restriction written in Web Ontology Language (OWL) [10]. Clouard *et al.* (2010) investigate the information used in the design and the evaluation of image processing software application and propose a computational language to describe them. Interestingly, the goal is defined using sample output images and task description [11].

The framework developed by Nadarajan *et al.* [12] focuses on automating different stages of video processing mainly design, workflow, and processing layer. The knowledge related to each task is abstracted in the three layers namely goal ontologies, video description, and capabilities. The workflow engine controls the complete system. It uses the knowledge related to the goal, video data and, capabilities and requests planner to create a plan for a given condition. Based on the plan, the workflow enactor creates an executable script and using the capabilities available in the processing layer, the plan is executed. The framework was evaluated using an ecological application of underwater video stream. The authors claim improvement in execution time by 90% as compared to manual processes.

There are many WMS systems that attempt to solve the problem of automating construction of a scientific workflow (construction of processing pipeline) [13–16]. Pegasus is one the leading workflow automation system used by scientist around the world from different domains including image processing researchers [15]. The Pegsus WMS maps the workflow description on distributed computing environment. The key concept of the system is the separation of workflow description and description of running environment. The scientific computation steps are represented as a graph of task nodes, which are connected with dependency edges. The workflow is manually created by an expert users. To the best of our knowledge, these WMS systems do not provide intelligence to select the services automatically. Other resources include image processing libraries, vision workbench [17–19] etc. These provide micro and macro level resources for programing image processing tasks. These resources are difficult to use for building a complex image processing pipeline, without a sound knowledge of image processing.

3 Proposed Approach

Figure 1 shows high level architecture of the system. The system takes problem details such goal description, details of input and context information and generates deployable solution executable code that meets the given goal and constraints.

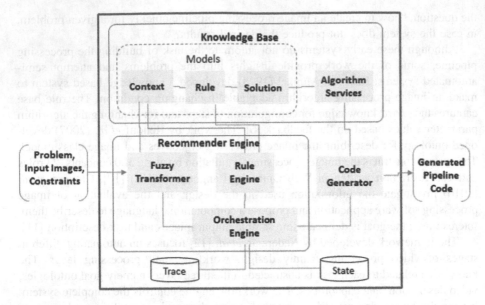

Fig. 1. System architecture

There are three main components of the systems:

1. **Knowledge Base:** The knowledge base consists of the models and the Algorithm Services.

   Models: The model comprises of the model for solution space (tasks, algorithms), model for the control logic or decision making knowhow using rules, and the object/context model for problem domain which covers domain, input and output context information.

   Algorithm Services: Algorithm Services are implementation options for solution space. These are the prebuilt custom made components, generic local services, or any services that are accessible through API. Algorithm Services and its sequence is recommended by the system, based on the given problem context information. Algorithm service is executed when user selects the recommended algorithm.

2. **Recommender Engine:** The Recommender Engine consist of Rule Engine, Fuzzy Transformer and Orchestration Engine.

   Rule Engine: The different type of rules are specified on the properties of the context model. Orchestration Engine controls the Rule Engine by suggesting which rules to execute. Rule Engine is created using Drools [20]. Drools supports the propositional and first order logic specification language for the rules. Rules specified in the rule model are transformed into Drools specification for execution.

   Orchestration Engine: The Orchestration Engine navigates Rule Engine through various tasks, shows retrieved algorithm recommendations for a task under consideration, provides interface to select parameters, provides visualization of the effects such as the context model changes as well as transformed images. It stores the state information to facilitate "undo" action by traversing back in a pipeline creation process by restoring execution to previous state. It generates the trace information that can be used in continuous improvement over solution building process as well solution usage.

Fuzzy Transformer: The Fuzzy Transformer transforms input data into normalize form. There are three options: (1) Expert can specify a value based on the judgement, (2) Set of initialization function calculate these values based on the numeric threshold, (3) A particular fuzzy membership defined over the attribute values space converts the numeric values into fuzzy variable.

3. **Code Generator:** On successful creation of a pipeline, the code is generated by the model based Code Generator, which can be used in standalone manner for actual deployment. The generation steps take care of invoking algorithms in a finalized pipeline in sequence by instantiating and interfacing with the inputs and output of algorithms.

4 System Meta Models

We used the model based approach for capturing the knowledge. Purpose specific meta models are defined. The knowledge is specified using the three main parts, that is, Context model, Rule model, and Solution model. The context model captures domain specific concepts. The rule model captures tacit knowledge from the domain expert in the form of rules. The solution model helps in defining granular, atomic reusable services. A reflexive modeling language compatible with OMG MOF [21] has been used to define the meta model of the system.

4.1 Context Meta Model

The problem under consideration is defined using *Problem* class (Fig. 2). It has property goalDescription to specify goal to be achieved through processing. Every *Problem* specifies *Context* information. Context is described by Property. Different types of context are *DomainContext*, *InputContext* and *ProcessingContext*.

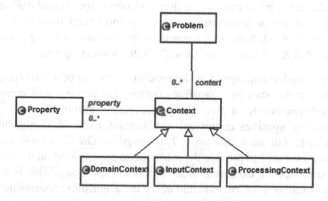

Fig. 2. Context meta model

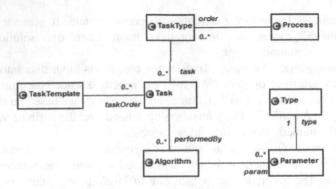

Fig. 3. Solution meta model

4.2   Solution Meta Model

Figure 3 shows the meta model to capture solution model. This meta model helps in decomposing solution space into granular, atomic computational services that can be used to perform a specific processing tasks.

Often, the computation intensive software follows a specific process that defines the order in which processing tasks should be performed. For example, first preprocessing of the input is done before the processing of the input to retrieve meaningful information. These processing tasks are categorized using *TaskType*. For example, the tasks that perform pre-processing are grouped, the task that focus on region of interest are grouped and so on. *Process* defines the default order in which multiple *TaskType* executed in processing pipeline. *TaskTemplate* helps in defining the tasks specific execution order using *taskOrder* association. A *Task* is performed by many *Algorithm*. *Algorithm* may take many *Parameter*. *Parameter* has a *Type*. *TaskType* and *Task* order information helps in navigating through the tasks for recommendations of algorithms.

4.3   Rule Meta Model

Figure 4 shows the rule meta model. *TaskTemplate* is ordered sequence of *Task*. Three types of the rules are used to express the domain knowledge: *TemplateRule*, *AlgoRule*, *PropRule*. All rules are expressed using properties and values from the context model using *RuleExpression*. Multiple *RuleExpression* are connected using *JointExpr*. *JointExpr* connects *RuleExpression* with "AND", "OR" logical operators.

TemplateRule: *TemplateRule* specifies the conditions for use of a *TaskTemplate*. These are executed at the start of a pipeline construction process and recommends the suitable *TaskTemplate* for a given image processing problem.

AlgoRule: *AlgoRule* specifies contextual conditions for use of an algorithm for performing a task. For each task in a *TaskTemplate OR TaskType,* corresponding *AlgoRule are* executed to provide the recommendations based on the context model. *Task* also specifies the execution order dependencies if any. This is used for generating rule's saliency information and hence the algorithm recommendations order.

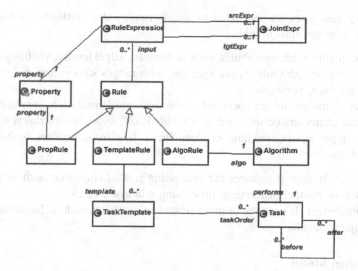

Fig. 4. Rule meta model

PropRule: *PropRule* specifies the derivation of property value from other property values. These are executed after the algorithm execution to cascade the effects of the context model changes.

5   Image Processing Models

The meta models described in the previous section are defined at higher level of abstraction and do not cover specifics of image processing. We intended to use the similar approach for other computation intensive problem domains to specify multiple problem domains. In this section we, describe its use for modeling image processing domain knowledge. The representative knowledge rules are described in the example Sect. 7.

5.1   Context Model

The context model is created as an instance of the context meta model shown in Fig. 2. The image processing *InputContext* specifies various properties: Image spectral and spatial characteristics, image contrast level, edge density, image format, noise information; Band related information such as directivity, entropy, linearity, periodicity, size and length; Sensor related information such as azimuth angle, band width, interval at which images are taken, look angle, spatial and temporal resolution, zenith angle etc.

Property data types are abstracted to specify range values instead of actual values. A few examples are shown below:

(1) Image quality related attributes such as contrast, edgeDensity, visibility, entropy, periodicity, image visibility are specified with ranges *<poor, low, belowaverage, average, high, veryhigh>*
(2) Spatial characteristic are specified as *<coarse, moderate, high, veryhigh>*
(3) Spectral characteristic specified as *<SWIR, VNIR, hyper, multi, thermal, visible>*
(4) Noise types considered are *<columnDrop, lineDrop, random, saltandPaper, speckled>*

ProcessingContext: It captures the processing related constraint such as time constraint, batch or parallel processing, processing window size etc.

DomainContext: It captures domain related information such as business domain, domain objects details.

5.2 Solution Model

The image processing tasks are classified into 5 main *TaskTypes* based on the functional characteristics: *Transform, Prepare, Focus, Perceive and Quantify. Transform* and *Prepare* convert input images to better image that can be processed. *Focus* highlights on meaningful attributes of the transformed image. Finally *Perceive* and *Quantify* interpret this information to generate the required output. Table 1 show a few examples of the tasks. These 5 types of processing are commonly carried out in the sequential manner for the image processing. For each task, there are several options for algorithms available that can be used in a specific conditions. Conditions are specified in the form rules defined over of the context model. Example of rules are given in the case study section.

Table 1. Task examples

Task type	Task
Transform	2D to 3D conversion, DNTransformation
Prepare	Filter, equalization, frame selection, image stitching, mesh creation, application of various filters, super resolution
Focus	Region detection and identification, background removal, crop, change detection, object proposal, saliency, super pixel generation
Perceive	Scene understanding and processing such as damage detection, object relation, object categories
Quantity	Count object, compute change statistics

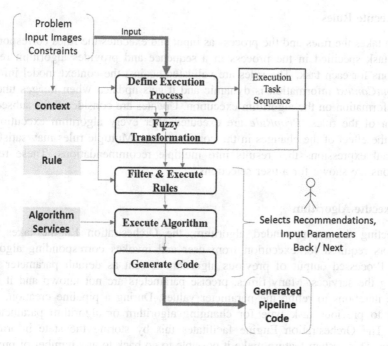

Fig. 5. Pipeline generation process

6 Pipeline Generation Process

System takes goal description, context parameters and input files from a user and generates the deployable code. The flow chart shown in Fig. 5 depicts the steps involved in generating the image processing pipeline, which is based on the architecture depicted in Fig. 1. The step by step methodology followed by the system, starting from deciding task sequence till final step of generating deployable code, is outlined here.

6.1 Define Execution Process

The Orchestration Engine provides instructions to the Rule Engine for executing specific rules. Orchestration Engine first executes *TemplateRule*. If *TaskTemplate* recommendation is retrieved then execution of subsequent rule is performed as per the task's order in the recommended template. Otherwise, the default task type sequence, that is, *Transform, Prepare, Perceive, Focus, Quantify* is used for the orchestration where in all tasks rules in a given task type are executed.

6.2   Execute Rules

This step takes the rules and the process as input and executes the rules corresponding to each task specified in the process in a sequence and provides algorithm recommendations for each task. The rules are validated against the context model information. *InputContext* information is dynamic and it gets updated when images undergo the transformation on the algorithm execution. Updates are considered for subsequent execution of the rules. *PropRule* are executed after every algorithm executions to cascade the effect of the changes in the context model. Multiple rules may satisfy the conditional expressions that results into multiple recommendations. These recommendations are shown for a user selections.

6.3   Execute Algorithm

On selecting the recommended algorithm, the Orchestration Engine takes input parameters required for execution from user and invokes corresponding algorithm service. Processed output of previous algorithm is sent as default parameter while executing the services. Many times, precise parameters are not known and it needs multiple iterations to refine the parameter values. During a pipeline creation, back-tracking to previous task type for changing algorithm or algorithm parameters is needed. The Orchestration Engine facilitates this by storing the state information execution. This system feature make it possible to go back to any number of previous tasks.

State of execution is stored as a stack of state entries. Every state entry is a tuple it contains *State Entry = tasktype, context model state, {algoName, <paramName, paramValue>*}*

This step also generates trace information that contains trace of entire navigation from start till end including back tracking.

6.4   Fuzzy Transformation

The Fuzzy Transformer has a collection of fuzzy membership functions. The appropriate fuzzy membership function for a fuzzification task is chosen by the system, based on the logical names. Once the fuzzy function is chosen, the numeric values are converted into fuzzy variables indicating degree such as high moderate low etc. For example, average brightness of the image are converted to qualitative range values such as <very high average low and very low>. This is a planned feature and is not present in the current scope.

6.5   Generate Code

On successful creation and validation of pipeline, finally code is generated. Generated code can be executed in standalone mode and is in ready to deploy form. Generators use model based code generation approach. Finalized pipeline is saved back into model repository in the form of algorithm execution sequence along with parameters used.

Generators encode accidental complexity involved in loading appropriate algorithm library classes, instantiation of classes, invoking algorithms with appropriate parameter values in appropriate sequence. This is a planned feature and hence described in brief.

7 Case Study

Motivation for analyzing aerial imagery from platforms such as drones, satellite etc. is to detect the changes over a large area frequently and quickly, which is not practically possible by manual efforts. We demonstrate one of such examples of detecting changes for a remote mine area.

7.1 Example

Mines and mining activities are regularly monitored for legal and environmental regulatory purposes. The anthropogenic activities related to mining adversely affect its surroundings. Degradation of green cover, encroachment on surrounding villages or towns are common problems. Monitoring expansion of the mining area is required for planning and other administrative activities of mine. Creating a pipeline of individual image processing algorithms/services in such a scenario is not a trivial task.

The challenges start from choosing a correct higher level task sequence. The change detection may be achieved by a simple image comparison as well as by a very complicated method such as the comparison of scene graphs of the two images. The system recommends an appropriate sequence by selecting an appropriate template from a set of templates. The choice is activated by the rules, which binds instance of the template to the basic image properties of the data. The chosen template states the tasks to be performed for each task category in a given situation. In the present example, the change detection in mine areas entail the changes are to be detected for LULC (Land Use Land Cover) using coarse classification granularity. The change detection in mine areas over time does not often involve detection of objects. The broad level LULC classes such as soil, vegetation, built-up etc. are sufficient. Hence, the appropriate template with the sequence of LULC classification and image comparison is selected by the system for the given goal.

The satellite images cover a large area (in this case). Processing the entire image is not computationally efficient. The appropriate attention model is required for selecting the sub image for further processing. The simplest way to define the scope of the further processing is to choose the area using Latitude-Longitude or Cartesian coordinates (row and column). After choosing the focus area, for more accurate results, the encoded digital numbers (DNs) for all the bands need to be converted to radiance values. Each satellite platform provides the calibration constants and they are used to transform the DNs to radiance values. In the present example, the property of the image acquisition platform is set as "multi" determines the step for the transformation.

As the multi-date imagery is involved in this scenario, the atmospheric correction or normalization of the atmospheric effects over multi-date image is necessary. The atmospheric corrections are applied or not is decided based on the goal, nature of the imagery, spectral properties of the imagery etc. For example, in the case of single date imagery and classification task, the atmospheric corrections can be ignored. It is necessary for hyperspectral data and multi-date multispectral data. The atmospheric correction are also of the two types, each one with its advantages and disadvantages. The physics-based methods need additional atmospheric data, which is not easily available. In absence of such detailed information, the image based methods are the viable option.

Finally, the classification algorithm is to be selected. The image characteristics and the goal determines the most suitable classification algorithm. Availability of training data is limiting factor for the deep learning approaches. In case, the statistically significant ample training data is not available, the feature based classification algorithm is an optimal choice. Once the classification algorithm is chosen, the comparison of the segmented images is a straightforward job, relatively.

The Sect. 7.2 provides the rule base for the example scenario as explained.

Year 2013   Year 2016

Fig. 6. Input images

7.2   Pipeline Generation

Following inputs are specified by user to the system for generating a pipeline.

Problem.goalDescription – change detection, mine area expansion or changes over time.

Input files – 2 images as shown in Fig. 6
Input properties -
>*ProcessingContext.goalType* = *"change detection"*
>*InputContext.spatialResolution* = *"moderate"*
>*Spectral characteristics* = *multi*
>*InputContext.spectralCharacteristics* = *"multi"*
>*DomainContext.domain* = *"mine"*
>*InputContext.atmosphericData* = *no*
>*InptContext.platform* = *satellite*
>*InputContext.singleDate* = *false*
>*ProcessingContext.visualAnalysisRequired* = *false*
>*ProcessingContext.aoi* = *RowColumn*

Example Related Rules
TemplateRule:

1. *processingContext.classificationGranularity* == *"coarse"* => *TaskTemplate* = *LULC_change_detection*
   This has following task sequences 1)Focus - Crop   2) Transform - DNTransformation , 3) Prepare - Filter 4) Perceive – RegionDetectionandIdentification 5) Quantify – ChangeStatistics.

PropRule:

1. *ProcessingContext.goalType* == *"change detection"* AND *DomainContext.domain* == *"mine"* => *Goal.goalType* == *"LULC classification"*
2. *Goal.goalType* == *"LULC classification"* => *processingContext.classificationGranularity* = *"coarse"*
3. *InputContext.spatialResolution* == *"moderate"* => *processingContext.classificationGranularity* = *"coarse"*
4. *InputContext.aerosolProfile* == *yes* AND *InputContext.co2Concentration* == *yes* AND *InputContext. h2oConcentration* == *yes* AND   => *InputContext.atmosphericData* = *yes*

AlgoRule:

1. *ProcessingContext.aoi* == *latlong* => *Focus.Crop.latlong*
2. *ProcessingContext.aoi* == *RowColumn* => *Focus.Crop.RowColumn*
3. *InputContext.platform* == *"satellite"* => *Transfrom.DNTransfromation. DNtoRadiance*
4. *ProcessingContext.visualAnalysisRequired* == *Yes* => *Prepare.Filter.Linear*
5. *InputContext.atmosphericData* == *no* => *Prepare.Filter.IAR*
6. *InputContext.atmosphericData* == *yes* => *Prepare.Filter.6SV*
7. *ProcessingContext.classificationGranularity* == *"coarse"* =>
   a. *Perceive.RegionDetectionandIdentification.KNN*
   b. *Perceive.RegionDetectionandIdentification.SVM*
8. *ProcessingContext.goal* == *"LULC classification"* => *Quantify.ChangeStatistics.ComputeChangeStatistics*
9. *InputContext.singleDateImage* = *false* AND *InputContext.spectralCharacteristics* = *"multi"* =>
   a. *Prepare.Filter.DarkObject*
   b. *Prepare.Filter.SolarAngle*

System selected "*LULC_change_detection*" template and executed rules marked in bold. Figure 7 shows the system view for pipeline construction for this example. It shows (1) Algorithm recommendation (2) Pipeline under creation (3) Initial context values (4) Effect on context values (5) Effect on image.

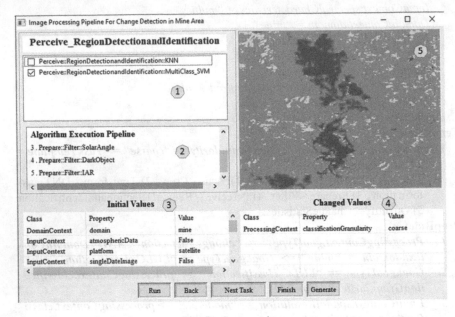

Fig. 7. System view

Pipeline recommendation is as shown below:
(1) Focus – Crop – RowColumn (2) Transform - DNTransformation – DNtoRadiance (3) Prepare - Filter – SolarAngle, (4) Prepare - Filter – Darkobject, (5) Prepare - Filter – IAR (6) Perceive – RegionDetectionandIdentification – SVM (7) Quantify – ChangeStatistics – ComputeChangeStatistics.

8   Lessons Learnt and Future Work

We have verified the system on a few examples of creating image processing pipeline. This section summarize the key findings from these experiments.

Knowledge Population: Population of knowledge was a challenging task. There is no single repository for comprehensive rule-base. Domain expert continue to play a critical role in seeding of the rule-base. We found brain storming session very useful for building the rule-base. Around 60 relevant properties have been identified so far that contribute in image processing pipeline decisions. ~40 tasks are identified, ~90 algorithm services are defined. Multiple rules were defined for the same algorithm in case the rules were orthogonal. As we work on more examples knowledge will get refined further. PropRule were found useful in cascading the effect of property automatically, at the beginning as well as during pipeline construction.

Knowledge Completeness and Consistency: System performance depends largely knowledge completeness and consistency. Maintaining up-to-date knowledge is iterative and continuing process. This can be a serious limitation of the system. To overcome this, we plan to incorporate learning functionality as an integral part of the system. System can learn new rules, and parameter values of the key rules in decision making and system performance. A simple feedback for the difference between the benchmark values and the current system output values can be effectively used. Other alternative is to reinforce the pathways based on its usage or objective function. Considering fuzzy or probabilistic rules is another option to make system more flexible and robust.

Configurability of System: Use of the compact models provided advantages as compared to generic ontology structure: it was helpful in connecting different concepts. Purpose specific user interface for defining various models helped domain experts to focus on knowledge definition than worrying about underlying execution technologies. System has taken care of eliminating accidental complexity involved by providing configurable models that can be easily extended by domain experts. System is configurable by design. Context, Rule and Solution Models can be configured for various computation intensive software systems. We plan to explore its use for different type of data and computation intensive usecases.

Evaluation of the System Performance: The efforts for creating the image processing pipeline for the working example was decreased by ~ 70–80% (from 16 person weeks to ~ 3 person weeks) as compared to the manual construction of such system. These are approximate numbers. We plan a more systematic evaluation as work progresses. Furthermore, we also plan to observe the accuracy of the output produced by the system pipeline and manual pipeline. Ideally, there should not be any degradation of the accuracy as a result of automation.

References

1. Eggert, J., Wersing, H.: Approaches and challenges for cognitive vision systems. In: Sendhoff, B., Körner, E., Sporns, O., Ritter, H., Doya, K. (eds.) Creating Brain-Like Intelligence. LNCS, vol. 5436, pp. 215–247. Springer, Heidelberg (2009). https://doi.org/10. 1007/978-3-642-00616-6_11
2. Zhaoping, L.: The Problem of Vision. Understanding Vision: Theory, Models, and Data. Oxford University Press, Oxford (2014)
3. LaValle, S.M.: The Physiology of Human Vision. Virtual Reality. Cambridge University Press, Cambridge (2019)
4. Vernon, D.: The space of cognitive vision. In: Christensen, H.I., Nagel, H.H. (eds.) Cognitive Vision Systems. LNCS, vol. 3948, pp. 7–24. Springer, Heidelberg (2009). https:// doi.org/10.1007/11414353_2

5. Binford, T.O.: Survey of model-based image analysis systems. Int. J. Robot. Res. **1**(1), 18–64 (1982)

6. Rost, U.: Knowledge-Based Configuration of Image Processing Algorithms (1998). ftp://ftp.tnt.uni-hannover.de/pub/papers/1998/ICCIMA-98-URHM.ps.gz

7. Malamas, E.N., Petrakis, E.G., Zervakis, M., Petit, L., Legat, J.-D.: A survey on industrial vision systems, applications and tools. Image Vis. Comput. **21**(2), 171–188 (2003)

8. Nagao, M., Matsuyama, T.: A structural analysis of complex aerial photographs. In: Nadler, M. (ed.) Advanced Applications in Pattern Recognition. Plenum Press, New York (1980)

9. Matsuyama, T.: Expert systems for image processing-knowledge-based composition of image analysis processes. In: 9th International Conference on Pattern Recognition, Rome, Italy, pp. 125–133 (1988)

10. Renouf, A., Clouard, R., Revenu, M.: How to formulate image processing application? In: International Conference on Computer Vision Systems, Bielefeld, Germany (2007)

11. Clouard, R., Renouf, A., Revenu, M.: An ontology-based model for representing image processing objectives. World Sci. Publ. **24**(8), 1181–1208 (2010)

12. Nadarajan, G., Chen-Burger, Y.-H., Fisher, R.B.: A knowledge-based planner for processing unconstrained underwater videos. In: IJCAI Workshop on Learning Structural Knowledge From Observations (2009)

13. Deelmana, E., et al.: Pegasus: a framework for mapping complex scientific workflows onto distributed systems. Sci. Program. J. **13**(3), 219–237 (2005)

14. Fahringer, T., et al.: ASKALON-A development and grid computing environment for scientific workflows. In: Taylor, I.J., Deelman, E., Gannon, D.B., Shields, M. (eds.) Workflows for e-Science, pp. 450–471. Springer, London (2007). https://doi.org/10.1007/978-1-84628-757-2_27

15. Deelmana, E., et al.: Pegasus, a workflow management system for science automation. Future Gener. Comput. Syst. **46**, 17–35 (2015)

16. Taylor, I., Shields, M., Wang, I., Harrison, A.: The Triana workflow environment: architecture and applications. In: Taylor, I., Deelman, E., Gannon, D., Shields, M. (eds.) Workflows for e-Science, pp. 320–339. Springer, New York (2007). https://doi.org/10.1007/978-1-84628-757-2_20

17. The openCV Library. https://opencv.org

18. Mathworks Inc.: Image Processing Toolbox. http://www.mathworks.com/products/image

19. NASA: NASA Vision Workbench (VW), Version 3. https://software.nasa.gov/software/ARC-15761-1A

20. Drools. https://www.drools.org

21. OMG-Object Management Group. http://www.omg.org/spec/MOF/2.0

Specification and Management of Methods - A Case for Multi-level Modelling

Ulrich Frank[✉] [iD]

University of Duisburg-Essen, Essen, Germany
ulrich.frank@uni-due.de
https://www.umo.wiwi.uni-due.de/en

Abstract. The digital transformation creates an increasing demand for projects to prepare and realize change. The professional management of projects demands for methods. In particular, there is not only need for method engineering, but also for managing the use of methods and for method maintenance. In this paper, it will be shown that traditional approaches to method engineering are not only limited with respect to reuse, they also do not support the integration of method engineering and method management. The approach presented in this paper addresses these limitations. It is based on a mult-level language architecture, which enables the common representation of models and code.

Keywords: Multi-level modelling · Language engineering · Method engineering

1 Introduction: The Need for Methods

In times of the digital transformation, many organizations need to regularly adapt their products, their operations and possibly their entire business model to stay competitive. In most of these cases, the adaptation will involve the conjoint analysis and modification of an organizations action system and its information system. Corresponding projects do not only target a contingent and challenging subject, they also require remarkable skills and substantial resources. Most organizations are not capable of staffing and managing those projects on their own. As a consequence, a huge consultancy industry has evolved over the last decades. The major companies in this industry alone employ hundreds of thousands of consultants, many of which are still novices or not far above. Therefore, it is essential for these firms as well as for other organizations running projects under similar conditions to promote a professional management of projects. Among other things, that recommends the use of appropriate *methods*. A method is suited to foster the reuse of existing knowledge, to reduce risk and, hence, to promote the economics of projects. However, general-purpose methods that can be used in a wide range of projects will usually not be satisfactory. Instead, it

© Springer Nature Switzerland AG 2019
I. Reinhartz-Berger et al. (Eds.): BPMDS 2019/EMMSAD 2019, LNBIP 352, pp. 311–325, 2019.
https://doi.org/10.1007/978-3-030-20618-5_21

seems more appropriate to focus on domain-specific methods. For this purpose, a consultancy firm would provide a repository of methods, a project manager can choose from and, if required, add modifications. An example of such an approach is IBM's "Component Business Modeling" (https://www.ibm.com/downloads/cas/6NMP1WEP). In any case, the management of method repositories faces serious challenges. On the one hand, it should allow for convenient adaptations of existing methods. On the other hand, it needs to ensure the integrity of a repository. While copy&paste might be regarded as a convenient way of creating new methods from existing ones, it is suited to create a maintenance nightmare. In academia, these challenges have been known for long. The field of method engineering is based on the assumption that the construction of particular methods should follow an engineering approach, which among other things recommends accounting for linguistic rigor, consistency and coherence as well as for the development of supportive tools. During the last 20 years, a plethora of approaches originating mostly in Requirements Engineering and Software Engineering have evolved (for an intermediate overview see [15]). The field has reached a stage of moderate maturity, which is also indicated by the existence of a respective ISO standard [1]. At the same time, it seems that research interest in method engineering has clearly declined during the last years. With respect to the current and further growing relevance of methods for mastering the digital transformation, this seems unfortunate. Against this background, the paper is intended to contribute to the revival of method engineering. It is structured as follows. First, an analysis of foundational terms will conclude with essential requirements related to the specification and management of modelling methods. Then, it will be shown that traditional approaches to meta-modelling have serious limitations that clearly compromise the specification and use of methods. Subsequently, a multi-level approach to the specification, modification and management of methods is presented. It improves reuse and adaptability. Furthermore, it enables the integration of method specification, method use, and project management.

2 Conceptual Foundation and Essential Requirements

Often, the term method is defined with respect to purpose: a method is aimed at solving a class of problems. However, such a functional definition is not sufficient for an approach to guide the specification and management of methods. To that end, a concept of method is required that reflects its constitutional elements. Only then, it is possible to specify a method referring to these elements and to represent a method in a repository. And only then, we can develop requirements to be satisfied by approaches that target the specification and management of methods.

2.1 Terminology

In systems development and method engineering various definitions of the term method can be found. "A method is based on models (systems of concepts) and consists of a number of steps which must/should be executed in a given order." [20, p. 7] While this definition could be misinterpreted in the sense that, e.g., a particular data model could be constitutive for a method, its intention seems to correspond to that of the definition proposed by Karagiannis and Fill who regard a modelling method as being composed of a "modelling language and a modelling procedure" [7, p. 8] Instead of using the term "modelling language", Lyytinen speaks of "a multitude of conceptual structures to describe, interpret and prescribe a field of phenomena" [16, p. 5]. In line with these definitions, we shall regard a method in general as consisting of a linguistic structure and a process model. A linguistic structure such as a technical terminology defines concepts that allow for structuring the problem domain in a purposeful way. In the field of system development, the concepts should be suited to structure both, the system to be built and the domain it is supposed to represent. A process model provides guidelines for how to proceed with developing a solution. A *modelling* method is a refinement of the general term. It consists of one or more modelling languages and a corresponding process model (for a more comprehensive description see [9, p. 40]).

This conception of (modelling) method focusses the syntax and semantics of the specification that describes a method as an artefact. In addition to that, the pragmatics of a method needs to be accounted for. The pragmatics of a method results from the practices it is used in. These practices may be in line with the guidelines specified with the artefact or may deviate from them. People may only pay lipservice to those guidelines, misinterpret them, or develop their own workarounds. Understanding these pragmatic aspects of a method is of pivotal relevance for their success, but not of particular relevance for the focus of our investigation.

2.2   Requirements

Metamodels are a common approach to specify the abstract syntax and semantics of modelling languages. A process model could be created with a modelling language designed for that purpose. Hence, methods could be specified as (meta) models: on the one hand, metamodels would represent the modelling languages that are being used in a method. On the other hand, a metamodel would be used to represent the corresponding process. The modelling method would then result from an integration of these metamodels, which could be stored and managed in model repositories. While this conclusion is not inappropriate, it would be wrong to regard it as the solution to our problem. An approach to the specification, use and management of modelling methods should account for the following generic requirements.

R1 - Support for reuse: the approach should feature abstraction concepts that foster reuse. In an ideal case, it should be possible to reuse all knowledge available in a domain for the specification of a method. *Rationale*: reuse of mature knowledge does not only reduce the costs of developing methods substantially, it should also contribute to method quality. This requirements has been at the core of research on method engineering for long.

R2 - Relax conflict between range of reuse and productivity of reuse: with respect to economies of scale, a method should have a wide range of reuse. That recommends the construction of methods which are not designed for specific purposes, but that cover a wider range of possible project types. However, the more generic a method is, the lower is its contribution to productivity and integrity of a particular project. *Rationale*: relaxing this conflict promises clear economic advantages. One could benefit from economies of scale without giving up on the customized methods that are designed to specific needs. This conflict also reflects a practical problem that every language designer is confronted with. For every relevant concept in a domain, it has to be decided whether it should be part of the language or rather be specified with a language. While there are a few guidelines that support this decision, none of those is entirely convincing [10]. For example: a concept like "Desktop Computer" could be part of a language for modelling IT infrastructures. Alternatively, it could be modelled as an instance of the more generic concept "Computer".

R3 - Support for integrity: an approach to specify methods should guide with the construction of methods that are consistent and coherent. *Rationale*: a method that lacks important aspects or that includes conflicting elements is likely to cause problems. Furthermore, method representations that lacks integrity compromise storing and retrieving of methods.

R4 - Integration of method and method use: the representation of a method's use, that is, a particular project should be integrated with a representation of the method. *Rationale*: method management is not restricted to the specification and dissemination of methods. It also includes the support of particular projects that use a method and their monitoring. Monitoring is required to assess a project's performance and to contribute to its improvement. If the representations of a method and its use are integrated, it is possible to use a method as a foundation for project management and to enable navigation between the two levels of abstraction.

As we shall see, satisfying these requirements is confronted with serious challenges.

3   Pitfalls of the Traditional Meta-Modelling Paradigm

Research on method engineering has resulted in various concepts to foster method configuration and reuse of existing knowledge. It also produced meta-modelling tools that feature the convenient and fast realization of specific model editors.

3.1   Patterns of Reuse and Tools

Classification is probably the most prominent abstraction concept to foster reuse in method engineering. It is addressed by the use of metamodels. A metamodel provides foundational concepts that can be instantiated to specify particular methods. In addition, composition is often referred to as a measure to achieve reuse. In that case, components of methods, referred to as "chunks" or "fragments", are stored in a repository. There seems to be no common definition of chunks and fragments. Henderson-Sellers et al. [13] suggest that a fragment can either represent a part of a process that constitutes a method or part of the product, that is, the documents (models, code ...) the creation of which a method is aimed at. According to this terminology, a chunk represents an aggregation of a fragment that represents part of a process with a corresponding fragment that represents part of a product. Both, classification and composition are well-known approaches to promote reuse in conceptual modelling. The use of metamodels corresponds to the construction of modelling languages. Reuse of knowledge is especially effective in the case of domain-specific modelling languages (DSML).

Both, instantiation and composition are supported by specific tools. Metamodelling environments such as Eclipse, MetaEdit [17], or ADOxx [7] enable the fast creation of modelling tools. For this purpose they take the metamodel that specifies the abstract syntax and semantics of a modelling language as an input. They also provide specific tools for the specification of the concrete syntax. Based on that, they generate a corresponding model editor. These tools usually focus on model editors and do not provide specific support for the specification of corresponding process models. Tools that focus on composition usually feature repositories. Chunks and fragments can be retrieved from a repository, e.g., through faceted classification [18], and somehow composed to a full method. However, the composition seems to be based on copy, paste & adapt [13].

Tools for method engineering are focussed on the specification of modelling languages and, in part, the configuration of methods. They usually do not allow for monitoring the use of a method, that is, they do not provide specific support for project management. However, this is not the case, because the use of a method is regarded as being out of scope. Instead, the application of methods is explicitly accounted for by various authors (e.g., [4,14]) as well as in the ISO 24744 standard. The authors speak of "endeavour" in the sense of a particular project that is instantiated from a method. As we shall see, there is a principal reason, why the instantiation of projects (or actual uses of methods) from a method is not covered by metamodelling tools: the semantics of prevalent object-oriented programming languages.

3.2   Limitations

To illustrate limitations of traditional approaches to method engineering we look at the fictitious example of a large consultancy firm that wants to develop a method repository. The simplified metamodel depicted in Fig. 1 serves as a language for defining specific methods. It can also be seen as a schema for storing methods. Note that this metamodel is not to be seen as a solution but as an illustration of a problem.

Let us assume the metamodel is used to define a method to guide the selection of an ERP system. The process model in Fig. 2 and the description of a selected activity in the process illustrate the method.

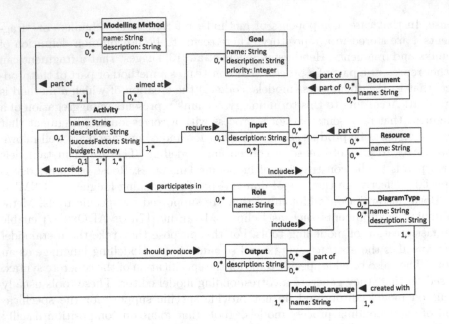

Fig. 1. Prototypical metamodel for the specification of modelling methods

Now let us see, how the method could be instantiated from the metamodel. Apparently, the activities that form the waterfall are instantiated from the meta-class `Activity`. The object that serves to represent the required input is instantiated from `Input` and linked to instances of `DiagramType` each of which would refer to one or more representations of modelling languages, instantiated from the metaclass `ModellingLanguage`. Similarly, one could instantiate objects to represent roles, goals, budget, resources, etc. But, maybe, this would not be sufficient. For example, a proper application of the method might require accounting for certain states. A business process map that is needed as input should, e.g., be in a state that includes the definition of certain performance indicators for each

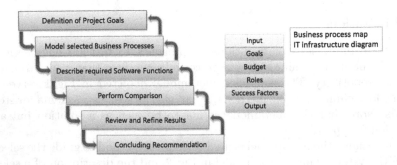

Fig. 2. Illustration of process model that is part of a modelling method

process type. Adding an attribute like "state" to DiagramType does not work, since we are not interested in the state of a diagram type, but rather in that of a particular diagram. While we could overload the object that represents a diagram type to also represent particular diagrams that would clearly compromise model integrity. It would also be impossible to define that two different instances of a diagram type were required in different states. Using two different meta types like "Diagram" and "DiagramType" would result in a loss of semanitics. This lack of expressiveness becomes even more obvious, if a particular method use should be represented. In that case, an instance of the metamodel would have to be further instantiated. While we know that each activity has a certain start and termination time, those cannot be expressed in the metamodel. Also, it is not possible to specify the actual budget available in a particular activity – or whether it was exceeded or not. Furthermore, it would be important to assign actors to roles. For this purpose, it would be required to instantiate a role type like "domain expert", which was instantiated from Role, into a particular role instance and link it to an instance of a class Actor. However, again that would not be possible, because in MOF like architectures the instantiation of a class cannot be further instantiated.

An approach to reuse method fragments would correspond to instantiating parts of a metamodel and reusing them with further instantiations. For example, a particular instantiation of Activity and associated instances of Goal, Input, Role, etc. could be stored in a repository and used for the creation of a new method. However, the challenge to avoid copy&paste semantics and the accompanying redundancy would remain: it is unlikely that the state of the components in the repository will be invariantly the same across all reuse cases. For example, within one method activity b may follow activity a, while another method requires activity b to follow activity x.

A further shortcoming of the traditional approach to method engineering becomes not immediately apparent. Imagine, a large company that frequently runs projects in areas such as software development, IT management, integration of IT infrastructures, etc. is using a metamodel like the one shown in Fig. 1. Each new method would have to be created from scratch using the rather generic concepts defined in the metamodel – maybe supplemented by using existing method fragments through copy&paste. Imagine, the company would instead use more specific meta modelling languages to define particular methods. There could, for example, be a meta-metamodel that reflects common knowledge about software development methods. It may include a meta-activity Analysis that defines what is generally known about analysis of software systems. The knowledge represented by this meta-meta model (or, in other words: this meta DSML) would then be reused for the definition of a more specific method, e.g., a method for developing distributed systems. Again, such an approach would require sequences of multiple instantiation, which are not supported by MOF like architectures. This limitation has been known for some time. Various authors suggest the use of powertypes to cope with it [4,12,14]. Powertypes are also supported by the ISO/IEC 24744 metamodel. Apart from powertype being a cumbersome concept that does not contribute to the readability of metamodels (even though that may be a subjective assessment), it is restricted by the fact that it is part of an extended MOF architecture, which means it can be used on M2 only, not on higher levels of classification. That would hinder the definition of multiple classification levels in order to define hierarchies of reusable DSML.

Even more important is a limitation that is not implied by the concept itself: as long as no programming language provides generic support for powertypes, they cannot be used for the design and implementation of tools, in particular they could not be used for tools that integrate the representation of methods with representations of method use ("endeavour"). Table 1 presents an assessment of traditional approaches to method engineering with respect to the generic requirements proposed in Sect. 2.2.

Table 1. Assessment according to generic requirements

R1	Classification allows for defining properties of direct instances. Composition allows for reusing particular instances. However, it is not possible to express knowledge related to instances of instances
R2	Each metamodel reflects a specific trade-off between range of reuse and productivity of reuse. The concepts defined with a certain method cannot be reused for the definition of further more specific methods – except for the reuse of method fragments. Therefore, the conflict between the two objectives of reuse can hardly be relaxed
R3	The integrity of a method depends on the extent of misleading interpretations its specification allows for. The more domain-specific a meta-model is, the better are the chances to constrain the specification of a model properly. However, it is not possible to define constraints on instances of instances, e.g. on specific states of diagrams
R4	From a conceptual perspective, methods could be further instantiated into specific method uses, because methods are conceptually specified on M1. However, apart from the use of powertypes, it is not possible to define properties (attributes, associations, etc.) for the classes that represent a method. Therefore, they cannot be further instantiated. But even with powertypes, the integration of methods with particular method instances is not possible, as long as there is no programming language that allows for multiple levels of classification

4   Prospects of Multi-level Language Architectures

The limitations of MOF like architectures as a foundation for method engineering call for language architectures that enable higher levels of abstraction. Multi-level modelling has been around for some time [3]. It provides concepts that allow for creating models on different levels of classification. The meta language and language engineering environment presented in this section follows this tradition.

4.1   Multi-level Methods in a Nutshell

While multi-level modelling may appear unusual to some, it supports in fact a natural way of using language. In the traditional paradigm, a language is always defined from scratch, that is, using the generic concepts of a generic meta-modelling language (see example in Fig. 1). However, that does not correspond to the creation and use of languages in advanced societies. If, for example, a company wants to create a method, it will very likely not start with generic concepts such as class or attribute to design a method that fits its needs. Instead, it will use domain-specific concepts that are known for a certain purpose, e.g., software development, and/or for a certain domain, such as a specific industry. These concepts in turn are also not defined from scratch, but by using some more general concepts known for describing methods and projects. The highest level of such a hierarchy could be regarded as the textbook level. It reflects generally applicable knowledge of a certain field. Figure 3 illustrates this idea. The boxes represent (meta-) models that define (meta-) methods. A certain method is defined by concepts that are part of a more general method. At the top level, the range of reuse is the highest. With every refinement step, the range of reuse decreases, but the productivity of reuse in a particular case increases. At the same time, the distinction between modelling language and model gets blurred. What is a model at one level, is a language at a higher level. That corresponds to the natural use of language. Usually, we do not bother with asking whether a term is part of a language (which it usually is) or whether it was defined with some other concepts (which is usually the case). Apparently, such a language architecture clearly contributes to satisfying requirements R1 and R2, because it fosters reuse in general and promotes range of reuse at a higher level, while it contributes to productivity of reuse on more specific levels. It is also suited to foster the integrity of methods (R3), since every refinement step introduces more specific concepts that constrain the construction of methods on the level below. Finally, it enables the integration of representations of a method and its use (R4), because objects on M0 that represent a particular use of a method (or in other words: a particular project) are part of the language architecture. Note that the relationship called "specified with" represents a specific kind of intrinsic instantiation (see the description of the FMML$^{\times}$), which in fact combines aspects of instantiation with aspects of inheritance.

In the remaining part of this section, it will be shown how a multi-level method architecture like the one illustrated in Fig. 3 can be accomplished – both at design and at run-time.

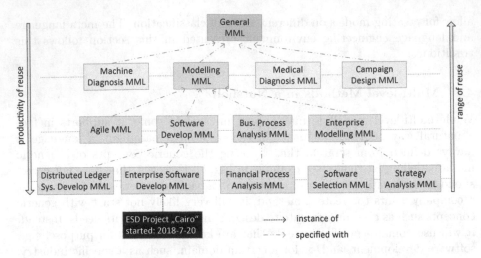

Fig. 3. Illustration of multi-level methods

4.2   An Executable, Multi-level Meta-Modelling Language

The Flexible Meta Modelling Language (FMML^x) [11] is an executable multi-level modelling language. It allows for modelling classes on an arbitrary number of classification levels. To enable multiple instantiation steps, intrinsic properties, that is, attributes, operations and associations can be defined for each class. For each intrinsic property, the intended instantiation level has to be defined, which allows for deferred instantiation. The examples in Fig. 4 illustrate the default notation of the FMML^x. The classification level of a class is indicated by the background color of the header field. The class `PeripheralDevice` is on level M3. Its intrinsic attribute `serialNo` is to be instantiated on M1 only. Since ever class is an object at the same time, it may have a state. For example, the class on M1 that represents a printer model includes data that represent technical properties and a price. Note that objects on M0 can be included in a model, too.

The FMML^x is implemented with XMF (eXecutable Metamodeling Facility) [5,6], which is a language execution engine that is based on a recursive metamodel, called Xcore. Modelling and programming languages that are specified as instances of Xcore can be executed within XMF. XMF allows accessing and modifying its own specification and its run-time system. Hence, there is no clear distinction between the language and a respective meta language. That is, XMF is reflective. Therefore, it facilitates navigation and introspection across all language levels represented in a particular system. XMF includes XOCL, an executable object constraint language. Xcore enables classes on an arbitrary number of classification levels. However, is not possible to assign a particular classification level to a class. Instead, the classification level of the metaclass `Class` is contingent. The particular classification level of its instances is determined dynamically, depending on the actual number of possible instantiation steps. It does not provide direct support for deferred instantiation either. By

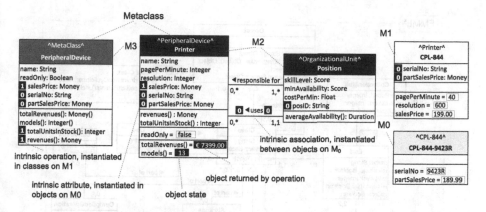

Fig. 4. Default notation of the FMML^x

default `Class` is on level M3 at first. A class that is instantiated from `Class` is on M2. If this class then inherits from `Class`, it is lifted to M3. The same procedure can be applied to its instances, which results in lifting the class higher to any intended level.

The specification and implementation of the FMML^x is based on an extension of Xcore and an intermediate layer that enables assigning a specific classification level to a class. Figure 5 illustrates the recursive architecture of Xcore and the extension (properties marked with green background) added for the FMML^x. The interface layer includes the class `MetaAdaptor`, which is an instance of `Class` and inherits from it at the same time. It is instantiated into the class `MetaClass`, which serves to create classes on particular classification levels. The instantiation methods implemented in `MethodAdaptor` hide the process of lifting a class to an intended level described above.

Apart from a slightly different terminology, the FMML^x shares core features such as multiple classification levels and deferred instantiation with other approaches to multi-level modelling [2,19]. However, it offers two distinct features that are of particular relevance for method engineering tools. Models defined with the FMML^x may comprise objects on different levels of classification – down to M0. Furthermore, it features a common representation of models and code. Hence, there is no need to generate code from models and to cope with the challenges implied by the synchronisation of models and code.

4.3   Application to Method Engineering

To demonstrate the benefits of multi-level languages for method engineering, we will refer to the concepts in Fig. 1 and the idea of a multi-level language hierarchy shown in Fig. 3. One essential principle of defining concepts of a language at any level is to express all knowledge available at that level. Only then, it is possible to avoid the redundant repetition of this knowledge at lower levels.

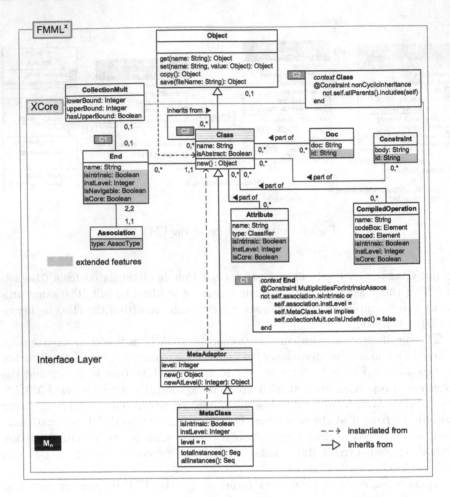

Fig. 5. Metamodel of the FMML^x as an extension of Xcore

The multi-level model shown in Fig. 6 illustrates how DSML can be defined with more abstract DSML. The model shows only a small excerpt of classes that are part of corresponding DSML, such as a hierarchy of DSML for modelling resources, or documents. The representation of associations is restricted to a few examples only. On a high level of classification certain associations that are to be instantiated on lower levels, may be known already, e.g. the association "requires" between the classes `Activity` and `Role`, which is to be instantiated on M1 only. The model illustrates a few important aspects of multi-level language architectures. There is no clear distinction between language and language application. Furthermore, a class may be associated with a class on any other level. Again, this corresponds to the use of concepts in natural language. Apparently, it is possible to integrate the representation of particular method

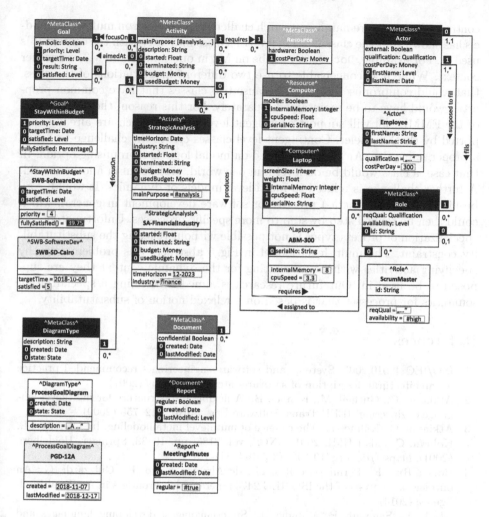

Fig. 6. Illustration of multiple levels of DSMLs integrated in one model[x]

uses on M0. The Xmodeler allows to execute the model hierarchy. In other words, the multi-level model becomes the conceptual foundation *and* the implementation of an integrated method specification and execution environment.

5 Conclusions and Outlook

The approach presented in this paper demonstrates the potential of multi-level language hierarchies for modelling language and models in the context of method engineering and method use. It is suited to relax the fundamental conflict between range of reuse and productivity of reuse. It also contributes to more consistent method definitions. The obvious prospects of multi-level modelling are contrasted with two remaining research challenges. Our work on multi-level models has shown that the classification level of a class may vary with the context it is used in. For example, Document may be on M2 in one context, on M3 in another context. While it is conceivable to use two different instantiations of the class, that would compromise integrity, because two classes that have common properties would have to be maintained separately. For this reason, the next version of the FMML^x [8] will support contingent level classes, which are already supported by the Xmodeler. Contingent level classes create the challenge to define a proper semantics. An approach based on modal logic is a promising option. In that case, a class would be on level n in one world, on level m in another world. A further challenge is related to multi-level models of dynamics. It would, e.g., be nice to define a (meta-) process for software development in general, which could then be refined step by step to more specific processes. Unfortunately, the specialization of process types is not possible without relaxing the substitutability constraint. The multi-level model in Fig. 6 abstracts this problem away by specifying activities without accounting for the dynamic context they are supposed to be used in. Our future research is aimed at defining a specialization semantics for processes that is based on a relaxed notion of substitutability.

References

1. ISO/IEC 42010:2007: Systems and software engineering - recommended practice for architectural description of software-intensive systems (2007)
2. Atkinson, C., Gutheil, M., Kennel, B.: A flexible infrastructure for multilevel language engineering. IEEE Trans. Software Eng. **35**(6), 742–755 (2009)
3. Atkinson, C., Kühne, T.: The essence of multilevel metamodeling. In: Gogolla, M., Kobryn, C. (eds.) UML 2001. LNCS, vol. 2185, pp. 19–33. Springer, Heidelberg (2001). https://doi.org/10.1007/3-540-45441-1_3
4. Borges Ruy, F., Perini Barcellos, M., de Almeida Falbo, R., Guizzardi, G.: An ontological analysis of the ISO/IEC 24744 metamodel. Frontiers in Artificial Intelligence (2014)
5. Clark, T., Sammut, P., Willans, J.: Superlanguages: developing languages and applications with XMF. Ceteva (2008)
6. Clark, T., Willans, J.: Software language engineering with XMF and XModeler. In: Mernik, M. (ed.) Formal and Practical Aspects of Domain-Specific Languages, pp. 311–340. Information Science Reference (2012)
7. Fill, H.G., Karagiannis, D.: On the conceptualisation of modelling methods using the adoxx meta modelling platform. Enterp. Model. Inf. Syst. Architectures **8**(1), 4–25 (2013)
8. Frank, U.: The flexible multi-level modelling language (fmmlx): Version 2.0: Analysis of requirements and technical terminology. ICB research report, no. 66, university of duisburg-essen (2018)
9. Frank, U.: Multi-perspective enterprise modelling: Background and terminological foundation. ICB research report, no. 46, university of duisburg-essen (2011)
10. Frank, U.: Domain-specific modeling languages - requirements analysis and design guidelines. In: Reinhartz-Berger, I., Sturm, A., Clark, T., Wand, Y., Cohen, S., Bettin, J. (eds.) Domain Engineering: Product Lines, Conceptual Models, and Languages, pp. 133–157. Springer, Heidelberg (2013)

11. Frank, U.: Multilevel modeling: toward a new paradigm of conceptual modeling and information systems design. Bus. Inf. Syst. Eng. **6**(6), 319–337 (2014)
12. González-Pérez, C., Henderson-Sellers, B.: Modelling software development methodologies: a conceptual foundation. J. Syst. Software **80**(11), 1778–1796 (2007). https://doi.org/10.1016/j.jss.2007.02.048
13. Henderson-Sellers, B., González-Pérez, C., Ralyté, J.: Comparison of method chunks and method fragments for situational method engineering. In: Proceedings of the Australian Software Engineering Conference (2008)
14. Henderson-Sellers, B., Ralyté, J.: Situational method engineering: state-of-the-art review. J. Univ. Comput. Sci. **16**(3), 424–478 (2010)
15. Henderson-Sellers, B., Ralyté, J., Ågerfalk, P.J., Rossi, M.: Situational Method Engineering. Springer, Heidelberg (2014). https://doi.org/10.1007/978-3-642-41467-1
16. Lyytinen, K., Smolander, K., Tahvanainen, V.-P.: Modelling case environments in systems development. In: Proceedings of CASE 1989, Stockholm (1989)
17. Kelly, S., Lyytinen, K., Rossi, M., Tolvanen, J.P.: Metaedit+ at the age of 20. In: Bubenko, J. (ed.) Seminal Contributions to Information Systems Engineering, pp. 131–137. Springer, New York (2013)
18. Kornyshova, E., Deneckère, R., Salinesi, C.: Method chunks selection by multicriteria techniques: an extension of the assembly-based approach. In: Ralyté, J., Brinkkemper, S., Henderson-Sellers, B. (eds.) Situational Method Engineering: Fundamentals and Experiences. ITIFIP, vol. 244, pp. 64–78. Springer, Boston, MA (2007). https://doi.org/10.1007/978-0-387-73947-2_7
19. Neumayr, B., Grün, K., Schrefl, M.: Multi-level domain modeling with m-objects and m-relationships. In: Link, S., Kirchberg, M. (eds.) Proceedings of the 6th Asia-Pacific Conference on Conceptual Modeling (APCCM), pp. 107–116. Australian Computer Society, Wellington (2009)
20. Rolland, C.: A primer for method engineering (1998)

Evaluation of Modeling Approaches (EMMSAD 2019)

The Usage of Constraint Specification Languages: A Controlled Experiment

Azzam Maraee[1,2] and Arnon Sturm[1(✉)]

[1] Ben-Gurion University of the Negev, Beer-Sheva, Israel
mari@cs.bgu.ac.il, sturm@bgu.ac.il
[2] Achva Academic College, Arugot, Israel

Abstract. Model-based software engineering places models in the center of the development process. To support this notion, multiple modeling languages are available, and the visual ones are widely used. Nevertheless, visual modeling languages are limited in their expressiveness and sometime might introduce ambiguity into the models. To overcome these limitations, model-based constraint languages have emerged, yet, their usage is limited, probably due to a misconception that they are difficult to work with. In this paper, we challenge this misconception by comparing the use of three constraint languages: OCL, Java, and natural language in understanding and developing model-based constraints. The comparison was made through a controlled experiment with 68 information systems engineering undergraduate students. We found out that using natural language results in shorter times to perform the tasks. Yet, using OCL results in increased accuracy for specifying new constraints, in particular, in complex settings.

Keywords: Modeling · Constraint language · OCL · Evaluation · Controlled experiment

1 Introduction

Model Based Software Engineering (MBSE) places models as the core artifacts of software development. Within the academia, research on MBSE has a long tradition and new directions are emerging [8]. Following the MBSE approach, models are used for various purposes such as communication, documentation, design means, and for the generation of various artifacts including code. Nevertheless, due to lack of formalization and due to some ambiguities that still exist in models, additional languages are required. To address this need, the Object Constraint Language (OCL) was devised [10, 15]. OCL was developed as a language that should be further attached to an existing (diagrammatic) modeling language, that might be lacking in its expressiveness. Such a language eliminates the misunderstanding occurs when humans read models and thus errors can be found in an early stage of the development process, as the intended meaning of the modeler is to clarify the specifications with the various stakeholders. OCL becomes even more important when there is an automatic system that further uses it for various tasks, such as generating simulation and tests, checking consistency, and generating other artifacts (including other models and code) [10, 15].

© Springer Nature Switzerland AG 2019
I. Reinhartz-Berger et al. (Eds.): BPMDS 2019/EMMSAD 2019, LNBIP 352, pp. 329–343, 2019.
https://doi.org/10.1007/978-3-030-20618-5_22

OCL is designed to be both a query and a constraint language which allow restrictions and further investigation of models. It is based on mathematical foundation (set theory and predicate logic), yet, avoids the use of mathematical symbols to increase its accessibility. It is strongly typed so to allow checking without the need to have an executable system. Finally, it is a declarative language that allows higher level of specification, eliminating the need to get into implementation details [15].

Following the OCL characteristics, its usage increases over the years and includes model validation, e.g., [3], testing, e.g. [1], and model querying [5]. Furthermore, a plethora of tools were developed as specified in [9].

Nevertheless, only limited attention was paid to test whether OCL is the best option for specifying constraints in various contexts. This include the impact of OCL on maintenance [2], the effect of OCL constraint quality on understanding [4], and the effect of improving OCL querying language to increase its usage [13]. Only recently, an evaluation of alternatives constraint specification languages was performed [17]. It was found that in general, the quality of constraints specified in Java and OCL were similar. In this work we are interested in a similar direction and extend the scope to the comprehension of constraints and also to check whether the use of natural language is more effective. Thus, in this paper we address the research question of:

Is OCL the best alternative for handling model-based constraints?

To do so, we design an experiment that examines the usage of three alternative languages: OCL, Java, and natural language. In particular, by usage we refer to comprehension and specification of constraints related to existing models.

The rest of the paper is organized as follows. In Sect. 2 we review studies related to the examination of OCL and other constraints languages utilization. In Sect. 3 we present the design of an experiment we performed to compare the utilization of constraint languages. In Sect. 4 we elaborate on the experiment results whereas in Sect. 5 we discuss those results. In Sect. 6 we indicate the threats to validity and finally, in Sect. 7 we conclude and set plans for future research directions.

2   Related Work

As mentioned before only few works have been used experimentation to evaluate the usage of OCL. In this section we examine these works in light of various characteristics: the experiment goal, classification of OCL constraints, and the system aspects that were examined.

The work of Briand et al. [2] was the first of its kind and aim at exploring the impact of OCL constraints on UML model maintainability. It emphasizes of whether the use of OCL constraints improves the comprehension of system functionality and logic and whether it improves the identification of required changes when new or changed requirements are introduced. The models include use cases, class diagrams and state machine diagrams. Based on the experiment the authors found out that the usage of OCL improved the comprehensibility and maintainability for either students with high ability and low ability.

Correa et al. [4] took a different view and examine the way syntactic complexity of constraints affect the understanding of OCL constraints. They devised a controlled experiment in which they had the same questions with different constraints. The results of the experiment revealed that the way constraints are written do affect their comprehension in both the correct interpretations and the time to reach them. This was also confirmed by the subject perceptions over the way the constraints were written.

Storrle [13] examined whether the addition of a friendlier interface to OCL increases the usability of OCL. In a controlled experiment, using queries of OCL and OCL with OQAPI (the improved language interface) and a set of responses, he asked the subjects to find appropriate matching, to write queries for given responses, and to assess the readability and writability of the two options, as well as the required effort and confidence. The results indicate that using the improved language interface improved the comprehension, the writability, the confidence and reduced the required effort.

Yue and Ali [17] examined the writeability of OCL versus Java. For two domains they specified ten constraints and asked their subjects to write those in OCL and Java and refer to the applicability and confidence when using these languages. Based on the results, the authors conclude that there are no much differences in using Java or OCL.

Most studies dealt with the comprehension of constraints, however, they did not compare OCL to alternative languages. The most recent work [17] did compare the writeability or the development of constraints and compare it to Java, yet the comprehensibility when using these alternatives was not examined.

Actually, the various comparisons refer to the essence of the language, i.e., whether it is imperative or declarative. In the context of transformation language, Sendall and Kozaczynski [12] claim that the essence of the language affects its usability. Declarative languages are concise and thus simplify the transformation rules, whereas imperative languages are more familiar and explicate the transformation procedure. In the context of business process modeling, Pichler et al. [11] differentiate among the language types as follows. An imperative language requires that all execution paths are specified explicitly (which might lead to over specification), whereas, using a declarative language required the specification of the essential parts and the addition of constraints, without the need to specify the procedure. In their experiment Pichler et al. found that although declarative languages seem to be simpler, the importance of the procedural aspect make the imperative one to be better understood.

The above understanding can be interpreted by the cognitive dimensions proposed by Green [6]. These include: (1) Hidden/explicit dependencies – that need to be accessible to complete a task; (2) Viscosity – that refers to modularity; (3) Premature commitment – that refers to the time of reaching a decision; (4) Role expressiveness – that refers to the tradeoffs between expressiveness and usability; and (5) Hard mental operations – that refer to the effort required to understand a model by transforming it to one's perceptions. As discussed above in the context of business process modeling, moving from declarative statements to procedural knowledge requires heavy mental transformation, whereas in the context of transformation moving from declarative statements to the required transformation is much easier. In the following, we aim at examining whether these considerations also apply in the case of specifying and understanding constraints over an existing model.

3   Experiment Design

To examine the effectiveness of the language essence we compare three constraints languages: OCL, Java, and Natural-Like Language (NLL) for understanding and developing constraints over models, via a controlled experiment. OCL represents a declarative language, Java represents an imperative language, and the NLL as it stands is also a declarative language, yet without the expected formalism. In this section we present the experiment design.

3.1   Hypotheses

We consider the use of the language in terms of correctness, time, and confidence with respect to both comprehension and development of constraints. We further make a difference between simple and complex constraints. Our conjectures regarding the utilization of a constraint language were the following:

- When referring to comprehension we believe that NLL is easier to understand than Java or OCL, as no syntax or formal semantics familiarity is required, and thus the mental transformation is limited. In particular, in simple constraints this would hold and in complex constraints the effect might be reduced. As invariant constrains do not require procedural knowledge, understanding constraints specified in OCL would be easier than constraints specified in Java, as Java provide much more information than required. That is, it further elaborates the implementation details.
- When referring to the development of constraints we believe that the benefit of using NLL in reduced as there is a need to refer to the model and its instances explicitly. Nevertheless, it will still outperform Java and OCL, as concrete syntax seems to negatively affect the language usability. When referring to Java and OCL, Java is more familiar, yet it requires further efforts, whereas OCL is less familiar, but requires less efforts. Thus, there is a tradeoff in using these languages.

We believe that our conjectures will hold for the three factors we measured: correctness, time to address the requirements, and confidence. Our hypotheses can be formalized as follows:

$$H_0^{CAT-TASK-ASPECT} : OCL^{CAT-TASK-ASPECT} = Java^{CAT-TASK-ASPECT} = Nav^{CAT-TASK-ASPECT}$$
$$H_1^{CAT-TASK-ASPECT} : OCL^{CAT-TASK-ASPECT} \neq Java^{CAT-TASK-ASPECT} \neq Nav^{CAT-TASK-ASPECT}$$

Where CAT refers to either all, simple, and complex constraints, TASK refers to development or comprehension and ASPECT refers to correctness, time, and confidence.

3.2   Design

In the following we describe the variables and their measurements, the subjects, and the tasks.

Independent Variables

The first variable is the approach according to which the constraints are set. It has three options: OCL, Java, and Natural-Like Language (NLL). In the following we present the three forms of specifying constraints using the example of Hotel Room Management system adopted from [15] as presented to the subjects. A partial model of that system appears in Fig. 1.

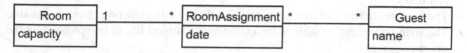

Fig. 1. A partial model of a hotel room management system

For the constraint that each room has a single assignment in each day and that assignment should fit the capacity of the room, the following specifications hold:

OCL	Context Room inv: self.roomAssignment->forAll (ra1, ra2 | ra1.date=ra2.date implies ra1=ra2) and self.roomAssignment-> forAll(ra| ra.guest->size()<=self.capacity)

Java	`public boolean roomCapcity(Room room){`
	  `result=true;`
	  `for(RoomAssignment ra1: room.roomAssignment){`
	    `for(RoomAssignment ra2: room.roomAssignment){`
	      `result=result && (ra1.date!=ra2.date || ra1==ra2)`
	    `}`
	  `}`
	  `for(RoomAssignment ra1: room.roomAssignment){`
	    `result= result && (ra1.guest.size()<=room.capacity)`
	  `}`
	  `return result;`
	`}`

NLL	There could not be two Assignment objects with the same date related to the same Room object, and the number of Guest objects associated with each Assignment is lower or equal to the capacity of the related Room of that assignment.

The second independent variable is the constraint complexity. The complexity is calculated based on the following metrics, inspired by the work of Yue and Ali [14]: Nesting level, Maximum number of traversals, Number of OCL Complex Operators/Operators, Number of oclAsType operations, and Number of clauses. Based on these metrics we classified the constraints as simple or complex. Although, complexity is an independent variable, we calculated these metrics to objectively determined the complexity of each constraint.

Dependent Variables

- The first dependent variable is the correctness of a developed constraint.
- The second dependent variable is the time it takes to develop a constraint.
- The third dependent variable is the confidence a subject has in the developed constraint.
- The fourth dependent variable is the correctness of comprehending a given constraint.
- The fifth dependent variable is the time it takes to comprehend a given constraint.
- The sixth dependent variable is the confidence a subject has in comprehending the given constraint.

Dependent Variables Measurements

The correctness of the constraint specification is determined based on the following. For each constraint we checked its correctness in light of a pre-defined solutions (i.e., gold standard), yet, with some flexibility (to allow valid, yet different solutions). We also considered the time it took to specify the constraint, as measured by the subjects themselves, and the confidence they had in their specified constraints in a 5-Likert scale.

The comprehension of constraints is checked using instances that either violate or adhere with a pre-specified constraint. Each constraint had 3 instance diagrams which need to be judged by the subjects for their alignment with the given constraint. Thus, the ranking would be 0–3 for each of the constraint. Here again, we also considered the time it took to understand the constraint, as measured by the subjects themselves, and the confidence they had in their answers in a 5-Likert scale.

Note that confidence measure for both the comprehension and construction is actually the subjects' subjective perspective on the language usability.

Subjects

The subjects of the experiment were third year students taking the course on Object-oriented Analysis and Design. The course consists of analyzing, designing, and implementing software based on the object-oriented paradigm. During the course the subjects learned the notion of modeling and in particular class diagram, they further learned OCL with the emphasize on invariants in class diagrams. They also practice class diagram and OCL. The students have previous experience in Java and other programming languages and also used these as part of the course. Some of them have already started practicing in the industry.

Recruiting the students was done on a volunteering basis. Nevertheless, they were encouraged to participate in the experiment by providing them additional bonus points to the course grade based on their performance. Before recruiting the students, we also approved the research via the ethics committee.

Task

We designed the experiment so that each subject will experience one language, yet, they all refer to the same domain and model, which is a hospital management system (adopted from [14]).

The experiment form consists of 3 parts: (1) a pre-task questionnaire that checks the background and knowledge of the subjects; (2) the actual task, in which subjects receive a class diagram of a Hospital Management system (as appears in Appendix B), and were asked to write 5 constraints based on natural language specification (development) and determine the validity of instance diagrams of 5 other constraints (comprehension); The expected constraints and their complexity appears in Appendix A; (3) the last part of the form reflects upon the subjects' perception of the used language.

Execution

The execution of the experiment took place during one of the lecture sessions and last approximately 1 h. The assignment of the groups (i.e., the language) to the subjects was done randomly. The distribution of groups was as followed: A–21; B–24; C–23.

4 Experiment Results

To check homogeneity among the three groups we had the pre-task questionnaire that refers to the subject background. Overall, no significant differences were found among the groups.

In the following we present the results of the experiment. Tables 1, 2, 3, 4, 5 and 6 present the descriptive statistics of the various variables divided into the development and comprehension tasks and in division to: all constraints (total), simple constraints, and complex constraints. The triplets within each cell represent the average, the standard deviation, and the number of answers. Bolded-underlined numbers indicate the best results, in each column (i.e., the language with the highest achievement).

Next, we perform a statistical analysis on the results. Table 7 includes the Anova test for the correctness and time variables along with Tukey test for post-hoc analysis, and the Kruskal-Wallis test for the confidence variable (as it is an ordinal variable). The *Sig* column indicates the difference significance whereas the Post-Hoc column indicates only statistical differences among the approaches.

The most noticeable difference among the usage of the three languages is that when using natural language, the time to reach to a solution (which is not necessarily correct) is lower than when using OCL and Java. This difference was statistically significant.

Other existing differences are that comprehending constraints is usually easier when following the natural language, and that developing new constraints is more correct when using OCL, in particular in case of complex constraints. Also, there are some indications that confidence is larger when using OCL. Nevertheless, the latter differences were not found to be of statistical significance.

Table 1. Descriptive statistics of the development variables for all constraints

Approach	Dev-Correctness	Dev-Time	Dev-Confidence
OCL	**0.76**, 0.16, 21	4.74, 1.99, 21	**4.71**, 1.11, 21
JAVA	0.7, 0.22, 22	6.86, 1.45, 22	4.58, 1.28, 22
NLL	0.64, 0.33, 16	**4.05**, 1.11, 16	4.36, 1.19, 16

Table 2. Descriptive statistics of the comprehension variables for all constraints

Approach	Comp-Correctness	Comp-Time	Comp-Confidence
OCL	0.87, 0.13, 21	3.34, 1.35, 21	5.6, 0.6, 21
JAVA	0.86, 0.15, 24	4.52, 1.69, 24	5.42, 0.98, 23
NLL	**0.9**, 0.1, 23	**2.43**, 0.84, 23	**5.79**, 0.86, 23

Table 3. Descriptive statistics of the development variables for simple constraints

Approach	Dev-Correctness	Dev-Time	Dev-Confidence
OCL	0.73, 0.22, 21	4.44, 1.85, 21	**4.84**, 1.2, 21
JAVA	**0.75**, 0.23, 22	6.51, 1.8, 22	4.7, 1.33, 22
NLL	0.67, 0.34, 16	**3.77**, 1.59, 16	4.39, 114, 16

Table 4. Descriptive statistics of the comprehension variables for simple constraints

Approach	Comp-Correctness	Comp-Time	Comp-Confidence
OCL	0.86, 0.17, 21	2.47, 1.1, 21	**5.86**, 0.55, 21
JAVA	**0.89**, 0.14, 24	3.65, 2, 24	5.51, 1.04, 24
NLL	0.85, 0.1, 23	**2.06**, 0.79, 23	5.72, 0.85, 23

Table 5. Descriptive statistics of the development variables for complex constraints

Approach	Dev-Correctness	Dev-Time	Dev-Confidence
OCL	**0.81**, 0.22, 21	5.19, 2.8, 21	**4.52**, 1.1, 21
JAVA	0.61, 0.31, 22	7.39, 2.34, 22	4.41, 1.33, 22
NLL	0.59, 0.39, 16	**4.47**, 1.62, 16	4.31. 1.33, 16

Table 6. Descriptive statistics of the comprehension for complex constraints

Approach	Comp-Correctness	Comp-Time	Comp-Confidence
OCL	0.89, 0.14, 21	4.47, 2.12, 21	5.21, 0.92, 21
JAVA	0.83, 0.21, 24	5.83, 2, 24	5.4, 1.17, 24
NLL	**0.98**, 0.14, 23	**3.00**, 1.21, 23	**5.89**, 0.98, 23

Table 7. Statistical analysis

	F	Sig	Post-Hoc
Total dev correctness	1.282	0.286	
Total dev time	16.816	0.00	NLL > Java
			NLL > OCL
Total dev confidence		0.629	
Total comprehension correctness	0.524	0.595	
Total comprehension time	14.277	<0.0001	NLL > Java
			NLL > OCL
Total comprehension confidence		0.447	
Simple dev correctness	0.525	0.595	
Simple dev time	13.04	<0.0001	NLL > Java
			NLL > OCL
Simple dev confidence		0.458	
Simple comprehension correctness	0.353	0.704	
Simple comprehension time	8.136	<0.0001	NLL > Java
			NLL > OCL
Simple comprehension confidence		0.699	
Complex dev correctness	3.021	0.057	
Complex dev time	8.241	0.001	NLL > Java
			NLL > OCL
Complex dev confidence		0.751	
Complex comprehension correctness	4.295	0.018	OCL > Java
			OCL > NLL
Complex comprehension time	14.316	<0.0001	NLL > OCL > Java
Complex comprehension confidence		0.066	

Back to the hypotheses, the following were rejected:

$$H_0^{Total-Dev-Time}, H_0^{Complex-Dev-Time}, H_0^{Simple-Dev-Time}, H_0^{Total-Comp-Time}$$
$$H_0^{Simple-Comp-Time}, H_0^{Complex-Comp-Time}, H_0^{Complex-Dev-Correctness}$$

The first six indicate that using NLL take less time to process. The last one indicates that in developing complex constraints using OCL yields better results than using Java or NLL. We were not able to reject the other hypotheses, a fact that indicates that using either methods yields similar results.

Examining the subjects' forms yields some insights regarding common errors that characterize the different languages. In the following we present examples of answers for some of the constraints and analyze the different answers.

Constraint 1: *"If a ward has at least three patients, then the number of doctors in teams responsible for that ward is greater than or equal to 3"*

Constraint 2: *"A ward and its patients have the same gender"*

Constraint 3: *"A team must have at least one junior doctor with a rank of 1"*

For Constraint 1, using Java received only 8 correct answers. Moreover, the subjects tended to use nested loops. Listing 1 presents such a solution. When using OCL, most subjects succeeded in formulating it correctly.

For Constraint 2, using Java gains only 65% success rate, whereas using OCL gains 72% success rate, and similarly to Constraint 1, the Java solutions included unnecessary nested loops (7 answers). Listing 2 presents an example of such code.

For Constraint 3, using Java gained an advantage over the usage of OCL. This constraint uses the type-related operations such as instanceof and casting. In OCL, 48% of the answers were correct or partially correct answers. This was due to omission of the oclAsType (casting in Java) operator. In addition, there were four answers that omits the operators select or oclIsTypeOf (instanceof in Java). On the other hand, using Java gain 56% correct or partially correct answers. The problems were similar to those when using OCL, i.e., accessing the rank field without casting. In addition, there were three answers with incorrect use or lack of use of instanceof operator. In general, analyzing the specification for all constraints, we found out that when using OCL the subjects had less logical mistakes and navigation errors than when using Java. Using OCL resulted in 27 logical mistakes and 17 navigation mistakes, whereas using Java resulted in 33 logical mistakes and 33 navigation mistakes.

```
public boolean check(Ward ward){
    List<Doctor> list = new List();
    if (ward.patient.size() >= 3) {
        for(Patient p: ward.patient){
            for(Doctor doc: p.team.doctor){
                if(!lis.contain(doc) lis.add(doc)}}}
    return (list.size>=3)}
```
Listing 1. A student solution for Constraint 1

```
for(int i=0; i<hospital.award.size,i++)
    for(int j=0; j<hospital.person.size;j++)
        if(hospital.ward[j].gender!=hospital.person[i].gender   return false;
    return true;
```
Listing 2. A student solution for Constraint 2

Constraints written in natural language suffer from unclarity and logic problems. The constraints were long and did not follow the guidelines. For example, an NLL answer to Constraint 1: *"The number of objects of the junior doctor, who have a grade 1 and associated with some instance, is less than or equal to one"*. The problem in this answer is using *some instance* without specifying the class (instance of what?). Another example is an answer for Constraint 2: *There is no object of a class that has 3 patients or more and the number of different doctors associated with team is less than 3"*. Here also the subject mentioned *class* without specifying the name of the class.

Reviewing the subjects' post-questionnaires, we found no difference in their perception or preference of using OCL or Java in specifying and comprehending constraints.

5 Discussion

The results indicate a few advantage of using OCL over using Java or NLL while developing new constraints, in particular, those with high complexity. Complex constraints require deep navigation of the elements within the models, collection manipulation and universal and existential quantification (such as, there exists, there are no two objects, and for all objects). While OCL naturally support these features, subjects showed difficulties in formulation these constraints in Java and NLL. Developing complex constraints in Java requires using loops, definition of local variables, and control expressions. Therefore, subjects were affected by a culture that values loop and control structures, which led to the unnecessary use of nested loops, and to further focus on implementation aspects. The inherit difference among both languages (i.e., imperative object-oriented paradigm vs. declarative paradigm) affects the way subjects express the constraints. Writing the constraints declaratively using object navigation, collections, collection operations and Boolean-valued expressions shifts the way student formulate (program) the constraints. We found out that using Java resulted in more errors compared to OCL and that using OCL achieved better results in case of complicated constraints. On the other hand, as mentioned in the previous section, Java had an advantage, for example, in Constraint 3. Using OCL resulted in more errors in accessing objects of the sub-class `JuniorDoctor`. Navigating to the objects of `JuniorDoctor` through the objects of the super-class `Doctor`, requires using *type introspection* which provided by OCL by `oclIsTypeOf` and in Java by the operator `instanceof`. We believe that the reason for that is the lack of the subjects' experience in OCL. In addition, both using OCL and using Java had the same percentage of errors in using the casting operator for accessing the `rank` field.

Constraints written in natural language suffer from unclarity and logic problems. The subjects tend to formulate the constraints, especially the complex ones, in a convoluted and unclear manner that included logical errors.

Based on the above results and discussion, we are in line with the work of Yue and Ali [17] and recommend using OCL as constraint language. Modeling should be independent from other software elements and OCL indeed provides such separation.

6 Threats to Validity

The above results need to be considered in view of several threats to validity categorized by [16] as construct, internal, conclusion, and external validity.

Construct validity threats, which concern the relationships between theory and observation, are mainly due to the method used to assess the outcomes of the tasks. In this experiment we examined three language types for specifying constraints, namely declarative, imperative, and natural language. It might be that the selection of the specific languages affects the results. Nevertheless, the chosen languages are widely used so in practice has a benefit as well.

Internal validity threats, which concern external factors which might affect the dependent variables, may be due to individual factors, such as familiarity with the domain, the degree of commitment by the subjects, and the training level the subjects underwent. These effects are mitigated by the experiment design that we chose. As the students belong to the engineering faculty, we believe that they did not have previous knowledge of how a hospital is running and being managed. The random assignments that was adopted should eliminate these kind of external factors. Although the experiment was done on a voluntary basis, the compensation of bonus points based on the students' performance, increased the motivation and commitment of the subjects as they took advantage of entire time allocated for the experiment.

Conclusion validity concerns the relationship between the treatment (the approach) and the outcome. We followed the various assumptions of the statistical tests when analyzing the results. In addition, we used a pre-defined solution for grading the subjects' answers and thus only a limited amount of human judgment was required.

Lastly, *external validity* concerns the generalizability of the results. The main threat in this area stems from the choice of subjects and from using simple tasks in the experiment. The subjects were undergraduate students with little experience in software engineering, in general, and in modeling and specifying constraints, in particular. The subjects had an extensive knowledge in Java and were trained and had practiced with OCL. Furthermore, the subjects were at an advanced stage in their studies and close to becoming software engineers and developers. Thus, they approximate the population intended to use models and constraints. More generally, Kitchenham et al. argue that using students as subjects instead of software engineers is not a major issue as long as the research questions are not specifically focused on experts [7], as is the case in our study. As we dealt only with one domain, it might be that the results are biased and there is a need to extend this experiment. We also believe that the types of constraints that were part of the experiment indeed represent the required capability in practical applications, and thus generalization of the results is applicable.

7 Summary

The usage of constraint languages in conjunction with model is quite limited both in academia and industry. Although, the Object Management Group, which currently leads the modeling standardization, also provide specification for such languages, in practice, it seems that their usage is limited. A major claim is that such languages are limited in their accessibility (i.e., ease of use).

In this paper, we make another step in evaluating whether constraint languages and in particular OCL indeed lack in their accessibility. For that purpose, we set a controlled experiment which examines the usage of OCL, Java, and natural language in terms of comprehension and development of model based constraints. We found out that using OCL achieved better results in developing new constraints, in particular, complex ones. We believe that this hold due to the fact that OCL as a declarative language omits the need to go into the implementation details and the way the procedure should work. This reduces the transformation efforts required to specify the constraints.

This work is another step in understanding the difficulties of using constraint languages. In the future, we plan to conduct additional evaluations, so to get further insights of what are the limitations of using constraint languages. This will allow us to call for their usage so model-based software engineering would benefit from additional improvements.

Appendix A – The Hospital Management System – Class Diagram

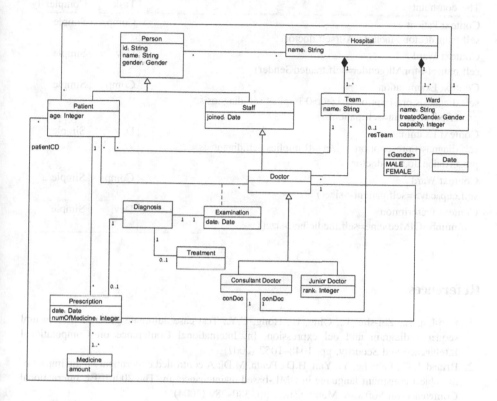

Appendix B – Constraints' Complexity

The constraint	Task	Complexity
Context Patient self.prescription->forAll(p1, p2| not(p1=p2) and p1.date=p2.date implies p1.medicine->intersection(p2.medicine)->isEmpty ())	Comp	Complex
Context Team self.doctor->select(oclIsTypeOf(JuniorDoctor))->collect(oclAsType (JuniorDoctor))->exists(rank=1)	Dev	Complex
Context Examination self.diagnosis.treatment->size()=1 implies self.doctor.oclIsTypeOf (ConsultantDoctor)	Comp	Complex
Context Ward self.patient->size()>=3 implies self.patient.team.doctor->asSet()- >size()>3	Dev	Complex

(*continued*)

(*continued*)

The constraint	Task	Complexity
Context Patient self.team.doctor->includesAll(self.doctor)	Comp	Simple
Context Ward self.patient->forAll(gender=self.treatedGender)	Dev	Simple
Context Examination self.diagnosis.prescription->size()>0 implies self.diagnosis. prescription.patient=self.patient	Comp	Simple
Context Examination self.diagnosis.prescription->size()>0 implies self.diagnosis. prescription.doctor=doctor	Dev	Simple
Context Ward self.capacity>=self.patient->size()	Comp	Simple
Context Prescription self.numberOfMedicine=self.medicine->size()	Dev	Simple

References

1. Bao-Lin, L., Zhi-shu, L., Qing, L., Hong, C.Y.: Test case automate generation from uml sequence diagram and ocl expression. In: International Conference on Computational Intelligence and Security, pp. 1048–1052 (2007)
2. Briand, L.C., Labiche, Y., Yan, H.D., Penta, M.Di: A controlled experiment on the impact of the object constraint language in UML-based maintenance. In: The 20th IEEE International Conference on Software Maintenance, pp. 380–389 (2004)
3. Chiorean, D., Bortes,M., Corutiu, D., Botiza, C., Cârcu, A.: Object Constraint Language Environment (OCLE). http://lci.cs.ubbcluj.ro/ocle/. Accessed Apr 2019
4. Correa, A., Werner, C., Barros, M.: An empirical study of the impact of OCL smells and refactorings on the understandability of OCL specifications. In: Model Driven Engineering Languages and Systems, pp. 76–90 (2007)
5. Eclipse, Eclipse OCL. https://projects.eclipse.org/projects/modeling.mdt.ocl, last accessed April 2019
6. Green, T.R.G.: Cognitive dimensions of notations. In: Sutcliffe, A., Macaulay, L. (eds.) People and Computers V, pp. 443–460. Cambridge University Press, Cambridge (1989)
7. Kitchenham, B.A., Pfleeger, S.L., Pickard, L.M., Jones, P.W., Hoaglin, D.C., El Emam, K., Rosenberg, J.: Preliminary guidelines for empirical research in software engineering. IEEE Trans. Software Eng. 28(8), 721–734 (2002)
8. Mussbacher, G., et al.: The relevance of model-driven engineering thirty years from now. In: Dingel, J., Schulte, W., Ramos, I., Abrahão, S., Insfran, E. (eds.) MODELS 2014. LNCS, vol. 8767, pp. 183–200. Springer, Cham (2014). https://doi.org/10.1007/978-3-319-11653-2_12
9. OCL Portal, OCL Tools. http://st.inf.tu-dresden.de/oclportal/index.php?option=com_content&view=category&id=8&Itemid=26. Accessed Apr 2019
10. OMG, Object-Constraint Language, version 2.4. https://www.omg.org/spec/OCL/2.4. Accessed Apr 2019

11. Pichler, P., Weber, B., Zugal, S., Pinggera, J., Mendling, J., Reijers, H.A.: Imperative versus declarative process modeling languages: an empirical investigation. In: Daniel, F., Barkaoui, K., Dustdar, S. (eds.) BPM 2011. LNBIP, vol. 99, pp. 383–394. Springer, Heidelberg (2012). https://doi.org/10.1007/978-3-642-28108-2_37

12. Sendall, S., Kozaczynski, W.: Model transformation: the heart and soul of model-driven software development. IEEE Softw. **20**(5), 42–45 (2003)

13. Störrle, H.: Improving the usability of OCL as an ad-hoc model querying language. In: The 13th International Workshop on OCL, Model Constraint and Query Languages, pp. 83–92 (2013)

14. UMLdiagrams.org, Hospital Management – UML Class diagram example. https://www.uml-diagrams.org/examples/hospital-domain-diagram.html. Accessed Apr 2019

15. Warmer, J., Kleppe, A.: The Object Constraint Language: Getting Your Models Ready for MDA. Addison-Wesley, Reading (2003)

16. Wohlin, C., Runeson, P., Höst, M., Ohlsson, M.C., Regnell, B., Wesslén, A.: Experimentation in Software Engineering. Springer (2012)

17. Yue, T., Ali, S.: Empirically evaluating OCL and Java for specifying constraints on UML models. Software Syst. Model. **15**(3), 757–781 (2016)

Dealing with Structural Differences in Serialized BPMN Models

Drazen Brdjanin[✉] and Stefan Ilic

Faculty of Electrical Engineering, University of Banja Luka,
Patre 5, 78000 Banja Luka, Bosnia and Herzegovina
drazen.brdjanin@etf.unibl.org, stefan92f@yandex.com

Abstract. The paper presents an approach to robust extraction of specific concepts from differently serialized BPMN models. Based on empirically identified structural differences in XSD-serialized BPMN models, we propose a rule-based approach to overcome such problems. The implemented extractor has been applied to several differently serialized BPMN models. The experimental results show that the proposed approach and implemented extractor enable robust extraction from differently serialized BPMN models with very high completeness and precision.

Keywords: BMRL · BPMN · Extractor · Robustness · Serialization · Structural differences · XMI · XSD

1 Introduction

Business process models (BPMs) are the key artifacts in several business process-related disciplines, such as business process management, business process (re)engineering, etc. They also play a very important role in the field of information systems serving as a basis for requirements specification, or even direct generation of software models in model-driven development approaches. We are particularly interested in using BPMs as a starting point for model-driven synthesis of data models. Several experiments (e.g. [1]) imply that well-formed data-centric BPMs enable a very effective and efficient automatic synthesis of conceptual database models.

BPM-driven tools for data model synthesis are very dependent on the source BPMs. Some of these dependencies are related to serialization specificities of the source models. In this paper we are particularly interested in the serialization specificities of BPMN [2] models. These specificities occur due to the platform specificities and various implementations of the standard in different modeling tools. Therefore, the standard also provides the serialization flexibility, since some attributes may be omitted or differently serialized. This may lead to significant differences in the serialized forms of BPMs, which may cause ineffectiveness of the transformation programs used for the transformation of the source BPMN model into the target data model. In the best case scenario, transformation programs are limited to a group of specifically serialized BPMN models.

© Springer Nature Switzerland AG 2019
I. Reinhartz-Berger et al. (Eds.): BPMDS 2019/EMMSAD 2019, LNBIP 352, pp. 344–358, 2019.
https://doi.org/10.1007/978-3-030-20618-5_23

It is therefore of interest to define an approach for efficient manipulation with structural differences of serialized BPMs, which will enable implementation of robust extraction tools of characteristic concepts from differently serialized BPMs, regardless of whether they are specific to the existing tools or specificities that will be subsequently identified. In this paper we propose a rule-based approach to robust extraction of specific concepts from differently serialized BPMN models, which is based on empirically identified structural differences in serialized BPMN models.

The paper is structured as follows. After the introduction, the second section presents the related work. The third section presents different ways of BPMN model serialization. The identified structural differences in the serialized BPMN models are presented in the fourth section. The fifth section presents the proposed approach. The experimental results are presented and discussed in the sixth section. The final section concludes the paper.

2   Related Work

This paper presents recent achievements of an ongoing research project devoted to automatic synthesis of conceptual database models driven by business process models (*BPM-driven CDM synthesis*). After the initial ideas and proposed approach [3] supported by the tools for automatic direct CDM synthesis based on BPMs represented by UML activity diagrams [4] and BPMN [2], recently we proposed a two-phase approach [5] to CDM synthesis. It is based on the introduction of a domain specific language named BMRL[1] as an intermediate layer between different source notations (to represent source BPMs) and the target notation (to represent the target CDM). With the intermediate layer, the CDM synthesis is split into two phases: (i) automatic extraction of specific concepts from the source BPM and their BMRL-based representation, and (ii) automatic CDM generation based on the BMRL-based representation of the extracted concepts. Finally, we implemented the first online two-phase BPM-driven CDM generator named M-lab Generator[2] [6], which is able to automatically generate the initial CDM (represented by UML class diagram [4]) based on BPMs (represented by BPMN or UML activity diagrams).

The existing extractor services within the M-lab Generator [6] are able to extract specific concepts only from the XMI[3]-serialized source BPMs, which represents a very significant limitation of the M-lab Generator. Therefore, the current implementation of the extractor services is based on Acceleo[4] transformations, which makes the extractor services unusable in the case of differently serialized BPMs. In this paper we propose a rule-based approach to overcome those problems, which enables the robust extraction of specific concepts from differently serialized BPMN models.

---

[1] Business Model Representation Language.
[2] Available at: http://m-lab.etf.unibl.org:8080/generator/.
[3] XML Metadata Interchange.
[4] http://www.eclipse.org/acceleo/.

There are several studies (e.g. [7–9]) considering structural specificities of serialized BPMN models and model interchange. The analysis [7] recognized more than 600 constraints, categorized in four categories (CARD, VAL, REF, EXT), which have to be fulfilled in order to obtain correctly serialized BPMN models. Similarity checks for structural specificities are implemented in BPMN-spector tool [9], which performs schema validation, referential integrity checks and EXT checks, and provides report on discovered deviations from the standard. The analysis [8] of standard conformance of open source BPMN tools showed that tested engines support 64% of tested features at most, while only 43% are portable between all of the tested engines.

The problem of finding structural differences among models that conform to the same metamodel still exists. To the best of our knowledge, there are no papers dealing with robust extraction of specific concepts from differently serialized process models. The research [10] shows that the majority of the existing papers focus on model versioning (e.g. [11,12]) and model clone detection (e.g. [13,14]).

3 Serialization of BPMN Models

This section presents different ways of BPMN model serialization and interchange. Additionally, we explain the structure of XSD[5]-serialized models and limitations of this form of BPMN model serialization.

BPMN Model Interchange. First versions of the BPMN standard focused solely on standardization of graphical modeling elements for BPMs, while the serialization format was left undefined. Due to this shortcoming, modeling tools were left to create their own serialization formats. BPMN model interchange between different tools was, for this reason, infeasible. This created a need for model transformations to other standards more suitable for model exchange.

First standardized model interchange, although indirectly, was partially possible since BPMN 1.2 version [15]. BPMN 1.2 provided a set of non-normative rules for mapping to WS-BPEL[6] which could be used to facilitate exchange. Flaws of this approach were ability to map only executable processes and losses due to difference in language capabilities which was especially visible in round-trip scenarios. Combined, these factors made using the WS-BPEL approach impractical. To solve this issue BPMN 2.0 [2] introduced two additional ways of model exchange based on XML, serialization using XSD and using XMI. XSD specifies structure and content of XML files while XMI represents the standard for exchange of metadata whose metamodel can be expressed using MOF[7]. Beside giving schemes for these formats, BPMN 2.0 standard defines constraints which have to be fulfilled in order to create well-formed models conforming to the standard. These constraints include the rules for graphical display of elements, executable semantics as well as a large number of rules relevant to model

---

[5] XML Schema Definition.

[6] Web Services Business Process Execution Language.

[7] Meta-Object Facility [16].

serialization. Conformance to these extra rules is essential to achieving correct model serialization, since the validation using only XSD or XMI is insufficient [7].

BPMN XML Schema. Although there are two methods of BPMN model serialization, serialization based on XSD is more prevalent in practice. A significant benefit of this form of serialization is a possibility to validate serialized models using XSD. Validating XML schema is also supported in most XML tools, which makes it widely available. For the given reasons, together with the fact that both serialization methods have the same expressive power, this paper is focused on BPMN XSD serialization. Additionally, BPMN standard defines XSLT[8] transformation for conversion between XMI and XSD formats.

Business processes in BPMN have two aspects: *process model* and *process diagram*. The process model contains only model semantics while the process diagram contains visual representation of the model such as information about layout of its elements. Based on this BPMN XML models are also comprised from two parts, one or more process models and one or more process diagrams. A part of the BPMN XML model which specifies visual representation is called BPMN DI[9].

XSD schema of BPMN metamodel consists of five files: BPMN20.xsd, Semantics.xsd, BPMNDI.xsd, DI.xsd, DC.xsd. BPMN20.xsd represents a central BPMN XSD file, which includes Semantics.xsd and imports BPMNDI.xsd. BPMNDI.xsd additionally imports DI.xsd and DC.xsd. DI and DC[10] are parts of the DD[11] standard [18] developed by OMG for modeling and exchange of graphical notations. BPMNDI.xsd uses and additionally expands definitions from DC and DD with attributes specific to BPMN.

Limitations of BPMN XSD. According to [19], limitations of BPMN model interchange can be divided in three categories: visual aspects of process diagrams which are not interchangeable, semantic aspects of process models which are not interchangeable and tool specific BPMN extensions. BPMNI DI provides mechanism for specifying only the basic layout of BPMN diagrams. This leads to variations in visual representation between different tools. Unsupported visual aspects include: colors of shapes and text, decorations (shadows, backgrounds, gradients, etc.), font and size of text, text wrapping and thickness and line style. Semantic differences are caused by interchange of unstandardized BPMN elements. These elements include: scripts in script tasks, implementations of user tasks and implementations of global user tasks. Semantic differences can also be caused when elements are not contained in the BPMN model itself, but referenced. This primarily happens in case of web services referenced by service, send and receive tasks. Serialized data from tool specific BPMN extensions is not interchangeable.

---

[8] eXtensible Stylesheet Language Transformation [17].
[9] Diagram Interchange.
[10] Diagram Common.
[11] Diagram Definition.

Besides these limitations, created due to lack of standardization, interchange of BPMN models is also affected by inadequacy of BPMN XSD. The analysis [7] of the BPMN standard identified 611 constraints which have to be fulfilled to correctly serialize BPMN process model. The identified constraints can be further divided into four categories: CARD (basic attributes – basic group of constraints which defines structure of BPMN models), VAL (basic value constraints and default values), REF (basic reference constraints), and EXT (extended set of constraints – all other constraints defined by the standard not belonging to the previous categories). The largest number of identified constraints (311) belong to the CARD category, followed by EXT 152, REF 107 and VAL 41. BPMN XSD covers most of CARD and VAL constraints, but REF and EXT categories are largely left out. In total, according to [7], BPMN XSD covers approximately 54% of constraints defined in the standard.

To help solve these problems, BPMN MIWG[12] was created inside OMG. The goal of this group is to lead and support BPMN tool makers with the purpose of creating a set of standard complying tools, identifying problems in the standard and enabling BPMN model interchange. BPMN MIWG defines a set of test BPMN models which can be used as reference for testing the import and export functionalities of modeling tools. Besides test models, the group also created a tool for an automatic recognition of interchange problems in modeling tools[13].

4   Structural Differences in Serialized BPMN Models

This section presents the results of an analysis of different serialization approaches and recognized structural differences in serialized BPMN models for the selected modeling tools. The analysis focuses on the selected BPMN elements having semantic capacity [1] for automatic CDM synthesis in M-lab Generator.

We selected and analyzed ten BPMN modeling tools. We tried to include different commercial and free-of-charge tools, as well as online tools. Two selected tools are implemented as plugins (CameoBusinessModeler for MagicDraw, and EclipseBPMNModeler for Eclipse). The sole prerequisite for the tool inclusion was its ability to serialize BPMN models in the XSD form.

Table 1 shows a list of the selected modeling tools. Each row shows *ID* (unique label for each tool) and the corresponding *name and version*, together with marks indicating the tool *type* (F=*Free*, C=*Commercial*, O=*Online*) and the corresponding *reference*. Some rows contain combined marks indicating a *free online* tool (FO) or a *commercial online* tool (CO). The considered set of modeling tools contains seven free and three commercial tools. Three tools are online.

Table 2 shows the results of the analysis of serialization approaches applied in the selected tools. The standard serialization of the selected modeling elements is marked with '✓', while the specific serialization approaches are marked with 'S'. The '–' sign indicates that the serialization of the corresponding modeling element is not supported in the given modeling tool.

---

[12] BPMN Model Interchange Work Group (http://www.omgwiki.org/bpmn-miwg/).
[13] BPMN MIWG tools (https://github.com/bpmn-miwg/bpmn-miwg-tools).

Table 1. Selected modeling tools

ID	Tool name and version	Type	Reference
T-01	BonitaStudioCommunity 7.7	F	https://www.bonitasoft.com/
T-02	Bpmn.io	FO	https://bpmn.io/
T-03	CameoBusinessModeler 18.5	C	https://www.nomagic.com/product-addons/magicdraw-addons/cameo-business-modeler-plugin
T-04	CamundaModeler 1.16.2	F	https://camunda.com/
T-05	Cawemo	FO	https://cawemo.com/
T-06	GenMyModel	CO	https://www.genmymodel.com/
T-07	EclipseBPMNModeler 1.5	F	https://www.eclipse.org/bpmn2-modeler/
T-08	Modelio 3.7.1	F	https://www.modelio.org/
T-09	VisualParadigmEnterprise 15	C	https://www.visual-paradigm.com/editions/enterprise/
T-10	Yaoqiang 5.3.12	F	http://bpmn.sourceforge.net/

Table 2. Serialization of the selected modeling elements in the selected tools

Modeling element		**Serialization:** Standard (✓), Specific (S), Not-supported (−)									
ID	BPMN metaclass	T-01	T-02	T-03	T-04	T-05	T-06	T-07	T-08	T-09	T-10
E-01	Participant	✓	✓	S	✓	✓	✓	✓	S	S	✓
E-02	Lane	✓	✓	S	✓	✓	✓	✓	✓	✓	✓
E-03	Task	✓	✓	✓	✓	✓	✓	✓	✓	✓	✓
E-04	DataObject	✓	S	✓	S	S	✓	✓	S	S	✓
E-05	DataObjectReference	−	S	S	S	S	S	✓	S	✓	S
E-06	DataStore	−	−	✓	−	−	−	✓	✓	✓	✓
E-07	DataStoreReference	−	S	✓	S	S	S	✓	✓	✓	S
E-08	Message	−	−	✓	−	−	S	✓	✓	✓	✓
E-09	MessageFlow	S	S	✓	S	S	S	✓	✓	✓	✓
E-10	DataInput	−	−	✓	−	−	−	✓	−	−	✓
E-11	DataOutput	−	−	✓	−	−	−	✓	−	−	✓
E-12	DataInputAssociation	S	✓	✓	✓	✓	✓	S	✓	✓	✓
E-13	DataOutputAssociation	S	✓	✓	✓	✓	✓	S	✓	✓	✓

There is no tool that supports all the considered modeling elements and applies the standard approach for their serialization. Only three tools (T-03, T-07, T-10) support all the considered modeling elements. The analysis (Fig. 1) shows that ∼58% of the considered modeling elements are serialized according to the standard in the considered tools, ∼23% of the considered modeling elements are serialized differently, and ∼19% of the considered modeling elements are not supported in the considered tools.

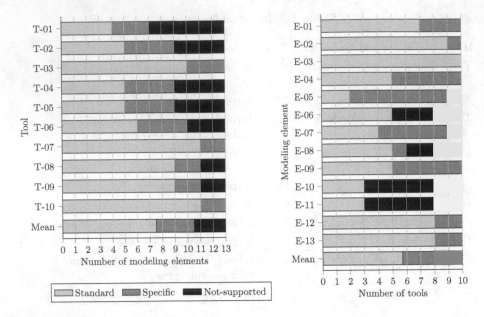

Fig. 1. Serialization of the selected elements in the selected tools: grouped by the tool (left), grouped by the modeling element (right)

5   Automatic Recognition of Structural Differences

By knowing the expected structure of the XSD-serialized BPMN models, it is possible to automatically recognize structural specificities in the models serialized by different tools. Here we focus on structural specificities of the serialized modeling elements having semantic importance for the automatic CDM synthesis in M-lab Generator. Since the BPMN standard [2] enables flexible modeling and generation of models at different levels of abstractions and details, the identified differences do not necessarily mean a mismatch with the standard, but a flaw in the context of extraction of considered modeling elements having semantic importance for automatic CDM generation.

5.1   Preliminary Model Purging and Checking

XPath[14] is used for accessing elements in the XSD-serialized BPMN models. In order to speed up XPath expressions execution, all unnecessary elements are removed from the model. We call this activity *model purging*. Those unnecessary elements are: (i) all elements related to diagram layout and visualization, (ii) tool-specific elements, (iii) other model elements that do not have semantic importance for the specific purpose (in our case, elements that are not necessary for automatic generation of the target class diagram).

---

[14] XML Path Language [20].

The namespaces could also be purged from the serialized models. They are defined in the format: `xmlns:<prefix>='<namespaceIdentifier>'` and could be used as elements/attributes prefixes in order to avoid naming or grouping conflicts. The complete qualified element/attribute name, also known as *QName*, is specified in the form `<prefix>:<name>`. In the considered set of tools, seven out of eleven tools use prefixes for BPMN elements. We identified four different prefixes. As there are no naming or grouping conflicts for the considered elements and attributes in the considered set of tools, the namespaces are also removed from the models in order to facilitate easier selection of the elements. An additional advantage of the model purging is related to the memory saving since XPath requires loading complete serialized models in the memory.

The purged model contains *essential* attributes of the considered elements (i.e. attributes that are required for the extraction) and other attributes that are required by the specificities of certain tools. After purging the model, the model structure is checked. This includes checking essential attributes and checking mutually dependent pairs of considered elements, such as `object` and `objectReference`, `dataStore` and `dataStoreReference`, `message` and `messageFlow`, etc.

5.2   Rule-Based Extraction

Flexibility of extraction is achieved by defining a set of rules containing `XPath` path expressions and additional metadata. The corresponding metamodel of this set of rules is shown in Fig. 2. The `Configuration` metaclass represents the extractor's configuration. It consists of multiple `Object` elements, each representing one BMRL concept. Objects contain an arbitrary number of `Rules`, each of which can contain `Subrules`. Both `Rules` and `Subrules` contain `Attributes` required for information retrieval. Subrules are used in case there is a shared part of the configuration between two or more different cases to simplify the configuration.

Based on the empirically identified structural specificities for the selected BPMN modeling elements in the selected modeling tools, we defined the corresponding set of rules (Fig. 3) in accordance with the aforementioned specified

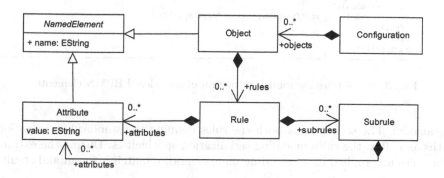

Fig. 2. Rules metamodel

```xml
<?xml version="1.0" encoding="UTF-8"?>
<bpmnExtractor>
  <participants>
    <rule namePath="/definitions/collaboration/participant"
          idAttribute="processRef"/>
    <rule namePath="/definitions/process"
          idAttribute="id"/>
    <rule namePath="/definitions/process/laneSet"
          idAttribute="id"/>
    <rule namePath="/definitions/process/laneSet/lane"
          idAttribute="id"/>
  </participants>
  <roles>
    <rule path="/definitions/process/laneSet/lane"
          recursive="/childLaneSet/lane"
          participantId="process"/>
    <rule path="/definitions/process/laneSet/lane"
          recursive="/childLaneSet/lane"
          participantId="laneSet"/>
    <rule path="/definitions/process/laneSet/lane/childLaneSet/lane"
          recursive="/childLaneSet/lane"
          participantId="lane"/>
  </roles>
  <dataObject>
    <rule path="/definitions/process/dataObject"
          namePath=""
          dataStorePath="/definitions/dataStore"/>
    <rule path="/definitions/process/dataObject"
          namePath="/definitions/process/dataObjectReference"
          dataStorePath="/definitions/dataStore"/>
  </dataObject>
  <dataObjectReference>
    <rule path="/definitions/process/dataObjectReference"
          dataInputPath="/definitions/process/ioSpecification/dataInput"
          dataOutputPath="/definitions/process/ioSpecification/dataOutput"
          dataStoreRefPath="/definitions/process/dataStoreReference">
      <subRule id="id"/>
      <subRule id="dataObjectReference"/>
    </rule>
  </dataObjectReference>
  <message>
    <rule path="/definitions/process/message"/>
    <rule path="/definitions/message"/>
    <rule path="/definitions/collaboration/messageFlow"/>
  </message>
  <task>
    <rule path="/definitions/process/"
          ownerPath="flowNodeRef">
      <subRule input="/dataInputAssociation/sourceRef"
               output="/dataOutputAssociation/targetRef">
      </subRule>
      <subRule input="/ioSpecification/dataInput"/>
    </rule>
  </task>
</bpmnExtractor>
```

Fig. 3. Set of rules for robust extraction of considered BPMN elements

metamodel. The set contains both the rules defining the standard serialization paths as well as the rules modeling serialization specificities. During the extraction, rules are applied in a cascading manner until a match is found and results are obtained or until the currently defined set of rules is exhausted. In case of rule exhaustion, extraction for the current element will yield no results.

There are two cases that can occur when expanding extractor's capabilities to handle the newly found structural specificities. If the extractor for the given element provides enough flexibility in options, we can simply define a new rule that will handle new structural differences. On the other hand, if the newly identified structural difference is significantly different than the one previously established for the given element, then the proposed rule-based approach will not provide the required flexibility and robustness since the extractor itself will require modifications.

5.3 Tool Implementation

Based on the proposed approach, we implemented a robust extractor service aimed at extracting specific BPMN elements with a semantic capacity for automatic CDM synthesis. After extraction, the extractor service generates the corresponding BMRL code, which is subsequently used for automatic CDM synthesis in M-lab Generator.

The extractor service itself is split into multiple extractors with a narrower scope, each focusing on a particular BMRL element. The separation of responsibilities between extractors reduces dependencies between extractors and cost of potential code changes. A high level overview of the extractor service architecture is given in Fig. 4. All extractors work only with BPMN models serialized according to BPMN XSD. For this reason, XMI-serialized models are converted

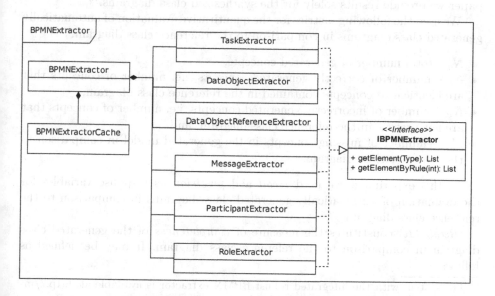

Fig. 4. Architecture of the extractor service

into XSD format by the XSLT transformation in the preprocessing step. Detailed implementation details are left out due to the paper length constraint.

6   Experimental Verification

This section analyzes effectiveness of the proposed approach and implemented extractor service.

Integration of the implemented extractor service with the preexisting M-lab environment alleviated the verification of the proposed extraction approach. Service-oriented architecture of the M-lab Generator allowed us to verify the implemented extractor service (by replacing the existing Acceleo-based extractor service) without changes to the rest of the orchestration.[15]

To verify the proposed approach and implemented extractor service, we created (in all selected tools) BPMN models that are the same (as much as possible) as the reference model representing the *Order processing* business process. This reference model (Fig. 5) has already been used in the experiment [1] to evaluate the effectiveness of BPM-driven CDM synthesis. This model is similar in complexity to real-world BPMN models since it contains most of the considered BPMN elements.

We applied the implemented extractor service to all models and analyzed the generated BMRL code, as well as the subsequently generated UML class diagrams. During verification, we took as reference, both the BMRL code and the corresponding UML class diagram, which were generated based on the reference model by the preexisting M-lab Generator. Due to length constraints, in this paper we provide results solely for the synthesized class diagrams.[16]

We used the following metrics for the quantitative evaluation of automatically generated class diagrams in comparison to the reference class diagram:

- N_g – total number of generated concepts,
- N_c – number of correctly generated concepts, i.e. number of concepts that are identical to concepts contained in the reference class diagram,
- N_w – number of incorrectly generated concepts, i.e. number of concepts that are not present in the reference class diagram, and
- N_m – number of missing concepts in the generated model in comparison to the reference class diagram.

In this experiment we used *recall* and *precision* as response variables for the evaluation of automatically generated class diagrams in comparison to the reference class diagram.

Recall (R) constitutes the measure of *completeness* of the generated class diagram in comparison to the reference class diagram. It may be defined as follows:

---

[15] The system with the integrated robust BPMN extractor is available at: http://m-lab.etf.unibl.org:8080/amadeos_test/.

[16] All source BPMs and the corresponding CDMs are available at: https://gitlab.com/F3real1/robustbpmnextractor.

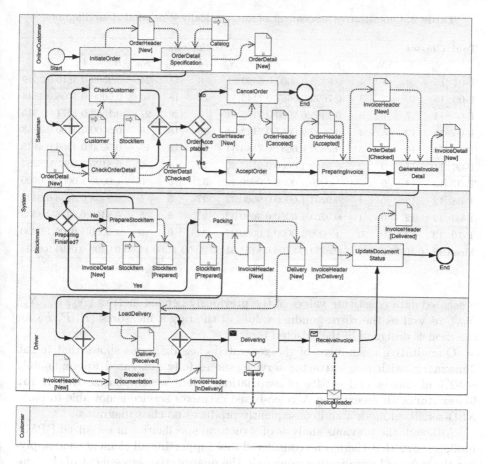

Fig. 5. Reference BPMN model of order processing [1]

$$R = \frac{N_c}{N_c + N_m}. \tag{1}$$

Precision (P) constitutes the measure of *correctness* of the generated class diagram. It may be defined as follows:

$$P = \frac{N_c}{N_c + N_w}. \tag{2}$$

F-measure (F) constitutes the measure of *effectiveness* of the approach. It represents the harmonic mean of precision (P) and recall (R), and it may be defined as follows:

$$F = \frac{2PR}{P + R}. \tag{3}$$

Table 3 contains the results of the assessment of automatically generated classes and automatically generated associations in the entire experiment. The

Table 3. Quantitative assessment of automatically generated class diagrams

Tool	Classes							Associations						
	N_g	N_c	N_w	N_m	R	P	F	N_g	N_c	N_w	N_m	R	P	F
T-01	15	9	6	4	0.6923	0.6000	0.6429	21	8	13	24	0.2500	0.3810	0.3019
T-02	15	10	5	3	0.7692	0.6667	0.7143	34	16	18	16	0.5000	0.4706	0.4848
T-03	14	7	7	6	0.5385	0.5000	0.5185	34	5	29	27	0.1563	0.1471	0.1515
T-04	15	10	5	3	0.7692	0.6667	0.7143	34	16	18	16	0.5000	0.4706	0.4848
T-05	15	10	5	3	0.7692	0.6667	0.7143	34	16	18	16	0.5000	0.4706	0.4848
T-06	11	11	0	2	0.8462	1.0000	0.9167	30	26	4	6	0.8125	0.8667	0.8387
T-07	13	13	0	0	1.0000	1.0000	1.0000	32	32	0	0	1.0000	1.0000	1.0000
T-08	12	12	0	1	0.9231	1.0000	0.9600	32	27	5	5	0.8438	0.8438	0.8438
T-09	12	12	0	1	0.9231	1.0000	0.9600	32	27	5	5	0.8438	0.8438	0.8438
T-10	13	13	0	0	1.0000	1.0000	1.0000	32	32	0	0	1.0000	1.0000	1.0000
Mean	13.50	10.70	2.80	2.30	0.8231	0.8100	0.8141	31.50	20.50	11.00	11.50	0.6406	0.6494	0.6434

presented data constitute values of the previously defined metrics (N_g, N_c, N_w, N_m), as well as the corresponding values of the target measures (R, P, F) for the models designed in the selected tools.

Quantitative assessment of the generated class diagrams shows that M-lab Generator, with new extractor service, successfully generated approximately $\sim 82\%$ of classes and $\sim 64\%$ of associations. Here we emphasize that M-lab Generator with preexisting Acceleo-based extractor service is not able to parse XSD-serialized models and consequently produces no class diagrams.

Although the previous analysis of structural specificities in serialized BPMN models shows that there is no considered tool supporting all elements and applying the standard serialization approach, the quantitative assessment of the generated class diagrams shows that M-lab Generator (with the new extractor service) generates complete models as expected (F=1.00) based on the models designed in T-07 and T-10. This fact proves that the implemented extractor service successfully resolved all structural specificities in the models designed in T-07 and T-10.

Models created in T-06, T-08 and T-09 yield very good results ($F > 0.91$ for classes and $F > 0.83$ for associations) despite identified serialization specificities. Missing classes and associations are caused by the process dataInput not being supported in the given tool (T-06), or being lost during serialization (T-08 and T-09). This also proves that all structural specificities were resolved successfully during extraction.

We obtain the same results for T-02, T-04 and T-05 tools. Although the calculated effectiveness is not so high (~ 0.71 for classes and ~ 0.48 for associations), a more detailed analysis shows that the low effectiveness is caused by unsupported elements in these tools. For instance, 10 out of 14 generated associations that do not match associations from the reference set differ only in the name (as a consequence of unsupported message names). This fact also proves that structural specificities were resolved successfully during extraction.

T-03 gives us weaker results. This happens as a result of wrong participants being created by the tool during serialization. Instead of expected participants, T-03 generates one with a name of diagram itself while user created participants and roles are created as roles and subroles of this participant. Since there are no structural specificities in the serialized model, the extractor service is unable to distinguish this case. As participant is one of the basic elements, this discrepancy produces a large total difference in comparison to the reference model.

We also applied M-lab Generator (with the new extractor service) to the reference model, which is XMI-serialized. The implemented extractor service transformed it firstly into the corresponding XSD-serialized model (by the built-in XSLT transformation). We found that this conversion results in some surplus tasks, but the extractor resolved these inconsistencies, and we obtained a class diagram as expected (the same as the reference class diagram). These results are not presented in Table 3.

Finally, based on the quantitative and qualitative analysis of the generated class diagrams, we can conclude that implemented extractor service successfully deals with structural specificities in serialized BPMN models, and enables robust extraction of the considered modeling elements from differently XSD- and XMI-serialized BPMN models.

7   Conclusions

In order to achieve robust extraction of specific concepts from differently serialized BPMN models, in this paper we proposed a rule-based approach for the representation of structural specificities. The proposed approach is based on the empirically identified structural specificities in different modeling tools, which are formally represented by a metamodel that enables flexible specifications of structural specificities for different modeling elements in different tools.

Based on the proposed approach, we implemented an extractor service and integrated it into an existing service-oriented online system for automatic business process model-driven synthesis of conceptual database models. The implemented extractor service enables extraction from both XSD- and XMI-serialized BPMN models.

The implemented extractor service has been applied to several differently serialized BPMN models. The experimental results show that the proposed approach enables robust extraction from differently serialized BPMN models since the implemented service successfully resolved all structural specificities.

Our future work will focus on further improvements of the approach and its application to other extractor services within M-lab Generator, in order to achieve robust extraction from differently serialized business process models represented by different notations. We will also try to explore some alternatives, such as techniques related to the semantic web, in order to overcome limitations related to the extensibility of the approach.

References

1. Brdjanin, D., Banjac, G., Banjac, D., Maric, S.: An Experiment in Model-Driven Conceptual Database Design. Software Syst. Model. (2018)
2. OMG: Business Process Model and Notation (BPMN), v2.0. OMG (2011)
3. Brdjanin, D., Maric, S.: An approach to automated conceptual database design based on the UML activity diagram. Comput. Sci. Inf. Syst. 9(1), 249–283 (2012)
4. OMG: Unified Modeling Language (OMG UML), v2.5. OMG (2015)
5. Brdjanin, D., Banjac, D., Banjac, G., Maric, S.: An approach to automated two-phase business model-driven synthesis of data models. In: Ouhammou, Y., Ivanovic, M., Abelló, A., Bellatreche, L. (eds.) MEDI 2017. LNCS, vol. 10563, pp. 57–70. Springer, Cham (2017). https://doi.org/10.1007/978-3-319-66854-3_5
6. Brdjanin, D., Banjac, D., Banjac, G., Maric, S.: An online business process model-driven generator of the conceptual database model. In: 8th International Conference on Web Intelligence, Mining and Semantics - WIMS 2018, 16:1–16:9. ACM (2018)
7. Geiger, M., Wirtz, G.: BPMN 2.0 serialization - standard compliance issues and evaluation of modeling tools. In: Proceedings of the 5th International Workshop on Enterprise Modelling and Information Systems Architectures - EMISA 2013, pp. 177–190 (2013)
8. Geiger, M., Harrer, S., Lenhard, J., Casar, M., Vorndran, A., Wirtz, G.: BPMN conformance in open source engines. In: 2015 IEEE Symposium on Service-Oriented System Engineering, pp. 21–30, March 2015
9. Geiger, M., Neugebauer, P., Vorndran, A.: Automatic standard compliance assessment of BPMN 2.0 process models. In: Kopp, O., Lenhard, J., Pautasso, C. (eds.) ZEUS 2017, CEUR-WS, vol. 1826, pp. 4–10 (2017)
10. Stephan, M., Cordy, J.R.: A survey of model comparison approaches and applications. In: Proceedings of Modelsward 2013, pp. 265–277. SCITEPRESS (2013)
11. Kolovos, S.D., Di Ruscio, D., Pierantonio, A., Paige, F.R.: Different models for model matching: an analysis of approaches to support model differencing. In: Proceedings of the ICSE Workshop on Comparison and Versioning of Software Models, pp. 1–6. IEEE (2009)
12. Ivanov, S.Y., Kalenkova, A.A., van der Aalst, W.M.P.: BPMNDiffViz: a tool for BPMN models comparison*. In: CEUR Workshop Proceedings, vol. 1418, pp. 35–39 (2015)
13. Strüber, D., AcreȚoaie, V., Plöger, J.: Model clone detection for rule-based model transformation languages. Software Syst. Model. 18(2), 995–1016 (2017)
14. Störrle, H.: Effective and efficient model clone detection. In: De Nicola, R., Hennicker, R. (eds.) Software, Services, and Systems, pp. 440–457. Springer, Cham (2015)
15. OMG: Business Process Modeling Notation, v1.2. OMG (2009)
16. OMG: Meta Object Facility Specification, v1.4. OMG (2002)
17. W3C: XSL Transformations (XSLT) v2.0. W3C (2010)
18. OMG: Diagram Definition (DD), v1.1. OMG (2015)
19. Kurz, M., Menge, F., Misiak, Z.: Diagram Interchangeability in BPMN 2. Recommended reading for the OCEB 2 BPMN 2 certification program (2014)
20. W3C: XML Path Language (XPath) 3.1. https://www.w3.org/TR/xpath-31/ (2017)

Evaluating Usefulness of a Fractal Enterprise Model Experience Report

Ilia Bider[1(⊠)] and Arian Chalak[2]

[1] DSV - Stockholm University, Stockholm, Sweden
ilia@dsv.su.se
[2] Försäkringskassan, Sundsvall, Sweden
arianchalak@gmail.com

Abstract. The paper presents an experience of evaluating the usefulness of a particular modeling technique called Fractal Enterprise Model (FEM). FEM connects enterprise processes with assets that are used in and are managed by these processes. The evaluation has been conducted in a somewhat unusual manner. A model that covers an essential part of an enterprise's activities has been built without any practical goal in mind, e.g. finding a cause of a problem, designing or completing a transformational change, etc. Then, it was presented to and discussed with the stakeholders that helped to build it. During the discussions, the stakeholders were asked to elaborate on the potential usages of the model in the practice of the enterprise. The result was a comprehensive list of possible usage of the model.

Keywords: Fractal Enterprise Model · Business process ·
Business process modeling · Process architecture · Experience report ·
Evaluation · Usefulness

1 Introduction

This paper reports on the experience of a project aimed at evaluating usefulness of Fractal Enterprise Model (FEM) [1] for practical purposes. FEM presents an enterprise/organization as a network of interconnected processes and assets. From one point of view, FEM can be considered as a model that expresses business process architecture [2, 3], as it shows interconnection between different business process that exist in an organization/enterprise. From the other point of view, FEM can be considered as an enterprise model (or an enterprise architecture [4]) in line with other enterprise models, e.g. Viable System Model (VSM) [5], work systems framework [6], or Business Model Canvas (BMC) [7], as it shows connection between the processes and enterprise's tangible and intangible assets (resources in the terminology of other modeling techniques).

© Springer Nature Switzerland AG 2019
I. Reinhartz-Berger et al. (Eds.): BPMDS 2019/EMMSAD 2019, LNBIP 352, pp. 359–373, 2019.
https://doi.org/10.1007/978-3-030-20618-5_24

The objective of the project was threefold:

1. Introduce modeling technique into a company. This was to be done by creating a model of the company business and then present it back to the company.
2. Find out new application areas for FEM, beyond those that were theoretically identified in [1], and partly investigated in other works, e.g. [8].
3. Test whether FEM can be built by a novice modeler in practical settings.

The objective has been achieved in a somewhat unusual manner. In normal practice, a model is being built for some specific practical task, e.g. building an IT system to support a process, educating new members of staff, finding a cause of a problem or a solution when the cause has been identified. Having a practical task in mind is quite justifiable, as building a model requires resources from the stakeholders when collecting data on which to build a model. People need to be interviewed, documents related to the object of modeling need to be provided, observation of activities need to be allowed, etc. Providing these resources without having any practical task for which the model should be built might be difficult to justify. However, in the case described in this paper, we were lucky to obtain permission to use the resources for creating and discussing our model without having a practical task to complete.

The strategy we used in this project was: (a) build a model based on information obtained from different groups of stakeholders, and (b) present the model to each stakeholders group separately and discuss for what purposes this model can be used in the enterprise. The goal with building the model was to show to the stakeholders its capabilities. As FEM is aimed at visualizing the interconnections between the enterprise business processes and its assets, this general goal was translated into discovering representative for the company business processes and assets and presenting as much interconnection between them in the model as it was possible to discover. As the project had limited resources, in terms of time and access to the information, there was no attempt to build a full model of the whole enterprise.

An organization, for which a FEM has been built is a typical IT solution provider that develops, supports, maintains and operates IT solutions for their customers. The team who created a model consisted of an MS student – the second author who did all fieldwork, and his thesis supervisor who guided the work via meetings held through a video conferencing system. The first member of the team had minimal experience of modeling in real practice in general and building FEM models in particular, though FEM was included in one of the courses the second author took. He also did not possess any domain knowledge, so the IT solution provider business was new to him. The second member of the team, supervisor, has an intimate knowledge of FEM as being one of the authors of the modeling technique, has long experience of building models of various types in practical settings, as well as he has knowledge of the IT solutions providers business in general, being for a long time engaged in such business personally.

The composition of the team allowed us to include the third goal in the project's objective, namely, "to test whether FEM can be built by a novice modeler in practical settings".

The plan of first building, and then showing the model was successfully implemented, though some stakeholders were a bit suspicious about the project as they did not understand the goal with the project. The second part of the project showing to and discussing the model with the stakeholders gave interesting results in both showing new areas of application of FEM, and providing a more specific form for those areas that were predicted in [1].

The rest of this paper is written according to the following plan. In Sect. 2, we present a short overview of FEM to give the reader a possibility to read this paper without studying the papers where FEM was originally introduced. Section 3 presents the business case, i.e. necessary information on the IT-provider, and the ways of how the FEM model has been built. Section 4 presents and explains the FEM model. Section 5 presents the stakeholders' views on how the model can be used in practice. Section 6 summarizes the findings.

2 Fractal Enterprise Model

As was mentioned in the introduction a Fractal Enterprise Model (FEM) belong to the class of enterprise models and thus has some common features with other modeling technique, and tools in this category. A full description of FEM, including its relationships with other enterprise modeling techniques and tools is presented in journal paper [1]. The latter has also explanation of why the model has been called fractal. The goal of this chapter is only to give the basic notions so that the reader does not need to become acquainted with [1] before reading this experience report.

FEM includes three types of elements: business processes, assets, and relationships between them, see Fig. 1 in which a fragment of a model is presented. The fragment is related to a business case considered in the next sections, and it will be explained in more details in these sections. Graphically, a process is represented by an oval; an asset is represented by a rectangle (box), while a relationship between a process and an asset is represented by an arrow. We differentiate two types of relationships in the fractal model. One type represents a relationship of a process "using" an asset; in this case, the arrow points from the asset to the process and has a solid line. The other type represents a relationship of a process changing the asset; in this case, the arrow points from the process to the asset and has a dashed line. These two types of relationships allow tying up processes and assets in a directed graph.

In FEM, a label inside an oval names the given process, and a label inside a rectangle names the given asset. Arrows are also labeled to show the type of relationships between the processes and assets. A label on an arrow pointing from an asset to a process identifies the role the given asset plays in the process, for example, *workforce*, *infrastructure*, *EXecution Template* (EXT), etc. A label on an arrow pointing from a process to an asset identifies how the process affects (i.e. changes) the asset. In FEM, an asset is considered as a pool of entities capable of playing given roles in given processes. Labels leading into assets from supporting processes reflect the way the pool is affected, for example, a label *acquire* identifies that the process can/should increase the pool size.

Note that the same asset can be used in two different processes playing the same or different roles in them, which is reflected by labels on the corresponding arrows. It is

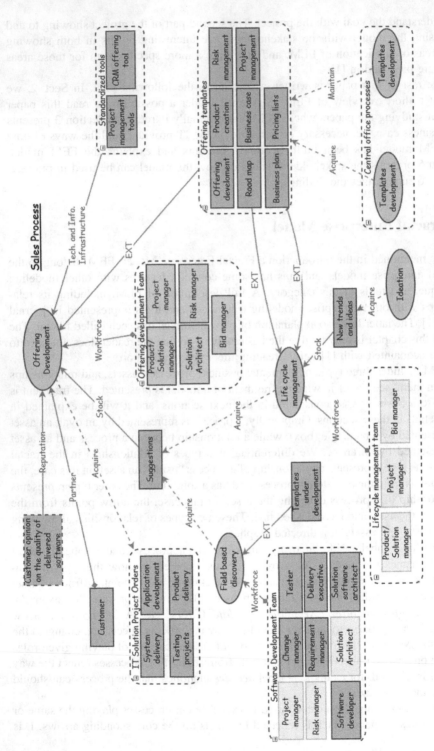

Fig. 1. A fragment of a FEM representing a process from our case study

also possible that the same asset can be used for more than one role in the same process; in this case, there can be more than one arrow between the asset and the process, but with different labels. Similarly, the same process could affect different assets, each in the same or in different ways, which is represented by the corresponding labels on the arrows. Moreover, it is possible that the same process affects the same asset in different ways, which is represented by having two or more arrows from the process to the asset, each with its own label.

Labels inside ovals, which represent processes, and rectangles, which represent assets, are not standardized. They can be set according to the terminology accepted in the given domain, or be specific for a given organization. Labels on arrows, which represent the relationships between processes and assets, however, can be standardized. It is done by using a relatively abstract set of relationships, like, *Workforce*, *Acquire*, etc., which are clarified by the domain- and context-specific labels inside ovals and rectangles. Standardization improves the understandability of the models.

While there are many types of relationships that show how an asset is used in a process (see example in Fig. 1), there are only three types of relationships that show how an asset is managed by a process – *Acquire*, *Maintain* and *Retire*.

To make the work of building a fractal model more systematic, FEM uses archetypes (or patterns) for fragments from which a particular model can be built. An archetype is a template defined as a fragment of a model where labels inside ovals (processes) and rectangles (assets) are omitted, but arrows are labelled. Instantiating an archetype means putting the fragment inside the model and labelling ovals and rectangles; it is also possible to add elements absent in the archetype, or omit some elements that are present in the archetype.

FEM has two types of archetypes, process-assets archetypes, and an asset-processes archetype. A process-assets archetype represents which types of assets that can be used in a given category of processes. The asset-processes archetype shows which kinds of processes are aimed at changing the given category of assets.

3 Project Overview

3.1 The Business Case

As was already mentioned in the introduction, this research has been completed at an IT Solutions Provider, which we refer to as ITSP in the rest of the text. Organizationally, ITSP is a local office of a large national concern that has many offices around the country. It works quite independently serving their customers but uses some services provided by the central office. ITSP develops, supports, maintains and operates IT solutions for their customers. The company has few significant customers for which it develops and operates solutions. Thus, their sales process is more directed at getting more orders from the existing customers than acquiring new customers.

3.2 The Project Strategy and Plan

As follows from the introduction, the project strategy was straightforward; the project plan consisted only of three steps presented in Fig. 2. At the same time, this strategy was a bit unusual. The project was not connected to any specific practical task, like a problem to solve, challenge to meet or improvement to introduce. Still, it required resources from the company for all three steps, like time for answering interview questions, time to participate in the presentations, and time for understanding the model and providing feedback. All these resources were requested without promising anything particular in return.

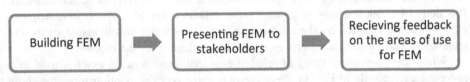

Fig. 2. Project plan

As was already mentioned in the introduction, all field work of building and presenting FEM has been done by the second author. The information for building a model has been gathered from different sources, such as interviewing people that play various roles in the processes, reading the documentation, and making observations while participating in the meetings of the software development team.

Navigation through the information sources was done according to the internal recursive structure of FEM. When a process of interest had been identified, a process-assets archetype, such as the one presented in Fig. 3, was used to produce a set of questions that needed answers, e.g. who participate in the process (*workforce*), what tools (*information & technical infrastructure*) are used in it, what templates/ guidelines/methods steer the process (EXTs -*execution templates*), etc. These questions were answered by interviewing the participants, who in turn could also point to other people participating in the process to be interviewed. Thus, a snowball-like method guided by archetypes was used for building the model.

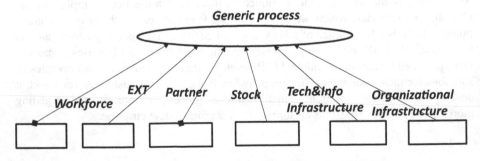

Fig. 3. A generic process-assets archetype (adapted from [1]).

As the time frame for the project was limited, there was no possibility to build full FEM of ITSP; thus only a limited, but an essential fragment of FEM has been built. It includes one primary process – *IT Solution delivery*, and one supporting process that belongs to a category of sales processes, called *Offering Development*. The first process delivers value to the customers for which they are ready to pay; that is why it is called primary in the FEM terminology of [1]. The second process aimed to get orders for the first process from the existing customers; that is why it is called supporting in the terminology of [1].

4 Fractal Enterprise Model of ITSP

4.1 FEM of a Primary Process

FEM for the primary process - *IT Solution Delivery* - is presented in Fig. 4. The process includes both developing and delivering solutions. The model has been built using a web tool called *InsightMaker* [9]. Though this tool is not designed for FEM diagramming, its expressive graphical power is enough for many FEM diagrams.

The root of FEM in Fig. 4 is an oval representing the primary process; the assets connected to it with the solid line arrows represent the assets that are used in this process. There are many assets of the same type, i.e. assets that are connected to the process with arrows that have the same labels. To make a diagram easier to grasp, assets are grouped. Each group is represented by a visual element of *InsightMaker* called *folder*. A folder is a group of visual elements that can be exploded or collapsed. As can be seen in Fig. 5, an arrow can be drawn between a folder and a process. This arrow means that each asset in the folder is connected with the corresponding process using the same type of arrows like the one which goes from the folder.

Figure 4 presents many assets that are used in the process of *IT Solutions Delivery*. It took quite some time to identify and group these assets. The three groups of assets - *Software Environment, Basic Software Platform,* and *Advance Software Platform* - represent environment/platform/tools used for solution development and employment. They are connected to the process by arrows labeled as *Tech. And Info. Infrastructure*. The fourth group connected by an arrow with the same label – *Standardized Tools* represents tools used to arrange the work of process instances of the primary process - actual projects that produce and deliver solutions.

The group called *Process Templates* is connected to the primary process by an arrow labeled *EXT* (EXecutable template). The group contains assets used for guiding different phases of process instances; each asset includes descriptions of routines used in the corresponding phase.

The group *Software Development Team* includes several assets that represent various roles people play in solution development and delivery. The group is connected to the primary process with an arrow labeled *Workforce*; each asset in this group represents a particular category of participants of the development and delivery process. These participants were the primary source of information for building the model. Representatives of each group were interviewed as well as their meetings were observed. Note that an arrow that leads from this group to the process has a diamond

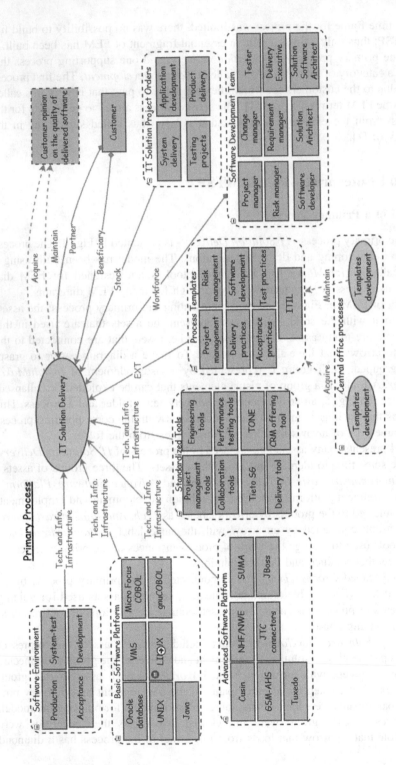

Fig. 4. FEM of the main process

start. The diamond start means that an asset or group represent a stakeholder of the process, which according to [1] warrants a special kind of acquiring archetype to be used when expanding this node.

The group, *IT solutions Projects Orders,* is connected to the primary process with the arrow labeled *Stock.* The stock of orders is an essential asset that ensures that the primary process can be run repeatedly. The stock always needs to be filled up, and this is a responsibility of another process discussed in the next section. The orders group consists of four different types of project orders, as shown in Fig. 4.

Customer is an asset that fulfills two functions. Firstly, the customer functions as a beneficiary for the process. Having a beneficiary, somebody who gets value from the process for which the company can get paid is mandatory for a primary process. Secondly, the customer actively participates in the process, thus fulfilling the role of *Partner.* Both arrows start with the diamond pointing out that this asset is of stakeholder type.

The last asset represented in Fig. 4 is *Customer opinion on the quality of delivered software.* It is not an asset needed for running the primary process, but an asset that is acquired and maintained by the process, which is represented by dashed arrows in Fig. 4. This asset is needed for another process, the one which is discussed in the next section. This asset belongs to the particular type of intangible assets that represent the opinion/reputation of some kind. Dashed borders highlight such assets.

For each asset represented in Fig. 4, there exist processes that manage it, e.g. hiring and training people, creating and maintaining platforms, etc. These are not represented in Fig. 4, except the ones that manage execution templates. The management processes for the templates are presented explicitly to mark that these processes do not run by the local company, but by the central office of the whole concern.

4.2   FEM of a Sales Process

The model for a sales process is presented in Fig. 1. The process belongs to supporting processes, more precisely it is a process the goal of which is to get new orders from the existing customers; this is why it is called *Offering Development.* This process serves as an *acquire* process for a group of assets *IT Solutions Orders,* which is represented by a dashed arrow from the process to the asset in Fig. 1. All other assets connected to the root process in Fig. 1, are assets that are used in the process.

As we see from Fig. 1, *customer* is an essential asset that functions as a *partner* in developing new offers which it then accepts. *Customer opinion* is also a valuable asset that makes the customer trust the companies even when all details of an offer are not completely clear. *Workforce* is represented by a group of assets that includes several roles. These are marked by a yellow background, which means that they also participate in other processes presented in Fig. 1; the cases of repetition are denoted by a light-yellow background. The offering process uses a number of *Offering templates* that are being developed and maintained by the central office. *Tech. & Info. Infrastructure* is represented by a group of assets that includes *Project management tools* and *CRM offering tool.*

As can be seen from Fig. 1, an important asset for the offering development process is a stock of suggestions. The stock is filled by two different processes *Field based discovery* and *Life cycle management*. Both are connected to asset *Suggestions* via dashed arrows labeled as *Acquire*. The *Workforce* for the first process is the *Solution development team*, the same as identified in Fig. 4. The idea is that the team should come with suggestions for new projects based on their knowledge of the existing systems and their communication with the customers. Though this source to generate suggestions is very important, there are no standardized working procedures on how this process should work. The latter is depicted in Fig. 1, by asset *Templates under development* which is connected to the discovery process by an arrow labelled as *EXT* (Execution template).

The second process that generates suggestions, *Life cycle management*, is based on the idea of each product (solution) having a natural life cycle. The suggestions are made to move the product to the next phase of the cycle, e.g. enhance the functionality, or create a new version. One of the sources of enhancing and improving the products is *New trends and ideas* coming from the ideation process. *Life cycle management* uses *Road map* and *Business plan* templates for guiding the process of generating suggestions. Three roles are included as *Workforce* for this process, these roles also participate in the offering development process itself.

4.3   Connecting the Models

After both models for the solution delivery and offering development had been completed, they were integrated to give a holistic view of the company's activities. This view is presented in Fig. 5, where the left-hand side represents the primary process, and the right-hand side represents the sales process. The most important common assets are represented once and connected to nodes on both sides. To these belong *Customer*, *Customer Opinion*, *IT solution project orders* and *Software development team*. Other assets that are included in both sides are represented by green background in the left-hand side and light green background in the right-hand side. In addition the yellow background is used in the right-hand side to show the assets that are used in several processes on this side. Again, the light color is used to indicate the second (or third) occurrence of the asset. Note also, that some groups of assets on the left-hand side are collapsed and do not show all details that can be seen in Fig. 4.

5   Stakeholders Views

After the model had been built, it was separately shown to and discussed with different stakeholders. Below, we summarize the feedback received from them. The summary is structured according to the issues named by various stakeholders. The summary below does not give all the details of the input, only the most important issues named by the stakeholders.

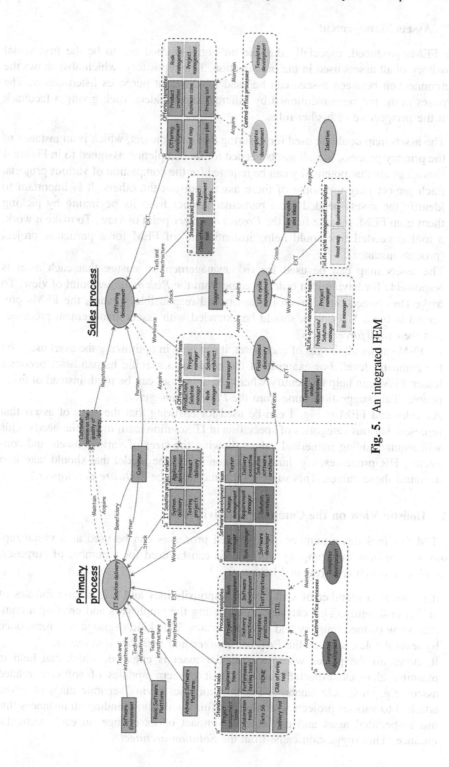

Fig. 5. An integrated FEM

5.1   Assets Management

The FEMs produced, especially the one on Fig. 4, turned out to be the first visual repository of all assets used in the organization. This repository, which also shows the interconnection between assets, can be used for different purposes listed below. The purposes in the list were mentioned by different stakeholders, each giving a feedback from the perspective of his/her roles.

1. The assets map could be used for ensuring that each project, which is an instance of the primary process, has all assets needed for its completion assigned to it. Figure 4 lists all assets that potentially can be required for the completion of various projects. Each project may use some of these assets, but not the others. It is important to identify the assets needed for a particular project from its beginning by picking them from FEM. It came from the *Project manager* point of view. To make it work, a tool is needed that could help "instantiation" of FEM for a particular project (process instance).
2. The assets map can be used for risk management to ensure that each asset is responsible for having it in order. It came from the *Risk manager* point of view. To make the connection between the assets and responsible persons, the FEMs presented in Figs. 1, 3 and 4, should be extended with assets management processes and their *workforce* assets.
3. As FEM shows all usages of each asset, it can help in optimizing the asset usage on the company level. For example, if the need for a specific human asset becomes lesser, FEM can help to identify where else this asset can be used, instead of firing people. This suggestion came from the *Project manager.*
4. An enhanced FEM is Fig. 4 can be used for ensuring that the sizes of assets that represent various categories of specialists in IT solution team match the needs. This will require adding numerical values showing the sizes of various assets and connecting HR processes, e.g. hiring and training, to the model that should take into accounts these values. This suggestion came from the *Software developers.*

5.2   Holistic View on the Company's Activity

A FEM that includes a number of connected processes can be used as a visual representation of how the company works. This can be used for a number of purposes, examples of which are presented below.

1. It shows to a member of staff his/her responsibilities and also responsibilities of his/her colleagues. This can help in educating the employees and creating a common view of the company and how it operates. This kind of usage was mentioned by several roles, such as the *Project manager* and *Software developers.*
2. It shows all the places where a particular asset is engaged, which can help in planning changes, especially changes that concern updates of software related assets, e.g. an Oracle database. For this purpose, having separate maps of assets attached to various projects would be helpful. It will allow finding all instances that use a specified asset and calculate the impact of its change on each particular instance. This suggestion came from the *Solution architect.*

5.3   Process Development and Improvement

As well as being a repository of assets, FEM can be considered as a repository of the company's processes. This repository can be used for a number of purposes, examples of which are presented below.

1. It is important to have EXTs for each process, as a process without EXTs will be run in an ad-hoc manner, which may affect both efficiency and effectiveness of the company. Also, each process template needs to have its managing processes and responsible persons for them. Missing this part in the organization may result in that the templates are never updated, thus resulting in them being not used in practice. FEM can both point to the processes without templates, and templates without proper managing processes and responsible persons. This suggestion came from the *Project manager.*
2. FEM shows the connections between various processes, which can help to avoid each process being handled in isolation. The latter may result in improvement (e.g. optimization) in one process decreasing the effectiveness of the company instead of increasing it. This suggestion came from the *Product solution manager.*

5.4   Field Based Discovery

Many stakeholders provided feedback related to a particular area of the FEM on Fig. 4, namely around the process called *Field based discovery*, which is one of the sources for generating suggestions for *Offering development.* The feedback related to this process came from the *Product solution manager* (in fact, most of his feedback was associated with this issue), *Project manager* and *Software developers.*

All stakeholder considered that FEM in Fig. 5 highlights the importance of *Field based discovery* and the need to involve in it the software development team fully. FEM in Fig. 5, shows that the *IT solution development* process requires orders from the customers. Otherwise, the development team will have nothing to do. At the same time creating these orders requires help from the developers, as they meet the customers and can obtain information about their needs that might be missed by the sales executives and managers. FEM also shows that the process does not have EXTs, which creates confusion among the developers. They are asked to participate in the process, and they are willing to do so, but there are no clear guidelines of how to do this.

In general terms, this particular usage falls in the categories already discussed in the previous sections. However, we decided to address it separately, as it seems to be one of the major issues in the company. Also, this issue is of importance not only for this particular company but can be found in many consulting companies that have similar problems with the engagement of consultants and developers in sales.

6   Lessons Learned

On the whole, the strategy accepted for this project proved to be successful. It was possible to build a model without having a specific purpose and present it to stakeholders for discussions and reflections. It showed that the stakeholders fully understood the model and were able to reflect on it, which allows to conclude that the *first goal* of our project, i.e. introduce FEM to the company has been successfully achieved. One of the significant factors that contributed to the success was that the model presented to and discussed with the stakeholders was not abstract, but showed their business activities, and in a visual way. This prompted a chain of ideas related to the problems and challenges each stakeholder experienced in his/her work.

The discussions with the stakeholders and their reflections also revealed a number of possible usages of the model in the organization, which was the *second goal* of our project. The areas of usage suggested by stakeholders are listed in Sect. 5. They fall into general categories discussed in [1]. However, in difference from [1], where the categories were defined in broad terms, the suggestions from the stakeholders were more specific. Some suggestions require a special kind of tools that were not thought of before.

As far as using the FEM technique by a novice modeler, it was both challenging and supporting. Challenging - because it was not clear in the beginning what questions to ask, and to whom to talk. Supporting means that when some process had been identified, it was relatively easy to unwind the FEM structure by finding things connected to the process according to the archetypes. Using FEM gives an alternative way to understand the business activities of the company. Instead of starting with the official statement of mission and vision, and then continuing to how they are implemented, FEM can help to dive into how the company works as soon as some of its primary processes have been identified. This may give a more reliable view of the company, as the official goals (e.g. vision and mission) may not correspond to what the company does in reality.

Despite the challenges, it was possible to build a FEM for a novice modeler with a limited assistance from an expert. This allows us to conclude that the question posed in our *third goal*, whether it is possible to build a FEM by a novice modeler, can be answered positively.

Note that the main goal of this project was investigating the usefulness of FEM, all issues related to syntactical or semantical correctness were left outside the scope of the investigation. In this respect, we follow the famous statement from [10]: "… essentially, all models are wrong, but some are useful", which puts the usefulness issue before the correctness.

Note also, that the results of our project support the statement of Patrick Hoverstadt for the need of an architectural model that shows the management of how the company works presented in [11]. Namely, many managers found the strength of FEM in giving them a holistic view of the company's business activities, and especially on the importance of taking into consideration interconnectedness of processes and assets.

References

1. Bider, I., Perjons, E., Elias, M., Johannesson, P.: A fractal enterprise model and its application for business development. Softw. Syst. Model. **16**(3), 663–689 (2017)
2. Green, S., Ould, M.: A framework for classifying and evaluating process architecture methods. Softw. Process: Improv. Pract. **10**(4), 415–425 (2005)

3. Koliadis, G., Ghose, A., Padmanabhuni, S.: Towards an enterprise business process architecture standard. In: 2008 IEEE Congress on Services-Part I, pp. 239–246 (2008)
4. EARF: Enterprise Architecture Definition: In: Enterprise Architecture Research Forum. http://samvak.tripod.com/earf.pdf. Accessed 2014
5. Beer, S.: The Heart of Enterprise. Wiley, Hoboken (1979)
6. Alter, S.: The Work System Method: Connecting People, Processes, and IT for Business Results. Work System Press (2006)
7. Osterwalder, A., Pigneur, Y.: Business Model Generation: A Handbook for Visionaries, Game Changers, and Challengers. Wiley, Hoboken (2014)
8. Josefsson, M., Widman, K., Bider, I.: Using the process-assets framework for creating a holistic view over process documentation. In: Enterprise, Business-Process and Information Systems Modeling, LNBIP, Stockholm, Sweden, vol. 214, pp. 169–183. Springer (2015)
9. Give Team: Insightmaker. http://insightmaker.com/. Accessed 2014
10. Box, G., Draper, N.: Empirical Model Building and Response Surfaces. Wiley, New York (1987)
11. Hoverstadt, P.: Why business should take enterprise architecture seriously. In: Gøtze, J., Jensen-Waud, A. (eds.) Beyond alignment, Systems, vol. 3, pp. 55–166. College Publishing (2013)

Author Index

Printed in the United States
By Bookmasters